Peer Interaction and Second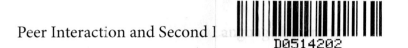

Language Learning & Language Teaching (LL&LT)

ISSN 1569-9471

The LL&LT monograph series publishes monographs, edited volumes and text books on applied and methodological issues in the field of language pedagogy. The focus of the series is on subjects such as classroom discourse and interaction; language diversity in educational settings; bilingual education; language testing and language assessment; teaching methods and teaching performance; learning trajectories in second language acquisition; and written language learning in educational settings.

For an overview of all books published in this series, please see
http://benjamins.com/catalog/lllt

Editors

Nina Spada
Ontario Institute for Studies in Education
University of Toronto

Nelleke Van Deusen-Scholl
Center for Language Study
Yale University

Volume 45

Peer Interaction and Second Language Learning
Pedagogical potential and research agenda
Edited by Masatoshi Sato and Susan Ballinger

Peer Interaction and Second Language Learning

Pedagogical potential and research agenda

Edited by

Masatoshi Sato
Universidad Andres Bello

Susan Ballinger
McGill University

John Benjamins Publishing Company

Amsterdam / Philadelphia

The paper used in this publication meets the minimum requirements of the American National Standard for Information Sciences – Permanence of Paper for Printed Library Materials, ANSI z39.48-1984.

DOI 10.1075/lllt.45

Cataloging-in-Publication Data available from Library of Congress:
LCCN 2016001357 (PRINT) / 2016009448 (E-BOOK)

ISBN 978 90 272 1332 7 (HB)
ISBN 978 90 272 1333 4 (PB)
ISBN 978 90 272 6717 7 (E-BOOK)

John Benjamins Publishing Company · https://benjamins.com

Table of contents

Acknowledgement of reviewers

In addition to the series editors, who were extremely efficient and helpful, the colleagues listed below have kindly served as anonymous reviewers at various times during the preparation of the volume. In printing their names here, we express our gratitude for their many hours and knowledgeable service. Their insightful and critical comments pushed the authors to improve their manuscripts and are well reflected in the overall quality of the book. Our sincere thanks go to (in alphabetical order):

Melissa Baralt (Florida International University); Ana Fernández Dobao (University of Washington); Tara Fortune (University of Minnesota); Pauline Foster (St. Mary's University); María del Pilar García Mayo (University of the Basque Country); Fred Genesee (McGill University); Laura Gurzynski-Weiss (Indiana University); Noriko Iwashita (University of Queensland); YouJin Kim (Georgia State University); Shawn Loewen (Michigan State University); Melinda Martin-Beltrán (University of Maryland); Neomy Storch (University of Melbourne); Diane Tedick (University of Minnesota); Jessica Williams (University of Illinois at Chicago).

Understanding peer interaction

Research synthesis and directions

Masatoshi Sato and Susan Ballinger

Universidad Andres Bello / McGill University

Introduction

Framework of this volume

While research on interaction between second language (L2) learners (peer interaction, henceforth) has been investigated since the early 1980s, this research domain has been given much less attention compared to another type of interaction – that between L2 learners and native speakers and/or language teachers. In this sense, our understanding of the nature of peer interaction, its effects on L2 development, and its pedagogical potential lag far behind our knowledge of teacher-student interaction. To date, research findings on peer interaction have clearly distinguished it from other types of L2 interaction and have pinpointed its unique role in L2 learning. In a recent comprehensive monograph of peer interaction, Philp, Adams, and Iwashita (2014) argued that peer interaction gives learners "a context for experimenting with the language" (17). Given the fact that student-teacher interaction and peer interaction are indeed different in many ways and that peer interaction occupies a significant amount of time in many L2 classrooms, it is high time to advance the research agenda by closely examining the nature of peer interaction, determining and testing mediating factors affecting L2 learning during that interaction, and seeking ways to maximize its pedagogical potential.

This book is the first collection of empirical studies focusing on peer interaction in L2 learning. It is designed to explore three central questions regarding (a) interactional patterns and learner characteristics, (b) tasks and interaction modality, and (c) learning settings. First, while past research has shown that L2 learners are capable of providing linguistic support to each other, it is evident that the effectiveness of peer interaction is mediated by other variables (e.g., quality of corrective feedback, degree of collaboration, learners' proficiency levels). Hence, the first question that the volume addresses is: How do interactional patterns and

DOI 10.1075/lllt.45.01int

learner characteristics affect L2 learning in peer interaction? Second, as applied linguistics has advanced our knowledge regarding how different types of tasks and/ or interaction modality affect interaction patterns and L2 learning, it is yet to be known how those factors play out in the peer interaction context. Thus, the second question posed in the volume is: How do tasks or interaction modality affect peer interaction and L2 learning? Third, one of the features that differentiates peer interaction from other types of interaction is that, unlike learner-teacher or learner-native speaker interactions, the learning that occurs between learners is susceptible to learning settings (e.g., two-way immersion, immigrants in L2 classes, minority language learning). Therefore, the third question that the book seeks to answer is: How do learning settings affect peer interaction and L2 learning?

Framework of this chapter

This chapter provides an overview of peer interaction research. We begin by examining the uniqueness of peer interaction both from research and practical perspectives. We then move on to discussing the theoretical underpinnings of peer interaction and L2 learning, noting that although researchers have traditionally relied on one of two theoretical accounts – either the interactionist or the sociocultural approach, there is a growing trend for researchers to use a sociocognitive, mixed methods approach to analyzing peer interaction. We then overview mediating variables that impact peer interaction, all of which are examined by the studies presented in this volume, and we describe the goals and organization of the book as well as the focus of individual chapters.

What is unique about peer interaction?

A distinct type of interaction

Since the interaction hypothesis was proposed over 30 years ago (Long 1981, 1983), researchers have compared peer interaction to interaction between learners and native speakers. This research has revealed that those two types of interaction are different in relation to four key interactional features: input modifications, corrective feedback, modified output, and self-initiated modified output.

Studies comparing the input provided by learners versus that provided by native speakers have found that native speakers provide lexically richer and syntactically more complex input than L2 learners (Pica, Lincoln-Porter, Paninos, & Linnell 1996; Porter 1986; Sato 2015a). However, high proficiency learners can be comparable or better input providers than native speakers. The participants in García Mayo and Pica's (2000) study, for instance, were English-major university students whose paper-based TOEFL scores ranged from 580–630. The researchers revealed that the learner-interlocutors produced structurally richer input to their partners than the native-speaking interlocutors. Although learners do sometimes conclude their interaction with nontarget-like solutions (e.g., incorrectly-resolved communication breakdowns) and provide their partners with grammatically incorrect input, research indicates that the directionality of error-related exchanges is usually toward correctness (see Bruton & Samuda 1980). In addition, the quality of native speakers' input, as opposed to presumably that of trained teachers, may not be as target-like as is generally assumed. Sato (2015a) focused on foreigner talk (a type of discourse that a native speaker tends to use when addressing a learner) and identified a significant reduction in grammaticality and complexity in native speakers' input which, in turn, affected learners' production. In sum, with regard to learners' input, Varonis and Gass (1985) concluded that peer interaction can be "a good forum for obtaining input necessary for acquisition" (83).

As far as feedback goes, research clearly indicates that learners are more willing to indicate that they do not understand what their partners have said when interacting with another learner. In one of the earliest studies comparing peer interaction with interaction between native and non-native speakers, Porter (1986) found that learners produced more language with other learners and that their quality of speech was similar in both types of interaction. Pica et al. (1996) compared peer interaction between Japanese learners of English with interaction between learners and native speakers. Half of the dyads engaged in a task in which the participants were asked to reproduce an unseen sequence of pictures by exchanging verbal descriptions. The remaining participants were given another task in which they were asked to compose a single story based on individually held pictures from the story line. The analysis of the number of signals indicating that learners did not understand what their partners had said – feedback – showed that there were significantly more such instances in peer interaction (for the story task). The researchers concluded that peer interaction "did offer data of considerable quality, particularly in the area of feedback" (80).

Sato and Lyster (2007) revealed that learners not only provided quantitatively more feedback but also arguably a more effective type of feedback than did native speakers. This study compared interactions between Japanese learners of English with interactions between these learners and native speakers. The analysis showed that learners provided more elicitation types of feedback than reformulation types, the former of which were deemed more effective because they can provide partners with opportunities to modify their initial erroneous utterances (see also Mackey, Oliver, & Leeman 2003). Alcón's (2002) comparison between peer interaction and learner-teacher interaction also exhibited a similar phenomenon. Her observation of EFL classes (one teacher-led and the other peer interaction focused) indicated that learners employed more requesting strategies with each other (i.e., a type of feedback) than when they interacted with the teacher (see also Toth 2008).

Research has also found that learners tend to react to feedback by modifying their initial errors (modified output) much more often during peer interaction than when they interact with native speakers. Sato and Lyster (2007) compared the frequency of modified output in the two interaction contexts. In the learner-native speaker dyads, they found that the amount of modified output was significantly less than other types of responses (e.g., topic continuation) regardless of the type of feedback that the native speakers gave. Moreover, the comparison across the types of interaction showed that learners modified their utterances more when they interacted with another learner than with a native speaker (see also McDonough 2004).

Finally, while much less investigated, a theoretically and pedagogically intriguing peer interaction phenomenon is that learners tend to self-correct more while interacting with each other than when they interact with native speakers. These "overt manifestations of the monitoring process" (Kormos 2006: 123) are hypothesized to facilitate L2 processing in the same way as modified output triggered by feedback (de Bot 1996). Shehadeh (2001) conducted an experiment with adult ESL learners in the UK with various L1 backgrounds and showed that 93% (496 out of 535) of self-initiation led to modified output during peer interaction. In the classroom context as well, Buckwalter (2001), based on over two years of audio and videotaping in Spanish language classes at a university in the United States, revealed that over 90% of the repair moves were self-initiated self-repair, as opposed to other-initiated (either by the teacher or other learners) (see also Fernández Dobao 2012; McDonough 2004; Sato 2007; Shonerd 1994; Smith 2009).

In sum, research that has compared peer interaction with other types of interaction indicates that it is different on many accounts. Despite the fact that native speakers are more likely to provide richer syntactical and lexical input, and learners may not always reach a target-like solution to language problems that arise during peer interaction, it seems that during peer interaction learners are able to shift their attention to formal aspects of the target language more than when they interact with native speaking partners or teachers. It is also clear that they engage in quantitatively richer interaction with each other in terms of output.

A facilitator of L2 processing

Although research has not fully explained why learners engage in more interactional moves during peer interaction, there is some evidence indicating that
learners feel more comfortable during peer interaction in comparison with student-teacher interaction. It can be argued that this comfort level positively affects
learners' L2 processing by helping them notice and point out errors in their partners' speech and encouraging them to modify their own errors when given feedback. Moreover, a greater comfort level seems to increase the amount of overall
language production, which leads to more opportunities for language practice.
Philp et al. (2014:198) asserted that peer interaction is "generally felt to be less
stressful than teacher-led interaction, precisely because it will not be carefully
monitored."

To examine learners' perceptions of peer interaction, Sato (2013) conducted
a factor analysis of learner questionnaire data. The results indicated a preference
for peer interaction (one of the statements in the questionnaire was, for instance,
"I enjoy communication activities with my classmates"). Although the quantitative
results were at best indicative of a positive perception, the follow-up interviews
added a dimension to understanding peer interaction psychology. Specifically in
comparison to a teacher-centered conversation, learners explained that they do
not have to worry about making errors while talking to each other. This result
is corroborated by some earlier studies. For example, Gass and Varonis (1989)
discussed the feeling of "shared incompetence" in peer interaction: They posited
that learners feel that they are more responsible for conveying their message to
a learner interlocutor and, therefore, they have to "work harder" to negotiate for
meaning (74). In the same line, by conducting in-depth interviews after dyadic
activities, Sato and Lyster (2007) found that, on the one hand, learners were under
pressure when interacting with native speakers because they believed that their
English was "broken English" and native speakers' English was "perfect English".
On the other hand, while working with their peers, they thought they had more
time to decide what to say and felt much more comfortable to test out what they
believed to be correct, that is, their linguistic hypotheses (see also Oliver 2002;
Shehadeh 1999, 2001).

Some studies have investigated perceptions of peer corrective feedback. In
Philp, Walter, and Basturkmen (2010), learners' retrospective interview data indicated that they hesitated to give feedback to their partners because of (a) their
proficiency (e.g., readiness to correct as a learner), (b) task-related discourses (e.g.,
interruption during a role-play), and (c) social relationship (e.g., face-saving). In
general, Philp et al. (2010) showed that, although the learners felt less anxious
during peer interaction compared to when interacting with the instructor, they

were reluctant to provide feedback to each other. These results do not mean, however, that learners do not prefer receiving feedback from their fellow learners. In fact, Sato (2013) revealed that learners strongly believed that they should receive feedback even when it was from their classmates. In this regard, Yoshida (2008) asserted that the learners' level of satisfaction is a deciding factor for feedback to be effective. That is, when learners were dissatisfied, feedback from their classmates was misunderstood or discarded. One learner in Yoshida's study reported that she believed in her partners' metalinguistic feedback because he sounded confident, which indicates learners' uncertainty in their classmates' feedback and inconsistency in the effectiveness of peer corrective feedback.

While it is still unclear whether learners' perceptions of peer interaction and peer feedback affect their choice of interaction moves or how these moves impact their L2 development, peer interaction indeed provides a context facilitative of learning in which learners experience greater levels of comfort.

A context for L2 development

Despite the amount of peer interaction research, only a limited number of studies have empirically shown the effectiveness of peer interaction on L2 development. In Sato and Lyster's (2012) pre-post design, there were four groups, two of which were given feedback training and communicative tasks. Another was given the communicative tasks only and a fourth acted as a control group. The results revealed that the peer interaction only group outperformed the control group for fluency development but not accuracy, while the feedback groups outperformed the rest of the groups both for accuracy and fluency. They postulated that engaging in communicative peer interaction tasks only may not be sufficient for developing grammatical knowledge. They suggested that to push accuracy development forward in peer interaction, some attention control device (e.g., corrective feedback) may be necessary. McDonough's (2004) study of EFL learners in Thailand exhibited the positive impact of shifting attention to L2 learning in peer interaction. In her study, learners who received more feedback and produced more modified output (categorized as a high-participation group) improved their accuracy during oral production (real and unreal conditionals) than those who were categorized as a low-participation group (see also McDonough & Chaikitmongkol 2010). In Kim's (2013) experiment, one of the two groups was given pre-task modeling before engaging in communicative tasks. The pre-post analysis of question formation development (see Pienemann & Johnston 1987) revealed that after several trials the experimental group advanced in question stages more than the control group. Kim concluded that the modeling helped the learners pay closer attention to their language production, which then pushed them to go to the next developmental stage (see also Kim & McDonough 2011). Although empirical evidence of peer interaction is accumulating, examination of L2 development using pre-post designs is a direction that peer interaction research should pursue in the future.

A versatile pedagogical option

Peer interaction can be used in a variety of formats (from pairs to small groups to larger groups), and it can be adapted for any type of task: The teacher can give a simple information-gap task (e.g., picture description) or a more creative task (e.g., a science project). The teacher can assign those tasks in any learning environment (in the classroom, outside the classroom for a group project, or in the virtual environment via computer-mediated communication). Furthermore, peer interaction is not limited to a specific learning context. It is as useful for task completion in traditional second language classes as it is in content-based classrooms for more elaborate collaborative projects, or in foreign language classrooms for tasks designed to promote L2 production.

In particular, in immersion settings there is a new pedagogical direction that takes advantage of the reciprocity of peer interaction. In the past, researchers pointed out problematic aspects of peer interaction; namely, North American immersion students tend to show an increased preference for speaking English with peers (McCollum 1999; Tarone & Swain 1995), and immersion students have been shown to focus on the communication of meaning over linguistic accuracy and to produce non-targetlike and seemingly fossilized linguistic structures (Lyster 1987; Swain 1985). These issues indicated the potential of two-way immersion where learners have the unique opportunity to engage with peers who are native speakers of their L2. While research has found that students also tend to prefer English during peer interaction in that context (Ballinger & Lyster 2011; Potowski 2007), other studies have demonstrated that they do offer each other linguistic support in the non-English language (Angelova, Gunawardena, & Volk 2006). Considering the fact that immersion learners are generally higher proficiency learners, and in two-way immersion, native speakers of some of their fellow students' L2, they are particularly suited to provide support during peer interaction. Thus, research that examines how to maximize the potential of peer interaction in these settings is needed.

In foreign language contexts, learners lack "access to NS models for their linguistic information and to actual samples from everyday social interaction" (García Mayo & Pica 2000: 273). This is also the case in the classroom setting, especially when the class is delivered in the learners' first language (Philp &

Tognini 2009). In addition, it is common that learners do not have opportunities to produce the target language inside or outside of the classroom (Sato 2013). This clearly suggests the importance of language classes in which learners could possibly engage in meaningful interaction by receiving the necessary input and producing spontaneous speech. The reality, however, indicates otherwise. A common pedagogical practice in these contexts is traditional grammar-translation methods. Fotos (1998: 301) summarized:

> [M]uch of the English language instruction in the world is not ESL-based, but takes place in the EFL situation, often with teachers who themselves are not native speakers of English. In many of these areas, the old ways are still the dominant educational paradigm, and communicative language teaching is just beginning to become an instructional option. Here, grammar teaching has never left the classroom.

After more than a decade, it seems that this reality has not improved in many foreign language contexts (see Kormos & Kiddle 2013; Shehadeh & Coombe 2012). Reasons for the failure to create a communicative environment and to give authentic activities vary: (a) the teacher's proficiency is insufficient to deliver the class in the target language (Gupta 2004); (b) the goal of L2 education focuses on passing certain language tests (e.g., university entrance examinations) which are usually written (Lam 2015); (c) the teacher is an absolute authority due to the cultural norms (see Pritchard & Maki 2006); and (d) the big class size makes it virtually impossible for each student to have a chance to engage in meaningful communication with the teacher (Khazaei, Zadeh, & Ketabi 2012).

For those pedagogical obstacles, peer interaction activities can be an ecological and effective tool. First, the teacher's proficiency in the target language is less of a concern (although he or she should be capable of facilitating peer interaction). Second, while learners tend to feel pressured when interacting with native speakers or when participating in a whole class activity, there is no hierarchy during peer interaction. Third, most importantly, peer interaction creates opportunities for everyone to speak. This is apparent when it is compared with teacher-centered activities, even including ones that are truly communicative. In sum, peer interaction is a viable and important pedagogical option in many learning contexts.

Theories of peer interaction

This book includes empirical studies of peer interaction in L2 learning from social, cognitive, and sociocognitive perspectives. Researchers have attempted to reconcile the gap between the cognitive and social approaches for a long time (see Bergman 2011; Hulstijn et al. 2014; Sato & Ballinger 2012). Although these approaches view L2 development differently, employ different methodologies, and seek different outcomes (generalizability vs. complete understanding of interaction data from one specific context), we believe that studies from both paradigms can inform and benefit our overall understanding of peer interaction and how it can be used in the classroom.

The cognitive perspective

Peer interaction has predominantly been investigated from the cognitive perspective. The interactionist approach dates back to the late 1970s when researchers examined discourse between native speakers and non-native speakers (e.g., Hatch 1978). Based on this research, Long (1983) proposed the interaction hypothesis. The premise of the hypothesis is that when an L2 learner engages in interaction with a native speaker of the target language, there necessarily occurs a situation where communication is impeded due to a comprehensibility issue (a communication breakdown). To resolve this breakdown, learners must engage in certain interactional moves labeled negotiation for meaning. The native speaker then modifies what he or she originally said to make it more comprehensible. This type of input – comprehensible input – promotes second language acquisition (Krashen 1982). Hence, interaction that includes comprehensible input via modified interaction is considered to promote second language acquisition. Long (1996) eventually revised his hypothesis to emphasize the importance of implicit feedback – such as conversational recasts – that native speakers give in response to learners' incomprehensible utterances. In other words, the revised interaction hypothesis no longer argues that comprehensible input alone is sufficient for acquisition. In a more recent publication, Long (2015) maintained his position and argued that "the positive and negative feedback that target-like and deviant learner output and some kinds of communication problems (but not only communication problems) elicit from interlocutors is of particular importance for acquisition" (53). While reviewing this research is beyond the scope of this paper, there is substantial evidence that interaction does promote L2 learning (for reviews and meta-analyses, see García Mayo & Alcón Soler 2013; Gass 2003; Loewen 2015; Mackey 2007, 2012; Mackey, Abbuhl, & Gass 2012; Mackey & Goo 2007; Pica 2013; Russell & Spada 2006).

Following Long's revised interaction hypothesis, research gradually started to focus on corrective feedback as the most important interaction move (for a review of corrective feedback, see Lyster, Saito, & Sato 2013). The effectiveness of corrective feedback can be accounted for by several theories. First, corrective feedback may trigger noticing. Proposing the noticing hypothesis, Schmidt (1990) argued that "noticing the gap" between what learners produce and input in the environment is necessary for L2 learning because only the noticed input becomes intake (see also Schmidt & Frota 1986). When learners are given corrective feedback, their attention temporarily shifts to the formal aspects of language while maintaining the main focus on delivering the intended message. Second, feedback may provide learners with an opportunity to produce meaningful output as they attempt to, consciously or unconsciously, correct the original L2 error. This process of noticing the gap between what the learner knows and what he or she can actually say arguably benefits L2 learning (i.e., the output hypothesis: Swain 1985). This argument has been backed up by empirical studies (e.g., Izumi 2003; Loewen & Philp 2006; McDonough 2005; Russell 2014). Third, some researchers draw on skill acquisition theory to explain feedback effectiveness in relation to enhanced L2 production. This theory explains the importance of engaging in repeated practice and receiving feedback to avoid entrenching wrong knowledge representation (Anderson 2005; DeKeyser 2007; Lyster & Sato 2013). The practice effect has been shown to be beneficial for L2 development by neurocognitive and neurolinguistic research as well (Paradis 2009; Ullman 2005).

While a theoretical account for peer corrective feedback is rare in the literature, Sato and Lyster (2012) drew on Levelt's (1989) speech production model in order to theorize peer corrective feedback in a classroom-based experiment in which learners were trained to provide feedback to each other. The longitudinal intervention (10 weeks) resulted in an increase in grammatical accuracy. The researchers explained the effect by invoking Levelt's (1983) perceptual loop theory and proposed that peer corrective feedback serves a dual function and benefits both the provider and the receiver. That is, in order to provide corrective feedback to their classmates, learners need to notice errors in their classmates' speech first. This monitoring process facilitates L2 learning in the provider. Sato and Lyster (2012) argued that during peer interaction, this process of detecting an error (feedback provider) and rehearsing the error-free solution in turn (feedback receiver) contributes to the process of making effortful production to more automatic use of the target language, that is, proceduralization.

One may argue that peer corrective feedback, as opposed to teacher corrective feedback, should be discounted because of its quality (Adams, Nuevo, & Egi 2011). For this criticism, we argue first that there are empirical studies that have linked peer corrective feedback and L2 development (e.g., Sato & Lyster 2012). Second, although teacher's corrective feedback may be qualitatively better, this is only the case when feedback is provided. A number of studies of teachers' perceptions of corrective feedback revealed that they often hesitate in correcting their students' errors (see Brown 2009; Jean & Simard 2011; Lasagabaster & Sierra 2005). It also should be noted that research has confirmed that native speakers who are not trained teachers tend to give recasts, which tend to go unnoticed by the learner. These features of teacher corrective feedback lend support for peer interaction generally and peer feedback specifically because learners are exposed to more feedback, which could compensate for its quality (e.g., inaccurate or unfocused feedback).

The sociocultural perspective

Peer interaction has also been examined from the perspective of sociocultural theory. For researchers who draw on this theory to guide their investigations, cognitive theories provide only a partial picture of the complexity of language acquisition (Palinscar 1998). According to sociocultural theory, cognition and knowledge are inherently social and are dialogically constructed (Lantolf 2012). Foster and Ohta (2005:403) summarized this idea by arguing that "knowledge is not owned solely by the learner, but is also a property of social settings and the interface between person and social context."

Central to sociocultural theory is the concept of the zone of proximal development (ZPD) which Aljaafreh and Lantolf (1994) defined as: "the framework, par excellence, which brings all of the pieces of the learning setting together – the teacher, the learner, their social and cultural history, their goals and motives, as well as the resources available to them, including those that are dialogically constructed together" (468). In the ZPD, a novice learner is provided support by an expert. This support and the subsequent language exchanges between people and social environment is called scaffolding. While the original account proposed by Vygotsky (1978) was limited to the support provided by a person who is more competent (e.g., a native speaker), L2 researchers have adapted the idea to explain peer interaction. For instance, Donato (1994) observed the classroom interaction of American college learners of French who worked on open-ended collaborative tasks. The researcher sought to determine whether learners were capable of providing each other with support or guidance to the same extent as a teacher. Analyses revealed that learners are indeed capable and skillful at scaffolding and routinely do so during classroom activities. Similar claims were made by Swain and Lapkin (1998, 2001, 2002) in a series of studies looking at how French immersion students collaborate when given a writing task (e.g., a dictogloss task). By identifying dialogues where learners "generate alternatives, assess alternatives, and apply the resulting knowledge to solve a linguistic problem" (Swain & Lapkin 1998:333), the researchers emphasized the importance of collaborative work. Ohta's (2001) corpus of adult learners of Japanese also showed that, by engaging in dialogic activities, even less proficient learners could support more proficient learners. In their review paper, Swain, Brooks, and Tocalli-Beller (2002) asserted that peers can support each other by "questioning, proposing possible solutions, disagreeing, repeating, and managing activities and behaviors" (173) within the ZPD.

The idea of scaffolding and co-construction of knowledge was conceptualized into four different relationship patterns by Storch's (2002) oft-cited paper. Storch's data set involved the recorded interactions of 10 pairs of university-level ESL learners in Australia who worked on a range of communicative tasks. In the data set, the researcher identified two dimensions that defined the degree of learner collaboration. The first dimension was equality and pertained to the extent of control that the learners exhibited over the direction of the task. The second dimension was mutuality and was related to learners' level of engagement with their partners' contributions during the task. Based on the degrees of the two dimensions (high vs. low), she categorized the pairs into four quadrants. For instance, when a pair showed high equality and high mutuality, this pair was labeled as a collaborative pair. When a pair showed low equality and high mutuality, this pair was labeled as an expert/novice pair (the other two quadrants were dominant/dominant and dominant/passive). Further, Storch analyzed the transcripts in light of possible L2 learning opportunities (e.g., instances suggesting evidence of a transfer of knowledge). The combined analyses of patterns of relationships and L2 learning opportunities revealed that the collaborative and expert/novice patterns were more conducive to L2 learning than the other patterns (see also Brooks & Donato 1994; Buckwalter 2001; Galaczi 2008; Storch 2009).

Peer corrective feedback is a move associated with scaffolding and thus it is also of interest for researchers working from a sociocultural perspective. Aljaafreh and Lantolf (1994) identified three features that make corrective feedback more effective for learning within the ZPD. First, assistance should be graduated with no more help than needed. They argued that over-assistance may raise learners' affective filter. Second, assistance should be contingent; that is, when the learner shows that he or she does not need assistance anymore, feedback should be removed. Finally, assistance should be dialogic with both the learner and teacher (or another learner) collaborating to solve the problem.

Nassaji and Swain (2000) designed a small-scale study with two learners and compared two types of corrective feedback called ZPD and non-ZPD help. One of the learners received ZPD feedback that met the criteria proposed by Aljaafreh and Lantolf (1994) and the other learner received feedback rather at random. Nassaji and Swain found that the ZPD feedback contributed to an increase in the correct use of English articles more than the non-ZPD feedback. Ballinger (2013) examined peer corrective feedback drawing on sociocultural theory as well. Her approach interfaced the notion of peer collaboration and the impact of feedback. Her analysis of the interactions of eight French immersion learner pairs revealed that more collaborative interaction does not necessarily mean that learners give more feedback to each other. Ballinger suspected that provision of corrective feedback may indicate either a collaborative mindset or excessive corrective behaviors depending on pair dynamics.

Sociocognitive perspectives

The interactionist and sociocultural approaches are distinct and useful in different ways (see, for a general discussion regarding social vs. cognitive approaches to L2 research, Hulstijn et al. 2014). However, both of these approaches impose certain limitations on data analysis and the extent to which researchers are able to interpret their findings. As a result, in recent years, peer interaction researchers have increasingly begun to combine social and cognitive approaches in analyzing their data. According to Batstone (2010: 5), "Sociocognition is based on the view that neither language use nor language learning can be adequately defined or understood without recognizing that they have both a social and a cognitive dimension."

By examining the same transcripts, Foster and Ohta (2005) investigated how quantifying certain interactional moves based on the interactionist approach (i.e., comprehension checks, confirmation checks, and clarification requests) represents learners' collaborative behaviors. The researchers concluded that the three negotiation moves did not fully capture what was going on during interactions. This was because, despite the low frequency of negotiation moves, the learners did work on repairing and rewording their own utterances and also on assisting each other to find the right form to achieve message comprehensibility. The researchers concluded that "it is possible, perhaps likely, that a learner in a successful interaction is able and willing to focus on form without having first to be shunted into a communication problem" (426: see also Sato 2015a).

While Foster and Ohta suggested the difference between social and cognitive approaches, Sato and Ballinger (2012) endeavoured to combine them, believing that the conflict between the two paradigms is "ultimately problematic when it comes to transferring findings from L2 research into practice" (173). Demonstrating this concept, Storch and Wigglesworth (2010) addressed discrepancies in findings related to the effectiveness of indirect and direct feedback on learners' L2 writings by using a mixed-methods and sociocognitive approach. The researchers analyzed language-related episodes (LREs) that occurred as learners attempted to revise their written work based on feedback and compared this to learner's uptake in their revisions as well as in later writings. The LRE analysis consisted of first quantifying the number of LREs that occurred to determine learners' noticing of errors as well as the number of turns that learners produced during LREs to determine their level of engagement with the feedback. The researchers then qualitatively analyzed interaction during LREs to look for other factors impacting learners' uptake of feedback. In their cognitive and quantitative examination of LREs, the researchers again found that neither of the feedback methods consistently led to learner uptake. A closer examination of learner interaction revealed that uptake was more dependent on whether the learners perceived the feedback as useful for their own goals and whether it accorded with their own understanding and beliefs about language use. In other words, the combined social and cognitive approach to analyzing their interaction data allowed Storch and Wigglesworth to find a possible reason for the types of discrepancies frequently found in comparisons of direct and indirect feedback.

Mediating variables affecting peer interaction

Due to limited teacher oversight and control over *how* learners engage in a given task during peer interaction, peer interaction activities are vulnerable to internal and external factors that mediate the ultimate effect on learning. It is therefore essential that peer interaction research investigate such variables. The studies included in this volume aim to unveil the impact of task type, mode of interaction, proficiency level, learner relationships, and pedagogical intervention on learners' interactional behaviors and language production.

Task type

In the literature on peer interaction, one variable that has attracted a great amount of research is task type, partly due to the popularity of task-based language teaching research which often focuses on peer interaction (see Skehan 2014). One of the earlier studies that examined the impact of task type on interaction patterns is Pica, Kanagy, and Falodun (1993) who compared five types of pair or group activities: jigsaw, information gap activity, problem-solving, decision-making, and opinion exchange. Among those, the researchers argued that the jigsaw and information-gap tasks promote the most beneficial interaction patterns. This is because during jigsaw tasks, paired learners must share their respective parts equally (i.e., two-way information exchange) and then try to converge on a single outcome. During information-gap tasks, only one person holds the pertinent information, which the other partner must solicit (see also Foster 1998). The benefits of these types of tasks have been confirmed in both laboratory and classroom settings (Gass, Mackey, & Ross-Feldman 2005) as well as in the context of computer-mediated communication (Yilmaz 2011). McDonough and Mackey (2000) examined a jigsaw task, a picture description task, and a story sequencing task in light of how many of those activities elicit negotiations of form (noun classifiers, quantifiers, and question forms in Thai). The results revealed that both tasks elicited negotiation over the target structures except for question forms.

In the context of peer interaction, (a) learners communicate via body language, (b) they complete the task by relying on simple acknowledgements such as "yes/no," or (c) they avoid using the targeted linguistic structures because it is often the case that "successful completion of the task does not require the form" (McDonough & Mackey 2000: 84). Hence, task types are an important variable for peer interaction and necessitate further research investigating not only interactional moves but also task effects on L2 learning outcomes (see McDonough, Crawford, & Vleeschauwer Chapter 7 this volume).

Proficiency level

Two groups of studies have investigated the proficiency effect on interaction patterns as well as on L2 learning. The first group of studies compared learner pairs of the same or different L2 proficiency levels (Same vs. Mixed). Some research suggests that pairing learners with different proficiency levels promotes interaction that is more conducive to learning. For example, Porter (1986) found that learners produced more language when interacting with advanced-level L2 speakers than they did with intermediate-level L2 speakers. Kim and McDonough (2008) examined peer interaction of adult Korean learners and found that mixed pairs resolved language-related issues more successfully (especially for LREs related to lexical issues). In Watanabe and Swain's (2007) design, the same learners were paired with both higher and lower proficiency learners. Their analysis on the degree of collaboration (the quantity and quality of LREs) indicated that learning outcomes were mediated more by how collaborative a pair was than by their interlocutor's proficiency level. This finding, which gives counterevidence to the previous research, was corroborated by a more recent study by Storch and Aldosari (2013). Having analyzed the LREs, amount of L2 production (words and turns), and relationship patterns (e.g., expert/novice) of EFL learners in Saudi Arabia, they concluded that to understand the relationship between proficiency levels and L2 learning "it is not only proficiency difference which needs to be taken into consideration, but also the kind of relationship learners form when working in pairs" (46). Bigelow and King (Chapter 13 this volume) examined the interactions of students who were 'asymmetrically paired' in terms of their experience with formal schooling, English L2 oral and reading proficiency as they engaged in a paired reading task. Bigelow and King concluded that the desire to complete the reading task, combined with positive social dynamics between the students contributed to their interaction but due to the mismatched text, the interaction did little to contribute to L2 or literacy learning (see also Choi & Iwashita Chapter 4 this volume; Young & Tedick Chapter 5 this volume).

Meanwhile, other researchers paired learners with the same proficiency level and compared high and low proficiency pairs. The findings from these studies have been mixed. Williams (2001) analyzed the amount and types of LREs that occurred between adult learners of English. The results indicated that pairs with a higher proficiency produced more LREs. Moreover, those learners scored better on the tailor-made post-test in which the grammatical or lexical items that appeared in the LREs were tested (see also Williams 1999). Williams claimed that higher proficiency learners can pay more attention to formal aspects of the target language. However, Iwashita's (2001) study with adult learners of Japanese failed to show such an effect for proficiency. She quantified the amount of corrective feedback and subsequent modified output that learners produced. The comparisons between pairs with different proficiency levels did not detect any statistical differences. Sato and Viveros (Chapter 3 this volume) compared intact classes in a high school that had been divided into high and low proficiency classes. Their analysis of the levels of collaboration of the two classes indicated that the learners in the lower class engaged in more collaborative interactions, suggesting more learning opportunities for the learners with lower proficiency level (see Oliver 2002).

Hence, unlike the implicit premise of the interaction hypothesis (i.e., the interlocutor needs to be a more competent learner to offer comprehensible input that is a step beyond what the learner has already acquired) or the sociocultural theory (i.e., the ZPD is mediated by a more capable person), it may be the case that the effectiveness of peer interaction is mediated more by the social relationship learners construct (e.g., how collaborative a pair is) than by their proficiency levels.

Modality of interaction

Oral vs. written

The defining difference between oral and written interaction is the amount of time learners have in order to process the L2 in the two modes. Kuiken and Vedder (2012: 366) summarized that written production is much slower; hence, "cognitive resources can be used for a longer period of time, from which information retrieval from long-term memory, as well as planning time, should benefit" (see also Kormos & Trebits 2012; Niu 2009). In the context of peer interaction, however, the comparison research is scarce. Adams and Ross-Feldman (2008) compared two tasks (decision-making and story-completion tasks) both of which entailed oral and written components. They found greater percentages of LREs during the written components for both of the tasks. In addition to the outcomes of LREs (addressed vs. ignored; resolved vs. unresolved; correctly resolved vs. incorrectly resolved), García Mayo and Azkarai (Chapter 9 this volume) looked at learners' level of engagement, operationalized as whether both of, one of, or none of the paired learners addressed the linguistic issue. As they predicted, more LREs were identified during the written activities; however, learners showed comparable levels of engagement between the oral and written tasks.

Perhaps it is not surprising that written activities prompt more attention to formal aspects of language considering that (a) learners have visual information of the language and (b) they have more time to process the information. What is warranted is the investigation of the effect of different modes on the development of L2 knowledge. On the one hand, it is possible that completing an oral task leads to the development of oral skills because knowledge is transfer-appropriate; that is, knowledge that is acquired during a written task tends to be best used during writing and that orally acquired language is more easily accessed and used during subsequent oral interaction (see, for transfer-appropriate processing, DeKeyser 2010; Lyster & Sato 2013). On the other hand, it may be the case that an interaction activity regardless of its mode contributes to the construction of L2 knowledge. Therefore, examinations of different L2 performance (or types of knowledge) are required to know the ultimate effect of tasks types.

Face-to-face vs. computer-mediated communication

A growing amount of research has comparatively examined face-to-face (FTF) and computer-based communication (CMC). This is perhaps not very surprising given the fact that this communication mode is getting more popular every day (Steel & Levy 2013) and is even replacing traditional classroom interaction in some cases. Several modalities exist within the category of synchronous CMC, namely, written chat, voice-based CMC, and video-based CMC (for reviews, see Ortega 2009; Sauro 2011).

As suggested in the section of written vs. oral modes, the difference between written and oral CMC in terms of learners' formal attention is considerable because in the written CMC mode learners have time to look at the text sent by their partner, process the linguistic information, produce the language at their own pace, and at times modify what they have already written before sending the message (see Sauro & Smith 2010; Smith 2009). They can also go back and check the feedback given earlier in the conversation (Gurzynski-Weiss & Baralt 2014). Consequently, these features of written CMC may enhance the accuracy and complexity of L2 production (Pasfield-Neofitou 2012). Nonetheless, empirical evidence suggests that written CMC does not yield a better learning context when it comes to the occurrence of certain interactional moves. For example, Yanguas (2010) compared written CMC and oral CMC and identified comparable amounts of negotiation for meaning. Similarly, as reported in this volume, Loewen and Wolff (Chapter 6 this volume) compared three modes (FTF, oral CMC, and written CMC) and discovered that oral modes (both FTF and CMC) yielded more confirmation checks and LREs than the written CMC mode.

When FTF and written CMC interactions are compared, FTF interaction still seems to construct a better learning environment as shown by, for instance, the amount of negotiation (e.g., Lai & Zhao 2006). While Loewen and Wolff's (Chapter 6 this volume) data did not show much difference between the FTF and oral CMC interaction, Baralt, Gurzynski-Weiss, and Kim's (Chapter 8 this volume) study supported FTF over CMC interactions. Baralt et al. operationalized the concept of engagement with the language into cognitive, affective, and social engagement. The mode comparison revealed that, first, learners' language awareness (including their attention to form) was higher in the FTF class. Second, learners' attitude toward the task was more positive in the FTF context. In addition, learners engaged with each other more in the FTF than in the CMC interactions. Finally, Rouhshad and Storch (Chapter 10 this volume) compared FTF (a traditional notebook) and CMC (Google Docs) interactions on a collaborative writing task. The researchers compared the audio-recorded interaction from the FTF context and chat script from the CMC context using the LREs as an analysis unit. The results indicated that learners were in general more collaborative when engaging in FTF interaction: They tended to contribute to the task completion together and to build on each other's suggestions.

It is interesting that research suggests that FTF interaction creates a more conducive learning environment than CMC, which has been evidenced by both cognitive (e.g., amount of feedback) and social researchers (e.g., level of engagement). While it is too early to draw any conclusions, given that this research area is still young, research so far does not support the direction of many language teaching institutions and companies promoting online learning. While this approach to teaching language may facilitate access to the language classroom for certain types of learners, it may also have its drawbacks. It is important to note, however, that many language teaching models, especially commercial ones, are not writing-based or voiced-based but video-based. Indeed, video-based synchronous CMC has not been extensively investigated to date. Also important to note is that the CMC examined in the previous research has been mostly dyadic, while FTF is operationalized as class-size interaction. Given that there are many online platforms that let us engage in video-based communication (video-conference software), investigating video-based synchronous CMC is a promising research direction (see Sato 2015b).

Learner relationships

The studies reviewed in the previous section dealt with variables that can be manipulated by the researcher or teacher. While those variables have certainly been found to affect learners' interaction behaviors to different degrees, research increasingly suggests that the inherently social nature of peer interaction works as a kind of filter through which all of the other factors must pass. Whether researchers refer to this aspect of peer interaction as learners' relationship, their mindset, their patterns of interaction, or their social dynamics, research findings tell us that learners' ability to profit from peer interaction is greatly affected by the social dynamics of their group or pair. This line of thinking is evident in many studies in this book as well (see chapters in this volume by García Mayo & Azkarai; Baralt, Gurzynski-Weiss, & Kim; Bigelow & King; Choi & Iwashita; Martin-Beltrán, Chen, Guzman, & Merrills; Moranski & Toth; Sato & Viveros; Rouhshad & Storch; Young & Tedick). For example, although Moranski and Toth (Chapter 11 this volume) sought to examine whether the amount and complexity (levels of analytical abstraction) of meta-analytic talk affected U.S. high school students' scores on grammaticality judgement tests, they found a more important link between levels of mutuality in collaborative group interaction and students' test scores.

Martin-Beltrán et al. (Chapter 12 this volume) examined high school students' interactions in an after-school language exchange program, finding that their use of relationship-building discourse helped them to build 'comity', which in turn may have opened opportunities for co-construction of knowledge and L2 learning. The researchers argue in favor of recognizing social discourse as a tool to expand language learning among peers. On the other hand, Fernández Dobao (Chapter 1 this volume) examined the role of the silent collaborator in group interactions, finding that learners who acted as silent observers of LREs still benefited from them in terms of vocabulary learning. Fernández Dobao's work not only highlights interaction researchers' over-adherence to measuring the benefits of peer interaction through students' language production, it also underscores the need to conduct more research that looks at how individuals' social behavior in previously unexamined patterns of peer interaction affects their and other group members' L2 learning.

Pedagogical interventions

Although one of the goals of peer interaction is to promote learners' autonomy and control, this does not imply that the teacher does not play a role in determining the success of peer interaction activities. To the contrary, in both preparing students for peer interaction and in scaffolding students' efforts during peer interaction activities, we believe that the teacher is an essential part of effective peer interaction.

Learner priming and training
Many L2 educators may have concerns regarding the quality of their students' language production and the utility of peer interaction as a source of L2 learning. For instance, learners may resort to their L1 to solve a communication issue and avoid negotiation (Loschky & Bley-Vroman 1993). Even when they are involved in the task, their communication could be as simple as a series of "yes" or "no" responses (Færch & Kasper 1983). As suggested by McDonough and Mackey (2000) learners tend not to shift their attention to form by themselves and thus corrective feedback on form rarely happens in communicative peer interaction. Even when a learner decides to work on a L2 error by pointing it out to his or her partner, the quality of corrective feedback may be low.

In order to overcome such obstacles, some researchers have manipulated the way in which learners engage in interaction. For instance, McDonough (2011) used priming to elicit a certain linguistic structure (English questions). This is a helpful technique given that learners may use a different structure (e.g., simple sentences) to express the same meaning when they are expected to practice a certain structure (e.g., relative clauses). Manipulating how learners interact with each other is also an important research and pedagogical direction, and some studies have attempted to engage in learner training for interaction. Kim (2013) modeled effective interaction to learners before they engaged in peer interaction. Ballinger (2013) created and taught a set of strategies designed to help learners learn from and teach one another during peer interaction. Sato and Lyster (2012) developed a teaching material designed to train learners how to provide corrective feedback to each other. The same initiative was taken by Fujii, Mackey, and Ziegler (Chapter 2 this volume) as well (see also Fujii & Mackey 2009; Naughton 2006; Sato & Ballinger 2012).

Teacher scaffolding
Henderson and Palmer (2015) note that peer interaction studies consistently overlook the teacher's role in supporting, or scaffolding the quality and quantity of students' L2 production during collaborative activities. Walqui (2006) outlined three

related pedagogical scales of scaffolding: *planned* curricular progression over time such as rituals or a series of tasks, the *procedures* used to organize a specific task, and the collaborative *process of interaction* that takes place during a task. While the priming and training studies described above reflect planned pre-task scaffolding, none of the studies in this volume explicitly examined the impact of the teacher's (or researcher's) procedures in organizing peer interaction nor their scaffolding through interaction with students during peer interaction.

Nevertheless, Sato and Viveros (Chapter 3 this volume) incidentally described how the teacher's attitude may affect learners' engagement during peer interaction activities. In that study, the teacher of the class in which lower collaboration was identified remained seated at his computer during peer interaction activities, while the teacher of the class in which higher collaboration was identified circulated among his students, offering support when necessary. While this may be an extreme case, it is safe to say that many teachers assign a peer interaction activity without giving students any instruction regarding how they should interact during what is meant to be a learning activity and without offering students ongoing support. Sato and Ballinger (2012) emphasized the importance of constructing a collaborative environment in the classroom prior to pair or group activities. Without the teacher's skillful set up, the potential of peer interaction activities can be wasted and classroom time lost.

Teachers cannot and probably should not manage all peer interaction, lest they override one of its key advantages – the absence of an authority figure and the resulting freedom students have to take risks and experiment with linguistic forms. Nevertheless, teaching students how to better interact during peer interaction, taking the time to make informed decisions in organizing such activities, and supporting students during those activities are all ways for teachers to play an active role in making their students more autonomous learners and increasing the effectiveness of peer interaction in their classrooms.

About this book

This book includes 13 empirical studies that involved more than 500 L2 learners. While the majority of what we know about peer interaction is based on reported adult ESL research from North America, New Zealand, and Australia, this volume includes learners whose first languages vary widely (e.g., Amharic, Arabic, Basque, Chinese, Korean, Japanese, Somali, Thai, Vietnamese), who are at different educational levels (elementary, high school, and university), and who are learning various target languages (e.g., English, French, Spanish). In addition, the data collection settings are varied. The studies, the majority of which were classroom-based, were conducted in Australia, the Basque Country, Canada, Chile, Japan, Spain, Thailand, and the United States.

Since one of the aims of this book was to present a variety of theoretical perspectives taken in examining similar phenomena, each chapter includes a section called "methodological framework" in which the authors justify their methodologies by explaining how they inform their research questions. Due to the persistent gap between research and practice, which leads to (a) researchers not taking the classroom context into consideration when constructing and analyzing their research and (b) teachers being uninformed regarding the latest research findings, all the chapters in this book also include a section for "pedagogical implications."

Section 1 addresses questions regarding interactional patterns and learner characteristics. In Chapter 1, Fernández Dobao examines the interactional behaviors and vocabulary learning of silent learners during group interaction to determine whether they can benefit from peer interaction without actively contributing to LREs. In Chapter 2, Fujii, Ziegler, and Mackey present an intervention in which they taught learners how to provide feedback to each other and examine the extent to which they can acquire the strategy. In Chapter 3, Sato and Viveros examine the effect of proficiency level on interactional patterns and L2 development by comparing classes with different proficiency levels. Similarly, in Chapter 4, Choi and Iwashita investigate how the interlocutor's proficiency level affects the dynamics of group work by mixing learners with different proficiency levels. Finally, in Chapter 5, Young and Tedick present the impact of social relationship on collaboration in groups with heterogeneous proficiency levels versus homogeneous proficiency levels.

In Section 2, questions surrounding tasks and interactional modality are examined. In Chapter 6, Loewen and Wolff examine interactional moves (e.g., negotiation for meaning and recasts) in FTF and CMC contexts. In Chapter 7, McDonough et al. looks at how summary-writing tasks affect learner interaction when they talk about language, content, and organization. In Chapter 8, Baralt, Gurzynski-Weiss, and Kim compare FTF and CMC modalities by examining how susceptible the modality is to tasks with different cognitive complexity. In Chapter 9, García Mayo and Azkarai compare oral vs. written tasks, focusing on how the two types of tasks influence peer interaction (e.g., LREs and level of engagement). In Chapter 10, Rouhshad and Storch conduct an in-depth analysis of collaborative patterns in FTF and CMC settings. Finally, in Chapter 11, Moranski and Toth present a study of learners' rule-generation processes during inductive consciousness-raising tasks.

Section 3, in which questions related to learning settings are explored, includes studies conducted in different L2 learning contexts. The data in Martin-Beltrán, Chen, Guzman, and Merrills study (Chapter 12) were collected in a multilingual setting where they examined how learners whose first language is either majority or minority together create learning opportunities during peer interaction. Bigelow and King's investigation (Chapter 13) involves immigrant populations in the United States who have learned their L2 without having developed strong literacy levels in their first language.

References

Adams, R., Nuevo, A., & Egi, T. (2011). Explicit and implicit feedback, modified output, and SLA: Does explicit and implicit feedback promote learning and learner-learner interactions? *Modern Language Journal*, 95, 42–63. doi:10.1111/j.1540-4781.2011.01242.x

Adams, R., & Ross-Feldman, L. (2008). Does writing influence learner attention to form? In D. Belcher & A. Hirvela (Eds.), *The oral-literate connection. perspectives on L2 speaking, writing, and other media interactions* (pp. 243–265). Ann Arbor, MI: The University of Michigan Press.

Alcón, E. (2002). Relationship between teacher-led versus learners' interaction and the development of pragmatics in the EFL classroom. *International Journal of Educational Research*, 37(3-4), 359–377. doi:10.1016/S0883-0355(03)00010-7

Aljaafreh, A., & Lantolf, J. (1994). Negative feedback as regulation and second language learning in the zone of proximal development. *The Modern Language Journal*, 78(4), 465–483. doi:10.1111/j.1540-4781.1994.tb02064.x

Anderson, J. (2005). *Cognitive psychology and its implications* (6 ed.). New York, NY: Worth Publishers.

Angelova, M., Gunawardena, D., & Volk, D. (2006). Peer teaching and learning: Co-constructing language in a dual language first grade. *Language and Education*, 20(3), 173–190. doi:10.1080/09500780608668722

Ballinger, S. (2013). Towards a cross-linguistic pedagogy: Biliteracy and reciprocal learning strategies in French immersion. *Journal of Immersion and Content-Based Language Education*, 1(1), 131–148. doi:10.1075/jicb.1.1.06bal

Ballinger, S., & Lyster, R. (2011). Student and teacher oral language use in a two-way Spanish/English immersion school. *Language Teaching Research*, 15(3), 289–306.

Batstone, R. (2010). Issues and options in sociocognition. In R. Batstone (Ed.), *Sociocognitive perspectives on language use and language learning* (pp. 3–23). Oxford: Oxford University Press.

Bergman, M. (2011). The good, the bad, and the ugly in mixed methods research and design. *Journal of Mixed Methods Research*, 5(4), 271–275. doi:10.1177/1558689811433236

Brooks, F., & Donato, R. (1994). Vygotskyan approaches to understanding foreign language learner discourse during communicative tasks. *Hispania*, 77(2), 262–274. doi:10.2307/344508

Brown, A. (2009). Students' and teachers' perceptions of effective foreign language teaching: A comparison of ideals. *The Modern Language Journal*, 93(1), 46–60. doi:10.1111/j.1540-4781.2009.00827.x

Bruton, A., & Samuda, V. (1980). Learner and teacher roles in the treatment of oral error in group work. *RELC Journal*, 11(2), 49–63. doi:10.1177/003368828001100204

Buckwalter, P. (2001). Repair sequences in Spanish L2 dyadic discourse: A descriptive study. *The Modern Language Journal*, 85(3), 380–397. doi:10.1111/0026-7902.00115

de Bot, K. (1996). The psycholinguistics of the output hypothesis. *Language Learning*, 46(3), 529–555. doi:10.1111/j.1467-1770.1996.tb01246.x

DeKeyser, R. (2010). Practice for second language learning: Don't throw out the baby with the bathwater. *International Journal of English Studies*, 10(1), 155–165.

DeKeyser, R. (Ed.). (2007). *Practice in a second language: Perspectives from applied linguistics and cognitive psychology*. Cambridge: Cambridge University Press.

Donato, R. (1994). Collective scaffolding in second language learning. In J. Lantolf & G. Appel (Eds.), *Vygotskian approaches to second language research* (pp. 33–56). Norwood, NJ: Ablex.

Færch, C., & Kasper, G. (1983). Plans and strategies in foreign language communication. In C. Færch & G. Kasper (Eds.), *Strategies in interlanguage communication* (pp. 20–60). London: Longman.

Fernández Dobao, A. (2012). Collaborative dialogue in learner–learner and learner–native speaker interaction. *Applied Linguistics*, 33(3), 229–256. doi:10.1093/applin/ams002

Foster, P. (1998). A classroom perspective on the negotiation of meaning. *Applied Linguistics*, 14(1), 1–23. doi:10.1093/applin/19.1.1

Foster, P., & Ohta, A. (2005). Negotiation for meaning and peer assistance in second language classrooms. *Applied Linguistics*, 26(3), 402–430. doi:10.1093/applin/ami014

Fotos, S. (1998). Shifting the focus from forms to form in the EFL classroom. *ELT Journal*, 52(4), 301–307. doi:10.1093/elt/52.4.301

Fujii, A., & Mackey, A. (2009). Interactional feedback in learner-learner interactions in a task-based EFL classroom. *International Review of Applied Linguistics in Language Teaching*, 47(3), 267–301. doi:10.1515/iral.2009.012

Galaczi, E. (2008). Peer-peer interaction in a speaking test: The case of the First Certificate in English Examination. *Language Assessment Quarterly*, 5(2), 89–119. doi:10.1080/15434300801934702

García Mayo, M. P., & Alcón Soler, E. (2013). Negotiated input and output / interaction. In J. Herschensohn & M. Young-Scholten (Eds.), *The Cambridge Handbook of Second Language Acquisition* (pp. 209–299). Cambridge: Cambridge University Press. doi:10.1017/CBO9781139051729.014

García Mayo, M. P., & Pica, T. (2000). L2 learner interaction in a foreign language setting: Are learning needs addressed? *International Review of Applied Linguistics*, 38(1), 35–58.

Gass, S. (2003). Input and interaction. In C. Doughty & M. Long (Eds.), *Handbook of second language acquisition* (pp. 224–255). Oxford: Blackwell. doi:10.1002/9780470756492.ch9

Gass, S., Mackey, A., & Ross-Feldman, L. (2005). Task-based interactions in classroom and laboratory settings. *Language Learning*, 55(4), 575–611. doi:10.1111/j.0023-8333.2005.00318.x

Gass, S., & Varonis, E. (1989). Incorporated repairs in nonnative discourse. In M. Eisenstein (Ed.), *The dynamic interlanguage: Empirical studies in second language variation* (pp. 71–86). New York, NY: Plenum Press. doi:10.1007/978-1-4899-0900-8_5

Gupta, D. (2004). CLT in India: Context and methodology come together. *ELT Journal*, 58(3), 266–269. doi:10.1093/elt/58.3.266

Gurzynski-Weiss, L., & Baralt, M. (2014). Exploring learner perception and use of task-based interactional feedback in FTF and CMC modes. *Studies in Second Language Acquisition*, 36(1), 1–37. doi:10.1017/S0272263113000363

Hatch, E. (1978). Discourse analysis and second language acquisition. In E. Hatch (Ed.), *Second language acquisition: A book of readings* (pp. 401–435). Rowley, MA: Newbury House.

Henderson, K., & Palmer, D. (2015). Teacher scaffolding and pair work in a pre-K bilingual classroom. *Journal of Immersion and Content-Based Language Education*, 3(1), 77–101. doi:10.1075/jicb.3.1.04hen

Hulstijn, J., Young, R., Ortega, L., Bigelow, M., DeKeyser, R., Ellis, N., Lantolf, J., Mackey, A., & Talmy, S. (2014). Bridging the gap: Cognitive and social approaches to research in second language learning and teaching. *Studies in Second Language Acquisition*, 36, 1–61. doi:10.1017/S0272263114000035

Iwashita, N. (2001). The effect of learner proficiency on interactional moves and modified output in nonnative-nonnative interaction in Japanese as a foreign language. *System*, 29(2), 267–287. doi:10.1016/S0346-251X(01)00015-X

Izumi, S. (2003). Comprehension and production processes in second language learning: In search of the psycholinguistic rationale of the output hypothesis. *Applied Linguistics*, 24(2), 168–196. doi:10.1093/applin/24.2.168

Jean, G., & Simard, D. (2011). Grammar teaching and learning in L2: Necessary, but boring? *Foreign Language Annals*, 44(3), 467–494. doi:10.1111/j.1944-9720.2011.01143.x

Khazaei, Z., Zadeh, A., & Ketabi, S. (2012). Willingness to communicate in Iranian EFL learners: The effect of class size *English Language Teaching*, 5(11), 181–187.

Kim, Y. (2013). Effects of pretask modeling on attention to form and question development. *TESOL Quarterly*, 47(1), 8–35. doi:10.1002/tesq.52

Kim, Y., & McDonough, K. (2008). The effect of interlocutor proficiency on the collaborative dialogue between Korean as a second language learners. *Language Teaching Research*, 12(2), 211–234. doi:10.1177/1362168807086288

Kim, Y., & McDonough, K. (2011). Using pretask modelling to encourage collaborative learning opportunities. *Language Teaching Research*, 15(2), 183–199. doi:10.1177/1362168810388711

Kormos, J. (2006). *Speech production and second language acquisition*. Mahwah, NJ: Lawrence Erlbaum Associates.

Kormos, J., & Kiddle, T. (2013). The role of socio-economic factors in motivation to learn English as a foreign language: The case of Chile. *System*, 41(2), 399–412. doi:10.1016/j.system.2013.03.006

Kormos, J., & Trebits, A. (2012). The role of task complexity, modality, and aptitude in narrative task performance. *Language Learning*, 62(2), 439–472. doi:10.1111/j.1467-9922.2012.00695.x

Krashen, S. (1982). *Principles and practice in second language acquisition*. Oxford: Pergamon.

Kuiken, F., & Vedder, I. (2012). Speaking and writing tasks and their effects on second language performance. In S. Gass & A. Mackey (Eds.), *The Routledge handbook of second language acquisition* (pp. 364–377). New York: Routledge.

Lai, C., & Zhao, Y. (2006). Noticing and text-based chat. *Language Learning & Technology*, 10(3), 102–120.

Lam, R. (2015). Language assessment training in Hong Kong: Implications for language assessment literacy. *Language Testing*, 32, 169–197. doi:10.1177/0265532214554321

Lantolf, J. (2012). Sociocultural theory: A dialectical approach to L2 research. In S. Gass & A. Mackey (Eds.), *The Routledge handbook of second language acquisition* (pp. 57–72). New York, NY: Routledge.

Lasagabaster, D., & Sierra, J. M. (2005). Error correction: Students' versus teachers' perceptions. *Language Awareness*, 14(2-3), 112–127. doi:10.1080/09658410508668828

Levelt, W. (1983). Monitoring and self-repair in speech. *Cognition*, 14(1), 41–104. doi:10.1016/0010-0277(83)90026-4

Levelt, W. (1989). *Speaking: From intention to articulation.* Cambridge, MA: The MIT Press.

Loewen, S. (2015). *Introduction to instructed second language acquisition.* New York, NY: Routledge.

Loewen, S., & Philp, J. (2006). Recasts in the adult English L2 classroom: Characteristics, explicitness, and effectiveness. *The Modern Language Journal*, 90(4), 536–556. doi: 10.1111/j.1540-4781.2006.00465.x

Long, M. (1981). Input, interaction, and second language acquisition. *Annals of the New York Academy of Sciences*, 379, 259–278. doi: 10.1111/j.1749-6632.1981.tb42014.x

Long, M. (1983). Linguistic and conversational adjustments in non-native speakers. *Studies in Second Language Acquisition*, 5(2), 177–193. doi: 10.1017/S0272263100004848

Long, M. (1996). The role of the linguistic environment in second language acquisition. In W. Ritchie & T. Bhatia (Eds.), *Handbook of second language acquisition* (pp. 413–468). San Diego, CA: Academic Press.

Long, M. (2015). *Second language acquisition and task-based language teaching.* Chichester, UK: Wiley Blackwell.

Loschky, L., & Bley-Vroman, R. (1993). Grammar and task-based methodology. In G. Crookes & S. Gass (Eds.), *Tasks and language learning* (pp. 123–167). Clevedon, UK: Multilingual Matters.

Lyster, R. (1987). Speaking immersion. *The Canadian Modern Language Review*, 43(4), 701–717.

Lyster, R., Saito, K., & Sato, M. (2013). State-of-the-art article: Oral corrective feedback in second language classrooms. *Language Teaching*, 46(1), 1–40. doi: 10.1017/S0261444812000365

Lyster, R., & Sato, M. (2013). Skill acquisition theory and the role of practice in L2 development. In M. G. Mayo, J. Gutierrez-Mangado, & M. M. Adrián (Eds.), *Contemporary approaches to second language acquisition* (pp. 71–92). Amsterdam: John Benjamins. doi: 10.1075/aals.9.07ch4

Mackey, A. (2007). Introduction: The role of conversational interaction in second language acquisition. In A. Mackey (Ed.), *Conversational interaction in second language acquisition: A collection of empirical studies* (pp. 1–26). Oxford: Oxford University Press.

Mackey, A. (2012). *Input, interaction, and corrective feedback in L2 learning.* Oxford: Oxford University Press.

Mackey, A., Abbuhl, R., & Gass, S. (2012). Interactionist approach. In S. Gass & A. Mackey (Eds.), *The Routledge handbook of second language acquisition* (pp. 7–23). New York, NY: Routledge.

Mackey, A., & Goo, J. (2007). Interaction research in SLA: A meta-analysis and research synthesis. In A. Mackey (Ed.), *Conversational interaction in second language acquisition: A collection of empirical studies* (pp. 407–452). Oxford: Oxford University Press.

Mackey, A., Oliver, R., & Leeman, J. (2003). Interactional input and the incorporation of feedback: An exploration of NS-NNS and NNS-NNS adult and child dyads. *Language Learning*, 53(1), 35–66. doi: 10.1111/1467-9922.00210

McCollum, P. (1999). Learning to value English: Cultural capital in a dual language bilingual program. *Bilingual Research Journal*, 23(1), 133–134. doi: 10.1080/15235882.1999.10668682

McDonough, K. (2004). Learner-learner interaction during pair and small group activities in a Thai EFL context. *System*, 32(2), 207–224. doi: 10.1016/j.system.2004.01.003

McDonough, K. (2005). Identifying the impact of negative feedback and learners' responses on ESL question development. *Studies in Second Language Acquisition*, 27(1), 79–103. doi: 10.1017/S0272263105050047

McDonough, K. (2011). Eliciting wh-questions through collaborative syntactic priming activities during peer interaction. In P. Trofimovich & K. McDonough (Eds.), *Applying priming methods to L2 learning, teaching and research* (pp. 131–151). Amsterdam: John Benjamins. doi:10.1075/lllt.30.10mcd

McDonough, K., & Chaikitmongkol, W. (2010). Collaborative syntactic priming activities and EFL learners' production of wh-questions. *The Canadian Modern Language Review, 66*(6), 817–841. doi:10.3138/cmlr.66.6.817

McDonough, K., & Mackey, A. (2000). Communicative tasks, conversational interaction, and linguistic form: An empirical study of Thai. *Foreign Language Annals, 33*(1), 82–91. doi:10.1111/j.1944-9720.2000.tb00893.x

Nassaji, H., & Swain, M. (2000). A Vygotskyan perspective on corrective feedback in L2: The effect of random versus negotiated help in the learning of English articles. *Language Awareness, 9*(1), 34–51. doi:10.1080/09658410008667135

Naughton, D. (2006). Cooperative strategy training and oral interaction: Enhancing small group communication in the language classroom. *The Modern Language Journal, 90*(2), 169–184. doi:10.1111/j.1540-4781.2006.00391.x

Niu, R. (2009). Effect of task-inherent production modes on EFL learners' focus on form. *Language Awareness, 18*(3–4), 384–402. doi:10.1080/09658410903197256

Ohta, A. (2001). *Second language acquisition processes in the classroom: Learning Japanese.* Mahwah, NJ: Lawrence Erlbaum Associates.

Oliver, R. (2002). The patterns of negotiation for meaning in child interactions. *The Modern Language Journal, 86*(1), 97–111. doi:10.1111/1540-4781.00138

Ortega, L. (2009). Interaction and attention to form in L2 text-based computer-mediated communication. In A. Mackey & C. Polio (Eds.), *Multiple perspectives on interaction: Second language research in honour of Susan Gass* (pp. 226–253). New York, NY: Routledge.

Palinscar, A. (1998). Social constructionist perspectives on teaching and learning. *Annual Review of Psychology, 49*, 345–375. doi:10.1146/annurev.psych.49.1.345

Paradis, M. (2009). *Declarative and procedural determinants of second languages.* Amsterdam: John Benjamins. doi:10.1075/sibil.40

Pasfield-Neofitou, S. (2012). *Online communication in a second language: Social interaction, language use, and learning Japanese.* Bristol, UK: Multilingual Matters.

Philp, J., Adams, R., & Iwashita, N. (2014). *Peer interaction and second language learning.* New York, NY: Routledge.

Philp, J., & Tognini, R. (2009). Language acquisition in foreign language contexts and the differential benefits of interaction. *International Review of Applied Linguistics in Language Teaching, 47*(3-4), 245–266. doi:10.1515/iral.2009.011

Philp, J., Walter, S., & Basturkmen, H. (2010). Peer interaction in the foreign language classroom: What factors foster a focus on form? *Language Awareness, 19*(4), 261–279. doi:10.1080/09658416.2010.516831

Pica, T. (2013). From input, output and comprehension to negotiation, evidence, and attention: An overview of theory and research on learner interaction and SLA. In M. G. Mayo, J. Gutierrez-Mangado, & M. M. Adrián (Eds.), *Contemporary approaches to second language acquisition* (pp. 49–69). Amsterdam: John Benjamins. doi:10.1075/aals.9.06ch3

Pica, T., Kanagy, R., & Falodun, J. (1993). Choosing and using tasks for second language instruction and research. In G. Crookes & S. Gass (Eds.), *Tasks and language learning: Integrating theory and practice* (pp. 9–34). Clevedon, UK: Multilingual Matters.

Pica, T., Lincoln-Porter, F., Paninos, D., & Linnell, J. (1996). Language learners' interaction: How does it address the input, output, and feedback needs of L2 learners? *TESOL Quarterly*, 30(1), 59–84. doi:10.2307/3587607

Pienemann, M., & Johnston, M. (1987). Factors influencing the development of language proficiency. In D. Nunan (Ed.), *Applying second language acquisition research* (pp. 45–141). Adelaide, Australia: National Curriculum Resource Center, Adult Migrant Education Program.

Porter, P. (1986). How learners talk to each other: Input and interaction in task-centered discussions. In R. Day (Ed.), *Talking to learn: Conversation in second language acquisition* (pp. 200–222). Rowley, MA: Newbury House.

Potowski, K. (2007). *Language and identity in a dual immersion school*. Clevedon, UK: Multilingual Matters.

Pritchard, R., & Maki, H. (2006). The changing self-perceptions of Japanese university students of English. *Journal of Studies in International Education*, 10(2), 141–156. doi:10.1177/1028315305283928

Russell, J., & Spada, N. (2006). The effectiveness of corrective feedback for the acquisition of L2 grammar. In J. Norris & L. Ortega (Eds.), *Synthesizing research on language learning and teaching* (pp. 133–162). Amsterdam: John Benjamins.

Russell, V. (2014). A closer look at the Output Hypothesis: The effect of pushed output on noticing and inductive learning of the Spanish future tense. *Foreign Language Annals*, 47(1), 25–47. doi:10.1111/flan.12077

Sato, M. (2007). Social relationships in conversational interaction: A comparison between learner-learner and learner-NS dyads. *JALT Journal*, 29(2), 183–208.

Sato, M. (2013). Beliefs about peer interaction and peer corrective feedback: Efficacy of classroom intervention. *The Modern Language Journal*, 97(3), 611–633. doi:10.1111/j.1540-4781.2013.12035.x

Sato, M. (2015a). Density and complexity of oral production in interaction: The interactionist approach and an alternative. *International Review of Applied Linguistics in Language Teaching* 53(3) 307–329. doi:10.1515/iral-2015-0016

Sato, M. (2015b). *The noticeability and effectiveness of corrective feedback in video-based interaction*. Selected plenary presented at *XVII International CALL Research Conference*, Tarragona, Spain.

Sato, M., & Ballinger, S. (2012). Raising language awareness in peer interaction: A cross-context, cross-method examination. *Language Awareness*, 21(1-2), 157–179. doi:10.1080/09658416.2011.639884

Sato, M., & Lyster, R. (2007). Modified output of Japanese EFL learners: Variable effects of interlocutor vs. feedback types. In A. Mackey (Ed.), *Conversational interaction in second language acquisition: A collection of empirical studies* (pp. 123–142). Oxford: Oxford University Press.

Sato, M., & Lyster, R. (2012). Peer interaction and corrective feedback for accuracy and fluency development: Monitoring, practice, and proceduralization. *Studies in Second Language Acquisition*, 34(4), 591–262. doi:10.1017/S0272263112000356

Sauro, S. (2011). SCMC for SLA: A research synthesis. *CALICO Journal*, 28(1), 1–23. doi:10.11139/cj.28.2.369-391

Sauro, S., & Smith, B. (2010). Investigating L2 performance in text chat. *Applied Linguistics*, 31(4), 554–577. doi:10.1093/applin/amq007

Schmidt, R. (1990). The role of consciousness in second language learning. *Applied Linguistics*, 11(2), 129–158. doi:10.1093/applin/11.2.129

Schmidt, R., & Frota, S. (1986). Developing basic conversational ability in a second language: A case study of an adult leaner of Portuguese. In R. Day (Ed.), *Talking to learn* (pp. 237–326). Rowley, MA: Newbury House.

Shehadeh, A. (1999). Non-native speakers' production of modified comprehensible output and second language learning. *Language Learning*, 49(4), 627–675. doi:10.1111/0023-8333.00104

Shehadeh, A. (2001). Self- and other-initiated modified output during task-based interaction. *TESOL Quarterly*, 35(3), 433–457. doi:10.2307/3588030

Shehadeh, A., & Coombe, C. (Eds.). (2012). *Task-based language teaching in foreign language contexts: Research and implimentation*. Amsterdam: John Benjamins. doi:10.1075/tblt.4

Shonerd, H. (1994). Repair in spontaneous speech: A window on second language development. In V. John-Steiner, C. Panofsky, & L. Smith (Eds.), *Sociocultural approaches to language and literacy: An interactionist perspective* (pp. 82–108). Cambridge: Cambridge University Press. doi:10.1017/CBO9780511897047.004

Skehan, P. (Ed.). (2014). *Processing perspectives on task performance*. Amsterdam: John Benjamins. doi:10.1075/tblt.5

Smith, B. (2009). The relationship between scrolling, negotiation, and self-initiated self-repair in an SCMC environment. *CALICO Journal*, 26(2), 231–245.

Steel, C., & Levy, M. (2013). Language students and their technologies: Charting the evolution 2006–2011. *ReCALL*, 25(3), 306–320. doi:10.1017/S0958344013000128

Storch, N. (2002). Patterns of interaction in ESL pair work. *Language Learning*, 52(1), 119–158. doi:10.1111/1467-9922.00179

Storch, N. (2009). *The nature of pair interaction: Learners? interaction in an ESL class: Its nature and impact on grammatical development*. Saarbrücken, Germany: VDM Verlag.

Storch, N., & Aldosari, A. (2013). Pairing learners in pair work activity. *Language Teaching Research*, 17(1), 31–48. doi:10.1177/1362168812457530

Storch, N., & Wigglesworth, G. (2010). Students' engagement with feedback on writing: The role of learner agency/beliefs. In R. Batstone (Ed.), *Sociocognitive perspectives on language use and language learning* (pp. 166–185). Oxford: Oxford University Press.

Swain, M. (1985). Communicative competence: Some roles of comprehensible input and comprehensible output in its development. In S. Gass & C. Madden (Eds.), *Input in second language acquisition* (pp. 235–253). Rowley, MA: Newbury House.

Swain, M., Brooks, L., & Tocalli-Beller, A. (2002). Peer-peer dialogue as a means of second language learning. *Annual Review of Applied Linguistics*, 22, 171–185. doi:10.1017/S0267190502000090

Swain, M., & Lapkin, S. (1998). Interaction and second language learning: Two adolescent French immersion students working together. *The Modern Language Journal*, 82(3), 320–337. doi:10.1111/j.1540-4781.1998.tb01209.x

Swain, M., & Lapkin, S. (2001). Focus on form through collaborative dialogue: Exploring task effects. In M. Bygate, P. Skehan, & M. Swain (Eds.), *Researching pedagogic tasks: Second language learning, teaching and testing* (pp. 99–118). Harlow, UK: Longman.

Swain, M., & Lapkin, S. (2002). Talking it through: Two French immersion learners' response to reformulation. *International Journal of Educational Research*, 37(3), 285–304. doi:10.1016/S0883-0355(03)00006-5

Tarone, E., & Swain, M. (1995). A sociolinguistic perspective on second language use in immersion classrooms. *The Modern Language Journal*, 79(1), 166–178. doi:10.1111/j.1540-4781.1995.tb05428.x

Toth, P. (2008). Teacher- and learner-led discourse in task-based grammar instruction: Providing procedural assistance for L2 morphosyntactic development. *Language Learning*, 58(2), 237–283. doi:10.1111/j.1467-9922.2008.00441.x

Toth, P., Wagner, E., & Moranski, K. (2013). 'Co-constructing' explicit L2 knowledge with high school Spanish learners through guided induction. *Applied Linguistics*, 34(3), 255–278. doi:10.1093/applin/ams049

Ullman, M. (2005). A cognitive neuroscience perspective on second language acquisition: The declarative/procedural model. In C. Sanz (Ed.), *Mind and context in adult second language acquisition* (pp. 141–178). Washington, DC: Georgetown University Press.

Varonis, E., & Gass, S. (1985). Non-native/non-native conversations: A model for negotiation of meaning. *Applied Linguistics*, 6(1), 71–90. doi:10.1093/applin/6.1.71

Vygotsky, L. (1978). *Mind in society: The development of higher psychological processes.* Cambridge, MA: Havard University Press.

Walqui, A. (2006). Scaffolding instruction for English language learners: A conceptual framework. *International Journal of Bilingual Education and Bilingualism*, 9(2), 159–180. doi:10.1080/13670050608668639

Watanabe, Y., & Swain, M. (2007). Effects of proficiency differences and patterns of pair interaction on second language learning: Collaborative dialogue between adult ESL learners. *Language Teaching Research*, 11(2), 121–142. doi:10.1177/136216880607074599

Williams, J. (1999). Learner-generated attention to form. *Language Learning*, 49(4), 583–625. doi:10.1111/0023-8333.00103

Williams, J. (2001). The effectiveness of spontaneous attention to form. *System*, 29(3), 325–340. doi:10.1016/S0346-251X(01)00022-7

Yanguas, Í. (2010). Oral computer-mediated interaction between L2 learners: It's about time. *Language Learning and Technology*, 14(1), 72–93.

Yilmaz, Y. (2011). Task effects on focus on form in synchronous computer-mediated communication. *The Modern Language Journal*, 95(1), 115–132. doi:10.1111/j.1540-4781.2010.01143.x

Yoshida, R. (2008). Learners' perception of corrective feedback in pair work. *Foreign Language Annals*, 41(3), 525–541. doi:10.1111/j.1944-9720.2008.tb03310.x

Interactional patterns and learner characteristics

CHAPTER 1

Peer interaction and learning

A focus on the silent learner

Ana Fernández Dobao
University of Washington

This chapter investigated whether all learners benefited from the lexical language-related episodes (LREs) produced in small group interaction, even when acting as silent observers of their peers' collaborative work. Using a pretest-posttest design, evidence was obtained confirming that silent learners did benefit from LREs. In fact, they were almost as likely to gain new knowledge as those learners who triggered the episodes. These findings indicate that silent learners were as actively engaged with the vocabulary being discussed in the LREs as their speaking peers. Other factors, such as the length of the episode and the amount of negotiation and repetition, seemed to have a stronger influence on learning than the actual opportunities to speak. The pedagogical implications of these findings are discussed.

Introduction

Both pair and small group activities constitute a very common practice in communicative second language (L2) classrooms. However, opportunities to speak are inevitably more limited in groups than in pairs. In fact, many teachers, and even students, tend to favor pair over small group work on the grounds that it offers more opportunities for practice and individual language use (for further discussion, see Fernández Dobao & Blum 2013). Furthermore, while in pairs learners are forced to speak, in groups it is easier for students to remain silent, for relatively short or long conversational intervals, thereby becoming observers of their group members' interaction. This chapter focuses on these silent learners. It examines L2 vocabulary learning during a collaborative writing task completed in groups of four. The goal is to identify whether all learners benefited from the interaction, even when they were acting as silent observers of their peers' collaborative work.

As discussed in the introduction of this volume (Sato & Ballinger 2016), second language acquisition researchers have approached the study of peer

DOI 10.1075/lllt.45.02fer
© 2016 John Benjamins Publishing Company

interaction and learning from both interactionist and sociocultural perspectives; and sometimes from a combination of both, as in Foster and Ohta (2005) or Sato and Ballinger (2012). Researchers adopting an interactionist approach have focused on the instances of negotiation of meaning and corrective feedback that occur during interaction. From a sociocultural perspective, interaction has been analyzed as an opportunity for learners to scaffold each other and to collaborate in the solution of their language-related problems. Sociocultural researchers argue that, because no two learners share the same weaknesses and strengths, when working together they can act as both novices and experts, and in this way provide scaffolded assistance to each other (Donato 1994; Ohta 2001). Research grounded in sociocultural theory has shown that when same-level learners collaborate, pooling their individual knowledge and resources, they are often able to solve each other's problems and co-construct new language knowledge (e.g., Antón & DiCamilla 1998; Donato 1994; Ohta 2000, 2001; Swain 2000; Swain & Lapkin 1998).

From this perspective, and as already mentioned in the introduction chapter to this book, the analysis of peer interaction has focused on language-related episodes (LREs), defined as "any part of dialogue where the students talk about the language they are producing, question their language use, or correct themselves or others" (Swain & Lapkin 1998:326). When learners talk about their grammar use, they produce grammatical LREs. Lexical LREs occur when they talk about vocabulary and collaborate to solve lexical problems.

LREs are instances of what Swain refers to as languaging, described as "the process of making meaning and shaping knowledge and experience through language" (Swain 2006:89). In LREs, learners use language to think and talk about language, and in this way build new language knowledge. From a sociocultural perspective, which views learning as a social activity mediated by language, languaging is a source of learning.

Empirical studies, conducted across a variety of languages and instructional contexts, have confirmed that the collaborative dialogue we see in LREs is "language learning in progress" (Swain & Lapkin 1998:321). One of the first studies to examine LREs as an opportunity for learning was Swain and Lapkin (1998). These authors analyzed the LREs generated by 12 pairs of French immersion students while completing a jigsaw task. They developed individualized posttests to trace learners' retention of those lexical and grammatical items discussed in their LREs, and found evidence that learners tended to remember the solutions reached in these episodes. Shekary and Tahirian (2006), Williams (2001), and Zeng and Takatsuka (2009) also developed tailor-made dyad-specific posttests to trace both grammar and vocabulary learning in LREs. They obtained similar positive results. Kim (2008) focused specifically on vocabulary acquisition, also finding a positive relationship between LREs and learning. Other studies that have found evidence of learners' independent use of the vocabulary and grammatical knowledge previously co-constructed in LREs include Lapkin, Swain and Smith (2002), Storch (2002, 2008), Swain and Lapkin (2002), and Watanabe and Swain (2007).

Most of these studies have analyzed peer interaction during collaborative writing tasks, defined as tasks that require learners to work in pairs or small groups and to produce one jointly written text (see Storch 2013). The joint authorship and shared responsibility for the text pushes learners to talk about the language they are using; that is, to language. The need to agree on what to say and how to best say it prompts them to question their language use and to collaborate in the solution of their language-related problems. This research has shown that, by promoting LREs, collaborative writing tasks promote L2 learning.

However, not all collaborative writing activities are equally conducive to learning. In the introduction, this volume, Sato and Ballinger review previous research showing how LRE production is influenced by both task and learner-related factors. More structured tasks, such as text reconstruction tasks, favor learners' attention to form and tend to elicit more grammatical LREs than meaning-oriented tasks. In meaning-oriented tasks, such as dictogloss, jigsaw, storytelling, or essay writing activities, lexical LREs are often more frequent than grammatical ones (e.g., Alegría de la Colina & García Mayo 2007; García Mayo 2002; Storch 2001a; Swain & Lapkin 2001). Other factors affecting the frequency, and sometimes the outcome, of both lexical and grammatical LREs are the learners' proficiency level (e.g., Choi & Iwashita 2016; Leeser 2004; Williams 1999), pair and group dynamics (e.g., Kim & McDonough 2008; Storch 2002; Storch & Aldosari 2013; Watanabe & Swain 2007; Young & Tedick 2016), and the mode of communication, face-to-face or online (e.g., Shekary & Tahririan 2006; Yilmaz 2011; Rouhshad & Storch 2016).

Some recent research has also observed that the number of participants in the task may affect both the frequency and the outcome of LREs. In a series of related studies (Fernández Dobao 2012, 2014a, 2014b), I found that, while completing the same writing task, learners working in groups of four focused their attention on language more often than learners working in pairs and were also more successful at solving language-related problems. Lasito and Storch (2013), comparing pairs and groups of three, obtained similar results, confirming that because groups share more knowledge and resources than pairs, they are able to solve a higher number and proportion of their LREs correctly.

These findings suggest that small groups may create more opportunities for L2 learning than pairs. But this previous research has also noticed that, because opportunities to speak are more limited in groups than in pairs, in small groups not all learners get to contribute to the dialogic resolution of all LREs. In Fernández Dobao (2012, 2014a, 2014b), LREs were often resolved by two or three members of the group, while the other group members remained silent. This raised the issue of whether LREs produced in small group interaction are as beneficial for learning as those in pair interaction, that is, whether learners can benefit from those LREs in which they act as silent observers of their peers' collaborative problem solving activity. This is the issue addressed in this chapter.

There is some evidence suggesting that learners can benefit from observing other learners' interaction. Ellis et al. (1994) analyzed the effect of negotiation of meaning on vocabulary acquisition. In this study, conducted from an interactionist perspective, some learners had the opportunity to engage in negotiation of meaning while others just listened to their peers negotiate. When comprehension and acquisition were measured, no differences were observed between the two groups of students. This led the authors to conclude that "active participation may be less important for acquisition than is sometimes claimed" (Ellis et al. 1994: 480). However, in a more recent study analyzing the role of output in L2 learning, Philp and Iwashita (2013) noticed that active language production may push learners to pay more attention to language form.

In the classroom context, Ohta (2001) observed how learners sometimes appropriate language they overhear from other learners' conversations. These findings are also supported by research on teacher-learner interaction. Studies on classroom language learning, such as Allwright (1980) or Slimani (1989), have provided evidence that learners can benefit from their classmates' contributions and from feedback provided by the teacher to other learners. In fact, Allwright's (1980) findings suggest that sometimes the quietest students in the class may actually be the ones who benefit the most from classroom interaction, precisely because they can take advantage of the extra attentional resources available to them when freed from the cognitive load of output production.

In Fernández Dobao (2014b), I compared the rate of retention of the lexical knowledge built in LREs for learners working in pairs and in small groups, and noticed no significant differences. On average, learners in small groups were as likely to remember the vocabulary discussed in their LREs as learners in pairs, even if they had had fewer opportunities to contribute to these episodes. The study presented in this chapter builds on this previous work and expands it by examining not only whether all the learners in the group benefited from the interaction, but also whether and how the learner's role in the LRE affected opportunities for L2 development. The study's final goal is to identify whether those learners who remain silent, acting as observers of their peers' collaborative problem solving activity, may benefit as much from the LRE as the learners triggering and/or solving the episode.

Method

Participants

The study was conducted in a Spanish as a foreign language classroom setting. All participants were enrolled in the same intermediate-level course offered for credit at a large public university in the United States. This course was part of the second year Spanish language program, which aims to develop learners' oral and written skills, as well as their vocabulary and grammar knowledge. Learners had been placed in the course after successful completion of the previous level class, or on the basis of their score on either the university placement test or the AP exam.[1] Since most of them had taken Spanish language classes before entering the university, they had been studying Spanish for an average of three and a half years.

Data was collected in six different classes. In each class, approximately half of the students completed the collaborative writing task in pairs and the other half in groups of four. A total of 25 dyads and 15 groups completed the task. This chapter analyzes the data collected from eight of these 15 groups. The ages of the learners in these eight groups ranged from 18 to 24 years. There were 18 females and 14 males, and they were all native English speakers.

Collaborative writing task

The writing task designed for the purposes of the study was based on a visual prompt. Each group and pair of students was given a set of 15 pictures and asked to rearrange them in order to create a story (see Appendix A). The pictures had no pre-established order. Learners had to sequence them in order to create their own original story and to write it down. Each pair and each group had to produce one jointly written text.

Vocabulary pretest and posttest

In order to test learners' retention of the vocabulary discussed in their LREs, a cloze task was designed. This task tested learners' productive knowledge of 20 vocabulary items, or more specifically, learners' ability to independently use, in a written text, the vocabulary previously used in collaboration with their peers.

---

1. Advanced Placement (AP) exams are college level exams administered to high school students in the United States so they can earn university credits and/or advanced placement in university courses.

A first version was administered as a pretest and a second version, including the same items but in a different order, as a posttest (see Appendix B).

This pretest-posttest design makes it possible to observe actual change and lexical development, as learners move from an incorrect to a correct response from the pretest to the posttest. But because it is impossible to predict what different learners will be talking about during an open-ended activity, the vocabulary task could only be expected to include a subset of the vocabulary items discussed by the learners in their LREs. To minimize this problem, the collaborative writing task was piloted with a group of 24 intermediate-level learners, who were enrolled in the same course as those in the main study, but in a different randomly selected class. Those words that created linguistic difficulties for these 24 learners were included in the vocabulary task (see Appendix C). It was expected that some of these words would also be unfamiliar for the learners in the main study and therefore discussed in their LREs.

Procedures

All the tasks designed for the study were completed during the class and were administered by the teachers as part of the regular course work. The course lasted 10 weeks and met 5 times per week for 50 minutes. Data was collected in weeks seven and eight, so that learners would be familiar with each other and used to working together both in pairs and in groups, a very common practice in these classes.

Each class was taught by a different instructor, but with the same syllabus, textbook, and teaching materials. The researcher met with the teachers twice to make sure they would all follow the same procedure and give the same instructions to their students.

The first day all learners completed the vocabulary pretest individually. The following day they performed the collaborative writing task, which lasted for approximately 30 minutes. Students chose to work in pairs or in groups, self-selecting their partners. Teachers made sure there was a balanced number of pairs and groups and also that all groups had four learners. Students were free to organize their work and choose who would write down their text, but they were specifically instructed not to use a dictionary or any other kind of reference materials. Teachers did not offer any linguistic help. One week later, learners completed the posttest, that is, the second version of the vocabulary task.

Data coding and analysis

As mentioned above, the data collected from eight of the 15 groups who completed the collaborative writing task was analyzed.[2] These eight groups were selected because of the quality of their audio recording and because they were gender-mixed, which allowed for a reliable identification of each learner's voice.

The data analyzed includes the individual pretests and posttests, and a total of 200 minutes of audio-recorded peer interaction – an average of 25 minutes per group. The oral interactions were transcribed and coded for lexical LREs. Then, the role each learner adopted in each LRE was identified. The pretests and posttests were analyzed for evidence of learning.

Lexical language-related episodes
Following Swain and Lapkin (1998), lexical LREs were conceptualized as segments of interaction in which learners talked about vocabulary, questioned their vocabulary use, or corrected their own or each other's lexical errors. These include segments in which learners collaborated to search for vocabulary, to choose between different lexical items, to clarify the meaning of a word, or to determine the correct spelling and/or pronunciation of a lexical item.[3]

In Example (1), Bob is searching for the Spanish equivalent of the English verb *to seem like*, which is provided by Ann in turn 2, confirmed by Jean in turn 3, and finally accepted and incorporated to the story line in turn 5: "*el once de septiembre parecía día normal*".

(1) 1 Bob: *co- cómo se dice* seemed like?
             (how do you say seemed like)
     2 Ann: *parecer*
             (to seem like)
     3 Jean: *parecer*
             (to seem like)
     4 Tom: *parece*
             (it seems like)
     5 Bob: *parece! que: … so … el once de septiembre parecía …*
             día normal
             (it seems like! so September 11 seemed like a normal day)

---

2. For an analysis of the data collected from the 15 groups and 25 pairs who completed the collaborative writing task see Fernández Dobao (2014b).

3. Spelling and pronunciation LREs were rather infrequent. Most LREs focused on word meaning and word choice difficulties. In this study, no distinction was made based on the focus of the LRE.

In Example (2), turn 1, Larry uses the word *rascacielos* (skyscraper), which Jenny does not recognize. In turn 4, Larry clarifies the meaning of the word, which is then accepted by the other members of the group.

(2) 1 Larry: uh: *entre dos rascacielos, grandes*
            (between two big skyscrapers)
     2 Ruth: *dos*
            (two)
     3 Jenny: *qué es?*
            (what is it?)
     4 Larry: skyscrapers
     5 Jenny: *rascacielos?* oh!
            (skyscrapers?)
     6 Ruth: *rascacielos rascacielos*
            (skyscrapers skyscrapers)
     7 Jenny: look at you
     8 Larry: *sí*
            (yes)
     9 Jenny: *rascacielos*
            (skyscrapers)
    10 Ruth: okay

All lexical LREs were classified as correctly resolved, unresolved, or incorrectly resolved. Examples (1) and (2) above illustrate two correctly resolved LREs. Example (3) presents an unresolved LRE. Learners are not able to find the word they are looking for, *extorsionar* (to extort).

(3) 1 Erin: *ella: gastó mucho dinero planeando … un viaje?*
            (she spent a lot of money planning a trip?)
     2 Don: we should say she extorted him … did something did
            something to:
     3 Erin: *no sé la palabra* ha-ha
            (I don't know the word)
            …
     4 Don: ha-ha … um … *ella … gastó*
            (she spent)

Finally, Example (4) illustrates an incorrectly resolved LRE. Learners agree on the use of *llover* (to rain), which is incorrect in this context. The word they are looking for is *llorar* (to cry).

(4)   1   Amy: let's say she's crying

             …

2   Danny: *ella: … llu- llover:*
               (she to rain)

3   Amy: she started to cry like

.

.

.

4   Danny: *ella empezó*
               (she started)

5   Martin: *a llover*
               (to rain)

             …

6   Danny: *a: llover*
               (to rain)

7   Amy: *a llover*
               (to rain)

             …

8   Danny: is it? *elle o ve e ere? … llover.*
               (ll o v e r … to rain)

9   Amy: think so

10 Danny: okay

11 Martin: *bien*
               (good)

12 Amy: yeah

13 Martin: okay

14 Danny: alright

Learners' roles

All lexical LREs were further analyzed and the role played by each member of the group in each LRE was identified. Four different categories emerged from this analysis: trigger, solver, contributor, and observer.

An LRE occurs in response to or as a result of a learner's problem or error. This learner is the trigger. He may trigger the LRE with a request for assistance, a confirmation check, a lexical error, or a problematic utterance that needs to be reformulated – for instance, an utterance that contains an L1 word. In Examples (1) and (2) above, Bob and Jenny trigger the LRE with a direct request for assistance: "*cómo se dice* seemed like?" – turn 1 in Example (1), and "*qué es?*" – turn 3 in Example (2). Examples (3) and (4) are triggered by Don and Amy, who prompt the search for the Spanish equivalent of the English verbs *to extort* and *to cry* – see turn 2 in Example (3) and turn 1 in Example (4).

The solver is the learner who provides the lexical item or information that will solve the LRE, either in response to a request for assistance, or as a confirmation, counter suggestion, or error correction. In Example (1), turn 2, Ann offers the word Bob asked for: *parecer*. She is the solver. Larry is the solver in Example (2) and Danny in Example (4) – see turn 4 in Example (2) and turn 2 in Example (4). In Example (3) the LRE is left unresolved and therefore there is no solver.

All learners who contribute at least one turn to the LRE, but are neither triggers nor solvers, are considered contributors. In Example (1), Jean and Tom repeat in turns 3 and 4 the input first offered by Ann, thus confirming its accuracy and in this way contributing to the resolution of the LRE. Ruth in Example (2), Erin in Example (3), and Martin in Example (4) are also contributors.

The silent learner, who does not have any turn in the LRE, was categorized as observer.[4] In Example (1), all four learners in the group contribute to the dialogic resolution of the lexical problem. However, Examples (2) and (4) are solved with turns from only three learners, and Example (3) from two. Sam in Example (2), Sophie in Example (4), and Lucy and Nora in Example (3) remain silent. They are acting as observers of their peers' collaborative problem solving activity.

Vocabulary learning

The vocabulary pretests and posttests were examined for evidence of learning. Learners' responses for those lexical items that had been the focus of an LRE, correctly or incorrectly resolved, were analyzed. Unresolved LREs were left out of the analysis. In unresolved LREs there is no agreed upon vocabulary item to be retained, therefore changes from the pretest to the posttest cannot be traced back to the episode.

A learner's independent use, in the posttest, of a word previously discussed in an LRE was considered evidence of learning. When the learner's response could not be traced back to the LRE, a missed opportunity for learning was noted. For the purposes of this study, learning is understood as both the acquisition of new knowledge and the consolidation of existing knowledge (see Swain 2000; Swain & Lapkin 1998; Storch 2008). To distinguish between these two kinds of learning, learners' responses to the pretest and posttest were compared. When the learner changed his response from the pretest to the posttest to incorporate the

---

4. These learners may be laughing, nodding, or using other forms of nonverbal communication. For the purposes of this study, which focused on oral data, nonverbal communication does not constitute a turn.

knowledge co-constructed in the LRE, it was considered that he had learnt new knowledge. When the word discussed in the LRE and retained in the posttest had already been used in the pretest, an instance of consolidation of knowledge was noted.

In the following LRE, we see Becky and Tim gaining new knowledge of the word *barco* (ship). Neither of these two learners was able to produce the word in the pretest, which suggests they have become able to use it as a result of their participation in the LRE – Becky as the trigger and Tim as a contributor. John is consolidating his previous knowledge of the word, while Sally is missing an opportunity for learning.

(5) 1 Becky: oh! *no sé la palabra para* ship
             (I don't know the word for ship)
     2 John: *barco*
             (ship)
     3 Tim: *barco?*
             (ship?)
     4 Becky: *barco?*
             (ship?)
     5 John: *barco*
             (ship)
     6 Sally: um

Vocabulary learning in the LRE: *barco* (ship)

Learner	Pretest	Posttest	Analysis
Becky	*bote grande* (big boat)	*barco*	Learning new knowledge
John	*barco*	*barco*	Consolidation of existing knowledge
Sally	*bargo* (nonexistent word)	*bargo*	Missed opportunity for learning
Tim	*barca* (boat)	*barco*	Learning new knowledge

Findings

The oral interactions between the groups as they collaborated to complete the writing task were analyzed for lexical LREs. Table 1 presents the results of the frequency and outcome analysis of these LREs.

Table 1. LRE frequency and outcome

	No.	*%*	*M**	*SD*
Correct LREs	125	70	15.63	4.14
Unresolved LREs	24	13	3.00	1.31
Incorrect LREs	30	17	3.75	2.12
All LREs	179	100	22.38	5.73

* Mean per group (8 groups)

Learners discussed their vocabulary use relatively often and were also quite successful at solving lexical problems. They produced a total of 179 lexical LREs, a mean of 22.38 LREs per group (*SD* = 5.73). One hundred and twenty five of these LREs, 15.63 per group (*SD* = 4.14), were correctly resolved; that is, groups solved correctly 70% of their lexical difficulties. They resolved 30 LREs incorrectly, 17% of the total, and left 24 episodes unresolved, 13% of all LREs. Although the number and percentage of correctly resolved episodes varied across groups, all groups were able to find a correct solution to the majority of their LREs.

To identify whether learners actually retained the lexical knowledge collaboratively built in these LREs, the pretests and posttests were analyzed. The results of this analysis are presented in Tables 2 and 3. Because two of the learners did not attend class on the date the posttest was completed, these tables present the results obtained for a total of 30 learners. As already discussed, the pretests and posttests could only provide evidence of learning for a subset of items, those vocabulary items included in the tests that were also discussed in an LRE – a total of 43 among the eight groups.

Table 2. Evidence of learning in correctly resolved LREs

	No.	*%*	*M**	*SD*
Learning new knowledge	38	33	1.27	1.28
Consolidation of existing knowledge	49	43	1.63	1.45
Missed opportunity for learning	27	24	.90	.96

* Mean per learner (30 learners)

Table 3. Evidence of learning in incorrectly resolved LREs

	No.	*%*	*M**	*SD*
Learning new knowledge	11	39	.37	.00
Consolidation of existing knowledge	3	11	.10	.00
Missed opportunity for learning	14	50	.47	.00

* Mean per learner (30 learners)

The results obtained for the correctly resolved LREs indicate that learners gained new lexical knowledge in 33% of the episodes analyzed. They consolidated existing knowledge in 43% and missed an opportunity for learning only in 24%. This means that they retained the solution reached in 76% of the correctly resolved LREs in which they participated.

As also documented in previous research, learning did not always occur in the desired direction. Learners also retained the solutions agreed upon in their incorrectly resolved LREs, that is, they also acquired incorrect lexical knowledge. But the number and percentage of words retained in these LREs were considerably lower. Table 3 shows that only 11 instances of learning and 3 of consolidation were identified.

Tables 4 and 5 show the number and percentage of words missed and retained by learners when acting as triggers, solvers, contributors, and observers. Not surprisingly, solvers have the highest rate of retention. They remembered and used in their posttests 90% of the words discussed in the correctly resolved LREs analyzed, missing an opportunity for learning only in 10% of these episodes. The solver is the learner who provides the word that eventually solves the LRE. It can therefore be assumed that he has some previous knowledge of this word. The comparative analysis of the pretests and posttests confirmed that, in correctly resolved LREs, solvers were mostly consolidating previously acquired knowledge. They consolidated existing knowledge in 71% of these LREs and learned new knowledge only in 19%.

Table 4. Evidence of learning in correctly resolved LREs by learners' roles

	Trigger		Solver		Contributor		Observer	
	No.	%	No.	%	No.	%	No.	%
Learning new knowledge	12	44	6	19	9	30	11	42
Consolidation of previous knowledge	8	30	22	71	12	40	7	27
Missed opportunity for learning	7	26	3	10	9	30	8	31

Table 5. Evidence of learning in incorrectly resolved LREs by learners' roles

	Trigger		Solver		Contributor		Observer	
	No.	%	No.	%	No.	%	No.	%
Learning new knowledge	3	43	2	28.5	3	37.5	3	50
Consolidation of previous knowledge	1	14	2	28.5	0	0	0	0
Missed opportunity for learning	3	43	3	43	5	62.5	3	50

Triggers, on the other hand, have the highest rate of learning. They gained new knowledge in 44% of the correctly resolved LREs analyzed. The trigger's lack of knowledge, or incorrect knowledge, is what sets off the LRE. He is therefore more likely to gain new knowledge than to consolidate existing knowledge. Still, there is a 30% of consolidation for the trigger which indicates that learners initiate LREs not only to ask for words they do not know, but also to confirm previously acquired, but possibly incomplete, lexical knowledge.

Contributors were almost as likely to retain the knowledge built in correctly resolved LREs as triggers. Contributors remembered the words discussed in 70% of these LREs and triggers in 74%. However, while triggers were mostly learning new knowledge, contributors were often consolidating previously acquired knowledge. They consolidated previous knowledge in 40% of the LREs analyzed and gained new knowledge in 30%.

Contributors make an attempt to collaborate in the solution of the lexical problem encountered, while observers remain silent, without contributing a single turn to the LRE. Table 4 shows that observers missed an opportunity for learning in 31% of the correctly resolved LREs analyzed, and remembered the words discussed in the other 69%. Their retention rate is therefore very similar to that of contributors, 70%, as well triggers, 74%. Furthermore, observers acquired new knowledge in 42% of the LREs. Contributors gained new knowledge in 30% and triggers in 44%. This means that observers were almost as likely to learn a new word as the learners who actually triggered the LREs.

As already discussed, the rate of retention was overall much lower for the incorrectly resolved LREs than for the correctly resolved ones. Table 5 shows this is true for all learners, regardless of their role in the LRE. It also reveals that triggers and observers were again more likely to gain new knowledge, albeit incorrect, than solvers and contributors.

In sum, the findings of the present study confirm that LREs were beneficial not only for those learners who triggered and solved them, but also for those who acted as peripheral participants, that is, contributors and observers. Silent learners, although apparently passive, were in fact active participants in the interaction. Their performance in the posttest indicates that they were actively engaged with the vocabulary being discussed in the LREs.

It should be noted however that not all learners adopted the observer's role with the same frequency – see Young and Tedick (2016) for similar findings and a discussion of possible reasons why a learner may choose to remain silent (or be silenced) during small group interaction. More importantly, when they did act as silent participants, they did not all benefit equally. In order to better understand this variation, the behavior of three different learners from three different groups was further analyzed. Jack, Chris, and David were selected for this qualitative analysis because they were frequent observers, plus, since they were males in groups composed mainly of women, their voices could be identified with great reliability.

Jack

Jack worked with Cindy, Emma, and Karen. This was quite an active group. They spent 26 minutes on task and produced a text that was 172 words long – while the average text had only 149 words. They also produced more LREs than most of the other groups: 28. Twenty-one of these episodes were correctly resolved and only one was left unresolved.

Jack contributed quite actively to the conversation, with 97 turns, 20% of the total, but not so much to the LREs. He acted as an observer in 17 LREs, that is, 61% of all the episodes produced by his group. This does not mean, however, he did not benefit from the interaction. His pretest and posttest indicate that he acquired new knowledge in 45% of the LREs analyzed, consolidated previous knowledge in 33%, and missed an opportunity for learning only in 24%.

Four of the 17 LREs in which he participated as a silent observer focused on a word included in the vocabulary tests: *tomar* (to take), *crucero* (cruise), *avión* (plane), and *adivino* (fortuneteller). In Example (6), we see the embedded LREs for *tomar* and *crucero*. These were relatively long LREs showing an elaborate level of engagement. An LRE shows limited engagement when one learner makes a suggestion that is simply accepted by another learner. Here, however, we see Cindy, Emma, and Karen deliberating over several turns before establishing a final agreement on the use of the words *tomar* and *crucero*. Both words are repeated several times by different learners in different turns. Previous research suggests that this multiple repetition and elaborate engagement with the target item facilitate its retention (see Storch 2008; Storch & Wigglesworth 2010; Wigglesworth & Storch 2012). The analysis of the vocabulary posttests showed that in fact all learners in this group remembered the verb *tomar* and three of them, including Jack, retained the word *crucero*.

(6) 1 Karen: *primero fue en avión al Caribe a: tomar un crucero? …*
            or coger?
            (first she went by plane to the Caribbean to take a
            cruise? or to take?)
     2 Emma: *para tomar*
            (to take)
     3 Cindy: *para tomar sí*
            (to take yes)
     4 Karen: *para tomar … … crucero? así?* ha-ha
            (to take cruise? like this?)
     5 Emma: *no sé*
            (I don't know)

6   Karen: *da igual, da igual*
             (it doesn't matter, it doesn't matter)
7   Cindy: *no tengo mejor palabra pero* ha-ha
             (I don't know a better word but)
8   Karen: *para pa- para tomar para tomar el crucero.*
             (to to take to take the cruise)

Vocabulary learning in the LRE: *tomar* (to take)

Learner	Pretest	Posttest	Analysis
Cindy	*tomo* (I take)	*tomaré* (I'll take)	Consolidation of existing knowledge
Emma	*tomo*	*tomaré*	Consolidation of existing knowledge
Jack	---	*tomará* (she'll take)	Learning new knowledge
Karen	---	*tome* (she takes)	Learning new knowledge

Vocabulary learning in the LRE: *crucero* (cruise)

Learner	Pretest	Posttest	Analysis
Cindy	*crucero*	*crucero*	Consolidation of existing knowledge
Emma	*barco* (ship)	*cruza* (he crosses)	Missed opportunity for learning
Jack	*un barco hermoso* (a beautiful ship)	*crucero*	Learning new knowledge
Karen	---	*crucero*	Learning new knowledge

Jack also retained the word *avión* discussed in another of the LREs he observed. He had not been able to use this word in the pretest, which suggests he acquired new knowledge, or at least some new knowledge, of the word in the interaction. He did not retain, however, the word *porvenista*, discussed in the following LRE.

(7)   1   Cindy: *fortunista?*
                   (fortuneteller)

                   .

                   .

                   .

      2   Emma: *pienso que es porvenista*
                   (I think it is fortuneteller)
      3   Karen: *cómo?*
                   (how?)

4   Emma: *porvenista?*
              (fortuneteller)
5   Karen: okay
6   Cindy: *es un hombre?*
              (it's a man?)
7   Emma: *pienso que sí*
              (I think so)
8   Cindy: *porvenista?*
              (fortuneteller)
9   Karen: okay

Vocabulary learning in the LRE: *porvenista* (nonexistent word)

Learner	Pretest	Posttest	Analysis
Cindy	---	*porvinista*	Learning new knowledge
Emma	*una persona que ve el porvenir* (a person who sees the future)	---	Missed opportunity for learning[5]
Jack	---	*un llamar de fortuna* (a fortune call)	Missed opportunity for learning
Karen	---	---	Missed opportunity for learning

This is an incorrectly resolved LRE. Learners are searching for *adivino* (fortune-teller). *Porvenir* (future) is a Spanish noun, but *porvenista* is not a Spanish word. The group creates this term to solve the lexical problem encountered. *Porvenista* appears in quotations in the collaboratively written text, "*entonces fue a un 'porvenista'*" (then she went to a fortuneteller), which suggests learners were probably aware this is a made up, nonexistent term. In fact, only one of the learners, Cindy, used it in the posttest.

In sum, Jack retained the lexical knowledge built in the three correctly resolved LREs analyzed here, in which he acted as an observer of his peers' collaborative work. The only item he did not retain was the incorrect, nonexistent term *porvenista*.

---

5.   When learners failed to retain the word discussed in the LRE, a missed opportunity for learning was coded. In this particular case, because *porvenista* is not a word in Spanish, failure to retain the word can actually be seen as a positive outcome, since it means that learners did not learn the incorrect knowledge built by their group.

Chris

Chris's group also adopted quite a diligent approach to the task. They worked for 25 minutes and wrote the longest of the eight texts: 206 words. They produced a total of 24 LREs.

A first look at the interaction would suggest that Chris was quite passive. The other three learners contributed to the conversation in an active and balanced way, but Chris produced only 58 turns, less than 12% of the total. We know, however, that he was actively involved in the task, because he was in charge of writing down the text. Furthermore, the results of the pretest and posttest indicate that he benefited more from the interaction than any of the other learners in the group. He gained new knowledge in 72% of the LREs analyzed, consolidated existing knowledge in 14%, and missed an opportunity for learning in the remaining 14%.

Chris acted as an observer in 11 of the 24 LREs produced by his group. Four of these 11 LREs focused on a lexical item included in the vocabulary tests. Three were correctly resolved and one incorrectly resolved. Example (8) presents the incorrectly resolved LRE, focused on the word *adivino* (fortuneteller). In turn 1, Sarah triggers the LRE and in turn 2 Pat offers *bruja* (witch) as a possible solution. The episode extends over 12 turns in which Sarah, Pat, and Alice repeat this word several times, in its feminine and masculine form, finally agreeing on the feminine, *bruja*. Chris is the only learner who does not contribute to the LRE, but we know he is paying attention to his peers' negotiation because he includes the word *bruja* in the collaboratively written text: "*una bruja muy fea que dijo el futuro*" (a very ugly witch who told the future). He also remembers and uses it in his posttest.

(8) 1   Sarah: *fue a: una persona que dice el futuro?*
                  (she went to a person who tells the future?)
                  ...
     2   Pat: *fue a un bruja* ha-ha
                  (she went to a witch)
     3   Alice: *bruja?* ha-ha
                  (witch?)
     4   Pat: *un brujo*
                  (a wizard)
     5   Sarah: *brujo:?*
                  (wizard?)
     6   Pat: *o es es un ... es un bruja*
                  (or it's it's a it's a witch)
     7   Sarah: ha-ha
                  ...

      8   Alice: *un brujo muy feo*
                   (a very ugly wizard)
      9   Pat: *un brujo?*
                   (a wizard?)
     10   Alice: *una bruja lo siento*
                   (a witch I'm sorry)
     11   Pat: alright *es una bruja* ha-ha … *que dice el futuro* ha-ha
                   (it's a witch who tells the future)

Vocabulary learning in the LRE: *bruja* (witch)

Learner	Pretest	Posttest	Analysis
Alice	*una persona que dice el futuro* (a person who tells the future)	*una bruja que dice el futuro* (a witch who tells the future)	Learning new knowledge[6]
Chris	*fortuna* (fortune)	*una bruja* (a witch)	Learning new knowledge
Pat	*una persona que dice el futuro*	*una persona que dice el futuro*	Missed opportunity for learning
Sarah	*una persona de fortún* (a person of [nonexistent word])	*una persona que dice el futuro*	Missed opportunity for learning

In the pretest, none of the four learners in this group was able to produce *corta-césped* or *cortadora de césped* (lawnmower). In the interaction, pooling their different pieces of knowledge, they co-construct *cortadora de césped*. Alice supplies *césped* (lawn) – turn 1, Pat suggests *cortar* (to cut) – turn 2, and Sarah adds the correct ending, *cortadora* (cutter) – turn 3. Chris is the only learner who does not contribute to the LRE, but he still benefits from the episode. Even though he does not retain the whole lexical unit, *cortadora de césped*, he does change his incorrect response in the pretest to incorporate the correct word *césped*.

     (9) 1   Alice: *porque necesita un … qué es? something de césped?*
                       (because she needs a what is it? something lawn)
          2   Pat: *el corta- cortabar:*
                       (the cut cutter)
          3   Sarah: *cor:tadora:*
                       (cutter)
          4   Pat: *cortadora, cortadora de césped*
                       (cutter, lawnmower)

---

6. The word *bruja* (witch) exists in Spanish, but it is not the word the learners were looking for and is not accurate in this context. Therefore, these learners are learning incorrect knowledge.

5   Alice: *cortadora de césped?*
         (lawnmower?)

6   Pat: *es porque: … ella tienen un: … mm … vida nueva*
         (it's because she has a new life)

Vocabulary learning in the LRE: *cortadora de césped* (lawnmower)

Learner	Pretest	Posttest	Analysis
Alice	*una cosa que cortar el cesped* (a thing to cut the lawn)	*una cortadora de cesped*	Learning new knowledge: *cortadora*
Chris	*maquina de cortar de cepa* (machine to cut vine)	*maquinas que cortan cesped* (machines that cut lawn)	Learning new knowledge: *césped*
Pat	*unas maquinas de cortar* (machines to cut)	*cortadores de cesped* (lawnmowers)	Learning new knowledge: *cortador de césped*
Sarah	*machinas de* lawn ([nonexistent word] of lawn)	*maquinas de corteza* (crust machines)	Missed opportunity for learning

The other two LREs focused on the words *crucero* (cruise) and *agencia de viajes* (travel agency). Chris did not contribute to the discussion around these two words. But both were incorporated in the collaboratively written text, which confirms he did notice them. The pretest and posttest indicate that Chris consolidated his previous knowledge of the lexical item *agencia de viajes* and gained new knowledge of the word *crucero*, once again benefiting from this double role as observer and writer.

David

David worked with Donna, Jason, and Mary. These learners took a much more relaxed approach to the task. They finished in 21 minutes and their text was only 115 words long. David contributed to the conversation with 20% of the turns, but the conversation was dominated by Mary, who was in charge of writing down the text and produced more than 36% of the turns. The group produced 20 LREs. David adopted the observer's role in eight of these episodes, 40% of the total.

In terms of vocabulary learning, David did not benefit much from the interaction, but neither did Jason and Mary – Donna did not complete the posttest. Five of the 20 LREs centered on lexical items included in the vocabulary tests. David consolidated his previous knowledge of two of these words – *contaminación* (pollution) and *esquiar* (to ski), and missed an opportunity for learning the other three words – *jardinería* (nursery), *boleto* (ticket), and *conocer* (to meet). Jason missed an opportunity for learning in 40% of these LREs and Mary in 60%, even though she was writing down the text.

Two of the LREs in which David acted as an observer focused on words included in the pretest and posttest: *jardinería*, Example (10), and *boleto*, Example (11). David did not retain either of these two words.

(10) 1   Mary: *trabaja en* eh *en la tienda?*
            (she works at the store?)

      2   Jason: *sí*
            (yes)

      3   Donna: *sí*
            (yes)

            .

            .

            .

      4   Mary: *necesito: … decir* um *una tienda de: jardinería o: o
                    solamente ésta? … no?* okay
                    (do I need to say a nursery store or or only this? no?
                    okay)

      5   Donna: *qué?*
            (what?)

      6   Mary: *no sé, está bien, … en … una: … … ferretería: y: …
                    jardinería:* um … okay
                    (I don't know, it's okay, in a nursery and hardware store
                    okay)

Vocabulary learning in the LRE: *jardinería* (nursery)

Learner	Pretest	Posttest	Analysis
David	---	*un tienda* (a shop)	Missed opportunity for learning
Jason	*la tiende* (the shop)	*una tienda de jardina* (a shop of [nonexistent word])	Missed opportunity for learning
Mary	*una tienda de jardín* (a garden shop)	*una tienda de gardín* (a garden shop)	Missed opportunity for learning

(11) 1   Mary: *comprar un: … para: comprar … una: una boleta?* un
                    boleto?
                    (to buy a to buy a ticket? a ticket?)

                    …

      2   Jason: uh: *sí, un boleto de: los* uh Swiss Alps
                    (yes, a ticket to the Swiss Alps)

Vocabulary learning in the LRE: *boleto* (ticket)

Learner	Pretest	Posttest	Analysis
David	---	*un código* (a code)	Missed opportunity for learning
Jason	*un boleto*	*un boleto*	Consolidation of existing knowledge
Mary	*un boleto*	*un boleto*	Consolidation of existing knowledge

Both LREs were relatively short and showed limited engagement with the target vocabulary. In Example (10), Mary poses the question that triggers the LRE and, with very little interaction from any other learner, decides that *jardinería* is the word the group will use in their text. In Example (11), Mary is unsure whether *boleto* is a feminine noun, ending in -a, or a masculine noun, ending in -o. Jason suggests that *boleto* is the correct form, and *boleto*, which is in fact the correct form, gets incorporated into the text without further discussion. The LRE is resolved in just two turns, with contributions from only two of the members of the group.

No learner retains and uses in the posttest the word *jardinería*. Mary and Jason remember the word *boleto*, but they already had some knowledge of this noun before the interaction. David, who did not know the word before, does not acquire new knowledge of this word, at least not at the productive level.

Previous research has noticed that "not all students work collaboratively when assigned to work on language tasks in pairs" (Storch 2002: 147). In her research on dyadic patterns of interaction, Storch observed that scaffolding and collaborative problem solving activities are frequent when learners adopt a collaborative approach, that is, when they are willing to share ideas and engage with each other's contributions (see Storch 2001b, 2002, 2004). But non-collaborative attitudes and patterns of behavior tend to correlate with low LRE frequency and limited opportunities for learning. The analysis of David, Donna, Jason, and Mary's interaction seems to illustrate a non-collaborative pattern of behavior. Their relaxed approach to the task and limited engagement with each other's problems, as observed in Examples (10) and (11), seem to be the reason for their low rates of vocabulary retention and subsequent poor performance on the posttest.

Conclusions

The collaborative writing task designed for the purposes of this study pushed learners to focus their attention on language and to collaborate in the solution of their vocabulary-related problems in ways that facilitate learning. Learners writing in groups of four discussed their vocabulary use relatively often and, pooling their individual knowledge and resources, solved most of their lexical LREs correctly. The analysis of the pretests and posttests showed how learners often retained and were able to make independent use of the vocabulary knowledge collaboratively built in these LREs. This data confirms that L2 vocabulary learning, understood as both the acquisition of new knowledge and the consolidation of previous knowledge, occurred in small group peer interaction.

The main goal of the study was to investigate whether all learners in the group could benefit from the lexical LREs produced. As already noted in previous research (Fernández Dobao 2012, 2014a, 2014b), LREs were often solved with contributions from only two or three learners, while the other members of the group remained silent, acting as observers of their peers' collaborative work. The findings of the present study confirm that these silent learners did also benefit from the LREs. In fact, they indicate that silent learners, adopting an observer's role, were almost as likely to acquire new knowledge as those learners who actually triggered the episodes and more likely than learners acting as contributors or solvers, who were mostly consolidating previously acquired knowledge.

In Fernández Dobao (2014b), some preliminary evidence was obtained suggesting that silent learners, though seemingly passive, may actually be active participants in their groups' LREs. They can participate as active listeners of their peers' collaborative work and in this way benefit from the episode. The findings of the present study confirm that silent learners were as actively engaged with the vocabulary being discussed in the LREs as their speaking partners, otherwise they would not have been able to retain this vocabulary with almost the same frequency as triggers and contributors.

The fact that a learner is silent does not mean he cannot be languaging. What we observe in LREs is the social form of languaging, what Swain calls collaborative dialogue, but languaging can also occur with oneself, via private speech (see Swain et al. 2011). Ohta (2001) showed how apparently non-participatory learners, who were not contributing in teacher-fronted activities, were in fact regulating their own learning through the use of vocal private speech. They were repeating, monitoring, correcting, rehearsing, and manipulating the language of the class. Ohta (2001) recorded and analyzed instances of vocal private speech (see also Saville-Troike 1988). But private speech can also be subvocal and therefore not directly observable – what some authors refer to as inner speech (e.g., Guerrero 2005). While in pair interaction, learners are forced to speak, in small group interaction one learner can momentarily disappear. A private space can thus emerge, a space in which the silent learner, through subvocal private speech, can repeat, manipulate, and internalize the vocabulary afforded by the interaction. Future research using stimulated recall techniques and video recorded data should be able to examine this hypothesis, and identify to what extent silent learners can engage in subvocal private speech during small group interaction and how this activity may impact their learning.

The findings of the present study also revealed that not all learners adopted the observer's role with the same frequency and, more importantly, they did not all benefit equally from this position. The analysis of Jack, Chris, and David's performances suggests that certain factors related to the LRE, and ultimately the nature of the interaction, may have a stronger influence on learning and retention than the learner's role in the episode. The length of the LRE, the level of engagement with the target vocabulary, and the amount of repetition it entails may be more important in shaping learning than the role the learner gets to play. In order to better understand when and why learning occurs, it would also be helpful to know the reasons underlying the learner's choice to remain silent in certain LREs but not others, and how these relate to group dynamics, affective factors, and/or learners' beliefs about language learning. Again, future research incorporating stimulated recall methods should be able to provide new and valuable insights in this regard.

In sum, although small scale and exploratory in nature, the present study shows that, in small group interaction, lack of contribution does not necessarily mean lack of participation or fewer opportunities to learn. Learners can benefit from small group interaction, both when they are speaking and when they are not, as long as they are actively engaged with the language.

Pedagogical implications

The findings of this study have important pedagogical implications. First, they confirm that same level learners can have a positive influence on each other's learning. When working collaboratively, they are able to solve each other's lexical problems and co-construct new vocabulary knowledge. These findings support the use in the L2 classroom of collaborative writing tasks. However, teachers need to remember that same level learners cannot always help each other as desired. Although in this study correctly resolved LREs were far more frequent than unresolved and incorrectly resolved ones, the analysis of the posttests revealed that learners retained the knowledge built in their correctly and incorrectly resolved LREs. As already observed by other researchers (see Swain & Lapkin 1998), this means that collaborative activities, when implemented in the classroom, need to be supervised by teachers who are able to provide appropriate feedback and assistance.

As discussed in the introduction to this chapter, in L2 classrooms, teachers often favor pair over small group work because it offers more opportunities for individual learners to speak. The analyses conducted in this study showed how indeed, in groups of four, learners sometimes acted as silent observers of their peers' interaction. But they also revealed that this did not necessarily mean they were not participating in the activity and benefiting from the interaction. Learners benefited from observing their peers' problem solving and knowledge building activities. While previous research on collaborative writing has highlighted the benefits of pair work, these findings support the use of collaborative tasks completed in small groups. As the analysis of Jack, Chris, and David's performances illustrates, the main concern for teachers should not be whether all learners get similar opportunities to speak, but rather the actual learning opportunities different groups create and how each individual learner takes advantage of these learning affordances.

References

Alegría de la Colina, A., & García Mayo, M. P. (2007). Attention to form across collaborative tasks by low proficiency learners in an EFL setting. In M. P. Garca Mayo (Ed.), *Investigating tasks in formal language learning* (pp. 91–116). Clevedon: Multilingual Matters.

Allwright, R. (1980). Turns, topics and tasks: Patterns of participation in language teaching and learning. In D. Larsen-Freeman (Ed.), *Discourse analysis in second language research* (pp. 165–187). Rowley, MA: Newbury House.

Antón, M., & DiCamilla, F. (1998). Socio-cognitive functions of L1 collaborative interaction in the L2 classroom. *The Canadian Modern Language Review*, 54, 314–342.
doi:10.3138/cmlr.54.3.314

Choi, H., & Iwashita, N. (2016). Interactional behaviours of low-proficiency learners in small group work. In M. Sato & S. Ballinger (Eds.), *Peer interaction and second language learning: Pedagogical potential and research agenda* (pp. 113–134). Amsterdam: John Benjamins.

Donato, R. (1994). Collective scaffolding in second language learning. In J. P. Lantolf, & G. Appel (Eds.), *Vygotskian approaches to second language research* (pp. 33–56). Norwood, NJ: Ablex.

Ellis, R., Tanaka, Y., & Yamazaki, A. (1994). Classroom interaction, comprehension, and L2 vocabulary acquisition. *Language Learning*, 44, 449–491.
doi:10.1111/j.1467-1770.1994.tb01114.x

Fernández Dobao, A. (2012). Collaborative writing tasks in the L2 classroom: Comparing group, pair, and individual work. *Journal of Second Language Writing*, 21, 40–58.
doi:10.1016/j.jslw.2011.12.002

Fernández Dobao, A. (2014a). Attention to form in collaborative writing tasks: Comparing pair and small group interaction. *Canadian Modern Language Review*, 14, 158–187.
doi:10.3138/cmlr.1768

Fernández Dobao, A. (2014b). Vocabulary learning in collaborative tasks: A comparison of pair and small group work. *Language Teaching Research*. doi:10.1177/1362168813519730

Fernández Dobao, A., & Blum, A. (2013). Collaborative writing in pairs and small groups: Learners' attitudes and perceptions. *System*, 41, 365–378. doi:10.1016/j.system.2013.02.002

Foster, P., & Ohta, A. (2005). Negotiation for meaning and peer assistance in second language classrooms. *Applied Linguistics*, 26, 402–430. doi:10.1093/applin/ami014

García Mayo, M. P. (2002). The effectiveness of two form-focused tasks in advanced EFL pedagogy. *International Journal of Applied Linguistics*, 12, 156–175.
doi:10.1111/1473-4192.t01-1-00029

Guerrero, M. C. M. de (2005). *Inner speech - L2: Thinking words in a second language*. New York, NY: Springer. doi:10.1007/b106255

Kim, Y. (2008). The contribution of collaborative and individual tasks to the acquisition of L2 vocabulary. *The Modern Language Journal*, 92, 114–130. doi:10.1111/j.1540-4781.2008.00690.x

Kim, Y., & McDonough, K. (2008). The effect of interlocutor proficiency on the collaborative dialogue between Korean as a second language learners. *Language Teaching Research*, 12, 211–234. doi:10.1177/1362168807086288

Lapkin, S., Swain, M., & Smith, M. (2002). Reformulation and the learning of French pronominal verbs in a Canadian French immersion context. *The Modern Language Journal*, 86, 485–507. doi:10.1111/1540-4781.00157

Lasito, & Storch, N. (2013). Comparing pair and small group interactions on oral tasks. *RELC Journal*, 44, 361–375. doi:10.1177/0033688213500557

Leeser, M. J. (2004). Learner proficiency and focus on form during collaborative dialogue. *Language Teaching Research*, 8, 55–81. doi:10.1191/1362168804lr134oa

Ohta, A. S. (2000). Rethinking interaction in SLA: Developmentally appropriate assistance in the zone of proximal development and the acquisition of L2 grammar. In J. P. Lantolf (Ed.), *Sociocultural theory and second language learning* (pp. 51–78). Oxford: Oxford University Press.

Ohta, A. S. (2001). *Second language acquisition processes in the classroom: Learning Japanese*. Mahwah, NJ: Lawrence Erlbaum Associates.

Philp, J., & Iwashita, N. (2013). Talking, tuning in and noticing: Exploring the benefits of output in task-based peer interaction. *Language Awareness*, 22, 353–370.
doi:10.1080/09658416.2012.758128

Rouhshad, A., & Storch, N. (2016). A focus on mode: Patterns of interaction in face-to-face and computer-mediated contexts. In M. Sato & S. Ballinger (Eds.), *Peer interaction and second language learning: Pedagogical potential and research agenda* (pp. 267–289). Amsterdam: John Benjamins.

Sato, M., & Ballinger, S. (2012). Raising language awareness in peer interaction: A cross-context, cross-methodology examination. *Language Awareness*, 21, 157–179.
doi:10.1080/09658416.2011.639884

Sato, M., & Ballinger, S. (2016). Understanding peer interaction: Research synthesis and directions. In M. Sato & S. Ballinger (Eds.), *Peer interaction and second language learning: Pedagogical potential and research agenda* (pp. 1–30). Amsterdam: John Benjamins.

Saville-Troike, M. (1988). Private speech: Evidence for second language learning strategies during the 'silent' period. *Child Language*, 15, 567–590. doi:10.1017/S0305000900012575

Shekary, M., & Tahririan, M. (2006). Negotiation of meaning and noticing in text-based online chat. *The Modern Language Journal*, 90, 557–573. doi:10.1111/j.1540-4781.2006.00504.x

Slimani, A. (1989). The role of topicalisation in classroom language learning. *System*, 17, 223–234. doi:10.1016/0346-251X(89)90035-3

Storch, N. (2001a). Comparing ESL learners' attention to grammar on three different classroom tasks. *RELC Journal*, 32, 104–124. doi:10.1177/003368820103200207

Storch, N. (2001b). How collaborative is pair work? ESL tertiary students composing in pairs. *Language Teaching Research*, 5, 29–53. doi:10.1177/136216880100500103

Storch, N. (2002). Patterns of interaction in ESL pair work. *Language Learning*, 52, 119–158.
doi:10.1111/1467-9922.00179

Storch, N. (2004). Using activity theory to explain differences in patterns of dyadic interactions in an ESL class. *The Canadian Modern Language Review, 60*, 457–480. doi:10.3138/cmlr.60.4.457

Storch, N. (2008). Metatalk in a pair work activity: Level of engagement and implications for language development. *Language Awareness, 17*, 95–114. doi:10.2167/la431.0

Storch, N. (2013). *Collaborative writing in L2 classrooms*. Bristol, UK: Multilingual Matters.

Storch, N., & Aldosari, A. (2013). Pairing learners in pair work activity. *Language Teaching Research, 17*, 31–48. doi:10.1177/1362168812457530

Storch, N., & Wigglesworth, G. (2010). Learners' processing, uptake, and retention of corrective feedback on writing. *Studies in Second Language Acquisition, 32*, 303–334. doi:10.1017/S0272263109990532

Swain, M. (2000). The output hypothesis and beyond. In J. P. Lantolf (Ed.), *Sociocultural theory and second language learning* (pp. 97–114). Oxford: Oxford University Press.

Swain, M. (2006). Languaging, agency and collaboration in advanced language proficiency. In H. Byrnes (Ed.), *Advanced language learning: The contribution of Halliday and Vygotsky* (pp. 95–108). New York, NY: Continuum.

Swain, M., Kinnear, P., & Steinman, L. (2011). *Sociocultural theory in second language education: An introduction through narratives*. Bristol, UK: Multilingual Matters.

Swain, M., & Lapkin, S. (1998). Interaction and second language learning: Two adolescent French immersion students working together. *The Modern Language Journal, 82*, 320–337. doi:10.1111/j.1540-4781.1998.tb01209.x

Swain, M., & Lapkin, S. (2001). Focus on form through collaborative dialogue: Exploring task effects. In M. Bygate, P. Skehan, & M. Swain (Eds.), *Researching pedagogic tasks: Second language learning, teaching and testing* (pp. 99–118). London: Longman.

Swain, M., & Lapkin, S. (2002). Talking it through: Two French immersion learners' response to reformulation. *International Journal of Educational Research, 37*, 285–304. doi:10.1016/S0883-0355(03)00006-5

Watanabe, Y., & Swain, M. (2007). Effects of proficiency differences and patterns of pair interaction on second language learning: Collaborative dialogue between adult ESL learners. *Language Teaching Research, 11*, 121–142. doi:10.1177/136216880607074599

Wigglesworth, G., & Storch, N. (2012). Feedback and writing development through collaboration: A socio-cultural approach. In R. Manchón (Ed.), *L2 writing development: Multiple perspectives* (pp. 69–100). Boston, MA: de Gruyter Mouton.

Williams, J. (1999). Learner-generated attention to form. *Language Learning, 49*, 583–625. doi:10.1111/0023-8333.00103

Williams, J. (2001). The effectiveness of spontaneous attention to form. *System, 29*, 325–340. doi:10.1016/S0346-251X(01)00022-7

Yilmaz, Y. (2011). Task effects on focus on form in synchronous computer-mediated communication. *The Modern Language Journal, 95*, 115–132. doi:10.1111/j.1540-4781.2010.01143.x

Young, A., & Tedick, D. J. (2016). Collaborative dialogue in a two-way Spanish/English immersion classroom: Does heterogeneous grouping promote peer linguistic scaffolding? In M. Sato & S. Ballinger (Eds.), *Peer interaction and second language learning: Pedagogical potential and research agenda* (pp. 135–160). Amsterdam: John Benjamins.

Zeng, G., & Takatsuka, S. (2009). Text-based peer-peer collaborative dialogue in a computer-mediated learning environment in the EFL context. *System, 37*, 434–446. doi:10.1016/j.system.2009.01.003

Appendix A

Collaborative writing task

González Sáinz, T. (1999). *Juegos comunicativos. Español lengua extranjera*. Madrid: SM (p. 87)

Appendix B

Extract of the vocabulary tests

Me gustan mucho los deportes al aire libre. Me gusta mucho _____ (*to ski*)
y también _____ (*to bike*). Pero cada vez hay más _____
(*pollution*) y eso me preocupa. Si no hacemos nada pronto tendremos que llevar
_____ (*gas masks*) para salir a la calle.

Appendix C

Vocabulary items in the tests

esquiar (to ski)
andar en bici (to bike)
contaminación (pollution)
máscara antigás (gas mask)

crucero (cruise)
aeropuerto (airport)
tomar (to take)
avión (plane)
barco (ship)
navegar (to sail)

adivino (fortuneteller)
futuro (future)
predecir (to predict)
conocer (to meet)
agencia de viajes
(travel agency)
boleto (ticket)
salir (to leave)

jefe (boss)
jardinería
(nursery)
cortacésped
(lawnmower)

CHAPTER 2

Peer interaction and metacognitive instruction in the EFL classroom

Akiko Fujii, Nicole Ziegler and Alison Mackey
University of the Sacred Heart / University of Hawai'i at Mānoa /
Georgetown University

This chapter examines the effects of metacognitive instruction on the provision
and use of interactional opportunities in learner-learner interactions in the
task-based EFL classroom. Learners ($N = 39$) drawn from three intact speaking
classes in an intensive academic EFL program were divided into a treatment
group and a control group. Learners in both groups completed a pretest and
posttest. The treatment group participated in a metacognitive instruction session, which demonstrated to learners the benefits of interactional feedback and
presented tips and practice on how to provide feedback to their peers. Overall,
findings indicate that metacognitive instruction led to greater provision and use
of interactional feedback in subsequent interactions, and that learners recognized the benefits for their second language learning.

Introduction

As second and foreign language educators increasingly embrace "communicative" and "task-based" methods of language teaching, learner-learner interactions
in the form of "pairwork" and "groupwork" are becoming more and more common in language learning classrooms (Adams, Nuevo, & Egi 2011; García Mayo
& Pica 2000; Philp & Tognini 2009; Sato & Ballinger 2016; Zhao & Bitchener
2007). Yet, despite seminal (Doughty & Pica 1986; Long & Porter 1985; Varonis
& Gass 1985) and more recent empirical research (e.g., Adams 2007; Mackey,
Oliver, & Leeman 2003) demonstrating that learner-learner interaction may facilitate second language (L2) learning, doubts exist about the practical effectiveness
of learner-learner interaction in the L2 classroom, particularly in foreign language
contexts (Philp & Tognini 2009). For instance, research has identified challenges in
learner-learner interactions, with findings showing that they may result in lower
frequency of negotiation (García Mayo & Pica 2000; Williams 1999) and less L2

DOI 10.1075/lllt.45.03fuj
© 2016 John Benjamins Publishing Company

development than teacher-learner interactions (Toth 2008). Although research has clearly demonstrated that interaction facilitates L2 development (see Keck, Iberri-Shea, Tracy-Ventura, & Wa-Mbaleka 2006; Mackey & Goo 2007; Ziegler 2015 for reviews), few studies have investigated the effects of explicit, metacognitive instruction on learners' use and provision of interactional features (although see Kim & McDonough 2011; Sato & Ballinger 2012; and Sato & Lyster 2012 for exceptions). This chapter addresses this gap in the literature by investigating whether learners can be explicitly taught to be better interactors and feedback providers, thereby maximizing their opportunities to positively benefit from interaction with their peers.

Interaction and second language development

The theoretical foundations for the benefits of interaction on L2 development have been established by a large body of research conducted over the course of the past two decades (Gass & Varonis 1994; Iwashita 2003; Leeman 2003; Loewen & Philp 2006; Mackey 2007; 2012; Mackey & Goo 2007; Mackey & Gass 2006; Mackey et al. 2003; Mackey & Oliver 2002; McDonough 2007). Previous empirical studies, as well as meta-analyses (Keck et al. 2006; Li 2010; Lyster & Saito 2010; Mackey & Goo 2007; Russell & Spada 2006; Ziegler 2015), have indicated that interaction plays a facilitative role in L2 development by providing learners with opportunities to receive modified comprehensible input and interactional feedback, to produce output, and to notice gaps between their interlanguage and the target language features through negotiation for meaning (Mackey 2012; Mackey, Abbuhl, & Gass 2012; Mackey & Gass 2006). These negotiations, which include conversational moves such as confirmation checks, and clarification requests made in response to failures in communication, can lead to interactional adjustments by a more competent interlocutor, thus facilitating acquisition through the "connection of input, internal learner capacities, particularly selective attention, and output in productive ways" (Long 1996: 451–452). The feedback that learners receive during these negotiations for meaning can crucially direct their attention to mismatches between interlanguage and target language features.

Interaction also provides opportunities for learners to produce modified output, which is an essential aspect of L2 development as it provides learners with opportunities to improve fluency and to test hypotheses about the target language (Gass & Mackey 2006; Long 1996, 2007; Mackey & Gass 2012; Swain 1985, 1995, 2005). In addition, research has demonstrated that the benefits of interaction are not limited to the laboratory setting, but apply in the classroom as well (Ellis 2007; Gass, Mackey, Ross-Feldman 2005; Keck et al. 2006; Mackey 2006; Mackey & Goo

2007; McDonough 2004). However, previous research has also suggested that the effects of interaction on L2 development may be influenced by differences in interlocutor, setting, and context (Mackey & Goo 2007; Sheen 2004).

Feedback in peer interaction

Numerous studies during the last three decades have specifically investigated learner-learner interaction. The results of such studies have demonstrated that learner-learner interaction can be rich in interactional modifications, such as negotiation for meaning, modified output, and feedback (Bruton & Samuda 1980; García Mayo & Pica 2000; Long & Porter 1985; Pica, Lincoln-Porter, Paninos, & Linnell 1996; Sato & Lyster 2007; Varonis & Gass 1985; Zhao & Bitchener 2007) (Also see Sato & Ballinger 2016 and Philp, Adams, & Iwashita 2014 for more discussion). For example, negotiation in learner-learner interactions has been linked to negative feedback, a crucial process in language development. Mackey et al. (2003) compared native-speaker (NS)-learner interactions with learner-learner interaction in an English as a Second Language (ESL) setting with reference to recasts and negotiation moves, such as confirmation checks and clarification requests, which occurred specifically in response to non-target-like utterances. In other words, they examined the occurrence of negotiation moves that functioned as negative feedback. Findings indicated that negative feedback was indeed provided by learners in learner-learner interaction in response to more than 30% of non-target-like utterances for both adult dyads and child dyads. Results also showed that NSs provided more negative feedback than learners did in adult dyads. However, adult learner-learner dyads produced more opportunities for modified output, and child learner-learner dyads produced more modified output. Similar results of increased modified output production in learner-learner interaction compared to learner-NS interactions were also found in a study of English as a Foreign Language (EFL) learners by Sato and Lyster (2007), whose findings demonstrated that learner-learner dyads provided more elicitation feedback than native speaker interlocutors. Finally, Adams (2007) examined the relationship between negative feedback and L2 learning in ESL learner-learner interactions and found that almost 60% of all feedback episodes resulted in learning the linguistic issues involved. However, Adams' findings also indicated that learners may provide each other with inaccurate feedback, lending support to previous research (García Mayo & Pica 2000).

Furthermore, studies have found that the quantity and quality of interactional feedback in classrooms may be variable and may be task or setting-dependent. In a study of information gap tasks carried out in in an ESL setting, Foster (1998) found wide individual variation in the quantity of learner negotiation, including a lack of negotiation by many of the participants. Based on these findings, Foster argued "'negotiation for meaning' is not a strategy that language learners are predisposed to employ when they encounter gaps in their understanding" (Foster 1998: 1). Foster and Ohta (2005) suggest that the low frequency of negotiation in Foster's (1998) study may be due to the fact that negotiation for meaning may be face-threatening and frustrating for learners. However, Gass, Mackey, and Ross-Feldman (2005) came to a different conclusion based on their data also collected in ESL classroom and laboratory settings, suggesting that task effects were more important than contextual differences.

Peer interaction and foreign language contexts

Limitations in adult peer interaction have been pointed out specifically with respect to EFL contexts, particularly in non-immersion settings where L2 input opportunities are often limited (Fujii & Mackey 2009; García Mayo & Pica 2000; McDonough 2004; Philp & Tognini 2009). For instance, in McDonough's (2004) examination of pair and group activities in a Thai EFL context, she found that only those learners who were highly participatory in feedback and modified output episodes benefited from the interaction. Learners may also fail to negotiate or provide feedback due to shared cultural beliefs, such as the need to avoid face-threatening linguistic behavior (Sato & Lyster 2007). For example, Fujii and Mackey (2009) investigated learner-learner interactions in a Japanese EFL context, finding that learners provided a relatively low rate of interactional feedback, possibly due to learners' shared cultural background. Studies have also demonstrated that learners from varied cultural backgrounds may be hesitant to provide feedback because they feel their interlocutors may find it socially inappropriate (Mackey et al. 2003). However, as Philp and Tognini (2009) suggest, despite these challenges, foreign language classrooms, where time and L2 exposure are limited, are exactly the kind of contexts where interaction is a valuable resource for learning. These learners may need direct instruction or preparation in order to participate actively and benefit fully from task-based language teaching (see also Mackey et al. 2013).

The learner's role in learning

The implementation of interactive tasks in the L2 classroom assumes a learner-centered approach to learning (Willis & Willis 2008). Development is driven by learners' efforts to achieve mutual understanding (Long 1996), and such interaction stimulates the unfolding of the learners' internal syllabi (Robinson 2001) by providing samples of language that learners can incorporate into their interlanguage when they are developmentally ready. In addition, Samuda (2001) has discussed the role of the learners themselves in shaping whether a task results in knowledge construction or skill practice. In other words, as Philp and Mackey (2011) point out, learners are active participants in their own learning process.

Empirical studies have investigated learners' perceptions about interaction from a wide range of perspectives, ranging from whether learners notice corrective feedback (Mackey, Gass, & McDonough 2000) to their perceptions about the role that social and personal factors play in peer interaction (Philp & Mackey 2011). Research has also examined the connection between learners' perceptions about interaction, their task performance, and resulting L2 development. For example, Mackey (2006) investigated 28 adult ESL learners' noticing of feedback, target features, and L2 development, eliciting their perceptions through journals, stimulated recalls, and questionnaires. Results indicated a positive relationship between learners' noticing of interactional feedback and their resulting L2 development, with learners who reported greater levels of noticing demonstrating greater improvements in their use of question forms. Egi (2007) also examined the relationship between learners' perceptions and their subsequent L2 development, with findings indicating that learners who had interpreted recasts as both negative and positive evidence had significantly higher scores on posttests than learners who interpreted recasts as meaning-focused responses.

In addition, studies have demonstrated that learners may benefit more from interaction if they are actively involved in negotiation (Mackey 1999), and that positive attitudes towards tasks may lead to improved willingness to communicate (Dörnyei & Kormos 2002), suggesting that learners' perceptions impact their participation in interactional tasks and therefore affect their opportunities to benefit from interactional processes. Mackey (2002) examined the extent to which learners' perceptions of interaction overlapped with researchers' claims, finding that learners' insights consistently corresponded to empirical claims surrounding comprehensible input, modified output, corrective feedback, and hypothesis testing. Overall, these findings suggest that learners' perspectives may play an important role in their use and provision of interactional opportunities and the developmental and social benefits they stand to gain.

Furthermore, it may be possible to improve learners' overall engagement and effectiveness in interactions by providing them with explicit instruction on interactional features and processes.

Targeted instruction

Recent studies have reported on efforts to instruct or train learners to improve their opportunities for learning through interaction. In a study of collaborative learning in interactive tasks, Kim and McDonough (2011) found that the quality of interaction was better with learners who had viewed models of collaborative learning prior to engaging in the task compared to learners who had not viewed the models. Mackey and Fujii (2009) provided an intact class of Japanese EFL learners with instruction on how to be more effective interactors. Following a presentation on the benefits of interaction, learners participated in a classroom-based picture-description task. Findings indicated a slight improvement in learners' rates of interactional feedback following training, suggesting that some learners might become better interlocutors when directly told about the benefits of interaction. Their findings suggest that direct instruction may be beneficial to learners' overall use of interaction in a variety of settings and contexts.

Sato and Lyster (2012) examined the impact of corrective feedback training on Japanese EFL learners' second language development. Learners in the experimental groups were trained to give corrective feedback in response to their partners' errors. Results indicated that the learners in the corrective feedback groups significantly improved on measures of accuracy and fluency, while the interaction-only group demonstrated greater gains in fluency than the control group. These findings suggest that learners' L2 development may improve as a result of training in corrective feedback. In addition, Sato (2013) reports that the training had a positive impact on learners' trust in their peers as learning resources, and in their willingness and confidence to provide each other with corrective feedback. Thus, these studies demonstrate the benefits of training learners to provide their peers with corrective feedback. There is a need for additional classroom research examining the impact of instruction on other interactional factors, such as negotiation for meaning and modified output opportunities.

Ballinger (2013) also reported on a study on learner training, which was conducted in the context of an English-French immersion classroom at the elementary school level and involved two intact classes. Both classes received instruction on the use of peer language learning strategies in interactional tasks. Quantitative and qualitative analyses examined the audio recordings of the learners' interactions for instances of pair collaboration, or language-related episodes (LREs), which can be defined as learners' implicit or explicit discussions regarding their or their interlocutors' language use and strategy use, including instances of corrective feedback. Findings suggest that although corrective feedback provision may encourage enhanced language awareness, its effectiveness was mitigated by the lack of collaboration or cooperation within learner pairs, with feedback provision sometimes leading to missed development opportunities rather than L2 learning. Sato and Ballinger (2012) suggested that these results provide evidence for the effectiveness of combining language awareness training with training for improved peer collaboration in order to improve learners' L2 development.

Although these studies suggest that learners' L2 development may improve as a result of training in the provision and use of interactional feedback during oral and written peer interactions, more research is necessary to further our understanding of how instructors can maximize learning opportunities through explicit training in conversational interaction. Previous research has established the benefits of interaction and negotiation for meaning on L2 development (for reviews, see Keck et al. 2006; Mackey & Goo 2007); however, the role learners themselves play in these learning processes remains unclear. As many teachers are already aware, learners often fail to negotiate over non-target-like utterances, thus missing out on the potential benefits of interaction. Although this is a common enough issue in ESL and EFL contexts, the research has not adequately addressed if and how instructors might improve learners' interactional abilities through explicit training.

The current research

This study focuses on how learners in classroom contexts might become better interlocutors by raising their awareness of the quality of their interactions. In other words, this study examines whether raising learners' awareness of their provision and use of interactional features through metacognitive instruction improves learner engagement in interactive tasks.

The following research questions were addressed:

1. How does metacognitive instruction affect learners' provision and use of interactional opportunities?
2. What do learners' reports suggest about their perceptions of metacognitive instruction and its effects on their language learning?

Method

Methodological framework

This quasi-experimental study conducted in an authentic classroom setting employed a pretest-treatment-posttest design in order to examine the effect of task-based metacognitive instruction on learners' provision and use of interactional feedback. The study was carried out within the framework of interactionist research (Mackey 2007; 2012). Data consisted of transcripts of learners' task-based interactions before and after the treatment session, which were coded following Mackey, Oliver, and Leeman (2003) for (a) instances of interactional feedback, (b) opportunities for learners to modify their output in response to the feedback provided by their peers, and (c) instances where learners actually modified their output in response to the feedback they received from their peers. These data were supplemented by learners' reports on perceptions about their learning, which were analyzed using a qualitative approach.

Participants

Participants were 39 learners from three intact classes in an intensive academic English program at a private university in Tokyo, Japan. Of these 39 learners, 13 were men and 26 were women. The learners were all native speakers of Japanese in their first year of university study with a mean age of 18.6 years. The learners began studying English at a mean age of 11, which is the age when English education usually begins in schools in Japan. They were placed in the low-intermediate level of the program (the lowest of three levels) based on an in-house placement test administered at the beginning of the term. The TOEFL PBT scores for this level ranged from 377–513, with an average score of 463. The participants in one of the three intact classes were assigned to a control group ($n = 16$), and participants in the other two intact classes were assigned to a single treatment group ($n = 23$). Because data collection was conducted during regular class periods, data was initially collected from all of the learners present. The number of participants reported here represent the learners for whom there were complete data sets. The academic speaking courses maintained an English-only policy during class, and the overall instructional methodology of the intensive language program followed a communicative, task-based approach. Since the tasks and instruction for the current research were conducted as part of the regular course curriculum, participants were not paid for their participation.

Materials

Tasks
The pretests and posttests consisted of tailor-made interactive tasks and others adapted from previous research (Ur 1981). Two types of information gap tasks were used as pretests and posttests. One task was a picture difference task in which learner dyads were given two different versions of a picture (each learner had a different version) and asked to identify differences between the pictures. The second

task was a problem-solving task. In this task, learners were each given one half of a comic strip depicting a mystery. The task was to exchange information about the pictures in order to solve the mystery. Information gap tasks were selected because previous studies suggest that required information exchange results in more negotiation (Ellis 2006; Foster 1998). The two different types of information gap tasks were selected in order to represent both closed outcome tasks, such as the picture-difference task, which may result in short, lexical exchanges, as well as conversational tasks, such as the picture-sequencing task, that may result in longer expressions of opinion. Previous research has demonstrated that these contrasting task types elicit different patterns of negotiation (Duff 1986; Nakahama, Tyler, & Van Lier 2001). The picture difference tasks were adopted from *Discussions that Work* (Ur 1981), while the problem-solving tasks were created based on stories from an internet mystery story website *MysteryNet's Kids Mysteries*. Different versions of both types of information gap tasks were used on the pretest and posttest, with the pretest consisting of a different picture difference task and problem-solving task than the posttest.

Metacognitive instruction session

The four-part instructional session was titled "How to be an active learner: Feedback, negotiation, and noticing," and delivered by the first author who was introduced to the class as a guest speaker. The instruction was conducted using PowerPoint slides all in English following the English-only policy in the program.

1. Explanation: Since the learners all came from a common background of form-based language instruction, the presentation began with an introduction of the characteristics and benefits of communicative, meaning-focused language instruction. After discussing the advantages and disadvantages of communicative language learning, specifically the concern that it may lead to development in fluency but not necessarily accuracy or complexity, the presenter explained how negotiation processes could facilitate the development of learners' accuracy and complexity.

2. Examples: The second phase of the instruction provided learners with examples of successful interactions. Negotiation processes were illustrated using video clips of a Japanese learner carrying out a decision-making task with an instructor. This video was supplemented with transcripts highlighting the negotiation processes, thereby providing support for both visual and aural learners. One of the slides used to highlight negotiation processes in the transcript is shown in Figure 1.

3. Useful phrases: The third phase presented learners with several phrases that could be used to elicit clarification or confirmation or for giving recasts, such as 'so you mean...' or 'I'm sorry, I don't understand'.

4. Practice: The final phase of the instruction session provided learners with one guided practice activity and one practice activity in learner-learner dyads. During this phase, the whole class completed a picture-difference task together, guided by the instructor, who initiated negotiation, modeled a variety of feedback moves, and also created contexts for the learners to initiate negotiation. Then, learners practiced a similar task in learner-learner dyads.

> Example (1)
>
> Hiro: I think that… to arrive oasis…
> Teacher: <u>to what?</u> you think…? ← **clarification question**
> Hiro: to arrive oasis
> Teacher: Oh, to arrive <u>at the oasis</u> ← **restate correctly (recast)**
> Hiro: yeah, oasis ← **NOTICE and corrects**

Figure 1. Sample slide from metacognitive instruction session

Exit questionnaire

The written exit questionnaire (Appendix A) consisted of 13 items designed to elicit learners' perceptions and evaluation of the instructional session. The questionnaire was administered in the learners' first language, Japanese. Learners were asked to rate their responses on a five-point Likert scale ranging from a score of one, "I strongly disagree," to a score of five, "I strongly agree."

Procedure

Data were collected during learners' regularly scheduled academic speaking class during two 70-minute class periods (referred to here as Session 1 and Session 2), which took place within the space of one week. For both the pretest and posttest, learners were given five minutes to carry out the picture-difference task and 10 minutes to carry out the problem-solving task. All interactions, which the learners completed in self-selected learner-learner dyads, were audio-recorded using portable digital audio-recorders. Learners worked with the same partner throughout the duration of the study except in unavoidable circumstances such as absence. Learners were accustomed to the English-only policy enforced across the program and therefore no Japanese was used in the classroom even during peer interaction.

Treatment group

Learners in two intact classes were assigned to the treatment group. During Session 1, they participated in the pretest, which was immediately followed by the four-part metacognitive instruction session described above. Session 2 began with a review of the metacognitive instruction. Following the review, participants completed the posttest, which consisted of different versions of the same type of tasks used during the pretest. Finally, learners carried out exit questionnaires that asked learners to recall and record what they had been thinking during the pretest and posttest tasks. All learners carried out the tasks with the same partners for both the pretest and the posttest. In order to mitigate the possibility of the Hawthorne effect, which suggests that participants might alter their behavior in a favorable way due to their being part of a research study, the instruction and tasks were carefully structured to follow the design and implementation of regular task-based class activities.

Control group
Learners assigned to the control group (one intact class) participated in the same pretest and posttest tasks as the treatment group. However, instead of receiving the task-based metacognitive instruction, they participated in regular class activities. In addition, the control group participants did not complete exit questionnaires. Figure 2 illustrates the procedure of the study.

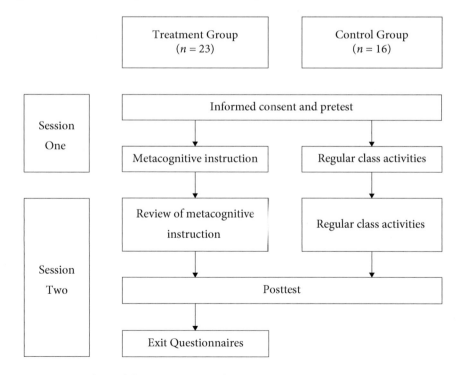

Figure 2. Procedure of the current research

Analysis

Data analyses were carried out using both quantitative and qualitative approaches. Quantitative measures addressed the effects of metacognitive instruction on the amount of feedback learners provided in response to their interlocutors' non-target-like utterances, as well as the amount of modified output opportunities and actual instances of learners' modified output. Qualitative measures investigated participants' experiences and perceptions about instruction from a more holistic perspective.

All audio recordings of learners' pretest and posttest tasks were transcribed. Following Mackey, Oliver, and Leeman (2003), learner utterances were first coded as target-like or non-target-like in order to identify contexts of interactional feedback provided in response to erroneous utterances. Because this study focused on learners' provision of interactional feedback, only responses to non-target-like utterances were included in the analyses. Interlocutors' responses to erroneous utterances were then categorized according to the type of feedback provided. Clarification requests, confirmation checks, and recasts were operationalized following previous research (Mackey et al. 2003; Fujii & Mackey 2009). Examples taken from the current study illustrate the types of feedback that were coded in the analyses:

(1) Clarification request
     Learner 1   yea, book. Book and uh..string?
     Learner 2   what?
     Learner 1   string…ball

(2) Confirmation check
     Learner 1   How many dots your picture?
     Learner 2   You mean how many arrows?
     Learner 1   Yes.

(3) Recast
     Learner 1   Found the broken glass.
     Learner 2   window.
     Learner 1   broken window.

Next, interactions were coded for modified output opportunities and the production of modified output. If an interlocutor provided feedback and then gave an opportunity for the reformulation of the original utterance, by pausing or hesitating in order to provide the interlocutor with an opportunity to respond, this was categorized as a modified output opportunity. Example (4) from the data illustrates an opportunity for modified output.

(4) Opportunity for modified output
  Learner 1 and the last scene, the left fishing boy said house, said house and
       sandwich, there is a house sandwich.
  Learner 2 House sandwiches?

In this example, Learner 2 asks for clarification, but instead of continuing, pauses and provides an opportunity for Learner 1 to reformulate the original utterance. Learner utterances immediately following feedback and modified output opportunities were then coded for the production of modified output that corrected or clarified the original utterance. Modified output is illustrated in Example (5) below.

(5) Modified output
  Learner 1 Levine work something in in his uh old chair.
  Learner 2 What you mean? Work in his chair?
  Learner 1 Work something..mm…write..write something.
  Learner 2 Oh write. Ok.

In sum, these analyses examined the amount of interactional feedback, modified output opportunities, and resulting modified output that learners provided in response to non-target-like utterances. Inter-rater reliability was calculated with a second rater on 25% of the data set with a simple percentage agreement of 95%. Alpha levels were set at .05, and in light of the small sample size, exact significance values are reported for all statistical tests.

Qualitative analyses were carried out on the exit questionnaire data to obtain a more holistic view of learners' perceptions and use of interactional feedback, as well as their opinions of the experience of the metacognitive instruction and how it might be related to their learning outcomes.

Results

The first research question addressed how providing metacognitive instruction on interaction would affect learners' provision and use of interactional opportunities. Since the data did not meet assumptions for normality underlying parametric statistics, Mann-Whitney U-tests were conducted to examine whether differences in the amount of feedback provided in response to non-target-like utterances between the control and treatment groups were significant over time. Results indicate that the different gain scores in the raw amount of feedback were significant across the treatment and control groups, $U = 324$, $p < .001$, with the control group providing an average of 8.25 ($SD = .63$) instances of feedback in response to non-target-like utterances during the pretest and 5.06 ($SD = .74$) during the posttest and the treatment group providing an average of 3.60 ($SD = .53$)

instances of feedback in response to non-target-like utterances during the pretest and 5.70 (SD = .62) instances during the posttest.

However, since raw counts of feedback may be misleading, to obtain a more accurate measurement of the amount of feedback produced in relation to non-target-like utterances, ratio percentage scores of feedback in the context of all non-target-like utterances were also subjected to Mann-Whitney U-tests, which indicated that the gain scores in the amount of feedback provided relative to the number of erroneous utterances was significantly different between the treatment and the control group, U = 288, p = .002. In the control group, feedback was provided an average of 14.68% (SD = 5.58) of the time in response to non-target-like utterances during the pretest and 11.38% (SD = 6.37) of the time during the posttest. For the treatment group, feedback was provided an average of 9.30% (SD = 5.53) of the time in response to non-target-like utterances during the pretest and 16.14% (SD = 10.19) during the posttest.[1]

Overall, these findings, as is shown in Figure 3, indicate that gains by learners in the treatment group were significantly higher in terms of the amount of feedback they provided in response to their interlocutor's non-target-like utterances when compared with gains in the amount of feedback provided by learners in the control group.

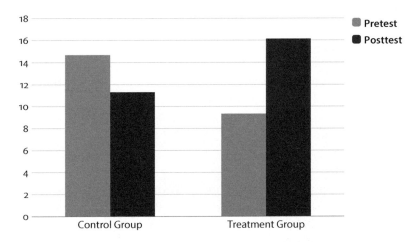

Figure 3. Percentage of non-target-like utterances provided with feedback

---

1.   The medium sized standard deviation (10.19%) seen in the posttest results of the treatment group suggests that there was a wider range of variability in the use and provision of interactional features when compared to the pretest results of those of the control group. Although the majority of learners in the treatment group fell within 5%–6% of the mean, three learners provided feedback over 30% of the time in response to their interlocutors non-target-like utterances, with one learner offering feedback on 45.45% of their partner's errors. This variation suggests that the impact of the instructional session may have differentially affected some learners.

Following the examination of quantity of feedback, analyses examining the quality of feedback were carried out. In other words, analyses then focused on the type of interactional feedback provided in response to non-target-like utterances. Mann-Whitney U-tests indicated that the gains in the treatment group were significantly greater than the gains in the control group in terms of provision of clarification requests, $U = 257$, $p = .037$. However, differences were not significant for confirmation checks, $U = 239.5$, $p = .114$, or recasts, $U = 133.5$, $p = .151$. Table 1 provides the descriptive statistics for the types of feedback for the treatment and control groups.

Table 1. Types of feedback provided in response to non-target-like utterances

Group	Control ($n = 16$)				Treatment ($n = 23$)			
	Pretest		Posttest		Pretest		Posttest	
	M	SD	M	SD	M	SD	M	SD
Clarification requests	.81	.91	.75	1.00	.61	.89	1.57	1.38
Comprehension checks	6.63	2.47	3.00	1.79	2.61	2.21	3.48	2.06
Recasts	.81	1.38	1.31	1.08	.39	.50	.48	.73

Next, analyses examining the provision of modified output opportunities were carried out. Gains in raw modified output opportunities differed significantly between the treatment and control groups, $U = 289$, $p = .002$. Although there was a clear difference in the mean of actual modification of output from pre to posttest for the treatment group, which can be seen in Figure 4, statistical analyses did not suggest that these differences were significant across groups, $U = 240$, $p = .114$.

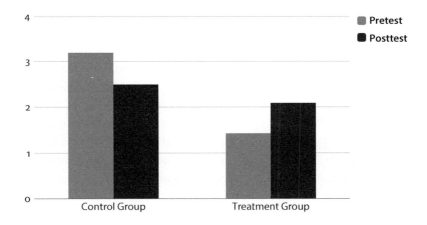

Figure 4. Mean amount of modified output produced by learners in response to modified output opportunities

Table 2 illustrates the trends in the raw numbers of learners' provision of modified output opportunities and the amount of modified output produced in response to these opportunities. However, since raw numbers do not take into account the possibility that learners may have more frequently modified output in relation to the opportunities they received, the proportion of learners' modified output to provided modified output opportunities was also examined. For the treatment group, learners produced modified output 47.97% (SD = 38.66%) of the time in response to modified output opportunities during the pretest, while learners in the control group produced modified output in response to 45.07% (SD = 26.31%) of the provided modified output opportunities. On the posttest, learners in the treatment group produced modified output for 48.18% (SD = 29.05%) of the modified output opportunities, while the control group learners produced modified output 56.63% (SD = 23.22%) of the time. Mann-Whitney U-tests indicate that gains in modified output produced in relation to the provided modified output opportunities was not significant across groups, U = 167, p = .641.

Table 2. Modified output in response to non-target-like utterances

Group	Control (n = 16)				Treatment (n = 23)			
	Pretest		Posttest		Pretest		Posttest	
	M	SD	M	SD	M	SD	M	SD
Opportunities for modified output	6.63	2.75	4.63	1.78	2.61	1.83	4.38	2.84
Modified output provided	3.19	2.20	2.50	1.15	1.43	1.59	2.09	1.78

The second research question examined learners' perceptions about metacognitive instruction and its impact on their language learning outcomes. Exit questionnaires collected from 22 out of the 23 learners in the treatment group were analyzed. Calculations of mean responses for each of the items indicated that learners generally "agreed" or "strongly agreed" with statements about understanding the purpose, benefits, and potential applications of interactional features and corrective feedback, as shown in Table 3 (see Appendix A for the complete questionnaire). Learners reacted positively to the instruction, with 19 out of 22 "agreeing" or "strongly agreeing" that they understood the concepts of negotiation, feedback, and noticing as a result of the training. The findings indicate that learners felt they understood how negotiation and feedback might both contribute to language learning, as well as improve their understanding of why it is important to provide feedback during conversational interactions.

Table 3. Exit questionnaire items with mean score of four or higher on a five-point scale

Questionnaire item	Mean	S.D.
1. I understood the concepts of negotiation, feedback, and noticing.	4.19	.68
2. I understood how negotiation, feedback, and noticing contribute to learning English.	4.05	.59
3. I was able to get an idea of how to give feedback.	4.00	.77
8. I think negotiation, feedback, and noticing are useful for improving my English.	4.28	.78
9. Specifically, negotiation, feedback, and noticing are useful for improving my ability to explain my thoughts.	4.29	.64
12. I think I will use what I learned in this workshop in the future.	4.00	.65

Additionally, responses to the open-ended questions showed that eight of the 22 learners stated that they would use what they learned in the workshop in their other English classes. Five of the 22 learners stated that they would use what they learned in the workshop in situations where they use English, including in study abroad situations and daily conversations, indicating that a portion of the learners were able to see beyond the classroom to the benefits of the instruction for authentic, real-world applications.

Summary of results

Significant differences between the gain scores of the treatment and control groups were found in the amount of overall interactional feedback in response to non-target-like utterances as a result of metacognitive instruction on the provision and use of interactional features. When feedback was examined by type, results showed that learners in the treatment group experienced significantly greater gains than the control group in their use of clarification requests. Additional analyses confirmed differences in the amount of learners' modified output opportunities and actual instances of learners' modified output. The treatment group experienced significantly greater gains for modified output opportunities, with trends in actual modified output being noted, although they were not statistically significant.

Exit questionnaires revealed that learners reacted positively to the instruction, with mean responses indicating that learners understood the concepts, learning benefits, and potential applications of negotiation and interactional feedback.

Discussion

Metacognitive instruction and learner interaction

Learners in this study were positively impacted by metacognitive instruction via task-based interaction in a number of ways, with the treatment group demonstrating an increase in the provision of interactional feedback, specifically clarification requests and modified output opportunities. In other words, learners in this group provided more feedback in response to non-target-like utterances, and provided each other with more opportunities for modified output. These results demonstrate that even a brief metacognitive instructional session like the one provided here can lead learners to become more productive providers of certain types of interactional feedback. Given that interactional feedback is associated with L2 development (Keck et al. 2006; Mackey & Goo 2007), it seems logical that if learners become more successful at providing each other with interactional feedback, they may increase their opportunities for L2 development.

As previous studies have indicated that learner-learner interactions may result in low instances of learner-generated feedback (García Mayo & Pica 2000; Fujii & Mackey 2009; Porter 1986), these results are particularly encouraging, suggesting that instructing learners in the 'hows' and 'whys' of interaction may improve both their ability and willingness to provide interactional feedback and modified output opportunities. These results also lend further support to recent research stating that learners can be trained to be 'better' interactors (Mackey & Fujii 2009) and 'better' corrective feedback providers (Sato & Ballinger 2012; Sato & Lyster 2012). In particular, the notion of becoming a better interactor has implications for learning during a variety of classroom activities and also extends beyond the classroom to learning in naturalistic settings.

Learner-learner interaction

The results also shed some light on several challenges existing in learner-learner interaction. For example, although the quantity of learner-provided feedback increased after the instructional session, the overall amount of negotiation and interactional feedback is still relatively low when considered in terms of the amount of non-target-like utterances. Learners in the control group provided feedback approximately 15% of the time on the pretest and 11% of the time on the posttest in response to their interlocutors' non-target-like utterances, while learners in the treatment group provided feedback approximately 9% of the time on the pretest and 16% of the time on the posttest. Although Mackey (2007) has suggested that the quality (in other words, the timing of interactional feedback, both in relation to learners' developmental levels and the flow of the discourse) is more important than the overall quantity of interactional feedback, it is important to consider the current findings in light of previous research. For example, Mackey et al. (2003) reported the provision of learner feedback on interlocutors' non-target-like utterances as 30%, suggesting that the current results, although they provide encouraging evidence for metacognitive training, might still be considered low when compared to this benchmark. However, the contexts of these studies differ, and it is important to consider the factors that may have impacted learner-learner interaction in the current study.

It remains unclear exactly why the learners in the control group produced less feedback in the posttest than in the pretest. Research has suggested that the success of corrective feedback and interaction can be influenced by a myriad of factors, including teacher and student classroom dynamics (Batstone & Philp 2013) and social or affective factors such as proficiency differences between learners, motivation, or attitudes to the tasks (Burrows 2008; Philp & Tognini 2009; Yoshida 2008). In the case of the control group for the current study, the pretest and posttest resulted in a sequence of task repetition separated by time. It could be that this repetition served to decrease the need for negotiation and/ or was simply a demotivating factor. In other words, it is possible that a decrease in negotiation is a natural tendency in the classroom when tasks are repeated, a point that only highlights further the benefits of explicit instruction about the importance of interactional feedback. Of course, further empirical research is needed in order to gain more insight into such trends.

In addition, the results of the study suggest that instructional sessions may also need to address learners' affective concerns, such as encouraging and supporting learners who seem shy in initiating negotiation or providing feedback in order to maximize the efficacy of metacognitive instruction. For example, the responses from the exit questionnaire showed that not all learners felt confident in their ability to actually give feedback to their peers. One learner stated that he felt he was unable to "teach grammar" to his interlocutor, while two other learners said that the tasks were difficult to discuss due to issues in grammar and vocabulary, thereby preventing them from providing feedback during the interaction. These comments lend further support to previous research findings that suggest learners' perceptions about proficiency differences (Yoshida 2008) and attitudes towards providing peer feedback (Philp, Walter & Basturkmen 2010; Sato 2013; Watanabe & Swain 2007) play a role in their willingness and ability to provide feedback during interactions. Although learners may possess the linguistic resources to adequately provide interactional feedback, their perceptions about their proficiency may prevent them from providing feedback or participating in negotiations with their interlocutor, highlighting the need for more time and/or more practice for learners to be able to put into action what they have understood at a metacognitive level.

In addition, the relatively low rates of learners' provision and use of feedback during peer interaction may be due to the focus, duration, and intensity of the metacognitive training session. Previous research has suggested that in order to alter learners' approaches to peer interaction, training is needed to not only raise learners' linguistic awareness, but also to improve peer collaboration (Sato & Ballinger 2012). Although the current study indicates that even a single metacognitive training session might lead to an increase in negotiation and feedback, intensive training sessions conducted over an extended period of time may lead to greater and more sustained gains. Multiple training sessions would provide learners with additional practice in giving and receiving feedback, as well as offer opportunities for the creation of a more supportive social learning environment, thereby potentially increasing the positive benefits of metacognitive training for learner-learner interaction.

Feedback and negotiation

Another point relates to the low quantity of recasts observed in the data. This is not an entirely unexpected result, as these learners were all at the low-intermediate level and may not have had the linguistic abilities necessary to provide recasts. This trend is also in line with other studies of peer interaction. Fujii and Mackey (2009) also found a low quantity of recasts in their study with EFL Japanese learners. In a comparison of learner-NS and learner-learner interaction Sato and Lyster (2007) found that only 30% of feedback in peer interaction were recasts, in contrast to 59% in learner-NS interaction. Interestingly, two learners did comment in the questionnaire that they did not feel there were many opportunities to learn grammar. In the current study, learners were instructed to resolve problems in communication, rather than to focus on their partners' linguistic errors and give recasts, as was the case in the studies conducted by Sato (Sato & Ballinger 2012; Sato & Lyster 2012). According to their exit questionnaires, learners indicated a neutral response ($M = 3.42$) to the statement that they had noticed more language, including errors and new expressions, in the interactions following the instruction. Thus, it appears that giving recasts, which requires attention to grammar, and knowledge of target-like forms, is a challenge for learners, especially at the lower proficiency levels. It may be that more focused training or more extended training is a necessary condition for a higher quantity of recasts.

Furthermore, negotiation is a learning opportunity that can be extended to contexts outside of the classroom (Sato 1986). Thus, it is especially noteworthy that, as reported above, some of the learners reported in their exit questionnaires their intention to apply what they had learned in the instructional session to other English classes and to other situations where they use English. Overall then, this study suggests that teaching learners about negotiation, feedback, and noticing may provide them with the tools necessary to be better learners through interaction in other contexts where they are in contact with English.

Limitations

Although this study provides interesting information regarding the effects of metacognitive instruction, it is necessary to acknowledge several limitations. The generalizability of the results is limited, as this study used a relatively small sample size from a single, academic context. Learners in other EFL or ESL environments may react differently, and further research is necessary to investigate the effects of metacognitive instruction in novel contexts. Learner proficiency may also have affected the results, particularly with regard to the provision of recasts. In order for learners to be able to provide a corrected reformulation of an interlocutor's utterance successfully, they must have knowledge of the correct grammatical or lexical form. For these low-intermediate learners, their language proficiency may not have allowed this level of interactional feedback, resulting in a lower provision of recasts compared to comprehension checks and clarification requests. Future research may wish to examine learners with more advanced language proficiency, as the instruction may potentially be more effective with more advanced learners.

Finally, the tasks used in this study were not designed to elicit a particular target feature, but rather, to provide learners with an environment in which to practice and build their interactional skills. Future research could consider the use of more targeted tasks in order to examine the impact of metacognitive instruction on the development of a wide range of L2 skills. In addition, particularly as previous research has suggested that learners may benefit from training sessions with greater intensity and longer duration (e.g. Sato & Ballinger 2012), studies using repeated instruction over a longer period of time should be conducted to further our understanding of the long-term effects of metacognitive instruction on learners' interactional skills and L2 development.

Conclusion and pedagogical implications

Overall, this short-term, small-scale study has demonstrated that providing learners with metacognitive instruction in the 'why', 'what,' and 'how' of interaction led to quantitatively increased use and provision of interactional strategies in subsequent interactions. In addition, the introspective data indicated that the learners both understood and enjoyed the instruction, suggesting that a metacognitive instruction component may be a useful and welcome addition to ESL and EFL classrooms. These findings may have important pedagogical implications, as they suggest that learners can be trained to be better providers of negotiation and interactional feedback, thus increasing their potential to benefit from interactional opportunities over time. These results provide useful information to instructors wishing to improve learners' engagement in task-based interactions in the foreign language classroom, and make important contributions to the considerations involved in task-based teaching curricula. Finally, this study highlights the role that learners themselves can play in their own learning process, particularly their ability to improve their provision and use of interactional feedback. However, further research is necessary to develop a greater understanding of the influence and benefits of metacognitive instruction on learner interactions and second language development.

References

Adams, R. (2007). Do second language learners benefit from interacting with each other? In A. Mackey (Ed.), *Conversational interaction in second language acquisition: A collection of empirical studies* (pp. 29–51). Oxford: Oxford University Press.

Adams, R., Nuevo, A., & Egi, T. (2011). Explicit and implicit feedback, modified output, and SLA: Does explicit and implicit feedback promote learning and learner–learner interactions? *The Modern Language Journal*, 95, 42–63. doi:10.1111/j.1540-4781.2011.01242.x

Ballinger, S. (2013). Towards a cross-linguistic pedagogy: Biliteracy and reciprocal learning strategies in French immersion. *Journal of Immersion and Content-Based Language Education*, 1(1), 131–148. doi:10.1075/jicb.1.1.06bal

Batstone, R., & Philp, J. (2013). Classroom interaction and learning opportunities across time and space. In K. McDonough & A. Mackey (Eds.), *Second language interaction in diverse educational contexts* (pp.109–125). Amsterdam: John Benjamins. doi:10.1075/lllt.34.09ch6

Bruton, A., & Samuda, V. (1980). Learner and teacher roles in the treatment of oral error in group work. *RELC Journal*, 11, 49–63. doi:10.1177/003368828001100204

Burrows, C. (2008). An evaluation of task-based learning (TBL) in the Japanese classroom. *English Today*, 24, 11–16. doi:10.1017/S0266078408000345

Dörnyei, Z., & Kormos, J. (2002). *Motivational determinants of the quality and quantity of student performance in communicative language tasks.* Paper presented at *the annual meeting of the American Association of Applied Linguistics*, Salt Lake City, UT.

Doughty, C., & Pica, T. (1986). "Information gap" tasks: Do they facilitate second language acquisition? *TESOL Quarterly, 20,* 305–325.

Duff, P. (1986). Another look at interlanguage talk: Taking task to task. In R. Day (Ed.), *Talking to learn: Conversation in second language acquisition* (pp. 147–81). Rowley, MA: Newbury House.

Egi, T. (2007). Recasts, learners' interpretations, and L2 development. In A. Mackey (Ed.), *Conversational interaction in second language acquisition: A collection of empirical studies* (pp. 249–268). Oxford: Oxford University Press.

Ellis, R. (2006). Researching the effects of form-focused instruction on L2 acquisition. *AILA Review, 19,* 18–41. doi:10.1075/aila.19.04ell

Ellis, R. (2007). The differential effects of corrective feedback on two grammatical structures. In A. Mackey (Ed.), *Conversational interaction in second language acquisition: A collection of empirical studies* (pp. 339–360). Oxford: Oxford University Press.

Foster, P. (1998). A classroom perspective on the negotiation of meaning. *Applied Linguistics, 14,* 1–23. doi:10.1093/applin/19.1.1

Foster, P., & Ohta, A. S. (2005). Negotiation for meaning and peer assistance in second language classrooms. *Applied Linguistics, 26,* 402–430. doi:10.1093/applin/ami014

Fujii, A., & Mackey, A. (2009). Interactional feedback in learner-learner interactions in a task-based EFL classroom. *International Review of Applied Linguistics, 47,* 267–301. doi:10.1515/iral.2009.012

García Mayo, M., & Pica, T. (2000). Interaction among proficient learners: Are input, feedback and output needs addressed in a foreign language context? *Studia Linguistica, 54,* 272–279. doi:10.1111/1467-9582.00066

Gass, S. M., & Mackey, A. (2006). Input, interaction, and output: An overview. *AILA Review, 19,* 3–17. doi:10.1075/aila.19.03gas

Gass, S., Mackey, A., & Ross-Feldman, L. (2005). Task-based interactions in classroom and laboratory settings. *Language Learning, 55,* 575–611. doi:10.1111/j.0023-8333.2005.00318.x

Gass, S., & Varonis, E. (1994). Input, interaction, and second language production. *Studies in Second Language Acquisition, 16,* 283–302. doi:10.1017/S0272263100013097

Iwashita, N. (2003). Negative feedback and positive evidence in task-based interaction. *Studies in Second Language Acquisition, 25,* 1–36. doi:10.1017/S0272263103000019

Keck, C. M., Iberri-Shea, G., Tracy-Ventura, N., & Wa-Mbaleka, S. (2006). Investigating the empirical link between task-based interaction and acquisition: A meta-analysis. In Norris, J. M. & Ortega, L. (Eds.), *Synthesizing research on language learning and teaching* (pp. 91–131). Amsterdam: John Benjamins. doi:10.1075/lllt.13.08kec

Kim, Y. J., & McDonough, K. (2011). Using pretask modelling to encourage collaborative learning opportunities. *Language Teaching Research, 15,* 183–199. doi:10.1177/1362168810388711

Leeman, J. (2003). Recasts and second language development. *Studies in Second Language Acquisition, 25,* 37–63. doi:10.1017/S0272263103000020

Li, S. (2010). The effectiveness of corrective feedback in SLA: A meta-analysis. *Language Learning, 60,* 309–365. doi:10.1111/j.1467-9922.2010.00561.x

Loewen, S., & Philp, J. (2006). Recasts in the adult English L2 classroom: Characteristics, explicitness, and effectiveness. *The Modern Language Journal*, 90, 536–556. doi:10.1111/j.1540-4781.2006.00465.x

Long, M. H. (1996). The role of the linguistic environment in second language acquisition. In W. Ritchie & T. Bhatia (Eds.), *Handbook of second language acquisition* (pp. 413–468). San Diego: Academic Press.

Long, M. H., & Porter, P. A. (1985). Group work, interlanguage talk, and second language acquisition. *TESOL Quarterly*, 19, 207–228. doi:10.2307/3586827

Lyster, R., & Saito, K. (2010). Oral feedback in classroom SLA: A meta-analysis. *Studies in Second Language Acquisition*, 32, 265–302. doi:10.1017/S0272263109990520

Mackey, A. (1999). Input, interaction, and second language development. *Studies in Second Language Acquisition*, 21, 557–587. doi:10.1017/S0272263199004027

Mackey, A. (2006). Feedback, noticing and instructed second language learning. *Applied Linguistics*, 27, 405–430. doi:10.1093/applin/ami051

Mackey, A. (2007). Introduction: The role of conversational interaction in second language acquisition. In A. Mackey (Ed.), *Conversational interaction in second language acquisition: A collection of empirical studies* (pp. 1–26). Oxford: Oxford University Press.

Mackey, A. (2012). *Input, interaction, and corrective feedback in L2 learning*. Oxford: Oxford University Press.

Mackey, A., Abbuhl, R., & Gass, S. (2012). Interactionist approach. In S. Gass & A. Mackey (Eds.), *The Routledge handbook of second language acquisition* (pp. 7–24). New York: Routledge.

Mackey, A. & Fujii, A. (2009). *Training learners to be more effective interactors*. Paper presented at the *3rd Biennial Conference on Task-Based Language Teaching*. Lancaster, UK.

Mackey, A., Fujii, A., Biesenbach-Lucas, S., Weger-Guntharp, H., Jacobsen, N. D., Fogle, L., Lake, J., Sondermann, K., Tagarelli, K., Tsujita, M., Watanabe, A., Abbuhl R., & Kim, K. (2013). Tasks and tradition practice activities in a foreign language context. In K. McDonough & A. Mackey (Eds.), *Second language interaction in diverse educational contexts* (pp. 71–87). Amsterdam: John Benjamins. doi:10.1075/lllt.34.07ch4

Mackey, A., & Gass, S. (2006). Pushing the methodological boundaries in interaction research: An introduction to the special issue. *Studies in Second Language Acquisition*, 28, 169–178.

Mackey, A., & Gass, S. (2012). *Research methods in second language acquisition: A practical guide*. Chichester, UK: Blackwell

Mackey, A., Gass, S., & McDonough, K. (2000). How do learners perceive interactional feedback? *Studies in Second Language Acquisition*, 22, 471–497. doi:10.1017/S0272263100004022

Mackey, A., & Goo, J. (2007). Interaction research in SLA: A meta-analysis and research synthesis. In A. Mackey (Ed.), *Conversational interaction in second language acquisition: A collection of empirical studies* (pp. 407–452). Oxford: Oxford University Press.

Mackey, A., & Oliver, R. (2002). Interactional feedback and children's L2 development. *System*, 30, 459–477. doi:10.1016/S0346-251X(02)00049-0

Mackey, A., Oliver, R., & Leeman, J. (2003). Interactional input and the incorporation of feedback: An exploration of NS-NNS and NNS-NNS adult and child dyads. *Language Learning*, 53, 35–66. doi:10.1111/1467-9922.00210

McDonough, K. (2004). Learner-learner interaction during pair and small group activities in a Thai EFL context. *System*, 32, 207–224. doi:10.1016/j.system.2004.01.003

McDonough, K. (2007). Interactional feedback and the emergence of simple past activity verbs in L2 English. In A. Mackey (Ed.), *Conversational interaction in second language acquisition: A collection of empirical studies* (pp. 323–338). Oxford: Oxford University Press.

Mystery Net: The Online Mystery Network (2009). *MysteryNet's Kids Mysteries*. Retrieved from: <http://kids.mysterynet.com/quicksolve/>

Nakahama, Y., Tyler, A., & Van Lier, L. (2001). Negotiation of meaning in conversational and interaction gap activities: A comparative discourse analysis. *TESOL Quarterly*, 35, 377–405. doi:10.2307/3588028

Philp, J., Adams, R., & Iwashita, N. (2014). *Peer interaction and second language learning*. New York, NY: Routledge.

Philp, J., & Mackey, A. (2011). Interaction research: What can socially informed approaches offer to cognitivists (and vice versa)? In R. Batstone (Ed.), *Sociocognitive aspects of second language learning and teaching*. Oxford: Oxford University Press.

Philp, J., & Tognini, R. (2009). Language acquisition in foreign language contexts and the differential benefits of interaction. *International Review of Applied Linguistics in Language Teaching*, 47, 245–266. doi:10.1515/iral.2009.011

Philp, J., Walter, S., & Basturkmen, H. (2010). Peer interaction in the foreign language classroom: What factors foster a focus on form? *Language Awareness*, 19, 261–279. doi:10.1080/09658416.2010.516831

Pica, T., Lincoln-Porter, F., Paninos, D., & Linnell, J. (1996). Language learners' interaction: How does it address the input, output, and feedback needs of L2 learners? *TESOL Quarterly*, 30, 59–84. doi:10.2307/3587607

Porter, P. (1986). How learners talk to each other: Input and interaction in task-centered discussions. In R. Day (Ed.), *Talking to learn: Conversation in second language acquisition* (pp. 200–222). Rowley, MA: Newbury House.

Robinson, P. (2001). Task complexity, task difficulty, and task production: Exploring interactions in a componential framework. *Applied Linguistics*, 22, 27–57. doi:10.1093/applin/22.1.27

Russell, J. & Spada, N. (2006). The effectiveness of corrective feedback for the acquisition of L2 grammar: A meta-analysis of the research. In J. Norris & L. Ortega (Eds.), *Synthesizing research on language learning and teaching* (pp. 133–164). Amsterdam: John Benjamins. doi:10.1075/lllt.13.09val

Samuda, V. (2001). Guiding relationships between form and meaning during task performance: The role of the teacher. In M. Bygate, P. Skehan, & M. Swain (Eds.), *Researching pedagogic tasks* (pp. 119–134). London: Longman.

Sato, C. J. (1986). Conversation and interlanguage development: Rethinking the connection. In R. Day (ed.) *Talking to learn*. Rowley, MA: Newbury House. 237–326.

Sato, M. (2013). Beliefs about peer interaction and peer corrective feedback: Efficacy of classroom intervention. *The Modern Language Journal*, 97, 611–633. doi:10.1111/j.1540-4781.2013.12035.x

Sato, M., & Ballinger, S. (2012). Raising language awareness in peer interaction: A cross-context, cross-method examination. *Language Awareness*, 20, 157–179. doi:10.1080/09658416.2011.639884

Sato, M., & Ballinger, S. (2016). Understanding peer interaction: An overview of the research. In M. Sato & S. Ballinger (Eds.), *Peer interaction and second language learning: Pedagogical potential and research agenda* (pp. 1–30). Amsterdam: John Benjamins.

Sato, M., & Lyster, R. (2007). Modified output of Japanese EFL learners: Variable effects of interlocutor vs. feedback types. In A. Mackey (Ed.), *Conversational interaction in second language acquisition: A collection of empirical studies* (pp. 123–142). Oxford: Oxford University Press.

Sato, M., & Lyster, R. (2012). Peer interaction and corrective feedback for accuracy and fluency development: Monitoring, practice, and proceduralization. *Studies in Second Language Acquisition*, 34, 591–626. doi:10.1017/S0272263112000356

Sheen, Y. (2004). Corrective feedback and learner uptake in communicative classrooms across instructional settings. *Language Teaching Research*, 8, 263–300. doi:10.1191/1362168804lr146oa

Swain, M. (1985). Communicative competence: Some roles of comprehensible input and comprehensible output in its development. In S. Gass & C. Madden (Eds.), *Input in second language acquisition* (pp. 235–253). Rowley, MA: Newbury House.

Swain, M. (1995). Three functions of output in second language learning. In G. Cook & B. Seidlhofer (Eds.), *Principle and practice in applied linguistics: Studies in honour of H. G. Widdowson* (pp. 125–144). Oxford: Oxford University Press.

Swain, M. (2005). The output hypothesis: Theory and research. In E. Hinkel (Ed.), *Handbook of research in second language teaching and learning* (pp. 471–483). Mahwah, NJ: Lawrence Erlbaum Associates.

Toth, P. D. (2008). Teacher- and learner-led discourse in task-based grammar instruction: Providing procedural assistance for L2 morphosyntactic development. *Language Learning*, 58, 237–283. doi:10.1111/j.1467-9922.2008.00441.x

Ur, P. (1981). *Discussions that work: Task centered fluency practice*. Cambridge: Cambridge University Press.

Varonis, E. M., & Gass, S. (1985). Miscommunication in native/nonnative conversation. *Language in Society*, 14, 327–343. doi:10.1017/S0047404500011295

Watanabe, Y., & Swain, M. (2007). Effects of proficiency differences and patterns of pair interaction on second language learning: Collaborative dialogue between adult ESL learners. *Language Teaching Research*, 11, 121–142. doi:10.1177/136216880607074599

Williams, J. (1999). Learner-generated attention to form. *Language Learning*, 49, 583–625. doi:10.1111/0023-8333.00103

Willis, D., & Willis, J. (2008). *Doing Task-based teaching*. Oxford: Oxford University Press.

Yoshida, R. (2008). Learners' perception of corrective feedback in pair work. *Foreign Language Annals*, 41, 525–541. doi:10.1111/j.1944-9720.2008.tb03310.x

Zhao, S. Y., & Bitchener, J. (2007). Incidental focus on form in teacher–learner and learner–learner interactions. *System*, 35, 431–447. doi:10.1016/j.system.2007.04.004

Ziegler, N. (2015). Synchronous computer-mediated communication and interaction: A meta-analysis. *Studies in Second Language Acquisition*, 0, 1–34. doi:10.1017/S027226311500025X

Appendix A

Questionnaire (translated from the original Japanese)

Questions	strongly agree	agree		disagree	strongly disagree
1	Through the power point presentation, I understood the concepts of negotiation, feedback, and noticing.	5	4	3	2	1
2	Through the power point presentation, I understood how negotiation, feedback, and noticing contribute to learning English.	5	4	3	2	1
3	Through the power point presentation, I was able to get an idea of how I could give feedback.	5	4	3	2	1
4	I was able to give my partner more feedback after the workshop than before the workshop.	5	4	3	2	1
5	I engaged in more negotiation after the workshop than before the workshop.	5	4	3	2	1
6	I noticed more feedback from my partner after the workshop than before the workshop.	5	4	3	2	1
7	I noticed more of my own errors, as well as new expressions or language in my production and in my peers, after the workshop than before the workshop.	5	4	3	2	1
8	I think negotiation, feedback, and noticing are useful for improving my English.	5	4	3	2	1

9	Specifically, do you think negotiation, feedback, and noticing are useful for improving the following aspects of your English?

	Very useful				Not useful at all
Fluency	5	4	3	2	1
New vocabulary	5	4	3	2	1
Accurate grammar	5	4	3	2	1
Explaining my thoughts	5	4	3	2	1
Clear pronunciation	5	4	3	2	1
Listening	5	4	3	2	1
Learning new grammar	5	4	3	2	1

10	If you answered "I disagree" "I strongly disagree" or "Not at all useful" to the two questions above, please explain why.

11	What were some especially effective aspects of the content or organization of the workshop? Were there any points that should be improved?

12	I think I will use what I learned in this workshop in the future.	5	4	3	2	1

13	If you answered "I agree" or "I strongly agree" in what context do you think you will use what you learned? If you answered "I disagree" or "I strongly disagree," explain why.

CHAPTER 3

Interaction or collaboration?

Group dynamics in the foreign language classroom

Masatoshi Sato and Paula Viveros
Universidad Andres Bello

This chapter reports on a classroom-based quasi-experimental study examining the relationship between interactional moves and collaborative patterns in peer interaction and their effect on L2 development, using proficiency as an independent variable. Participants were from two parallel Grade 10 English classes in Chile, divided into low and high proficiency classes by the school ($N = 53$). A series of communicative group work activities was designed and implemented during the regular classes. L2 development was investigated by examining past tense usage and vocabulary size. Focus groups from the two classes ($n = 10$) were used for analyses of interactional features. Results indicated that learners in the low proficiency group (a) provided more corrective feedback and produced more modified output, (b) engaged in more collaborative interaction, and (c) exhibited a greater L2 development gain, than the high proficiency group. In order to interpret the results and conceptualize the links among interaction-collaboration-learning, the findings are discussed in relation to a theory in social psychology referred to as social interdependence theory. It is concluded that while proficiency does have an impact on learners' interactional behaviours, a collaborative mindset – a learner's psychological approach towards the partner and/or task – may be a stronger mediating factor for L2 development.

Introduction

In many second language (L2) classrooms, teachers organize group work activities by dividing students into different groups based on their proficiency levels. The same can be observed at the institutional level where learners take a placement test and are subsequently divided into different classes. The rationale behind this pedagogical decision is that separation is beneficial for L2 learning, a belief which partly stems from the teacher's or institution's assumption that learners with higher proficiency levels do not benefit from engaging in a task with lower proficiency learners (see Leeser 2004). As for lower proficiency learners, it is often

DOI 10.1075/lllt.45.04sat

assumed that they are incapable of collaboratively completing a task due to their insufficient L2 knowledge (Alexander 2012). Based on this belief, teachers sometimes avoid communicative group work activities as a pedagogical option. While previous research has compared pairs with mixed vs. similar proficiency levels (e.g., Choi & Iwashita 2016; Kim & McDonough 2008; Storch & Aldosari 2013; Young & Tedick 2016), the current study addresses the assumption that lower proficiency learners are incapable of successfully participating in group work. This will be done by comparing occurrences of certain interactional moves as well as patterns of collaboration between learners with higher and lower proficiency.

Theoretically and methodologically distinct approaches have been used to understand peer interaction and L2 development. In the interactionist paradigm, on the one hand, much research has examined whether interactional moves such as feedback between learners (henceforth, peer CF) facilitate L2 learning (e.g., Sato & Lyster 2012). In this approach, it is posited that CF triggers restructuring of inaccurate L2 knowledge and pushes the learner to self-correct (see Mackey 2012; Pica 2013 for reviews). On the other hand, in the sociocultural paradigm, a burgeoning number of studies have examined peer interaction using language-related episodes (LREs) as a measurement of its effectiveness (e.g., Storch & Aldosari 2013). Sociocultural researchers draw on the idea of co-construction of knowledge within LREs as an account for L2 learning. Co-construction of knowledge (or scaffolding) emphasizes collaboration. As Lantolf and Poehner (2011) put it, interaction in the zone of proximal development (ZPD) is "an extensive and intensive collaborative experience" (29). To this end, it is not yet known how interactional moves, which are argued to trigger beneficial cognitive processing, and collaboration, which supposedly substantiates scaffolding, are related to each other or whether they are related at all. That is, it is possible that learners who constantly provide CF to peers are not collaborative, and it is also possible that collaborative learners do not always provide CF. The current study first operationalized collaboration by creating different collaborative categories and then investigated how those collaborative behaviours were related to interactional moves that are typically considered in the literature to be facilitative of L2 learning – peer CF and modified output (MO).

Literature review

Peer corrective feedback and L2 learning

Peer interaction creates learning opportunities that qualitatively and quantitatively differ from interaction with native speakers or language teachers. Studies comparing the two types of interaction have revealed that when learners interact with each other, they tend to use more interactional moves that are arguably beneficial for L2 learning compared to when they interact with native-speaking partners. García Mayo and Pica (2000), for instance, demonstrated that L2 learners are able to provide each other with simplified input that is more accessible to their developmental level by engaging in negotiation for meaning (input modification). In Sato and Lyster (2007), learners provided arguably a better type of feedback (i.e., prompts) significantly more than native speakers by creating more opportunities for their partners to modify their initial incomprehensible and/or ungrammatical utterances. These opportunities were taken up significantly more during peer interaction than during learner–native speaker interaction (i.e., MO). Alcón's (2002) classroom observation study also revealed that learners employed more requesting strategies with each other than when they interacted with the teacher (see, for similar findings, Fernández Dobao 2012; Pica, Lincoln-Porter, Paninos, & Linnell 1996; Sato 2015; Toth 2008; Varonis & Gass 1985).

While this research supports the overall effectiveness of peer interaction (see Philp, Adams, & Iwashita 2014 for review), there are conflicting findings regarding the causality between peer CF and L2 development. Adams, Nuevo, and Egi (2011) investigated interaction between adult ESL learners in the United States. The correlation analyses between the frequency of feedback and the gain scores from the pre- to post-tests showed that not only was there no correlation but that the provision of an explicit type of feedback was negatively correlated with the development of the past tense. They concluded that "feedback may not play as important a role in learner–learner interaction as it plays in NS–learner interactions" (56). On the contrary, in a study where learners were trained to provide feedback to each other, Sato and Lyster (2012) showed significant positive correlations between CF as well as MO and L2 development. Given the negative correlation in Adams et al. (2011), as opposed to a non-significant correlation, the differential finding in the two studies should not lie in the quantity of CF; rather, it seems to be the case that the CF that the learners gave each other in the two studies were qualitatively different and, thus, it affected their L2 development differently.

One possible factor that may have contributed to the qualitative difference may be that of the learners' collaborative mindset entailing readiness to pay attention to and to accept their peer's feedback. That is, the training component included in Sato and Lyster's (2012) study (i.e., raising learners' awareness of peer interaction and peer CF; giving them a separate CF training activity) might have helped learners become more collaborative by making them pay more attention to what their peers had to say and support each other's contribution. This collaborative mindset, in turn, might have accelerated CF effectiveness. This leads to a hypothesis that learners' attitudes towards each other and/or towards the task affect the effectiveness of peer CF. That is, because of the nature of peer CF – distrust in each other's linguistic abilities, social awkwardness in providing feedback, embarrassment over being corrected by their peers (see Fernández Dobao 2012; McDonough 2004; Sato 2013; Yoshida 2008, 2013) – establishing an environment where learners feel comfortable providing and receiving feedback may accelerate its effectiveness. The present study adds to this line of research by examining the relationship between collaborative patterns and provision of peer CF.

Collaborative peer interaction and L2 learning

Collaboration between learners is often explained using sociocultural theory which views language as a cognitive tool to make meaning within a social context. Researchers who are grounded in sociocultural theory view scaffolding as a crucial element in learning, whereby a learner is enabled to do something with assistance from another person (expert) that he or she would not have been able to do alone (Wood, Bruner, & Ross 1976). While the original conceptualization of scaffolding focused on learning opportunities created by a learner and a person with higher skills (e.g., native speakers, teachers, learners with higher proficiency), Donato (1994) expanded the idea by proposing the concept of *collective scaffolding* arguing that scaffolding is not necessarily unidirectional, from expert to novice, but bidirectional in collaborative peer interaction. He showed that learners are indeed capable and willing to help each other for learning an L2 (see also Davin & Donato 2013; Ohta 2001). The way in which learners assist each other (or not) was conceptualized into categories in Storch (2002). Her analysis involved transcripts from pair work in a college ESL classroom in which she identified four different types of collaboration based on the level of control or authority (i.e., equality) and engagement with each other's contribution (i.e., mutuality) that learners displayed. Storch found that when a dyad constructs either collaborative or expert/novice relationships, both of which entail high levels of equality and mutuality, peer interaction was linked to positive effects on language learning (see also Galaczi 2008; Rouhshad & Storch 2016).

Methodologically, the most common unit of analysis used to understand peer collaborative dialogues is the LRE. This measurement was defined by Swain and Lapkin (1998: 326) as "any part of a dialogue in which students talk about the

language they are producing, question their language use, or other- or self-correct."
By identifying and analyzing LREs, a number of studies evidenced varying degrees
of collaboration (see Storch 2011). What is unknown, however, is how differential
degrees of collaboration are related (or unrelated) to occurrences of interactional
moves (CF and MO) that arguably facilitate beneficial cognitive processing. In
this regard, Foster and Ohta (2005) attempted to integrate a sociocultural perspective into a cognitive analysis, focusing on how well negotiation for meaning
represents learners' collaborative interaction. Having analyzed the interaction data
pertaining to adult learners of English at a college in London and college learners
of Japanese in the United States, they claimed that three negotiation moves (i.e.,
comprehension checks, confirmation checks, and clarification requests) do not
fully capture what is going on in peer interaction. This was because these feedback
moves did not occur frequently, yet the learners demonstrably worked on repairing and rewording their own utterances while also assisting each other to find the
right form in order to achieve message comprehensibility. They concluded that
"it is possible, perhaps likely, that a learner in a successful interaction is able and
willing to focus on form without having first to be shunted into a communication problem" (426). Thus, it is possible that frequencies of MO and CF, which
entail negotiation moves such as clarification requests, may not reflect the extent
of how collaborative a learner pair is (see also Gagné & Parks 2013; McDonough
& Chaikitmongkol 2010; McDonough & Mackey 2008).

Research that has examined the link between interactional moves and collaboration is scarce. Ballinger (2013), who studied interaction between Grade 3
French immersion students, showed that more collaborative interaction does not
necessarily mean that learners give more CF to each other. Ballinger suspected
that provision of CF may indicate either a collaborative mindset or excessive corrective behaviours depending on pair dynamics (see also Sato & Ballinger 2012).
Focusing on adolescent foreign language learners, the present study examines the
relationship between cognitive-based interactional moves (i.e., CF and MO) and
collaborative patterns that we operationalized in that specific context.

Proficiency and interactional moves

The effect of proficiency on interactional moves has been examined from two different perspectives: (a) the effect of proficiency levels when learners are grouped
according to their proficiency levels (i.e., high-high vs. low-low pairs) and (b) the
impact of pairing learners with different proficiency levels (i.e., same vs. mixed
pairs). With regard to the first type of inquiry, the previous findings are mixed.
Williams (2001) analyzed the amount and types of LREs between adult learners
of English. The results indicated that the higher the learners' proficiency was, the

more LREs they produced together. Also, it was found that the higher proficiency learners scored better on the tailor-made post-test in which the grammatical or lexical items that appeared in the LREs were tested (see also Williams 1999). Williams claimed that learners with higher proficiency can pay more attention to formal aspects of the target language and, thus, are able to provide linguistic support for each other. However, Iwashita's (2001) study with adult learners of Japanese failed to show such an effect for proficiency. She quantified the amount of CF and the subsequent MO. The comparisons between pairs with higher and lower proficiency levels did not detect any statistical differences (see also Choi & Iwashita 2016; Young & Tedick 2016).

Meanwhile, the second type of inquiry suggests that pairing learners with different proficiency levels promotes beneficial interaction. By examining interaction between adult learners of Korean, Kim and McDonough (2008) found that mixed pairs resolved language-related issues more successfully (especially for LREs related to lexical issues). Watanabe and Swain (2007) designed a study to examine the impact of interlocutor's proficiency levels (by pairing the same learners with higher or lower proficiency learners) on the degree of collaboration (by the quantity and quality of LREs). They found that learning outcomes were mediated more by how collaborative a pair was than by whom they interacted with. This finding was corroborated by Storch and Aldosari (2013), who concluded that to understand the relationship between proficiency levels and L2 learning "it is not only proficiency difference which needs to be taken into consideration, but also the kind of relationship learners form when working in pairs" (46). The current study investigated learner relationships by examining how learners' proficiency levels affect both their interactional moves (i.e., CF and MO) and their collaborative behaviours. Two research questions were formed:

1. How do proficiency levels affect interactional moves – CF and MO – and collaborative patterns during group work?
2. How are CF and MO during group work related to collaborative patterns?

Methodology

Methodological framework

The cognitive and sociocultural approaches in the field of peer interaction have historically followed separate paths, and collaboration between researchers from the two fields has been rare (for collaborative efforts, see Foster & Ohta 2005; Sato & Ballinger 2012). This is due to the fact that these approaches tend to view language development differently, employ different methodologies (quantitative vs.

qualitative analyses of interaction data), and seek different outcomes (generalizability vs. detailed understanding of interaction data) (see also Hulstijn et al. 2014; Sato & Ballinger 2016). Nonetheless, the authors believe that studies from both theoretical paradigms can inform and benefit our overall understanding of peer interaction and how it can effectively be used in the classroom. Methodologically also, the authors are convinced that quantitative and qualitative approaches are complementary rather than conflictive when understanding L2 learning (see Riazi & Candlin 2014). Thus, the current study analyzed interaction data by borrowing from the two methodological approaches.

Chilean EFL context

The study was conducted in Chile, where traditional grammar-translation methods still prevail and learners struggle to develop communicative skills. In many Chilean classrooms, which may contain more than 40 students, English is often taught using the learners' L1 (i.e., Spanish) where lessons focus primarily on grammar teaching and vocabulary memorization, and interaction between the teacher and students as well as between the students is limited (see Kormos & Kiddle 2013, for the demographic information of the context). In such a context, learners may develop grammatical knowledge, but the development of communicative skills suffers (see Berns 1990; Block 2003). The results of a pilot Cambridge test given by the Ministry of Education in 2004 showed that the scores were so low that a new category had to be created in order to classify Chilean learners of English (Farías & Abrahams 2008). Though a diagnostic test (TOEIC Bridge) given to 240,000 third-grade students in 2010 showed some improvement (Sistema de Medición de la Calidad de la Enseñanza), the average English proficiency of EFL learners in Chile still remains basic.

   Considering the generally low English proficiency of Chilean learners, it seems likely that a more communicative approach to L2 teaching could benefit their typically traditional grammar-based instruction (Lyster 2007; Sato 2011). Nevertheless, although there was a time in the 1990s when the national curriculum recommended communicative approaches, in 1998, the curriculum returned to an emphasis on developing receptive (reading and listening) skills over productive skills, and Chilean L2 education reverted to a focus on the development of grammatical knowledge. Perhaps this is due to Chilean teachers' perception of methodologies, such as group work, which tend to accompany the communicative approach. In McKay's (2003) survey of 50 Chilean English teachers, 83% of the respondents did not value group work. Rather, they showed appreciation for the 1998 curriculum change. In general, both the curriculum and teachers are "de-emphasizing the use of CLT [Communicative Language Teaching] on the grounds that it is not appropriate to the local Chilean context" (McKay 2003: 144). One of the concerns shared by the teachers in McKay's study was skepticism of the students' autonomy. In other words, teachers believed that students would not work together without the teacher's control. Based on a belief that peer interaction creates an ideal context where learners engage in authentic interaction, especially in foreign language contexts (see Lyster & Sato 2013; Philp & Tognini 2009; Sato 2007), the current study designed communicative group work activities and investigated how learners create learning opportunities within these activities.

Participants

Two parallel 10th grade (15–16 years old) English classes at a private school in Santiago, Chile, participated in the study (N = 53). Following the national curriculum, the school implemented five hours of English classes a week, following the teaching methods described above; that is, the participants had been exposed to teacher-centered, grammar-based lessons. Hence, it was novel for participants to interact with their classmates in English as well as to engage in communicative activities. In other words, the context was ideal for examining the impact of group work on L2 learning specifically in foreign language contexts.

The school had divided students into three levels according to the paper-based exit exam given at the end of 9th grade. In the current study, the lowest and highest classes, which were administratively grouped by the school, were compared and they were labeled as low proficiency (LP: n = 27: 11 males and 16 females) and high proficiency (HP: n = 28: 14 males and 14 females) groups, respectively.

Intervention

The LP class was taught by a Chilean teacher with native-like English proficiency while the HP class had an American teacher who was a native speaker of English. Conducted entirely in English, which was an effort particularly for those classes, the speaking classes met four times a week for 40 minutes. For a four-week period, one meeting per week was devoted to the intervention (totalling 160 minutes of group work). The intervention targeted the development of past tense forms.

For the intervention lessons, the classes were divided into groups of 4–6 students and the students stayed in the same groups during the intervention period. The teachers were instructed not to provide explicit grammar instruction during the intervention period so as to make the two classes comparable. In addition, they were asked not to give feedback to the learners during group work. It is important to mention that the two teachers took different approaches during peer interaction activities, which might have affected the result of the current investigation. More precisely, the American teacher in the HP class tended to remain seated during the activities, while the Chilean teacher in the LP class actively walked around the classroom in order to make sure that the students were engaging in the tasks. This issue will be further discussed in the discussion section along with the results.

With the aim of promoting autonomous and collaborative group work, communicative activities were developed that comprised four stages: Presentation, Awareness, Guided Practice, and Communicative Practice. In the first stage, students were shown a movie clip that lasted around 5 minutes (Presentation). After watching the segment, they worked together on a fill-in-the-gap sheet in which sentences depicting the clip contained verbs in the base form that students were asked to conjugate in the past tense (Awareness). The third stage was role-play in which the group members played the main characters of the movie (Guided Practice). In this stage, students were encouraged to use the sentence structures that they had seen in the previous stage. In the final stage, discussion questions designed to connect the movie and the students' personal lives were given (Communicative Practice).

All stages were designed to help learners shift their attention to the target linguistic feature – past tense forms. For instance, after the trial scene from the movie *The Shawshank Redemption* (Darabont 1994) was shown, the following sentence among others was given in the Awareness stage: "I ____ (go) to a few bars first. Later, I ____ (drive) to his house to confront them. They ____ (be) not home. I ____ (park) in the turnout and ____ (wait)." Then, in the Guided Practice stage, one of the students had to act as the defendant while the rest of the group acted as the prosecutor, interrogating the person; hence, the learners were naturally guided to use the past tense. In the Communicative Practice stage, they were asked to discuss real court stories that they had previous knowledge of and to exchange their opinions. By providing opportunities for contextualized practice (see DeKeyser 2010) and gradually shifting students' attention to formal aspects of language, we hoped to see learners engaging in authentic interaction that aids grammatical development (Lyster & Sato 2013; Ranta & Lyster 2007). Three more lesson plans with the same structure but with different materials were also developed.

Data collection and analysis

The data to be presented in this chapter come from a larger study in which two data sources were used to investigate the effects of proficiency levels on (a) L2 development, (b) interactional moves (CF and MO), and (c) collaborative patterns during peer interaction. L2 development was operationalized as learners' productive knowledge of the English past tense (see Salaberry 2000) as well as oral productivity (vocabulary size: see Stæhra 2008) and examined by the pre- and post-tests given to the two classes ($N = 53$). The statistical analyses of L2 development tests showed that the lower proficiency group benefited from the intervention whereas the higher proficiency group did not. The results led the authors to suspect that there was a variable, other than learners' proficiency, that mediated the effect of the intervention. In this chapter, we will briefly summarize the L2 development results when interpreting the recorded interaction data. However, the primary focus is on the interaction data, obtained from two focus groups, in order to investigate the relationship between collaborative behaviours and interactional moves as well as the effect of proficiency levels on those interactional features.

A focus group was randomly chosen from each group (five students from LP and five students from HP) and their conversations were audio-recorded throughout the four intervention lessons. The data, comprising 320 min (40 min per class × 4 weeks × 2 proficiency levels), were transcribed and coded using two analytical frameworks. First, the frequencies of CF and MO were tallied. Then, interaction data were qualitatively explored to look for patterns of collaboration (for similar procedures, see Ballinger 2013; Foster & Ohta 2005). Three collaborative patterns emerged from the transcripts, and their frequencies were compared across groups: (a) Language-related collaboration; (b) Task-related collaboration; and (c) Collaborative sentence completion. While the operational definitions of some of those categories overlap with the previous literature, the authors created an original coding system following the inductiveness of the grounded theory methodology (i.e., avoidance of imposing existing ideas on the data: see Corbin & Strauss 2008). This methodological decision was also based upon the assumption that behaviours in peer interaction were susceptible to contextual variables (e.g., second vs. foreign language learning: see Sato 2011). In this section, the definitions of those categories will be presented, while actual examples will appear in the results section. Thirty-five percent of the transcripts were coded by the two researchers and the inter-rater reliability reached $\alpha = .92$.

Language-related collaboration (LRC) was operationally similar to LREs as defined by Swain and Lapkin (1998: 326): "any part of a dialogue where the students talk about the language use, or correct themselves or others." Unlike Swain and Lapkin's (2002) conceptualization of LREs which included *private speech*, however, LRC in the current study strictly focused on exchanges of language between the learners where they are engaging with each other.

Task-related collaboration (TRC) included interaction whereby learners engaged in exchanges which did not revolve around linguistic issues. More specifically, these were exchanges in which learners identified and analyzed the task at hand. In other words, the sole difference between TRC and LRC was the topic of conversation – language-related or task-related. The task-related category was thought to be useful in order to identify what kind of peer collaboration contributes to L2 development.

Collaborative sentence completion (CSC) was identified when a learner struggled to finish his or her utterance and another learner supplied the rest of the sentence. A similar behaviour was identified by Foster and Ohta (2005) as "co-construction." This category is different from LRC in that the exchanges were relatively shorter – A learner stops in the middle of a sentence and another learner completes it, often by adding a noun. Because of its nature, all the instances of CSCs in the current data set were lexical.

Quantitative results

Corrective feedback and modified output

In the 160-min peer interaction data pertaining to the LP group, 32 instances of CF were identified. Of those, 18 instances were followed by modifications of the initial incomprehensible or erroneous utterances. The learners in the HP group provided CF nine times in total of which four were followed by MO (see Table 1).

Collaborative behaviours

The learners in the LP group engaged in LRC 21 times; the HP group engaged in LRC 9 times. The analysis of TRC showed that the LP learners discussed the tasks 40 times while the learners in the HP group discussed the tasks 63 times. Regarding the CSC instances, the learners in the LP group supplied words or phrases to each other 13 times, while the HP group supplied words or phrases to each other 8 times (see Table 1).

Table 1. Frequencies of collaborative and interactional moves

	CF	MO	LRC	TRC	CSC
Low proficiency	32	18	21	40	13
High proficiency	9	4	9	63	8

Qualitative results

Qualitative transcript analyses showed that LRCs and CSCs may represent the learners' collaborative mindset which permitted them to support each other's ideas and to appreciate one another's contribution to L2 learning. In Excerpt 1, which was coded as an LRC in the LP group (names appearing in this manuscript are pseudonyms), Pablo initiated an exchange regarding the verb *trip*.

Excerpt 1 (LP)

1	Pablo:	Trip *es...* (trip is…)
2	Carla:	Trip *es viajar* (trip is to travel)
3	Vale:	*Cómo va a ser viajar al suelo?* (How can it be to travel to the floor?)
4	Pablo:	*Cómo... dio un pequeño viaje en el piso? Cierto?* (Like…did he make a small travel to the floor? Right?)
5	Carla:	*Yo creo que...* (I think that…)
6	Pablo:	*Se resfaló o algo así* (He trips or something like that)
7	Pancha:	*Sí,* I think, I think.
8	Pablo:	*Caerse!* (Fall down!).

As can be seen above, multiple learners attempted to solve the linguistic problem. Learners are engaged with each other's ideas (lines 3 and 7), they assist each other (lines 2 and 6), and they together aim to solve the given problem. Also, it can be observed that the learners took turns without dominating the exchange or serving either as experts or novices. Rather, their role as an expert is fluid: In line 2, Carla leads the conversation, while Pablo makes an assertive comment in line 6. This type of interaction may fall under Storch's (2002) definition of the collaborative relationship in which learners are "willing to offer and engage with each other's ideas" (128). Note here that it was not CF that initiated this LRC, yet Pablo reached the accurate meaning of the word by discussing it with his team mates. LRCs, therefore, did not include CF necessarily (see Foster & Ohta 2005).

CSCs seem to represent learners' collaborative mindset as well. In Excerpt 2 from the LP group, learners supplied words to support each other.

Excerpt 2 (LP)

1	Carla:	He answered I don't know! And the guard doesn't…doesn't
2	Pancha:	permit
3	Carla:	so the wine is good for your…
4	Pablo:	health

Carla tried to express her ideas (line 1); however, she stops and repeats an auxiliary verb *doesn't*. Presumably, in this exchange, her lexical knowledge was insufficient when attempting to complete her utterances. Pancha (line 2) and Pablo (line 4) assisted Carla by supplying the words. Though short in length, this type of exchange can also be argued to be collaborative because the learners are (a) engaged in each other's ideas and their exchanges are reciprocal, and (b) comparable in terms of the control over the direction of interaction. In other words, both mutuality and equality are reasonably present. Again, Pancha's and Pablo's utterances are by definition not CF because they did not follow any incomprehensible or ungrammatical utterances.

While the LRCs and CSCs seem to show learners' collaborative mindset, the opposite direction was observed in TRCs. In Excerpt 3, the learners in the HP group tried to organize the roles for the role-play activity:

Excerpt 3 (HP)

1	Jorge:	Who will be the guilty men? You are going to be the guilty one. You.
2	Matias:	No
3	Natalia:	I'm the guilty one. Who is the suspect of the murder? I... I... I...
4	Matias:	No no no. I'm the guilty one.

In this exchange the learners indeed tried to complete the task by working together. However, in this excerpt, Matias was controlling the direction of the group (lines 2 and 4), while the other members did not have much chance to contribute to it. This type of interaction may be identified as passive/dominant according to Storch's (2002) categorization in which "the level of equality and mutuality are both moderate to low" and the dominant participant "takes an authoritarian stance and seems to appropriate the task" (129). In the current data base, TRCs tended to entail one participant in the group dominating the conversation.

Discussion

The effect of proficiency on interaction and collaboration

The frequencies of CF in the two groups demonstrated that the learners in the LP group indicated when they did not understand what their classmates said (negotiation for meaning) and/or corrected each other's grammatical errors (negotiation for form) more than those in the HP group. Furthermore, the LP learners followed feedback from their peers by modifying their original incomprehensible or ungrammatical utterances more than the HP learners. This result does not support preceding research showing that the amount of CF and MO a learner produces is linked to the amount of linguistic knowledge they possess. Williams (2001) asserted that learners with lower proficiency levels were "somewhat less ready or able to integrate the new input" (336) generated during peer interaction. On the contrary, the current data suggest that there was another factor than learners' proficiency levels that played a role in determining those interactional moves during group work. One possibility is learners' collaborative mindset; that is, because the LP learners were supportive of each other's ideas and ready to accept their peers' contribution, they might have given more CF and produced more MO. The effect of collaborative mindsets will be discussed further in a later section.

It is difficult to interpret the fact that the HP learners engaged in more TRCs than the LP learners. Even if TRCs happened to involve passive/dominant interaction, it is unlikely that the learners' proficiency level constructed this type of social relationship in the HP group. For this, one can only speculate that the HP group was more focused on completing the tasks, the reason of which could lie in the classroom environment. The teacher in the HP group was sitting at his desk during the group work activities, as opposed to circulating around the class in order to make sure that the students were engaging in the tasks. Although the teacher's involvement is beyond the scope of the current study, Guk and Kellogg's (2007) study is relevant. The researchers compared the ZDP in peer interaction and peer-teacher interaction and revealed the importance of the teacher's lead (e.g., providing exemplar language) for peer interaction to be meaningful (see also Gillies, Ashman, & Terwel 2008). It might be the case, then, that in the HP class of the current study, the scaffolding environment was absent, which led the learners to focus on task completion as opposed to collaborative language learning when approaching to the given task.

To answer the first research question, the findings suggest that the grouping based on proficiency did have an impact on both interactional moves and collaboration in peer interaction. In the current study, the learners placed in the LP group provided more CF and produced more MO than those in the HP group, and, at the same time, those learners exhibited more collaboration. We suspect, however, that the differential occurrences of the interactional behaviours may not be due to learners' proficiency levels but to their psychology towards the tasks or towards their partners. The following sections focus on learners' collaborative mindset.

Interactional moves and collaborative patterns

The results indicated a link between interactional moves and collaborative patterns. Not only were LRCs and CSCs found more in the LP group, but instances of CF and MO were also found to occur more in this group. This result may not be surprising given that some of the CF and MO were identified also in the LRCs. Some studies, however, suggest that collaborative patterns are not necessarily linked to CF provision. Having operationalized collaborative interaction as partner-directed, on-task conversational turns, Ballinger (2013) posited that CF could be a rude behaviour and create "conflictive interactions" (144), as opposed to collaborative, depending on pair dynamics. Conceivably, the difference lies in age and context. The participants in her study were Grades 3/4 students who may have seen language learning differently compared to the high school students in this study. The learners in the current study, especially those in the LP group, may have been more capable of comfortably correcting each other's errors by being aware of the goal of English classes. Also, the learners in Ballinger's study were learning French as a second language in immersion programs in Montreal, Canada, whereas English was a foreign language in the current study's context. It may be the case that foreign language learners tend to regard the target language as a skill to acquire, while for second language learners, it is a medium of communication. Arguably, this contextual difference may contribute to differences in learners' interactional behaviours. That being said, the results do not imply by any means that giving CF was easy for those learners (see Philp, Walter, & Basturkmen 2010). Rather, given their low proficiency, it is safe to assume that the learners found it difficult to correct their classmates' errors.

Collaborative interaction, which was linked to interactional moves in the current study, may be a key factor for peer interaction to be conducive to L2 learning. In the larger study, the LP group, who showed more collaborative patterns, exhibited a greater L2 development gain. Based on sociocultural theory pertaining to the importance of scaffolding, it can be said that LRCs and CSCs are facilitative of L2 development (although Excerpt 1 is lexical-based, similar patterns were identified for grammatical issues). By collaboratively solving linguistic issues and/or supporting each other's lack of linguistic knowledge, learners may be able to assist each other's L2 development in the ZDP. The finding that the HP group engaged in more TRCs conversely supports the positive effect of LRCs on L2 development. Note that the difference between LRCs and TRCs is whether or not they are related to linguistic issues. As far as the development of L2 grammatical knowledge is concerned, therefore, TRCs may not be related to L2 learning. Being collaborative is important but learners need to work on language-related issues. Hence, the focus of collaboration matters.

In answering the second research question then, we argue that CF and MO are related to patterns of collaboration, operationalized as LRCs, TRCs, and CSCs. Importantly, it seems that proficiency is a weaker mediating variable than collaborative interaction in relation to the provision of CF and production of MO. On the one hand, the data from the current study provide counterevidence to Watanabe and Swain (2007) because the LP learners benefited more from peer interaction than the HP learners did. On the other hand, the data support their study in the sense that collaborative interaction is the key for peer interaction to be conducive to L2 learning (see also Fernández Dobao 2012; Storch & Aldosari

2013). It may be the case that, unlike previous research claiming that linguistic knowledge increases the chance of learners' paying attention to language-related issues, the more collaborative a group is, the more CF they provide and the more MO they produce regardless of the learners' proficiency levels.

Collaborative mindset-interactional moves-L2 learning

The two theoretical frameworks used in the current chapter – interactionist and sociocultural – both rely on interaction data to understand L2 learning. In the previous section, drawing on the interaction data, we discussed the interactional moves and collaborative patterns may be related based on their occurrences during communicative peer interaction. However, what we still do not know is *why* certain learners tend to produce beneficial interactional moves or engage in collaborative interaction. To this end, we draw on a theory in social psychology known as social interdependence theory that might be useful to infer possible causes for certain interactional behaviours, that is, the learner's collaborative mindset.

Social interdependence theory rests upon the idea that (a) the social relationship between group members and (b) the psychological processes that individuals experience while engaging in group tasks, are independent variables that affect individual learning outcomes. The theory, which has been widely tested in different areas of development and/or learning (e.g., moral development and psychological health: see Roseth, Johnson, & Johnson 2008, for a meta-analysis), emphasizes the effect of *positive interdependence* on final achievement whenever humans form a group. This type of social relationship exists when "individuals perceive that they can attain their goals if and only if the other individuals with whom they are cooperatively linked attain their goals" (Johnson & Johnson 2009: 366). In addition to the emphasis on psychology of collaboration, the theory explains that group psychological formation leads to specific types of interaction. Nihalani, Wilson, Thomas, and Robinson (2010), for example, looked for types of interaction within group work that determine academic achievement (measured by, for instance, class attendance and quiz scores in an educational psychology class) and reported that the groups who engaged in "a democratic discussion" reached higher levels of achievement.

The relationship between interactional moves and collaboarative patterns explored in the current study could be traced back to the learners' psychology. If we hypothesize that the amount of LRCs and CSCs reflect the degree of learners' collaborative mindset, then we may also posit that a stronger collaborative mindset may help learners give CF and modify their initial erroneous utterances when corrected by their peers. In other words, a collaborative mindset may free learners from hesitation in correcting their peers and testing out their linguistic hypotheses, which, in turn, drives L2 development forward. On the contrary, the TRCs identified in the current groups may represent learners' negative psychology that prevented the group members from appreciating each other's contribution. In Nihalani et al.'s (2010) data, the groups whose achievement levels were relatively low exhibited strikingly similar discourse patterns to those of the current study's in which one learner dominated the exchange. Borrowing social interdendence theory, we conclude that the positive causality links among a collaborative mindset (*a positive peer relationship,* in social interdependence theory terms), collaborative interaction (*promotive interaction*), and L2 development (*achievement*) were found in the LP group more than the HP group. The difference might have been caused by the overall collaborative environment in each classroom rather than the learners' proficiency levels. This means, at the same time, that proficiency does not define how much of a collaborative mindset the learners may possess.

Limitations

The current study has several limitations. First, the data source for interactions was quite limited (10 students), posing a generalizability issue. We focused on the interactions of two groups with one variable in place (i.e., proficiency). This indicates that it is possible that the group dynamics in the two groups were not representative of the other groups in both classes and that there may be other variables that caused difference in the L2 development results. On the same spectrum, it seems that the two teachers' involvement may have affected the overall collaborative environment in the classrooms and subsequently how the learners approached the tasks. This was an unexpected circumstance and we call for a study where the teacher variable is controlled (one teacher being in charge of different peer interaction groups). Therefore, we do not intend to proclaim that the lower a learner's proficiency level is, the more collaborative mindset she/he tends to have. Finally, more fine-grained analyses of interactional features may have shed light on the proficiency effect on interaction (e.g., grammatical vs. lexical exchanges; successful vs. unsuccessful exchanges: see García Mayo & Azkarai 2016). For this, we call for a larger study where this type of categorical analysis would be numerically viable.

We invoked social interdependence theory to draw a link between a collaborative mindset, interactional moves, and L2 learning. Admittedly, this interpretation does not go beyond speculation. Future research may separately investigate learners' psychology (e.g., via a questionnaire about peer interaction and peer CF) and examine how the way learners approach to the task influences their interactional behaviors and, consequently, the learning outcomes.

Pedagogical implications

Anecdotally, many teachers are uncertain about providing group work activities to learners with low proficiency levels because teachers believe that their students do not have sufficient linguistic tools to work autonomously. In an experiment in which learners were trained to provide CF to each other, Sato and Lyster (2012) also shared a concern that the training may not work with learners with lower proficiency levels due to their lack of linguistic knowledge. In this regard, the findings of the current study encourage those teachers to use group work regardless of learners' proficiency levels. In addition, the results indicate that the type of approach in Sato and Lyster's (2012) experiment (i.e., transforming learners to CF providers) may work with lower proficiency learners as well.

The current study does not imply that learners are able to develop their language skills without the teacher's support. On the contrary, we argue that the teacher's guidance is crucial because it may define the ultimate learning outcome of peer interaction. If the types and extent of collaboration play a strong role in L2 development, teachers should focus on creating a collaborative classroom environment. Dörnyei and Malderez (1997:75) asserted that "the group's disposition and commitment to the group goals and norms will follow that of the teacher." We concur with this claim and emphasize the importance of teachers' guidance and interventions during pair/group work activities.

References

Adams, R., Nuevo, A., & Egi, T. (2011). Explicit and implicit feedback, modified output, and SLA: Does explicit and implicit feedback promote learning and learner-learner interactions? *Modern Language Journal, 95*(1), 42–63. doi:10.1111/j.1540-4781.2011.01242.x

Alcón, E. (2002). Relationship between teacher-led versus learners' interaction and the development of pragmatics in the EFL classroom. *International Journal of Educational Research, 37*(4), 359–377. doi:10.1016/S0883-0355(03)00010-7

Alexander, O. (2012). Exploring teacher beliefs in teaching EAP at low proficiency levels. *Journal of English for Academic Purposes, 11*(1), 99–111. doi:10.1016/j.jeap.2011.12.001

Ballinger, S. (2013). Towards a cross-linguistic pedagogy: Biliteracy and reciprocal learning strategies in French immersion. *Journal of Immersion and Content-Based Language Education, 1*(1), 131–148. doi:10.1075/jicb.1.1.06bal

Berns, M. (1990). 'Second' and 'foreign' in second language acquisition/foreign language learning: A sociolinguistic perspective. In B. VanPatten & J. Lee (Eds.), *Second language acquisition/Foreign language learning* (pp. 3–11). Clevedon, UK: Multilingual Matters.

Block, D. (2003). *The social turn in second language acquisition.* Washington, DC: Georgetown University Press.

Corbin, J., & Strauss, A. (2008). *Basics of qualitative research: Techniques and procedures for developing grounded theory* (3 ed.). Thousand Oaks, CA: Sage.

Davin, K., & Donato, R. (2013). Student collaboration and teacher-directed classroom dynamic assessment: A complementary pairing. *Foreign Language Annals*, 46(1), 5–22. doi:10.1111/flan.12012

DeKeyser, R. (2010). Practice for second language learning: Don't throw out the baby with the bathwater. *International Journal of English Studies*, 10(1), 155–165.

Donato, R. (1994). Collective scaffolding in second language learning. In J. Lantolf & G. Appel (Eds.), *Vygotskian approaches to second language research* (pp. 33–56). Norwood, NJ: Ablex.

Dörnyei, Z., & Malderez, A. (1997). Group dynamics and foreign language learning. *System*, 25(1), 65–81. doi:10.1016/S0346-251X(96)00061-9

Farías, M., & Abrahams, M. (2008). Innovation and change in the Chilean ITT curriculum for teachers of English. *II Latin American Congress on Language Teacher Education (II CLAFPL)*, 26–29.

Fernández Dobao, A. F. (2012). Collaborative dialogue in learner–learner and learner–native speaker interaction. *Applied Linguistics*, 33(3), 229–256. doi:10.1093/applin/ams002

Foster, P., & Ohta, A. (2005). Negotiation for meaning and peer assistance in second language classrooms. *Applied Linguistics*, 26(3), 402–430. doi:10.1093/applin/ami014

Gagné, N., & Parks, S. (2013). Cooperative learning tasks in a Grade 6 intensive ESL class: Role of scaffolding. *Language Teaching Research*, 17(2), 188–209. doi:10.1177/1362168812460818

Galaczi, E. (2008). Peer-peer interaction in a speaking test: The case of the First Certificate in English Examination. *Language Assessment Quarterly*, 5(2), 89–119. doi:10.1080/15434300801934702

García Mayo, M., & Pica, T. (2000). L2 learner interaction in a foreign language setting: Are learning needs addressed? *International Review of Applied Linguistics*, 38(1), 35–58.

García Mayo, M. P., & Azkarai, A. (2016). EFL task-based interaction: Does task modality impact on language-related episodes? In M. Sato & S. Ballinger (Eds.), *Peer interaction and second language learning: Pedagogical potential and research agenda* (pp. 241–266). Amsterdam: John Benjamins.

Gillies, R., Ashman, A., & Terwel, J. (Eds.). (2008). *The teacher's role in implementing cooperative learning in the classroom*. New York, NY: Springer. doi:10.1007/978-0-387-70892-8

Guk, I., & Kellogg, D. (2007). The ZPD and whole class teaching: Teacher-led and student-led interactional mediation of tasks. *Language Teaching Research*, 11(3), 281–299. doi:10.1177/1362168807077561

Hulstijn, J., Young, R., Ortega, L., Bigelow, M., DeKeyser, R., Ellis, N., Lantolf, J., Mackey, A., & Talmy, S. (2014). Bridging the gap: Cognitive and social approaches to research in second language learning and teaching. *Studies in Second Language Acquisition*, 36, 1–61. doi:10.1017/S0272263114000035

Iwashita, N. (2001). The effect of learner proficiency on interactional moves and modified output in nonnative-nonnative interaction in Japanese as a foreign language. *System*, 29(2), 267–287. doi:10.1016/S0346-251X(01)00015-X

Johnson, D., & Johnson, R. (2009). An educational psychology success story: Social interdependence theory and cooperative learning. *Educational Researcher*, 38(5), 365–379. doi:10.3102/0013189X09339057

Kim, Y., & McDonough, K. (2008). The effect of interlocutor proficiency on the collaborative dialogue between Korean as a second language learners. *Language Teaching Research*, 12(2), 211–234. doi:10.1177/1362168807086288

King, S. (Writer) & Darabont, F. (Director). (1994). *The shawshank redemption* [Motion picture]. United States of America: Columbia Pictures.

Kormos, J., & Kiddle, T. (2013). The role of socio-economic factors in motivation to learn English as a foreign language: The case of Chile. *System*, 41(2), 399–412. doi:10.1016/j.system.2013.03.006

Lantolf, J. P., & Poehner, M. E. (2011). Dynamic assessment in the classroom: Vygotskian praxis for second language development. *Language Teaching Research*, 15(1), 11–33. doi:10.1177/1362168810383328

Leeser, M. (2004). Learner proficiency and focus on form during collaborative dialogue. *Language Teaching Research*, 8(1), 55–81. doi:10.1191/1362168804lr134oa

Lyster, R. (2007). *Learning and teaching languages through content: A counterbalanced approach.* Amsterdam: John Benjamins. doi:10.1075/lllt.18

Lyster, R., & Sato, M. (2013). Skill acquisition theory and the role of practice in L2 development. In M. García Mayo, J. Gutierrez-Mangado, & M. M. Adrián (Eds.), *Contemporary approaches to second language acquisition* (pp. 71–92). Amsterdam: John Benjamins. doi:10.1075/aals.9.07ch4

Mackey, A. (2012). *Input, interaction and corrective feedback in L2 classrooms.* Oxford: Oxford University Press.

McDonough, K. (2004). Learner-learner interaction during pair and small group activities in a Thai EFL context. *System*, 32(2), 207–224. doi:10.1016/j.system.2004.01.003

McDonough, K., & Chaikitmongkol, W. (2010). Collaborative syntactic priming activities and EFL learners' production of wh-questions. *The Canadian Modern Language Review*, 66(6), 817–841. doi:10.3138/cmlr.66.6.817

McDonough, K., & Mackey, A. (2008). Syntactic priming and ESL question development. *Studies in Second Language Acquisition*, 30(1), 31–47. doi:10.1017/S0272263108080029

McKay, S. (2003). Teaching English as an International Language: The Chilean context. *ELT Journal*, 57(2), 139–148. doi:10.1093/elt/57.2.139

Nihalani, P., Wilson, H., Thomas, G., & Robinson, D. (2010). What determines high- and low-performing groups? The superstar effect. *Journal of Advanced Academics*, 21(3), 500–529. doi:10.1177/1932202X1002100306

Ohta, A. (2001). *Second language acquisition processes in the classroom: Learning Japanese.* Mahwah, NJ: Lawrence Erlbaum Associates.

Philp, J., Adams, R., & Iwashita, N. (2014). *Peer interaction and second language learning.* New York, NY: Routledge.

Philp, J., & Tognini, R. (2009). Language acquisition in foreign language contexts and the differential benefits of interaction. *International Review of Applied Linguistics in Language Teaching*, 47(3-4), 245–266. doi:10.1515/iral.2009.011

Philp, J., Walter, S., & Basturkmen, H. (2010). Peer interaction in the foreign language classroom: What factors foster a focus on form? *Language Awareness*, 19(4), 261–279. doi:10.1080/09658416.2010.516831

Pica, T. (2013). From input, output and comprehension to negotiation, evidence, and attention: An overview of theory and research on learner interaction and SLA. In M. García Mayo, J. Gutierrez-Mangado, & M. Martínez Adrián (Eds.), *Contemporary approaches to Second Language Acquisition* (pp. 49–69). Amsterdam: John Benjamins. doi:10.1075/aals.9.06ch3

Pica, T., Lincoln-Porter, F., Paninos, D., & Linnell, J. (1996). Language learners' interaction: How does it address the input, output, and feedback needs of L2 learners? *TESOL Quarterly*, 30(1), 59–84. doi:10.2307/3587607

Ranta, L., & Lyster, R. (2007). A cognitive approach to improving immersion students' oral language abilities: The Awareness-Practice-Feedback sequence. In R. DeKeyser (Ed.), *Practice in a second language: Perspective from applied linguistics and cognitive psychology* (pp. 141–160). Cambridge: Cambridge University Press.

Riazi, A. M., & Candlin, C. N. (2014). Mixed-methods research in language teaching and learning: Opportunities, issues and challenges. *Language Teaching*, 47(2), 135–173. doi:10.1017/S0261444813000505

Roseth, C., Johnson, D., & Johnson, R. (2008). Promoting early adolescents' achievement and peer relationships: The effects of cooperative, competitive, and individualistic goal structures. *Psychological Bulletin*, 134(2), 223–246. doi:10.1037/0033-2909.134.2.223

Salaberry, M. R. (2000). The acquisition of English past tense in an instructional setting. *System*, 28(1), 135–152. doi:10.1016/S0346-251X(99)00065-2

Sato, M. (2015). Density and complexity of oral production in interaction: The interactionist approach and an alternative. *International Review of Applied Linguistics in Language Teaching*, 53(3), 307–329. doi:10.1515/iral-2015-0016

Sato, M. (2013). Beliefs about peer interaction and peer corrective feedback: Efficacy of classroom intervention. *The Modern Language Journal*, 97(3), 611–633. doi:10.1111/j.1540-4781.2013.12035.x

Sato, M. (2011). Constitution of form-orientation: Contributions of context and explicit knowledge to learning from recasts. *Canadian Journal of Applied Linguistics*, 14(1), 1–28.

Sato, M. (2007). Social relationships in conversational interaction: A comparison between learner-learner and learner-NS dyads. *JALT Journal*, 29(2), 183–208.

Sato, M., & Ballinger, S. (2012). Raising language awareness in peer interaction: A cross-context, cross-method examination. *Language Awareness*, 21(1-2), 157–179. doi:10.1080/09658416.2011.639884

Sato, M., & Lyster, R. (2012). Peer interaction and corrective feedback for accuracy and fluency development: Monitoring, practice, and proceduralization. *Studies in Second Language Acquisition*, 34(4), 591–262. doi:10.1017/S0272263112000356

Sato, M., & Lyster, R. (2007). Modified output of Japanese EFL learners: Variable effects of interlocutor vs. feedback types. In A. Mackey (Ed.), *Conversational interaction in second language acquisition: A collection of empirical studies* (pp. 123–142). Oxford: Oxford University Press.

Storch, N. (2002). Patterns of interaction in ESL pair work. *Language Learning*, 52(1), 119–158. doi:10.1111/1467-9922.00179

Storch, N. (2011). Collaborative writing in L2 contexts: Processes, outcomes, and future directions. *Annual Review of Applied Linguistics*, 31, 275–288. doi:10.1017/S0267190511000079

Storch, N., & Aldosari, A. (2013). Pairing learners in pair work activity. *Language Teaching Research*, 17(1), 31–48. doi:10.1177/1362168812457530

Stæhra, L. (2008). Vocabulary size and the skills of listening, reading and writing. *Language Learning Journal*, 36(2), 139–152. doi:10.1080/09571730802389975

Swain, M., & Lapkin, S. (2002). Talking it through: Two French immersion learners' response to reformulation. *International Journal of Educational Research*, 37(3), 285–304. doi:10.1016/S0883-0355(03)00006-5

Swain, M., & Lapkin, S. (1998). Interaction and second language learning: Two adolescent French immersion students working together. *The Modern Language Journal*, 82(3), 320–337. doi:10.1111/j.1540-4781.1998.tb01209.x

Toth, P. (2008). Teacher- and learner-led discourse in task-based grammar instruction: Providing procedural assistance for L2 morphosyntactic development. *Language Learning*, 58(2), 237–283. doi:10.1111/j.1467-9922.2008.00441.x

Varonis, E., & Gass, S. (1985). Non-native/non-native conversations: A model for negotiation of meaning. *Applied Linguistics*, 6(1), 71–90. doi:10.1093/applin/6.1.71

Watanabe, Y., & Swain, M. (2007). Effects of proficiency differences and patterns of pair interaction on second language learning: Collaborative dialogue between adult ESL learners. *Language Teaching Research*, 11(2), 121–142. doi:10.1177/1362168806070074599

Williams, J. (1999). Learner-generated attention to form. *Language Learning*, 49(4), 583–625. doi:10.1111/0023-8333.00103

Williams, J. (2001). The effectiveness of spontaneous attention to form. *System*, 29(3), 325–340. doi:10.1016/S0346-251X(01)00022-7

Wood, D., Bruner, J., & Ross, G. (1976). The role of tutoring in problem solving. *Journal of Child Psychology and Psychiatry*, 17(1), 89–100. doi:10.1111/j.1469-7610.1976.tb00381.x

Yoshida, R. (2008). Learners' perception of corrective feedback in pair work. *Foreign Language Annals*, 41(3), 525–541. doi:10.1111/j.1944-9720.2008.tb03310.x

Yoshida, R. (2013). Conflict between learners' beliefs and actions: Speaking in the classroom. *Language Awareness*, 22(4), 371–388. doi:10.1080/09658416.2012.758129

Young, A., & Tedick, D. (2016). Collaborative dialogue in a two-way Spanish/English immersion classroom: Does heterogeneous grouping promote peer linguistic scaffolding? In M. Sato & S. Ballinger (Eds.), *Peer interaction and second language learning: Pedagogical potential and research agenda* (pp. 135–160). Amsterdam: John Benjamins.

CHAPTER 4

Interactional behaviours of low-proficiency learners in small group work

Hyunsik Choi and Noriko Iwashita
University of Queensland

Building on empirical studies investigating the relationship between interlocutors' proficiency and learning opportunities in pair work, this chapter examines how group members' proficiency affected the occurrence and outcome of language related episodes (LREs) and also how their proficiency level affected their perception of working within a small group. Two low-proficiency ESL learners engaged in three small group discussion tasks. For each task, the two learners were grouped into one of three proficiency levels: high-proficiency dominant, low-proficiency dominant, and low-proficiency. The interactional data of the three groups was analysed in terms of the types and outcomes of LREs. While the occurrence and outcome of LREs appeared to be dependent on the interlocutors' proficiency levels, their perceptions of and contributions to group work were largely dependent on the interlocutors' attitudes toward sharing ideas in completing the task.

Introduction

Since the communicative approach was introduced in the 1970s, the use of a second language (L2) has been encouraged not only to generate meaning, but also to communicate with others in authentic contexts (Rance-Roney 2010). A substantial body of second language acquisition (SLA) research has demonstrated that learner-learner interactions provide optimal conditions for language learning, and are associated with creating suitable environments for meaningful use of the target language as well as opportunities for its production (e.g., Adams 2007; Fujii & Mackey 2009; Philp, Adams & Iwashita 2013; Sato & Lyster 2012; Sato & Ballinger 2016). Pica (1994) also claimed that target language interactions are abundant sources of linguistic input, and they play a major role in facilitating L2 acquisition. However, other researchers such as Hellermann (2008) note that L2 acquisition via peer interaction is not merely an individual process. Rather, it

DOI 10.1075/lllt.45.05cho

involves socially situated and jointly constructed aspects of L2 learning in which language user's ability, personality, and specific context are closely interrelated. That is, peer interaction intertwines with a range of variables that create unique environments for L2 learning (Sato & Ballinger 2016).

Based on Vygotsky's (1986) notion that cognition and knowledge are built through social interaction, Swain, Brooks and Tocalli-Beller (2002) claimed that the socially constructed nature of L2 interaction plays a significant role in SLA. Therefore, L2 interaction should be regarded as a verbal mediation through which learners are able to achieve control of tasks through speaking with others. Swain (2000) introduced the concept of *collaborative dialogue*, which signifies a discourse where language learners are engaged in knowledge building and problem-solving. Learners use language as a tool to build knowledge, as well as to communicate with each other in both their L1 and L2. Taking this concept further, Swain, Kinnear and Steinman (2011) argued that collaborative dialogue functions to mediate cognition and suggested the term 'languaging' which indicates the social use of language to mediate the process of thinking. In this context, languaging is employed not only as a method of internalisation, but also as a method of externalisation. This construct establishes language as a tool used to transform thoughts and allow deeper understanding of complex events.

Collaborative dialogue has received considerable attention in SLA research and much empirical research has specifically attempted to investigate to what extent interaction between peers is effective for creating learning opportunities. One of the predominant methods of quantifying collaborative dialogue is using language related episodes (LREs). Swain and Lapkin (1998: 326) defined this concept as "any part of a dialogue in which learners talk about the language they are producing or question their language use." (326). Studies on collaborative dialogues have shown that L2 learners engage with new lexical items and correct grammatical forms when carrying out various pair and small group tasks (e.g., Leeser 2004; Williams 1999). Furthermore, recent research revealed that one major set of variables in the occurrence of LREs over a collaborative dialogue are learner characteristics, which encompass gender, cultural background (e.g., Ross-Feldman 2007), and proficiency (e.g., Leeser 2004; Storch & Aldosari 2013; Watanabe 2008).

This chapter focuses on learner proficiency as the main factor affecting LREs in peer interaction and also examined how learners' perspectives of peer interaction were shaped contingent on their interlocutors' proficiency levels. Furthermore, focusing on two low English proficiency learners, the study observed to what extent these different proficiency-level groupings impacted on the participants' perceptions of working within a group.

Learner proficiency

A concern for many researchers of peer interaction is the way in which learner proficiency affects the quality and quantity of interactions. For example, Leeser (2004) compared LREs produced by three different types of dyads (high-high, high-low, or low-low) in a content-based adult L2 Spanish course. High-proficiency learner dyads (high-high) produced the greatest number of LREs and were more likely to produce grammatical LREs compared to low-proficiency learner dyads, which focused more often on lexical items. Although correct resolution of LREs was prevalent across the dyads, low-proficiency dyads showed a considerable number of unresolved LREs compared with the other two dyadic formations (high-high and high-low). This indicates that low-proficiency learner dyads may not be as capable of solving problematic linguistic forms as more proficient learner dyads.

Kim and McDonough (2008) investigated to what extent eight intermediate Korean L2 learners produced LREs when collaborating with an interlocutor of the same proficiency level, compared with their collaboration with an interlocutor of a higher proficiency level. Significantly more lexical LREs and correctly resolved LREs were observed in the collaborative dialogue of advanced learners. Furthermore, the questionnaire data showed that if learners perceived that their language proficiency was less developed than that of their interlocutors, they were more likely to adopt a less dominant role in the task, even though they participated as equal contributors. In contrast to the findings of Kim and McDonough, Watanabe (2008) found that interlocutors' language proficiency is not a decisive factor affecting the nature of peer assistance. Three participants were recruited as core participants, and interacted with two non-core participants who had either higher or lower English proficiency than each core participant. The result showed that, regardless of the interlocutors' proficiency, peer interaction provided learning opportunities when participants worked collaboratively. Furthermore, all the core participants agreed that their interlocutors' proficiency was not their major concern in successful collaboration, but rather it was their willingness to share their ideas and help the core participant in completing the task.

In line with Watanabe's study, Storch and Aldosari (2013) investigated ways to maximise the effectiveness of pair work by taking L2 proficiency as a main variable. Thirty university students participated in this study to complete a short composition. They were divided into similar proficiency pairs and mixed proficiency pairs. When learners are engaged in fluency-based tasks, low-proficiency learners were more likely to produce longer L2 turns when paired with those of a similar proficiency level, while high-proficiency learners were less likely to be affected by the proficiency level of their interlocutors. However, if the goal of the task centred on language use, low proficiency learners paid more attention to this goal when grouped with higher proficiency learners. This finding indicates language proficiency is not a major variable in maximising the effectiveness of pair work when compared to the goal of the activity and the dyadic relationship.

The empirical studies above have shown that learner proficiency plays an important role in directing the occurrence and outcome of LREs (see also Sato & Viveros 2016). The LREs in these studies were mainly generated in the course of dyadic interaction. However, there are many occasions in which oral interactions are not confined to dyadic contexts. Small group peer interactions, involving more than two learners, have been one of the most frequently used formats of interactional dynamics in language classrooms. Therefore, it would be beneficial to examine what patterns of small group interaction emerge, depending on interlocutors' proficiency levels. Furthermore few studies have focused on the perspectives of low-proficiency learners in small group work (see Young & Tedick 2016). Therefore, it is important to study how low-proficiency learners position themselves as novices who need developmentally appropriate help from experts and to what extent they receive assistance from peers in the various patterns of small group work. Moreover, the role of relatively low proficiency learners in interaction and LRE production is more likely to be influenced by interlocutors' proficiency than that of high-proficiency learners (Kim & McDonough 2008). Hence, the current study addressed the following research questions.

RQ 1:   How do the characteristics of LREs differ when low-proficiency learners collaborate with interlocutors of various proficiency levels?

RQ 2:   Does the proficiency level of other group members play a key role in directing low-proficiency learners' participation in small group work?

Methodology

Participants

The participants were 14 Korean L1 speakers (five males and nine females) with a mean age of 22 who were studying English in Australia. Twelve participants were recruited from one language study club, and two extra female participants were recruited through a noticeboard in the campus. Grouping of the learners according to proficiency level was decided using their IELTS (International English Language Testing System) score based on a nine-band scale. All participants had taken the IELTS test no more than one year before the data were collected. The exact ranges for categorising learners' proficiency levels were carefully considered to maintain a distinct proficiency gap between the two groups and to mitigate any minor increases or decreases in the proficiency level of the participants between the IELTS test and this research. There were eight low-proficiency participants (IELTS band score 4.5–5) and six high-proficiency participants (IELTS band score 6.5–7).

The study was designed so that two low-proficiency learners (the core learners) would engage in three group work sessions, each involving a different group of three other L2 learners (the non-core learners) whose English proficiency was either at a higher level or at the same level as the core participants. One male and one female were chosen at random as the core participants.

The first core participant (C1), Michael (pseudonym), aged 21, had been in Australia for approximately nine months. His IELTS score was 5.0. The second core participant (C2), Susan (pseudonym), aged 20, had been in Australia for approximately six months. Her IELTS score was also 5.0. Both Michael and Susan came to Australia to study English in order to enhance their employment opportunities upon their return to Korea. To avoid any impact of pre-determined ideas about interlocutors' proficiency on the overall interactions, the English proficiency levels of other participants were not discussed with the core participants prior to the small-group work. However, since most participants were recruited from the same language study club, the core participants had prior knowledge of the English proficiency levels of other members. Table 1 illustrates a brief profile of each participant.

Table 1. Profiles of non-core participants

	Name	Age	Sex	IELTS scores
Non-core participants for Michael (C1)	L1	23	Male	5.0
	L2	24	Female	5.0
	L3	22	Female	5.0
	H1	20	Female	6.5
	H2	22	Female	6.5
	H3	21	Male	6.5
Non-core participants for Susan (C2)	L4	21	Male	4.5
	L5	23	Female	5.0
	L6	20	Female	5.0
	H4	22	Female	6.5
	H5	24	Female	7.0
	H6	22	Male	6.5

Notes: Pseudonyms were used for all participants. Low proficiency learners are labelled L1-6 (e.g., L1 = low proficiency 1, L2 = low proficiency 2, L3 = low proficiency 3). High proficiency learners are labelled H1-6 (e.g., H1 = high proficiency 1, H2 = high proficiency 2, H3 = high proficiency 3). Each was randomly assigned to a core participant.

Task design

The task used for interaction was a discussion task in which a group of four learners discussed a possible outline of a section of the movie *Toy Story 3* after viewing the segment. Three different segments were chosen for each of the three sessions. Before the group began the discussion, the core participant and one other member were shown the target scene with Korean subtitles in order to enhance opportunities to understand the overall segment and employ this information while interacting with other group members. Subsequently, they watched the target scene again, this time with two other group members, and without sound or subtitles. In this process, the members who had watched the target scene earlier with subtitles and sound were expected to describe the scene and discuss it with the other members in English. Then the group was required to write a possible ending for the scene. All group members were encouraged to complete the task using the target language as much as possible. Since some participants had seen the movie already, they were asked to create their own storyline, which did not relate directly to the original. The participants were encouraged to interact in free-conversation using English and to focus on successful communication rather than grammatical precision. That is, all participants were reminded that the focus of the given task was not about accessing their grammatical knowledge, and they were reassured that the focal point of the task was to complete the task successfully. This unstructured task was chosen to encourage learners to engage in LREs effectively while completing a task (Philp, Walter & Basturkmen 2010).

Methodological framework

Data collection

After the basic design of the task was explained to all participants, each core participant carried out three discussion tasks based on different scenes from the movie with different group members over three days with an interval of three days between each session to avoid possible task repetition effect on performance. Each session was completed within 13–19 minutes. All group interactions were audio-recorded, and the researcher (the first author) attended each session to observe the interactions. Table 2 provides a brief procedure of the overall study.

Finally, semi-structured interviews were conducted with the core participants in order to integrate perspectives of their own behavior during each small group work session. The interview questions were inspired by Ewald (2008), who aimed to investigate learners' perceptions toward small group work (see Appendix A).

Core participants also listened to their recorded interaction data with different group members. After listening to the recorded interaction data, the researcher asked about the core participants' perceptions while they were engaged in LREs and their overall impressions of each small group task. During the interviews and stimulated recall sessions, the participants were encouraged to express their thoughts about each interaction freely. All the interviews were conducted in Korean and audio-recorded. The average duration of each interview was just under 90 minutes.

Table 2. Research procedure

Day	Task	Research procedure	
Day 1		Introduction of the task, Introducing the participants	
Day 2	Discussion Topic #1	High-proficiency dominant group interactions (H1, H2, H3) (C1)	Low-proficiency group interactions (L4, L5, L6) (C2)
Day 3	Discussion Topic #2	Low-proficiency dominant group interactions (H1, L1, L2) (C1)	Low-proficiency dominant group interactions (H4, L4, L5) (C2)
Day 4	Discussion Topic #3	Low-proficiency group interactions (L1, L2, L3) (C1)	High-proficiency dominant group interactions (H4, H5, H6) (C2)
Day 5		Stimulated recall. Interview with the researcher	

Notes: The interval between each group work session was three days. C1 – Michael, C2 – Susan.

Data analysis

To investigate how participants co-construct L2 learning opportunities through collaborative dialogues, the numbers and the types of LREs were observed. Learner participation in group work was also examined by counting the turns taken by all group members. First, to quantify the core participants' contribution to each group work task, the total number of turn-taking for all group work was calculated based on transcripts of the interactions. Adopting *the sequential-production model* (Sacks, Schegloff & Jefferson 1974), the current study defines turn-taking as turn constructional units which are characterised by prosodic, syntactic, and pragmatic aspects that usually occur when speakers change. Oreström (1983) suggested that transitions from one turn to the next occur either in a soft way or in a non-soft way. Pauses and synchronisation are the main elements that construct soft turn transition. These elements underpin a collaborative cooperative interaction, where the listener waits until the other speaker's turn is completed. Non-soft transitions occur through interruption, overlapping and interpersonal communication that is modified in the course of the interaction (Erickson 1996). Grounded in these concepts, the transitions were counted as an analytical unit. Therefore, the transcribed data of each group interaction was carefully coded in order to quantify core participants' contributions. Even though the interactional data were analysed in terms of soft and non-soft transition, these two distinctions were employed as one unit of turn-taking when coded.

Furthermore, the transcribed data of each interaction was analysed in order to quantify the core participants' involvement in LREs relative to other group members' proficiency level. This study mainly focused on grammatical and lexical LREs, and correctly resolved, unresolved and incorrect LREs, based on participants' oral output following previous studies. In coding each LRE, the definition by Williams (1999) was adopted, which states that lexical LREs indicate an occasion in which learners focus on the meaning of a lexical item, the spelling and/or pronunciation of a word. Example (1) shows a lexical LRE in which a core participant questioned the meaning of a word.

(1)   C1:   And they are about to (.2); mmm. What is the 쓰레기봉지 (trash bag) in English?=
      H2:   =Trash bag
      C1:   Trash bag?
      H2:   Yes
      Note: C1 – Core participant one, Michael, H1 – Non-core high-proficiency participant one   (high-proficiency dominant group, topic #1)

Grammatical LREs are classified as occasions in which learners are mainly concerned with an aspect of morphology or syntax. In Example (2), a high-proficiency learner assisted a core participant in producing the correct adverbial form of the word 'slow'.

(2)   H4: = You mean Barbie should give the crazy monkey some poisoned banana?
      C2:   Yes, yes, (.3). I don't know how Barbie can escape from that monkey. I think (.4) she run slow.
      H4:   Slowly.
      H6:   Isn't it slow?
      C2:   I always say 'slow' hah!
      H4:   Slowly is correct. It's adverb.=
      C2:   =Adverb?=
      H6:   = Oh o::k
      Note: C2 – Core participant two, Susan, H4 and H6 – Non-core high-proficiency participants four and six.
                               (high-proficiency dominant group, topic #3)

As for the outcome of LREs, the current study classified three different types of outcomes following Leeser (2004). Examples (3) and (4) relate to occasions in which the core participants resolved their problematic discourse correctly, with the help of peers, or by themselves. While Susan resolved her incorrect past tense form of the verb 'drive' by herself in Example (3), Michael resolved his incorrect pronunciation of the word 'owner' with the help of another participant in Example (4). The frequency of LREs in which the core participants were involved and LREs in which the core participants were not involved was calculated separately.

(3) C2: And the truck driver drived the truck. No, no…droved. No, drove… hah.
   Note: C2 – Core participant two, Susan
(low-proficiency dominant group, topic #2)

(4) C2: Daisy was the honour of the baby doll?
   L5: Owner: 아니에요? (Isn't it Owner?)
   C2: Yes, Owner, Owner, Owner…
   Note: L5 – Non-core low-proficiency participant five.
(low-proficiency dominant group, topic #2)

LREs that were not resolved in the interaction were classified as unresolved LREs. These mainly occurred when learners abandoned their problematic linguistic items without an attempt to resolve them fully (see Example (5)). This type of LRE was excluded from the total number of lexical and grammatical LREs.

(5) L2: mm (.3); Do you know '고아원'? (Orphanage)
   C1: 몰라..그게뭐지 (I don't know… What is it in English?)
   L3: 그냥넘어가자… (Well… Let's skip it)
   Note: C1 – Core participant one, Michael, L2 and 3 – Non-core
      low-proficiency participant two and three.
(low-proficiency group, topic #3)

LREs which were resolved incorrectly were also coded in the study. Learners usually received assistance from other peers in solving their problematic linguistic outcomes. However, other peers occasionally provided an incorrect form, as shown in Example (6).

(6) C1: How about the big baby doll?
   L2: You mean 'Daisy' doll? Mmm… I don't know…
   C1: He might want to 복수하다. (Revenge)
   L1: Mmm (.4); kill…
   Note: C1 – Core participant one, Michael, L2 – Non-core low-proficiency
      participant two.   (low-proficiency group, topic #3)

To establish inter-coder agreement, a second coder coded 10% of the LRE data independently; the inter-coder agreement rate was calculated to be 92.3%.

Findings

To examine the correlation between the occurrence and outcomes of LREs and the interlocutors' proficiency levels in small groups, the transcribed data for each small group work session was categorised into different types and outcomes of LREs as shown in Table 3 and 4. More LREs were generated in the high-proficiency dominant groups than the low-proficiency dominant and low-proficiency only groups. Both core participants engaged in more resolved LREs when grouped with high-proficiency learners than with other low-proficiency learners.

In general, lexical LREs were generated more often than grammatical LREs. The frequency of grammatical LREs increased in the high-proficiency dominant groups, but the number of grammatical LREs to which the core participants contributed was relatively low. The low-proficiency groups produced the least number of both grammatical and lexical LREs. These findings suggest that low-proficiency learners were less likely to produce LREs when grouped with other low-proficiency learners than with high-proficiency learners. Furthermore, one can argue that the higher frequency of lexical LREs can be attributed to the characteristics of the task. The discussion task used in the current study itself focuses on learners' ability to express their opinions fluently rather than to employ the correct form of the target language. In this sense, this study reflects previous findings that lexical LREs are more likely to occur in fluency-based tasks which are characterised by a lack of explicit pre-instruction on grammatical forms by the instructor (Philp et al. 2010). As was shown earlier by Swain and Lapkin (2002) and Leeser (2004), learners are more likely to engage in grammatical LREs than in lexical LREs when completing grammar-oriented activities such as dictoglosses. In those earlier studies, in order to complete a grammar-oriented task successfully, learners needed to focus on the

Table 3. Frequency of resolved LREs in each group

	HD (H, H, H, core)		LD (H, L, L, core)		L (L, L, L, core)	
	C1	C2	C1	C2	C1	C2
GG						
Gram	6	6	2	4	1	3
Lexical	8	9	9	13	5	9
Total	14	15	11	17	6	12
CG						
Gram	2	2	2	2	1	2
Lexical	5	7	3	6	2	4
Total	7	9	5	8	3	6

Notes: GG – Group Generated, CG – Core Generated, C1 – Michael, C2 – Susan; HD – High-proficiency dominant group, LD – Low-proficiency dominant group, L – Low-proficiency group, Gram – Grammatical.

correct form extensively. During this process, grammatical LREs were more likely to be generated in collaborative dialogue than were lexical LREs. Compared with the dictogloss task, the task used in the current study did not require the participants to pay as much attention to form as in other tasks.

Table 4 summarises the outcomes of LREs over the three different group work sessions. Both core participants were more likely to engage in correctly resolved LREs when grouped in a high-proficiency dominant group. This illustrates that core participants are more likely to be exposed to appropriate mediation from other group members in a high-proficiency dominant group. The number of unresolved LREs and incorrect LREs was greater in the low-proficiency groups than in the high-proficiency dominant and low-proficiency dominant groups. This indicates that core participants were less likely to receive appropriate mediation that might lead to solving core participants' problematic linguistic knowledge from other peers when grouped with low-proficiency learners.

Table 4. Outcome of LREs (core participants)

	HD (H, H, H, core)		LD (H, L, L, core)		L (L, L, L, core)	
	C1	C2	C1	C2	C1	C2
Resolved	7(1)*	9	5(1)*	7(1)*	1	2
Incorrect	0	0	0	1	2	4
Unresolved	1	2	1	2	3	5

Notes: C1 – Michael, C2 – Susan. *The number in brackets represents self-initiated, correctly resolved LREs. HD – High-proficiency dominant group, LD – Low-proficiency dominant group, L – Low-proficiency group.

Core participants' contributions to the group work were investigated by counting the numbers of each core participant's utterances, and the number of turns taken by the core participants versus the total number of turns as summarised in Table 5.

Table 5. Core participants' participation patterns across groups

	HD (H, H, H, core)		LD (H, L, L, core)		L (L, L, L, core)	
	C1	C2	C1	C2	C1	C2
Total turns	263	295	282	353	413	312
C's turns	85	78	89	113	139	105
	(32.3%)	(26.4%)	(31.6%)	(32.0%)	(33.6%)	(33.6%)
Writer of the storyline	H2	H3	H1	H1	C1	L3

Note: C1 – Michael, C2 – Susan, HD – High-proficiency dominant group, LD – Low-proficiency dominant group, L – Low-proficiency group, H – 1, 3 – High-proficiency level participants, L 3 – Low-proficiency participant.

While Michael (C1) had roughly the same opportunity to take turns in the three different small group dynamics, Susan (C2) was more likely to speak in the low-proficiency group, and less likely to participate in the high-proficiency dominant group. The transcribed data revealed many occasions in which both participants were engaged in off-task topics and spoke in the L1 when grouped with low-proficiency learners. Even though the results revealed that both participants produced more speech in the low-proficiency groupings as shown in Table 5, it does not mean that every utterance generated was related to the task. Moreover, unlike Susan's participation in the high-proficiency dominant group, Michael's data suggests that he had more opportunities to respond to others, and took more opportunities to express his opinion. In this group dynamic, the transcribed data showed that the other high-proficiency learners encouraged him to engage in the task, and invited his opinion. In the end, they actually reflected his opinion in the final decision-making, as shown in Example (7) below.

(7)   H1:   I think it's better for Woody not to jump into the trash bag.
        H3:   I think so too, what do you think?
        C1:   (.2) mmm, I think Woody can steal the knife. It's not a bad idea.
        H3:   How can Woody get the knife?
        C1:   Mmm, maybe in the kitchen?
        H2:   That's a good idea.=
        H1:   = ha I like that.
        C1:   He can cut the trash bag with the knife.
        H2:   You are right. It's better than using the dog.
        H3:   Yes, he is too slow anyway.
        C1:   Yes. That dog has short leg. I think it's impossible (.) to (.3) mm=
        H2:   = help them escape?
        C1:   Yes. Escape.
        H1:   That makes sense. Let's write this.
        Note: C1 – Core participant one, Michael, H1, H2 and H3 – Non-core high-proficiency participants one, two and three.
                        (high-proficiency dominant group, discussion topic #1)

In terms of the final decision-making and writing, Table 5 shows that both core participants were less likely to take the writer's role. Neither core participant was actively involved in the writing stages in either the high-proficiency or low-proficiency dominant groups, as shown in Example (7). In both these two groups, a high-proficiency learner took charge of putting all the members' ideas together on the task paper. This indicates that more skilled peers were more likely to take a leading role when it came to the writing stage. Furthermore, this result suggests that the level of contribution to the decision-making process by each core participant varied, contingent on the group dynamics. Excerpt 1 offers further insight into the overall participation of the core participant in each group work session.

Excerpt 1

Michael (C1): I think I contributed more on the task when the other group members asked my opinion, and when they actually carefully listened to what I said, and reflected on my opinion in relation to the overall task. I would not want to put any effort in if other group members ignored my contributions. I think it is important to have someone who shares a lot of ideas, and respects other group members' opinions.

Excerpt 2

Susan (C2): It is a matter of personality. No matter how well they speak English, if group members create a comfortable atmosphere to communicate with each other, I will share my ideas more actively. If I detect something uncomfortable between group members, I usually remain silent or became very passive. And I think it is very important to see each group member as equal. If someone reacts in a way which says that my opinion is wrong, because my English skill is not good enough, I would not want to be in the group work anymore.

Both core participants maintained their opinion that group member proficiency level was not a major factor in directing their overall participation in the group work. In relation to encouraging productive participation from each group member, the interview data revealed that it is important for each group member to be aware of the value of collaboration. In other words, seeing each group member as an equal contributor should be taken into consideration to facilitate more constructive participation by each member. Furthermore, as Susan pointed out in Excerpt 2, creating a comfortable atmosphere in the group should also be seen as one of the factors directing learners' participation.

Discussion

Interlocutors' proficiency levels and LREs

The current study investigated to what extent low-proficiency L2 learners engage in small group work with interlocutors of varying proficiency levels. In the same vein, the overall contribution to the task of small group interactions was examined as well as the extent to which these interactions facilitate opportunities for low-proficiency learners to explore their L2 knowledge with the aid of peers.

The results show that both the occurrence and the outcomes of LREs for the core participants were somewhat dependent on the proficiency levels of the group member. As shown in Table 3, the core participants were more likely to generate LREs when interacting in the group with high-proficiency learners and in the group with one high-proficiency learner and two low-proficiency learners than in the group consisting solely of low-proficiency learners. These findings support similar studies on pair work (Leeser 2004; Kim & McDonough 2008; Watanabe & Swain 2007; Williams 2001), which show that low-proficiency learners tend to produce more LREs when paired with a high-proficiency learner. This indicates a possibility that learners in the low proficiency group might be unsure as to their role – for example, whether they can seek help from or offer help to other members (Ballinger 2013; Sato 2013; Sato & Ballinger 2012). Another notable feature of the LREs that was observed in this study is that grammatical LREs were generated mainly between high-proficiency learners, especially during the writing stage, supporting Leeser's (2004) finding. The frequency of grammatical LREs generated by the core participants was considerably lower than it was for the high-proficiency learners. This may indicate that low-proficiency learners were busy deciphering the meaning of other members' discourses during small group work rather than focusing on form. Furthermore, most grammatical LREs occurred between high-proficiency learners while they were engaged in the writing stage; the limited contributions of the core participants may account for their relatively small numbers of grammatical LREs. As Yule and Macdonald (1990) pointed out, when low-proficiency learners are given the role of controlling the overall task, a higher percentage of negotiated solutions are more likely than when high-proficiency learners take control. Therefore, it would be beneficial to investigate to what extent low-proficiency learners in small group work focus on form when they have to play the role of the writer synthesising other group members' opinions.

In terms of the outcomes of LREs, the low-proficiency learner group produced the lowest number of correctly resolved LREs and the highest number of unresolved LREs and incorrect LREs. These findings confirm the results of previous studies (Kim & McDonough 2008; Lesser 2004; Watanabe & Swain 2007; Williams 2001) in that the occurrence of correctly resolved LREs is greater when participants engage in interactions with advanced interlocutors. Moreover, the high frequency of unresolved and incorrect LREs by the core participants in low-proficiency groups indicates that being grouped exclusively with low-proficiency learners might have increased the likelihood of learners being exposed to incorrect information from their peers (e.g., Ohta 2001). If learners realised that peer mediations provided incorrect linguistic knowledge, this also could lead to learners acquiring negative perspectives of L2 peer interaction due to the perception of peers as unreliable learning sources.

Learners' perception of group work and interlocutors' proficiency levels

Even though the occurrence of LREs was somewhat dependent on interlocutors' proficiency, core participants' perspectives of the group work were shaped in a different manner. To investigate whether core participants' perspectives are in line with the occurrence of the quantity of LREs and interlocutors' proficiency levels, the researcher sat with each of the core participants and listened to the recorded interaction data in which the participant was involved. While prompting his memory by listening to the recorded interaction data, Michael (C1) maintained the perspective that group members' proficiency would be a factor in propagating interactions of small group work, but not a major factor. He asserted that high-proficiency members' help with his linguistic problems aided the expansion of his L2 knowledge. Nevertheless, his perception of the link between a successful group work environment and L2 learning did not rely on group members' proficiency levels.

Excerpt 3
Michael: It was good to have someone who had a better English skill than me in the group. I think I learned some new words from them. But I think that high-proficiency group members are not particularly necessary to have a productive group. I have encountered many occasions in which groups made up of similarly proficient members were very successful. Actually, it is not a matter of proficiency, it's a matter of how you interact with other people, how much you want to help and contribute to overall group work.

Excerpt 4
Susan: I was too afraid to talk when I was grouped with high-proficiency learners. I felt a little embarrassed to talk or give my opinion, because their English skill was better than mine. Sometimes, they said things to each other that I didn't understand. Every time that happened, I felt left out. When one of the members in the group kept correcting my English, I even felt humiliated. However, the other two groups were quite different. H4 (a high-proficiency learner in low-proficiency dominant group) helped other members, and me, a lot to complete the task. It was good to have her in our group. When I had a problem to explain the story to the other members, she helped me to finish the sentence correctly, not like the other group (high-proficiency dominant group). When completing the task with group members of the same proficiency level, I felt comfortable. But I felt we spoke often in Korean. That wouldn't help me to learn English, but I still had a lot of fun in that group (low-proficiency group). In my opinion, it's good to have one or two high-proficiency learners in the group, but we could still complete the task without high-proficiency group members.

Despite the difficulty she encountered, Susan (C2) also stated that peer assistance from group work was beneficial in facilitating an optimal L2 learning environment. Nevertheless, both Michael and Susan remained sceptical about group members' proficiency as the main factor for collectively beneficial group work that provides optimal conditions for L2 learning opportunities. Furthermore, as Excerpts 3 and 4 revealed, both core participants agreed that group members' proficiency might have increased their exposure to correct L2 items. However, it did not directly lead to an overall positive view of their group work. The current study demonstrated that group members' proficiency might relate to the occurrence of LREs, but is not necessarily linked to learners' perspectives of collaborative group work. Additionally, as Excerpt 4 shows, the core participants' perceptions of high-proficiency learners were somewhat different in the high-proficiency and low-proficiency dominant group. Susan stated that high-proficiency learners in the high-proficiency dominant group were somewhat intimidating and dismissive of her contributions, but a high-proficiency learner in a low-proficiency dominant group was willing to provide appropriate mediation for her linguistic problems. One could argue that these results arose from personal difference or group arrangement. However, the current study did not conduct any post-interviews with high-proficiency learners to investigate this issue further. Therefore, in future studies it would be worth investigating to what extent the interactional behaviour of high-proficiency learners in small group work differs depending on group members' proficiency levels.

Peer interaction

Excerpt 5
Michael: I was not sure of the correct spelling of the word 'quiet'. I knew the word before, but was not sure if the correct spelling was 'q-u-i-t-e' or 'q-u-i-e-t'. Thanks to other group members, now I'm sure of the correct spelling of the word 'quiet'.

Excerpt 6
Susan: I felt it was definitely beneficial to talk in English with other group members. Especially, it was good to listen to and use some words I've heard before but I wasn't sure of, from other group members.

As the above interview data revealed, the core participants stated that peer assistance was beneficial in reinforcing previous knowledge that they were unsure of. This phenomenon could be explained by the concept of ZPD. As Aljaafreh and Lantolf (1994) argue, the condition which facilitates an ideal ZPD through mediation is that the assistance given by the expert should provide no more help than is necessary. In the same vein, Lapkin, Swain and Psyllakis (2010) claim that assistance should be attuned to the specific needs of the learner and should be provided when learners have internalised the new knowledge within their ZPD. Applying this concept to the findings of the current study, as Ohta (2000) argues, L2 development through ZPD does not occur if new knowledge is too sophisticated or too simplistic for core participants. In this sense, Excerpts 5 and 6 indicate that some peer mediations received by core participants were in their ZPD. Unlike these excerpts, most of the other lexical and grammatical LRE items that core participants were engaged in seemed too difficult for them to comprehend; in other words, they might have been too sophisticated to facilitate effective mediation in their ZPD. In summary, peer assistance in small group work is effective for learners to create L2 learning opportunities as long as the provisions of peer mediation are within each novice's ZPD. Therefore, regardless of the disparity between the proficiency levels of members in small groups, it is imperative for learners to understand that effective small group work can be achieved given the existence of experts who are capable of providing developmentally appropriate mediation.

Learners' participation and successful small group work

The second research question concerns the extent to which group member proficiency levels influence low-proficiency learners' participation in small group work. As the interview data and the frequency of participation for both core participants in Table 3 indicate, group members' proficiency levels did not play a decisive role in directing core participants' contributions to small group work. The interview data also revealed that their participation was largely dependent on other interlocutors' characteristics rather than their proficiency. In other words, the effective mediation of each other's learning is somewhat related to a level of sensitivity when providing developmentally appropriate help and an awareness of other learners' contributions to the task in a collaborative manner. This finding is in line with arguments from previous studies (Watanabe & Swain 2008; Watanabe 2008) which claim that seeing other interlocutors as equal contributors and sharing many ideas through collaborative dialogue plays a significant role in facilitating both learners' participation and the effectiveness of peer assistance. To facilitate successful small group work, it is important for learners to acknowledge that collaboration entails not only the awareness of individuals as part of a cooperative activity, but also the recognition of the contribution from each individual in completing the larger goal (Donato 2004).

In summary, the results of this study provide further insights, through the perspectives of low-proficiency learners, into the dynamics of small group work, contingent on group members' proficiency levels. The findings show that both core participants engaged in different patterns of group interaction depending on the members of the three groups. However, one notable aspect of this result is that, even though the occurrence and outcomes of LREs were somewhat dependent on interlocutors' proficiency levels, each core participant's perception of and contribution to the group work was reliant on the level of equality between learners (Storch & Aldosari 2013).

Pedagogical implications

The present study suggests several implications for pedagogy. First, in terms of the grouping of students for small group work, considering who plays the role of the expert is necessary to create optimal learning environments. The present study suggests that having an expert who can provide developmentally appropriate assistance in small group work, regardless of their proficiency, can help to create a positive L2 learning environment, which might lead to L2 development in learners' ZPD through effective peer mediation. Therefore, when arranging small group works, teachers should consider how learners would place themselves as novice or expert. Rather than assigning small group members based on their proficiency, appointing effective and collaborative members as a mediator in small group work would enhance the creation of cooperative classroom environment (Sato & Viveros 2016). To achieve this, it is imperative that teachers should train learners to acquire a collaborative mindset in terms of peer interaction. Additionally, teachers should understand learners are able to adopt their expert or novice roles in a very fluid manner (Young & Tedick 2016). These roles are not solely based on their language proficiency. Secondly, to facilitate each learner's participation in small-group work, it is important for teachers to encourage students to acquire a positive attitude towards other group members as equal contributors in completing small-group work. As mentioned earlier, learners' perspectives toward constructive group work is highly contingent on interlocutors' sensitivity and responsiveness and therefore, it is advantageous to train learners to be efficient interlocutors, as suggested by Kim and McDonough (2011).

Conclusion

The current study attempted to gain a deep insight into peer interactions in small group work contingent on the interlocutors' proficiency. The findings indicate that proficiency levels affect the occurrence and outcomes of LREs. However, according to the subsequent interview data, group members' willingness to share ideas and engage positively with the group played a more substantial role in encouraging the core participants to partake in the task, than did interlocutors' proficiency.

Since the study followed two core participants in depth, it is difficult to discuss the generalizability of its findings. Additionally, as Swain and Lapkin (1995) argue, it is necessary to administer tailor-made post-tests to measure the relationship between collaborative dialogues and L2 learning opportunities. However, since the present study employed semi-constructed interview sessions in order to clarify to what extent learners acknowledged peer assistance, the tangible evidence of L2 learning through each group work session was not covered. Another limitation of the study could be familiarity between participants. Familiarity and affiliation are two of the main factors which can change overall peer interaction (Philp et al. 2010). Since the two non-core participants were not recruited from the same language school, unlike the other participants, they did not have a chance to interact with the other participants beforehand. This factor should be taken into consideration as one of the effective variables that might influence the overall findings of this study. Lastly, Mackey and Gass (2005) suggested that retrospective interviews are better carried out as soon as possible after the event to acquire reliable data. The current study had a relatively long interval of nine days between the interview session and the first small group interaction session for each core participant. This long interval might have affected the core participants' overall recollection of each small group session. Furthermore, since the core participants engaged in the same format task three times, the familiarity and the repetition of the task might have influenced the overall outcome of the study. Therefore, these aspects should be taken into consideration in analysing the findings.

The current study mainly focused on the interactional behavior of low-proficiency learners in small group work. Therefore, it would be beneficial for further studies to investigate how the perspective of high-proficiency learners was formed while engaging in each different group work session, and to what extent they generate different types of LREs depending on different group dynamics. As the findings in this study indicated, the sensitivity and readiness to produce developmentally appropriate assistance were mainly generated from the learner that took on the expert role. Therefore, it would be imperative to understand and examine the perspective and linguistic features of high-proficiency learners contingent on different group members in further investigations. Integrating these two different perspectives from different proficiency learners would help to identify specific circumstances which facilitate effective peer mediation.

Overall, the present study shed light on the fact that effective mediation between peers is important for the construction of productive groups. As Lantolf and Aljaafreh (1995) suggested, effective help from other peers indicates graduated and contingent assistance. Given this notion of collaborative peer interaction in small group work, each group member's proficiency level might affect the quantity of LREs. However, to create more optimal learning conditions, one should consider to what extent the overall collaborative group work is affected by a learner's sensitivity towards and awareness of other peers as either an expert who is able to provide effective mediation or as a novice who requires assistance.

References

Adams, R. (2007). Do second language learners benefit from interacting with each other? In A. Mackey (Ed.), *Conversational interaction in second language acquisition* (pp. 29–51). Oxford: Oxford University Press.

Aljaafreh, A., & Lantolf, J. (1994). Negative feedback as regulation and second language learning in the zone of proximal development. *The Modern Language Journal*, 78, 465–483. doi:10.1111/j.1540-4781.1994.tb02064.x

Ballinger, S. (2013). Towards a cross-linguistic pedagogy: Biliteracy and reciprocal learning strategies in French immersion. *Journal of Immersion and Content-Based Language Education*, 1(1), 131–148. doi:10.1075/jicb.1.1.06bal

Donato, R. (2004). Aspects of collaboration in pedagogical discourse. *Annual Review of Applied Linguistics*, 24, 284–302. doi:10.1017/S026719050400011X

Erickson, F. (1996). Going for the zone: The social and cognitive ecology of teacher-student interaction in classroom conversations. In D. Hicks (Ed.), *Discourse, learning, and schooling* (pp. 29–62). Cambridge: Cambridge University Press. doi:10.1017/CBO9780511720390.002

Ewald, J. (2008). The assumption of participation in small group work: An investigation of L2 teachers' and learners' expectation. *Issues in Applied Linguistics*, 16, 151–174.

Fujii, A., & Mackey, A. (2009). Interactional feedback in learner-learner interactions in a task based EFL classroom. *International Review of Applied Linguistics in Language Teaching*, 47, 267–301. doi:10.1515/iral.2009.012

Hellermann, J. (2008). *Social actions for classroom language learning*. Clevedon, UK: Multilingual Matters.

Kim, Y., & McDonough, K. (2008). The effect of interlocutor proficiency on the collaborative dialogue between Korean as a second language learners. *Language Teaching Research*, 12, 211–234. doi:10.1177/1362168807086288

Kim, Y., & McDonough, K. (2011). Using pretask modelling to encourage collaborative learning opportunities. *Language Teaching Research*, 15(2), 183–199. doi:10.1177/1362168810388711

Lantolf, J., & Aljaafreh, A. (1995). Second language learning in the zone of proximal development: A revolutionary experience. *International Journal of Educational Research*, 23, 619–632. doi:10.1016/0883-0355(96)80441-1

Lapkin, S., Swain, M., & Psyllakis, P. (2010). The role of languaging in creating zones of proximal development: A long-term care resident interacts with a researcher. *Canadian Journal on Aging*, 29, 477–490. doi:10.1017/S0714980810000644

Leeser, M. (2004). Learner proficiency and focus on form during collaborative dialogue. *Language Teaching Research*, 8, 55–81. doi:10.1191/1362168804lr134oa

Mackey, A., & Gass, S. (2005). *Second language research: Methodology and design*. Mahwah, NJ: Lawrence Erlbaum Associates.

Ohta, A. (2000). Re-thinking interaction in SLA: Developmentally appropriate assistance in the zone of proximal development and the acquisition of L2 grammar. In J. Lantolf (Ed.), *Sociocultural theory and second language learning* (pp. 51–78). New York, NY: Oxford University Press.

Ohta, A. (2001). *Second language acquisition processes in the classroom: Learning Japanese*. Mahwah, NJ: Lawrence Erlbaum Associates.

Oreström, B. (1983). *Turn-taking in English conversation*. Lund: Gleerup.

Philp, J., Adams, R., & Iwashita, N. (2013). *Peer interaction and second language learning*. New York, NY: Taylor & Francis.

Philp, J., Walter, S., & Basturkmen, H. (2010). Peer interaction in the foreign language classroom: what factors foster a focus on form? *Language Awareness, 19,* 261–279.
doi: 10.1080/09658416.2010.516831

Pica, T. (1994). Research on negotiation: What does it reveal about second-language learning conditions, processes and outcomes? *Language Learning, 44,* 493–527.
doi: 10.1111/j.1467-1770.1994.tb01115.x

Rance-Roney, J. (2010). Reconceptualizing interactional groups: Grouping schemes for maximizing language learning. *English Teaching Forum, 1,* 20–26.

Ross-Feldman, L. (2007). Interaction in the L2 classroom: Does gender influence learning opportunities? In A. Mackey (Ed.), *Conversational interaction in second language acquisition* (pp. 53–77). Oxford: Oxford University Press.

Sacks, H., Schegloff, E. A., & Jefferson, G. (1974). A simplest systematics for the organization of turn-taking in conversation. *Language, 50,* 696–735. doi: 10.1353/lan.1974.0010

Sato, M. (2013). Beliefs about peer interaction and peer corrective feedback: Efficacy of classroom intervention. *The Modern Language Journal, 97*(3), 611–633.
doi: 10.1111/j.1540-4781.2013.12035.x

Sato, M., & Ballinger, S. (2012). Raising language awareness in peer interaction: A cross-context, cross-method examination. *Language Awareness, 21*(1-2), 157–179.
doi: 10.1080/09658416.2011.639884

Sato, M., & Ballinger, S. (2016). Understanding peer interaction: Research synthesis and directions. In M. Sato & S. Ballinger (Eds.), *Peer interaction and second language learning: Pedagogical potential and research agenda* (pp. 1–30). Amsterdam: John Benjamins.

Sato, M., & Lyster R. (2012). Peer interaction and corrective feedback for accuracy and fluency development: Monitoring, practice, and proceduralization. *Studies in Second Language Acquisition, 34*(4), 591–626. doi: 10.1017/S0272263112000356

Sato, M., & Viveros, P. (2016). Interaction or collaboration?: The proficiency effect on group work in the foreign language classroom. In M. Sato & S. Ballinger (Eds.), *Peer interaction and second language learning: Pedagogical potential and research agenda* (pp. 91–112). Amsterdam: John Benjamins.

Storch, N., & Aldosari, A. (2013). Pairing learners in pair work activity. *Language Teaching Research, 17*(1), 31–48. doi: 10.1177/1362168812457530

Swain, M. (2000). The output hypothesis and beyond: Mediating acquisition through collaborative dialogue. In J. Lantolf (Ed.), *Sociocultural theory and second language learning* (pp. 97–114). Oxford: Oxford University Press.

Swain, M., Brooks, L., & Tocalli-Beller, A. (2002). Peer-peer dialogue as a means of second language learning. *Annual Review of Applied Linguistics, 22,* 171–185.
doi: 10.1017/S0267190502000090

Swain, M., Kinnear, P., & Steinman, L. (2011). *Sociocultural theory in second language education: An introduction through narratives.* Bristol, UK: Multilingual Matters.

Swain, M., & Lapkin, S. (1995). Problems in output and the cognitive processes they generate: A step towards second language learning. *Applied Linguistics*, 16, 371–391. doi:10.1093/applin/16.3.371

Swain, M., & Lapkin, S. (1998). Interaction and second language learning: Two adolescent French immersion students working together. *The Modern Language Journal*, 82, 320–337. doi:10.2307/329959

Swain, M., & Lapkin, S. (2002). Talking it through: Two French immersion learners' response to reformulation. *International Journal of Educational Research*, 37, 285–304. doi:10.1016/S0883-0355(03)00006-5

Vygotsky, L. (1986). *Thought and language.* Cambridge, MA: The MIT Press.

Watanabe, Y. (2008). Peer-peer interaction between L2 learners of different proficiency levels: Their interactions and reflections. *The Canadian Modern Language Review*, 64, 605–635. doi:10.3138/cmlr.64.4.605

Watanabe, Y., & Swain, M. (2007). Effects of proficiency differences and patterns of pair interaction on second language learning: Collaborative dialogue between adult ESL learners. *Language Teaching Research*, 11, 1–22. doi:10.1177/1362168806074599

Watanabe, Y., & Swain, M. (2008). Perception of learner proficiency: Its impact on the interaction between an ESL learner and her higher and lower proficiency partners. *Language Awareness*, 17, 115–130. doi:10.1080/09658410802146651

Williams, J. (1999). Learner-generated attention to form. *Language Learning*, 51, 303–346. doi:10.1111/j.1467-1770.2001.tb00020.x

Williams, J. (2001). The effectiveness of spontaneous attention to form. *System*, 29, 325–340. doi:10.1016/S0346-251X(01)00022-7

Young, A., & Tedick, D. (2016). Collaborative dialogue in a two-way Spanish/English immersion classroom: Does heterogeneous grouping promote peer linguistic scaffolding? In M. Sato & S. Ballinger (Eds.), *Peer interaction and second language learning: Pedagogical potential and research agenda* (pp. 135–160). Amsterdam: John Benjamins.

Yule, G., & Macdonald, D. (1990). Resolving referential conflict in L2 interaction: The effect of proficiency and interactive role. *Language Learning*, 40, 539–556. doi:10.1111/j.1467-1770.1990.tb00605.x

Appendix A

Question 1:   When you are studying English, do you work in small groups?

Question 2:   Can you describe the three small group work sessions you participated in?

Question 3:   Which group work session do you think was the most beneficial and the least beneficial to you?

Question 4:   Do you think it's better for students to work in small groups with different proficiency learners rather than with learners of the same level?

Question 5:   What factors encouraged you to contribute to the overall group work?

Question 6:   Do you think you have learnt something while engaging in small group work?

CHAPTER 5

Collaborative dialogue in a two-way Spanish/English immersion classroom
Does heterogeneous grouping promote peer linguistic scaffolding?

Amy Young and Diane J. Tedick
New York University / University of Minnesota

This chapter contributes to the field of language education by comparing peer interaction patterns during homogeneous and heterogeneous (based on language proficiency) small group work in a two-way immersion context. Using Vygotsky's sociocultural theory as a theoretical framework, researchers analyzed 16 audio-recorded sessions of student Spanish interactions in a 5th grade (10 to 11 year-old students) two-way immersion classroom. Centered on four focal students, the study explored the relationship between group composition, student interaction, and collaborative dialogue. While homogeneous group work produced more collaborative dialogue, a micro discourse analysis using positioning theory, found student interactions were affected by expert and novice positioning leading to marginalization and silencing of less proficient students during heterogeneous group work. The study recommends ways teachers and students can facilitate collaborative interactions in two-way immersion contexts.

Introduction

Two-way immersion (TWI) programs in the U.S., which serve combined student populations of language minority (e.g., Spanish home language) and language majority (e.g., English home language) learners, have been identified as an innovative educational option effective at facilitating both academic achievement and additive bilingualism for a wide range of students (e.g., Lindholm-Leary 2001; Thomas & Collier 2012). The goals of TWI programs include academic achievement at or above grade level and development of high levels of proficiency in students' home language as well as their additional language (Howard, Sugarman, & Christian 2003).

DOI 10.1075/lllt.45.06you
© 2016 John Benjamins Publishing Company

The wide range of language proficiencies in most TWI programs creates a challenge for teachers. Both English home language (EHL) students and Spanish home language (SHL) TWI students (who are often U.S.-born and enter school with varying levels of Spanish proficiency) may not be achieving their Spanish language learning potential (Potowski 2007). Teachers struggle to attend to individual language learning needs (Wiese 2004) while at the same time facilitating Spanish language use between peers (Ballinger & Lyster 2011; Potowski 2004).

One strategy to promote Spanish language learning among TWI students with varying proficiency levels is to group them heterogeneously by language background and proficiency. Heterogeneous grouping is recommended in the literature (Carrera-Carillo & Smith 2006; Howard & Christian 2002; Howard, Sugarman, Perdomo, & Temple Ager 2005), apparent in practice (Senesac 2002), and presented as an opportunity to take advantage of the language learning potential created through interaction between "native speakers" and "second language learners." Howard et al. (2005), for example, state that heterogeneous grouping will "…help ensure that all groups will be able to complete the task successfully, and that all individuals within each group will participate and understand what they have done" (142). Other researchers have recommended a variety of grouping strategies (Parkes, Ruth, Anberg-Espinoza, & de Jong 2009), yet there has been relatively little research on how TWI students interact in different small group configurations.

Some studies have shown that TWI students do engage in peer interaction that facilitates language learning (e.g., Angelova, Gunawardena, & Volk 2006; Martin-Beltrán 2010a; Olmedo 2003), and other researchers have called for ways to enhance such interactions (de Jong & Howard 2009). De Jong and Howard (2009), for example, have suggested that, "…the benefits of native/non-native speaker integration must be considered in relationship to its impact on bilingual development, particularly regarding access to and development of the minority language as a first and foreign language" (93). Despite researchers' call for strategies to facilitate increased peer interaction in TWI to enhance bilingual development (e.g., de Jong 2002), to date there have been no studies examining the dynamics of peer interaction specifically during heterogeneous and homogeneous group work in TWI classrooms. The present study responds to this call by analyzing interaction patterns contributing to collaborative dialogue during small group work.

Collaborative dialogue as a scaffold for student learning

Scaffolding – a process that happens when a more able peer "expert" enables a "novice" to carry out a task beyond his or her unassisted efforts (Wood, Bruner, & Ross 1976) – can occur through peer interaction when students participate in collaborative dialogue (CD), or "dialogue that constructs linguistic knowledge" (Swain 2006: 97). While Vygotsky posited that learning is culturally mediated through available "tools" (Rogoff 2003), Swain used CD as a construct to talk about the role interaction plays as one such tool to mediate language learning. The current study uses the construct of CD to explore specifically the role that grouping practices play in promoting peer linguistic scaffolding and peer language modeling.

Proficiency levels, peer interaction and CD

As explained by Sato and Ballinger in the introductory chapter to this volume, a number of studies have examined proficiency level as a mediating variable affecting peer interaction. Relatively few studies have investigated the effects of adolescents' proficiency levels on peer interaction. Kowal and Swain (1994) examined the relationship between proficiency level and collaboration among Grade 8 French immersion students and found students collaborated more when paired homogeneously for proficiency. More proficient students tended to dominate discussion in heterogeneous pairs, thereby producing less collaborative learning environments. Martin-Beltrán (2010b), studying interactions of 5th grade Spanish-English TWI students, highlighted the particular importance of perceived proficiency, defined as "the discursive construction and evaluation of interlocutors' communicative competence" (264). Student participation was constrained and student access to classroom discussions restricted when peers and teachers positioned students as less proficient. Although Martin-Beltrán did not recommend specific grouping strategies, she did argue for orchestrated learning contexts that promote CD and "re-position students as proficient language users" (257). In a study involving Grade 10 learners of English in Chile, Sato and Viveros (2016) found that, in general, learners with lower proficiency engaged in more collaborative behaviors than those with higher proficiency. A qualitative analysis of the interactions led them to conclude that a collaborative mindset may be a stronger mediating factor for L2 development than language proficiency.

While these few studies with adolescent learners (Grade 5, 8, 10) generally found interaction among peers with similar proficiency levels (real or perceived) to be beneficial, studies involving adult learners have yielded different results. Iwashita (2001) found that lower proficient learners interacted more when paired with higher proficient learners and that higher proficient learners modified output more when interacting with peers at a similar level. Similarly, Choi and Iwashita (2016) found that adult low-proficiency learners of English in Australia engaged in more language-related episodes (LREs) that were resolved when they were grouped with high-proficiency learners or a combination of high- and low-proficiency learners than with other low-proficiency learners exclusively. Several studies have shown that adult learners produce more CD in heterogeneous pairs (Kim & McDonough 2008; Watanabe & Swain 2007; Williams 2001). At the same time, Watanabe and Swain (2007) found that learners could benefit from interacting with peers having similar and different proficiency levels provided that the interaction was collaborative. In other words, they claimed that pattern of interaction co-constructed by learners appeared to be more important than proficiency differences per se, similar to Sato and Viveros' (2016) claim that a collaborative mindset is more important. Choi and Iwashita (2016) also reported on the importance of peer relationships and attitudes toward each other's ideas in group work. The complexity of the relationship between proficiency and peer interaction merits close examination in order to determine optimal strategies for facilitating peer linguistic scaffolding in TWI.

Our intent with the present study is to contribute further to our understanding of how proficiency levels and group configurations impact peer interaction. Research questions guiding the study were: How do small group configurations (heterogeneous vs. homogeneous) affect CD? How do these two types of small group configurations hinder or encourage student participation?

Methodology

Theoretical/methodological framework

This study is informed by Vygotsky's theory of mind, or sociocultural theory, which views learners as participants in a developmental process mediated through interaction (Vygotsky 1986). Additionally, this study is informed by Vygotsky's conceptualization of learning as occurring in a Zone of Proximal Development (ZPD) wherein more knowledgeable peers and/or teachers (experts) scaffold a (novice) student's learning. According to Vygotsky (1978) learning is the internalization of the social interaction. Vygotsky (1986) also highlighted peer interaction, termed "conversation," and ways that it leads to student learning. For purposes of this study, it is assumed that CD mediates language learning for each student.

A second framework informing this study is positioning theory (Davis & Harré 1990). Davies and Harré (1990) define 'positioning' as, "the discursive process whereby selves are located in conversations as observably and subjectively coherent participants in jointly produced story lines" (48). Student characteristics, including proficiency levels, may be conceived of as interactionally and discursively negotiated. In applying positioning theory to a 5th grade TWI classroom, Martin-Beltrán (2010b) argues that this theory makes possible an analysis that examines how students are positioned and "how they engage in positioning of self and others" (259). Deictics (linguistic forms providing contextual information regarding person, place, and time) have been used to identify student alignment and positioning in relation to peers (Wortham 2001). For example, words such as "we" and "they" suggest how individuals place themselves in relation to others. Researchers have argued that deictics play a key role in establishing classroom relationships with pronouns such as "we" both "referring to and establishing an interactional group" (Wortham 1996:6). Studies applying positioning theory to language classrooms (Abdi 2011; Talmy 2004) have identified social factors affecting learning environments positively or negatively. There is a need for studies that apply positioning theory to look at specific interactional patterns that affect opportunities for peer interaction during small group work in TWI classrooms.

Setting, data collection, and analysis

The study took place in an urban Midwestern U.S. TWI program. A strand within an English-medium school, this program follows an 85/15 model, meaning students receive 85% of instruction in Spanish and 15% in English in kindergarten with an increase in English instructional time thereafter. The ratio shifts to 50% English, 50% Spanish by Grade 3 and continues as such through Grade 5, the grade level of study participants.

The data examined came from a classroom-based study on form-focused instruction (FFI) during language arts and social studies instruction (Tedick & Young 2014). Targeted linguistic structures for FFI were the Spanish past tense-aspects, imperfect and preterit. As part of the original study, researchers developed activities in which students worked in heterogeneous and homogeneous groups during and after FFI lessons.

To determine Spanish proficiency levels for all students, researchers considered teacher recommendations, a Spanish reading score, and ratings of each student's oral proficiency based on an analysis of transcripts using a modified version of the Foreign Language Oral Skills Evaluation Matrix (FLOSEM), a teacher-rating tool developed and validated at Stanford University (Padilla & Sung 1999). FLOSEM is a 6-level scale that assigns ratings for oral fluency, grammar, vocabulary, pronunciation, and listening comprehension. Scores are then totaled to identify overall proficiency levels ranging from Pre-production (PP, 0-5) to Speech Emergent (SE, 11-15), Low-Intermediate (LI, 16-20), High Intermediate (HI, 21-25), and Advanced/Native-Like (A, 26-30).

For the present study, heterogeneous and homogeneous group work transcripts (16 lessons of 30 to 60 minutes each, captured using four recorders) were coded using first cycle coding (Saldaña 2013) to identify interaction patterns that occurred. Four focal students were then chosen using guidelines for purposeful sampling (Patton 2002). They met the following selection criteria: (1) each represented a key classroom demographic in regards to language proficiency and home language, and (2) students' individual patterns were similar to trends found in interactional patterns across all students in the classroom and did not represent discrepant cases. We selected one focal student at the SE level (EHL), two at LI (one EHL, one SHL), and one at the A level (SHL). Table 1 displays student characteristics. Focal students included two EHL and two SHL students with varying levels of Spanish proficiency in order to explore the relationship between language background, proficiency, and CD during peer interaction.

Table 1. Focal student and peer characteristics

Name	Home language	Free/ reduced lunch	Ethnic/racial background	Spanish reading level[a] /grade level	Spanish proficiency[b]
Focal students					
Hannah	English	yes	African American	below (14)	SE
Anna	English	no	White	below (40)	LI
Julio	Spanish	yes	Hispanic	below (34)	LI
Nadia	Spanish	yes	Hispanic	above (60)	A
Peers grouped with focal students					
Andrés	Spanish	yes	Hispanic	at grade level (50)	HI
Armando	Spanish	yes	Hispanic	above (60)	A
Carlos	Spanish	yes	Hispanic	below (34)	LI
Cristina	Spanish	yes	Hispanic	at (50)	A
Diego	Spanish	yes	Hispanic	at (50)	HI
Elena	Spanish	yes	Hispanic	above (60)	A
Irene	Spanish	partial	Hispanic	above (60)	A
José Antonio	Spanish	yes	Hispanic	at (50)	LI
Juliana	Spanish	yes	Hispanic	above (60)	A
Lorena	Spanish	yes	Hispanic	at (50)	A
Paco	Spanish	partial	Hispanic	at (50)	HI
Peggy	English	yes	White	below (20)	SE
Theresa	English	yes	African American	below (28)	SE

[a]   Reading level determined by the EDL2 (Spanish version of DRA) (50=grade level)

[b]   Oral proficiency as determined by the modified FLOSEM

Two homogeneous (40 minutes total) and two heterogeneous (40 minutes total) group work sessions were selected for each focal student from the existing data set. These 16 interactions (a total of 80 minutes per focal student) were chosen because they generally represented typical patterns found in the data set. The chosen interactions then underwent second cycle coding (Saldaña 2013) which first involved identifying incidents of CD during heterogeneous and homogeneous group activities. In order to determine the frequency of CD incidents during each period of group work, selected transcripts were coded for interactions showing examples of CD in which focal students participated in co-constructing language knowledge. CD incidents were identified as language-related episodes (LREs) (e.g., Swain, Brooks, & Tocalli-Beller 2002) in which focal students collaboratively used language to discuss form (morphology, grammar, syntax or discourse) or lexis (vocabulary, spelling) during their interactions (Swain & Lapkin 2001; see also Choi & Iwashita 2016; Fernández Dobao 2016). Examples include:

(1) Form-based, morphology:
     Student A: *Ella es pintora.* (She is a painter.)
     Student B: *Era.* (Was.)
     Student A: *Era. Pintora.* (Was. A painter.)

(2) Lexis-based, spelling:
     Student A: *Usaban. ¿Cómo escribes hielo?* (Used. How do you spell ice?)
     Student B: *hi. elo.*
     Student C: *h.*
     Student B: *h-i-e-l-o.*

(3) Lexis-based, vocabulary:
     Student A: *No entiendo golpecitos.... ¿Cómo galope?* (I don't understand tapping. Like gallop? [incorrect word])
     Student B: *No galope. Golpe. Como si te pegan.* (Not gallop. Hit. Like if they hit you.)
     Student C: *Aha. Así.* (Aha. Like this.)
     Student B: *Si te pegan o les pegas.* (If they hit you or you hit them.)

For each focal student, the number of total minutes of student interaction in the data set was divided by the number of identified CD incidents. This measure provides an overall picture of the relative occurrence of CD during homogeneous and heterogeneous group work.

A micro discourse analysis was then conducted to identify positioning patterns that appeared to scaffold focal student learning or to constrain it. Informed by positioning theory (Davis & Harré 1990), the micro discourse analysis examined how students positioned self and others through discursive patterns during peer interaction. This analysis of transcripts was completed for each focal student (as a unit of analysis) (see Appendix for transcription conventions). Using open to axial coding (Corbin & Strauss 2008), the transcripts were coded by recursively (1) reading through each transcript repeatedly to identify salient issues in the data set, and then (2) closely rereading discourse related to acts of positioning and specific categories identified for each focal student. Data sources also included two interviews with the teacher, one before and one following data collection.

Findings

Preliminary analysis of status positioning in relation to CD

As seen in Table 2, for all focal students there were more episodes of CD during homogeneous group activities. All focal students engaged in CD on average every three minutes during homogenous group work whereas during heterogeneous group work they engaged in CD on average once every seven to 20 minutes. Although all focal students participated in more episodes of CD during homogeneous small group work than during heterogeneous work, each focal student exhibited unique interactional patterns that reflected differences in their CD episodes. Micro discourse analysis provides a closer look at how each focal student interacted with peers during group work and illustrates themes representing episodes of peer linguistic scaffolding and language modeling.

Table 2. CD episodes among focal students during heterogeneous and homogeneous small group work

Name	Home language	Spanish oral proficiency	Average CD during homogeneous group work	Average CD during heterogeneous group work
Hannah	English	SE	1 per 3 minutes	1 per 12 minutes
Anna	English	LI	1 per 3 minutes	1 per 7 minutes
Julio	Spanish	LI	1 per 3 minutes	1 per 18 minutes
Nadia	Spanish	A	1 per 3 minutes	1 per 20 minutes

Micro discourse analysis

Individual focal student interaction patterns that may have led to differences during homogeneous and heterogeneous group activities are presented with examples from the data set. While all focal students appeared to participate in more CD during homogeneous group work, specific factors affecting participation differed for each.

Hannah in homogeneous group: co-creation of meaning with peer scaffolding

Hannah (EHL, SE) had very low Spanish proficiency (SE), despite having participated in the TWI program since kindergarten. One of only two African American students in the class, Hannah was performing well below grade level in both English and Spanish. During homogeneous group work with Theresa (EHL, SE) and Peggy (EHL, SE), however, she interacted with fairly even turn-taking (albeit producing many utterances in English). During one 20-minute session, for example, Hannah produced 70 turns, Theresa 55, and Peggy 82, all equally dispersed throughout the activity. Although there was an apparent struggle for initial control of the process, Hannah's homogeneous team scaffolded each other's learning through their interaction. The similarity of proficiency levels appears to have legitimated the students' equal participation in the learning process, promoting "respect" for linguistic expertise (Kowal & Swain 1994) and facilitating more collaborative interaction patterns in which students adjusted their language to facilitate acquisition (Angelova et al. 2006; Olmedo 2003).

In Excerpt 1, Hannah was comparing her answers with her group members'. The students were categorizing verbs found in a reading. Their use of deictics such as "let's" and "we" (turns 8, 11, 14) indicated that the group positioned themselves as a collective of individuals working together to co-create meaning. The students can be seen giving and receiving information leading to proficiency-level appropriate CD, such as when Theresa assisted Peggy in identifying the word they were writing (turn 3) and Hannah repeated the word as she wrote it (turn 5). The students also negotiated whether they were finished with the task and agreed to continue working. The girls shared control to complete the task. They took direction from one another, giving and accepting feedback and suggestions. They began to speak in unison, as seen towards the end of the excerpt (turns 14, 15).

Excerpt 1

1.	Hannah: did you write this one?	
2.	Theresa: *¿iba, iba y?*	Theresa: went, went, and?
3.	Peggy: *admimiraba*	Peggy: admired (mispronounced)
4.	Theresa: *admiraba*	Theresa: admired
5.	Hannah: *ad. mir.*	Hannah: ad. mir.
6.	Peggy: *ok. amarillo* (pages turning)	Peggy: ok. yellow.
7.	Theresa: *ya.*	Theresa: ok.
8.	Peggy: ok. let's (incomprehensible)	
9.	Theresa: *y fue.*	Theresa: and went.
10.	Peggy: *no. ya tenemos.*	Peggy: no. we already have that one.
11.	Hannah: we don't have all of them.	
12.	Theresa: *no, verdad.*	Theresa: no, right.

13. Hannah: *ok. um.*	
14. Peggy. *ok. we start here. so we gotta go* [apodaron.	Peggy. *ok. we start here. so we gotta go* [nicknamed.
15. Hannah: [apodaron.	Hannah: [nicknamed.

Hannah in heterogeneous group: positioned as nonparticipant/ silenced through peer feedback

In contrast to the equal participation that Hannah experienced during homogeneous group activities, during heterogeneous work Hannah was marginalized. The other students in her group, Juliana (SHL, A) and Andrés (SHL, HI), positioned her as a less able group member and mocked some of her attempts at participation. It is important to note that the teacher had directed all students to provide each other with corrective feedback during the heterogeneous group work that occurred after the FFI lessons in the original study from which this data set was drawn.[1] In these groups, students took turns reading aloud to each other, clarifying which words they didn't understand, and identifying main ideas. Hannah's group members saw her as a less able member and enacted their perceived superior proficiency by eliminating any attempts at "brokering" (Martin-Beltrán 2010; Olmedo 2003) or co-constructing (Angelova et al. 2006) language development. Instead of scaffolding Hannah's learning, Juliana and Andrés corrected her on nearly every word she read and then aligned themselves with each other (using "we" referring to themselves and "she" referring to Hannah, as seen in turns 10, 11, 21 in Excerpt 2). They also used commands to indicate their control during the activity (turns 6, 10, 17, 21). Juliana and Andrés began to discuss with each other how best to give peer feedback to Hannah (turns 10, 11). The marginalization that occurred during the interactions communicated a clear message that Andrés and Juliana were "expert" speakers and learners with control over the task and Hannah was a "novice" speaker/learner.

Excerpt 2

1. Hannah: *veinte cuando apa:re:ce, aparecieron-* (reading slowly)	Hannah: twenty when they appe:, appeared
2. Andrés: (groans)	
3. Hannah: *auto: movilos-*	Hannah: auto: movilos-

---

1.   Researchers were not present when the teacher instructed students to give each other corrective feedback during heterogeneous interactions. We are, therefore, unsure of exactly how students were taught to do this.

4.	Juliana: *¿automóvilos o automóviles?* (speaks louder)	Juliana: automobiles (mispronounced) or automobiles?
5.	Hannah: *las personas.*	Hannah: the people.
6.	Andrés: *léelo otra vez.*	Andrés: read it again.
7.	Juliana: *sí. ¿dice automovoles o automóviles?*	Juliana: yes. does it say automobiles (mispronounced) or automobiles?
8.	Hannah: *automóviles. los personas.*	Hannah: automobiles. the people.
9.	Juliana: *¿los? ¿o las?* (raising her voice)	Juliana: the (los)? or the (las)?
10.	Andrés: *es que léelo. estamos dándole la repuesta*	Andrés: just read it. we are giving her the answer.
11.	Juliana: *oh. sí es cierto. tiene la pregunta. porque si no, no va a saber.*	Juliana: oh. yes you are right. she has the question. if not, she won't know.
12.	Andrés: *yeah. ya puedes leer.*	Andrés: *yeah.* now you can read.
13.	Juliana: *disculpa.*	Juliana: sorry.
14.	Hannah: *la, las personajes.*	Hannah: the characters.
15.	Juliana: *persona.*	Juliana: person.
16.	Andrés: *ahorita. otra vez.*	Andrés: right now. again.
17.	Juliana: *otra vez. léele.*	Juliana: again. read it again.
18.	Hannah: *pensaba que los-*	Hannah: it was thought that the-
19.	Juliana: *los?*	Juliana: the?
20.	Hannah: *las costos podían mejorar mucho-* (reading slowly).	Hannah: the costs could improve-
21.	Juliana: *vuélvalo a leer. dijo prácticas.*	Juliana: read it again. she said practice.

Whereas Hannah interacted with her homogeneous group as a capable peer, her heterogeneous group peers positioned her as incompetent. Their interactions reinforced the existing classroom expert/novice hierarchy instead of promoting more collaborative roles that could have afforded transformative learning (Vygotsky 1986). Large proficiency differences may have affected expert roles claimed by Juliana and Andrés as well as students' attempts to use corrective feedback during interactions. CD during heterogeneous group interaction occurred once every 12 minutes and mainly concerned Hannah's pronunciation (turns 7, 8) and lexis (with a few instances focused on form). The low frequency of CD was contrary to the teacher's belief that more proficient students would scaffold learning for learners with low proficiency. In her second interview she said:

> [I chose heterogeneous grouping] … because of how [speech emergent students] are reading, it was helpful to have them heterogeneously placed, so that they could have support in, "What does this word mean? What is it that I'm reading?"

The teacher's directive to students to provide each other with peer feedback during heterogeneous group work may have led to Juliana and Andrés to position Hannah as a novice.

Anna in homogeneous group: on-going collaborative dialogue

In Excerpt 3, Anna (EHL, LI) worked with students having similar proficiencies to identify important ideas about Frida Kahlo's life, which they had learned from a biography. Anna, a white student who had been in the program since kindergarten, was the only student who did not receive free/reduced price lunch (a proxy for low socioeconomic status) and had the highest Spanish proficiency level of the EHL students. Excerpts reveal Anna participated about every 4th or 5th turn during work with peers having similar proficiency (Peggy-EHL, SE;[2] José Antonio-SHL, LI; Carlos-SHL, LI; Julio-SHL, LI). Students enacted collaborative interaction patterns that would support Vygotsky's (1978) assertion that learning occurs, "only when the child is interacting with people in his environment and in cooperation with his peers" (90). In Excerpt 3, the group determined whether to use present or past tense when writing about Frida Kahlo's polio. Participation was fairly equal, with students defending their answers and using everyone's contributions to agree on an answer.

Excerpt 3

1.	Anna: *que Frida sacó el (incomprehensible) o ¿qué sacó?*	Anna: so Frida got (incomprehensible) or what did she get?
2.	Peggy: *que ella tenía el polio.*	Peggy: she had polio.
3.	Carlos: *ella.*	Carlos: she.
4.	Peggy: *no, ella.*	Peggy: no, she.
5.	Carlos: *ella tenía polio.*	Carlos: she had polio.
6.	Peggy: *¡tiene polio!*	Peggy: she has polio!
7.	Anna: *tenía.*	Anna: she had.
8.	José Antonio: *tenía.*	José Antonio: she had.
9.	Peggy: *ok. ella tenía*	Peggy: ok. she had

Anna in heterogeneous group: silenced by being ignored

Although Anna was an active participant in homogeneous group discussions, her participation decreased dramatically during heterogeneous interactions. Anna contributed 36 out of 171 turns during one 20-minute homogeneous group activity. In contrast, she only produced 10 of 82 student turns during a 20-minute heterogeneous group interaction [as compared to her peers: 41 total turns by Armando (SHL, A) and 31 by Diego (SHL, HI)]. Two of her turns were short clarification questions (*Diego, ¿por qué?* and *¿Qué página?*). Four turns were responses

---

2. Peggy was not typically a member of Anna's homogeneous group but joined it on this particular day because both her group members were absent.

to teacher prompts, and two were requests for vocabulary definitions. Only two of Anna's turns in this interaction were actual contributions to task completion.

During this heterogeneous group activity, she positioned herself as a novice through questioning and repetition of peer responses. Anna and her group members implicitly evaluated their perceived proficiency levels (Martin-Beltrán 2010) and enacted roles accordingly. In Excerpt 4, one of Anna's few comments (turn 3) reinforced expert positioning of Armando, the advanced speaker.

Excerpt 4

1.	Armando: *yo creo que traían. a hielo. o buscaban cuevas.*	Armando: I think that they brought. ice. or they looked for caves.
2.	Diego: *¿tú qué piensas?*	Diego: what do you think?
3.	Anna: *pienso como que, que dijo Armando.*	Anna: I think that, what Armando said.

Later during discussion on that same day, Anna participated only minimally during a 2- to 3-minute interactional sequence (Excerpt 5). And she even used some English, which was very atypical for her.

Excerpt 5

1.	Diego: *ya. ¿qué logró Clarence Birdseye?*	Diego: ok. what did Clarence Birdseye achieve?
2.	Anna: *what?*	
3.	Diego: *¿qué logró Clarence Birdseye?*	Diego: what did Clarence Birdseye achieve?
4.	Armando: *Birdseye.*	Armando: *Birdseye.*
5.	Diego: *yo creo que dice en el primer párrafo lo que logró.*	Diego: I think that it says in the first paragraph what he achieved.
6.	Armando: *aha. (reads.) allí está.*	Armando: aha. (reads) there it is.
7.	Diego: *pero hay que hacerlo más cortito.*	Diego: but we need to make it shorter.
8.	Armando: *ok.*	Armando: *ok.*
9.	Diego: *um. inventó un.*	Diego: um. he invented a.
10.	Armando: *¡no! desarrolló un método de congelado rápido.*	Armando: no! he developed a method for quick freezing.
11.	Diego: *ok.*	Diego: *ok.*
12.	Armando: *de alimentos.*	Armando: for food.
13.	Diego: *no. ¡de alimentos no!*	Diego: no. for food no!
14.	Armando: *sí. de alimentos. y luego dice para que la comida blah: y para que esto también.*	Armando: yes. for food. and then it says that the food blah: and for that too.
15.	Diego: *um. yo estoy acuerdo con eso.*	Diego: um. I agree with that.
16.	Armando: *para hacerlo más corto sólo escribes desarrolló un método rápido de congelamiento de alimentos.*	Armando: to make it shorter, just write developed a method for quick freezing food.
17.	Anna: *sí.*	Anna: yes.
18.	Diego: *ok.*	Diego: *ok.*

Armando and Diego spent almost five minutes co-constructing a written answer for the question they were working on during the activity, and Anna did not participate at all during this time. It should be noted that Anna's lack of participation does not necessarily mean that she learned nothing at all from the interaction. In a study with university-level learners of Spanish, Fernández Dobao (2016) found that learners who remained silent during group work still benefited from the lexis-based LREs that were produced by other group members. Nevertheless, Kowal and Swain (1994) assert that highly heterogeneous groups may constrain interaction due to "too much of a discrepancy" (85) in language competence when students' language learning needs are not within each other's zones of proximal development. Moreover, our data suggest that *enacted* perceived proficiency may affect interaction patterns as much as *actual* proficiency differences. The added complexity of TWI programs, where students are both second and heritage language learners, may render perceived proficiency especially important.

Julio in homogeneous group: trajectory of biliterate proficiency

Julio (SHL, LI) was one of the least proficient SHL students in the class, despite having been in the program since kindergarten. His lack of Spanish proficiency may have been related to a language delay when he was younger (which the teacher shared during the initial interview) or it could have been related to the trend towards English dominance that many SHL students experience despite TWI participation (Potowski 2007). During homogeneous group work, Julio worked with Anna (EHL, LI), José Antonio (SHL, LI), and Carlos (SHL, LI). As seen in Excerpt 6, Julio facilitated participation by asking the next question (turn 1), clarifying the focus of the question (turn 7), and later reminding Anna to weigh in (turn 9). This excerpt shows how students supported each other's learning through peer teaching strategies (Angelova et al. 2006) including prompts, cues, repetition, and corrective feedback.

Excerpt 6

1.	Julio: *¿cuándo vivió?*	Julio: when did she live?
2.	Anna: *um... como... nada más una vez en el.*	Anna: um. like. only one time.
3.	José Antonio: *vivió*	José Antonio: she lived (preterit)
4.	Carlos: *en México.*	Carlos: in Mexico.
5.	José Antonio: *¡ah! ¡en México!*	José Antonio: ah! in Mexico!
6.	Anna: *en México. sí.*	Anna: in Mexico. right.
7.	Julio: *no. ¿cuándo?*	Julio: no. when?

8.	Carlos: *viví, viviera.* wait, *vivió.*	Carlos: (I) lived, lived (subjunctive). wait, lived.
9.	Julio: (whispering) *¡Anna!*	Julio: Anna!
10.	Anna: Huh? *vivió.*	Anna: Huh? lived.

Julio in heterogeneous group: linguistic bullying and potential for language attrition

During heterogeneous group work, Julio (SHL, LI) was grouped with Lorena (SHL, A) and Cristina (SHL, A), who were both at grade level in Spanish. While his peers did not ignore or silence him (in the manner that Anna was ignored and Hannah was silenced), they ridiculed him extensively, perhaps due to his lower Spanish proficiency level. While young students have been shown to be "sensitive to language skills of their peers" (Olmedo 2003: 143), in this case the more proficient students used this sensitivity not to adjust their language and mediate comprehension, but instead to discourage participation of "non-legitimate" speakers (Martin-Beltrán 2010).

Although the frequency of Julio's contributions was similar in both homogeneous and heterogeneous groups, the nature of the interactions differed considerably. Excerpt 7 is an example of a pattern that emerged where Lorena and Cristina positioned themselves as experts, and Julio wavered back and forth between accepting and resisting the role of novice. Julio began to read to the group after having been corrected repeatedly during the previous 25 minutes. He began his turn at reading with extended hedges and pauses. When he faltered with the word *producir* (turn 1), he was quickly corrected by Lorena, who followed her correction with a sarcastic, "you're welcome" (turn 2). Julio then emphatically asked the group to allow him to figure out the language by himself, implying he did not want their corrective feedback (turn 3). Nevertheless, both girls chose to correct the manner in which he made this request (turns 4) and continued to correct his pronunciation and errors thereafter. They also laughed at his mistakes (turns 4, 6, 10, 11, 13, 14).

Excerpt 7

1.	Julio: *ok. hm. hm. hm. ah. como los carros ahora podían po: ro: do: cir=*	Julio: ok. hm. hm. hm. ah. since the cars now could po: pro: ro: du: ce=
2.	Lorena: *=producirse. ¿pro. du. cir. se? de nada.*	Lorena: =produced. pro. du. ced? you're welcome
3.	Julio: *yo lo necesito decir, <u>mi</u> mismo.*	Julio: I need to say it, <u>me</u> myself.
4.	Cristina: *(hhh) <u>yo</u> mismo.*	Cristina: (hhh) <u>myself.</u>
5.	Julio: <u>*dije eso.*</u>	Julio: <u>that is what I said.</u>

6.	Lorena: *mi mismo. (hhh)=*
7.	Julio: *=ok. um. "se basa en un. pe:riodo junto, el costo de, los, automóviles bajo de, y muchas personas, pu:dieron com- c:om. pra:r." °comprar° no.*
8.	Lorena: *tu mismo.*
9.	Julio: *era bien vencido más de.*
10.	Cristina: *vendido.* [(hhh)
11.	Lorena: [(hhh)
12.	Julio: *yo necesito decir.* [*mi mismo.*
13.	Lorena: [*yo =*[*mismo. (hhh)*
14.	Cristina: [*yo =*[*¡mismo!* (hhh)
15.	Julio: =[*yo mismo. a:h.*
16.	Cristina: *ok. pues.*

	Lorena: me myself. [(hhh) =
	Julio: =ok. um. it was based on a. pe:riod together, the low cost of, the, automobiles of, and a lot of people, cou:ld bu- bu:y. °buy° no.
	Lorena: yourself.
	Julio: it was overcome more than.
	Cristina: sold [(hhh)
	Lorena: [(hhh)
	Julio: I need to say. [me myself.
	Lorena: [myself (hhh)
	Cristina: [myself! (hhh)
	Julio: =[myself. a:h.
	Cristina: ok. then.

Lorena and Cristina also aligned themselves with each other through their co-creation of expert voice. This was illustrated by their simultaneous overlapping as well as the supportive comments and laughter they provided each other (turns 10–14). The girls defiantly positioned themselves as experts as reflected in their disregard for Julio's requests and their relentless corrections. At the start of Excerpt 8, Cristina interrupted Julio and told him to stop reading, then changed her mind and asked him to continue, scaffolding the reading for him with a sentence starter "it wasn't…" (turn 1). Julio, after complaining ("oh man"), continued to read (turn 2). He demanded to know why the girls were laughing (turn 5) as they used simultaneous laughter and repetition as a pejorative form of corrective feedback when he mispronounced the word "necessary" (turns 3, 4, 6, 7, 9, 10, 14).

Excerpt 8

1.	Cristina: *ya. oh. un poco más. ¿ya no…?*
2.	Julio: °*o:h man*° ha. *ya no era necesisario del el=*
3.	Lorena: =[(hhh)
4.	Cristina: =[(hhh)
5.	Julio: *¿ahora de qué se están riendo?*
6.	Lorena: [*necesisario.* (hhh)
7.	Cristina: [*necesisario.* (hhh)
8.	Julio: a:h. *necesisario.*
9.	Lorena: [(hhh)
10.	Cristina: [(hhh)
11.	Julio: *¿qué?*
12.	Lorena: *ne:ce:sa:rio.*

	Cristina: that's enough. oh. a little more. it wasn't…?
	Julio: °o:h man° it wasn't nececcessary for the= [reading]
	Lorena: =[(hhh)
	Cristina: =[(hhh)
	Julio: now what are you both laughing at?
	Lorena: [nececcessary. (hhh)
	Cristina: [nececcessary. (hhh)
	Julio: o:h. nececcessary.
	Julio: what?
	Lorena: ne:ce:ssa:ry.

13. Julio: *dije eso. a:h.*	Julio: I said that. oh.
14. Lorena: *no. necesesario.* (hhh)	Lorena: no. nececcessary. (hhh)
15. Julio: *ne:ce:sario. depende. del importe el público puede vivir rápido.* (reading) *a:h.*	Julio: ne:ce:ssary. depends on. the importance the public gives to living quickly. [reading] a:h.
16. Lorena: *viajar.* (hhh)=	Lorena: traveling. (hhh)=
17. Cristina: *=ya. ya no te vamos a corregir ya. ¿ok? ¿de qué se trató?*	Cristina: enough. we are not going to correct you anymore. ok? what was this about?

In turn 17 Cristina acknowledged the dynamic occurring, although this time she used the first person plural (we) to let him know that she and Lorena will no longer correct him. Through use of deictics, we can see more clearly how Lorena and Cristina aligned themselves in opposition to Julio. Olmedo (2003) has introduced the term "bilingual echo" as a metaphor for the process by which bilingual children "make judgments about the bilingual proficiency of their peers" and "provide scaffolds to maximize communication of their peers" (143). However, in these examples, the students' enactment of "(il)legitimate speakers" restrained Julio's access to learning experiences and opportunities for collaborative dialogue. Martin-Beltrán (2010) has argued that this positioning of (non)legitimacy has direct consequences to affordances for language learning.

Nadia in homogeneous group: resistance to "expert" positioning

Nadia (SHL, A) was above grade level in both English and Spanish and was always eager to participate during large and small group interactions. She often attempted to position herself as expert during small group interactions. However, when she worked within the homogeneous group of other SHL advanced speakers, she found that her peers pushed back on her attempts to appropriate the task and take on the teacher role. Their resistance to her expert role may have increased their own opportunities to play the role of expert and facilitated Nadia's linguistic "respect" for her peers. Respect can facilitate language learning in that, "participants must trust one another's opinions and all participants need to be considered as playing a legitimate role in the learning process" (Kowal & Swain 1994: 86). She initially worked very hard to ingratiate herself with her peers, as seen in turns 2 and 4 of Excerpt 9. Later, as Nadia and Juliana (SHL, A) discussed a point and presented hypotheses about what differences could be between the imperfect and preterit verbs identified in the reading, Armando (SHL, A) resisted Nadia positioning herself as expert (turn 8). A few minutes later he again rejected her attempts to control the activity (turn 9).

Excerpt 9

1. Juliana: *a:h. y algo que yo noté que con las palabras verdes, los de imperfecto, que casi todas terminan en "a" o "ían" como i, a, n o a, n.*

   Juliana: o:h. and something that I noticed was that all of the green words, the imperfect ones, almost all of them end in "a" or in "ían" like i, a, or a, n.

2. Nadia: *¡muy bien Juliana! ¡muy bien! ¡excelente!*

   Nadia: very good, Juliana! very good! excellent!

3. Armando: *bravo.* (sarcastically.)

   Armando: *bravo.*

4. Nadia: *no, es que está muy bien. ¡bravo!* (clapping) *muy bien.*

   Nadia: no it's that it is very good. bravo! very good.

   …   …

5. Juliana: *no, yo no tampoco. ¿pero alguien tiene alguna diferencia para la de imperfecto en vez de como que terminan en la misma palabra? como que probablemente que estaba en el pasado para ver si en el presente, ¿algo así?*

   Juliana: no, me neither. but does someone have something different for imperfect instead of that it ends in the same word? like probably that it was in the past to see if it is in the present. something like that?

6. Nadia: *yo tengo que, ¿se notaron que la mayoría de las palabras terminan en la palabra "a"? ¿del, del imperfecto?*

   Nadia: I have that, did you notice that the majority of the words end in the letter 'a'? the imperfect ones?

7. Armando: I don't know. Smarty pants.

   …   …

8. Nadia: *¿ya terminaste, Irene?¿ya terminaste, Armando?*

   Nadia: did you finish yet, Irene? did you finish yet, Armando?

9. Armando: *¡ya me preguntaste eso como mil veces!*

   Armando: you already asked me that like a thousand times!

10. Nadia: *ok. no te enojes.*

    Nadia: ok. don't get mad.

Later on students worked together to construct an explanation of their common understanding of the grammatical concepts. Their increased positioning of fluid expert and novice roles appeared to lead to their ability to co-construct new meaning using CD (Excerpt 10).

Excerpt 10

1. Nadia: *que ganaba era que ganaba muchas veces.*

   Nadia: that won (imperfect) was that he won many times.

2. Juliana: *y ganó es que nada más esa vez.*

   Juliana: and won (preterit) is just that one time.

   …   …

3. Armando: *¡oh! ¡yo sé! que ganó, ganaba, ganó. ¡es casi lo mismo!*

   Armando: oh! I see! that won (preterit), won (imperfect), won (preterit). it is almost the same thing!

On another day, the group worked to review peer writing on flipchart paper and to identify possible corrections to what they judged to be inaccurate. The discussion about language in Excerpt 11 shows participants (a group of advanced students including Elena-SHL, A) were experiencing high levels of fluidity between expert and novice roles and student scaffolding of language.

Excerpt 11

1.	Nadia: (reading) "...*en 1993 tras una huelga de hambre que duró 36 días.*" *el verbo es duró, y es um... °pretérito°.*	Nadia: in 1993 a hunger strike lasted 36 days. the verb is lasted. and it is. um. °preterit°.
2.	Elena: (reading) "*Carlos Chávez tenía una esposa llamada Elena.*"	Elena: "Carlos Chávez had a wife named Elena."
3.	Armando: *tenía.*	Armando: had.
4.	Nadia: *tenía es la acción.*	Nadia: had is the action.
5.	Juliana: *es que la tuvo por. lo siguió haciendo, no por un tiempo y la rechazó.*	Juliana: it's that he had her for. he continued doing it. not for a time and then he rejected her.
6.	Nadia: *¿entonces pretérito?*	Nadia: so preterit?
7.	Juliana: *es imperfecto.*	Juliana: it's imperfect.
8.	Armando: *¡oh! sí, sí porque sigue pasando.*	Armando: oh. yes. yes because it continues happening.

Nadia in heterogeneous: excessive languaging

In contrast to Nadia's homogeneous group interactions, when Nadia worked with her heterogeneous group, she used her expert positioning to dominate task direction, appropriating the task and taking on the role of teacher. While at times she included her peers, Paco (SHL, HI) and Carlos (SHL, LI), and CD did occur (turn 17) occasionally, she often tried to control their learning and impose her own ideas. This led to what could be called, "excessive languaging" in that she used language to mediate her own thinking and in so doing often confused the other members of her team, who appeared to assume what she said was the correct answer, given her expert positioning. Nadia's languaging in turn 4 shows how while "language serves as a vehicle through which thinking is articulated" (Swain 2006: 97), her extensive explanation of her thinking may have confused her less proficient peers. In Excerpt 12 she used a number of commands to impose her will on task completion (turns 4, 9, 11). Although Paco attempted to follow her instructions, her excessive languaging likely confused him, leading Nadia eventually to enlist Carlos' help to get Paco to erase all of the writing he had completed (turns 11, 17, 18).

Excerpt 12

1.	Nadia: *a ver. ¿lo puedes leer lo que escribiste? por favor.*	Nadia: let's see. can you read what you wrote? please.
2.	Paco: *la gente exploraba cuevas frescas para su comida.*	Paco: people explored cool caves for their food.
3.	Carlos: *y arroyos. y.*	Carlos: and streams. and.
4.	Nadia: *eh. y. y.* (incomprehensible) *decía, mira decía que si no había hielo en algún lugar buscaban cuevas frescas,* (incomprehensible), *sótanos o almacenaban la comida envuelta en un lago frío o en el corriente de algún arroyo. tienes que escribir eso. porque eso es lo que te ayuda a conservar la, para contestar la pregunta de conservar, puedes decir. también caba. sótanos, almacenaban la comida envuelta en un lago frío o en el corriente de algún arroyo. buscaban cuevas frescas. es decir.*	Nadia: um. and. and. (incomprehensible) it said, look it said that if there wasn't any ice in the place then they would look for cool caves. (incomprehensible), basements or they kept their food covered in a cool lake or in the current of a stream. you have to write this. because that is what helps you to conserve it, to answer the question of what to conserve, you can say that. also each basement, they kept the food wrapped up in a cold lake or in the current of a stream. they looked for cool caves. that is to say.
5.	(The group is silent while Paco writes.)	
6.	Nadia: *aquí dice Paco. en el, tu, en tu paquete.*	Nadia: here it says Paco. in the, your, in your packet.
7.	Paco: *la gente exploraba cuevas o en ríos fríos, ríos frías.*	Paco: people explored caves and cold rivers, rivers that were cold (incorrect gender).
8.	Nadia: *fríos. y almacenaban la comida envuelta en un lago fr, un lago frío es lo que dicen o en la corriente de algún arroyo. al. macenaba. al.*	Nadia: cold (corrects gender). and the kept food covered in lakes that were co- a cold lake is what they say or in the current of a stream. sto. red.
9.	Paco: *al.*	Paco: sto.
10.	Nadia: *no:. a ver. déjame ver lo que escribiste. y que. no sólo tiene sentido. la gente. explo. explora. bórrale.*	Nadia: no. let's see. let me see what you wrote. and that it doesn't make sense. the people. explo. explored. erase that.
11.	Paco: *¿todo?*	Paco: all of it?
12.	Nadia: *¿verdad? Carlos. ¿crees que se está bien? a ver. léelo. tú a ver si está bien. yo no.*	Nadia: right? Carlos. do you think it is ok? let's see. read it. you to see if it is ok. not me.
13.	Carlos: *la gente explora.*	Carlos: people explore.
14.	Nadia: *exploró.*	Nadia: explored.
15.	Carlos: *aha.*	Carlos: aha.
16.	Nadia: *explora.*	Nadia: explore.
17.	Carlos: *porque explora es como ahorita.*	Carlos: because explore is like right now.
18.	Nadia: *ve, ¿crees que tu, que lo tenga que, tiene que hacerlo de nuevo? como así para=*	Nadia: see. do you think that you, that he should, he has to do it over again? like this so that-
19.	Carlos: *=u:m. si. como para hacerlo mejor.* (Paco can be heard erasing.)	Carlos: =u:m. yes. like to do it better.

By implicitly positioning Nadia as the identified expert in this heterogeneous group configuration, the other SHL students were surprisingly positioned as non-expert participants despite their Spanish language abilities. It is important to remember that even students from the same language background working together can become excluded from the discourse community when pedagogy facilitates "social positioning and accommodation practices [that perpetuate] the discursive construction of proficiency" (Martin-Beltrán 2010: 265).

Discussion/implications

Pedagogical implications: The false promise of heterogeneous grouping

A deep understanding of small group work is especially important in TWI programs. Purposeful use of heterogeneous and homogeneous groups can help teachers take advantage of the diversity of language proficiency and backgrounds (Commins & Miramontes 2005) but can lead to positive or negative experiences for language learners. It is helpful to look at how students and teachers enact expert and novice roles during their interactions and mediate learning through their interactions. Teachers and administrators may assume heterogeneous grouping will lead to more student participation in TWI programs. However, if teachers are not aware of potential pitfalls during heterogeneous group construction, students may experience less positive group interactional patterns and participate in less CD.

At the same time, there are strategies teachers can use to increase student participation in heterogeneous group work. The teacher in this study, for example, often used visual charts with examples of target language forms posted in the room to assist students. Students referred to them during their interactions, and these scaffolds helped to increase their ability to participate as equal members during the activity. The teacher also provided word banks and sentence starters that helped homogeneous groups to work without teacher assistance and this, in turn, helped students prepare material that could later be shared in their heterogeneous groups.

Nevertheless, strategies that negatively affected positioning were also present. The teacher questioned students during their group work to check comprehension. To do this, she often chose to call on the student who she felt was most in need of assistance. This strategy appeared to clearly identify to each group who was the weakest student. She also assumed more proficient speakers should be assigned "facilitator" roles that exacerbated unequal status in each group. Facilitators often assumed a teacher stance that at times led to excessive languaging (assuming more proficient students had the "right" answer) and silencing of students who were less proficient.

Additionally, instruction to provide peer feedback in heterogeneous group activities appeared to lead to an over- or mis-application of feedback. Less proficient students were not allowed to express their ideas or read aloud to the group without explicit corrections of their grammar or pronunciation. This over- or mis-use of peer feedback both positioned certain students as novices and served as a tool to silence them. Although some less proficient students resisted such positioning, in general peer feedback appeared to cause conflict and a culture of silencing during these activities.

As explained previously, the teacher assigned heterogeneous groups for tasks involving reading a challenging text, and explained she believed more proficient speakers would be able to assist less proficient speakers in comprehending. This assumption – that heterogeneous groups will naturally lead to peer assistance – may reflect a "false promise" of heterogeneous grouping unless teachers carefully prepare students for and carefully structure the activity.

Perhaps if the teacher had provided more scaffolds for students (visual charts, word banks, sentence starters for answers, shorter text excerpts, different questions) or if she had differentiated readings (same topic, different readings for various levels), heterogeneous group activities would have been more successful and would have led to more equal participation and increased CD. She could have also adjusted role assignments (not have more proficient students as facilitators) or rethought implementation of peer feedback during that activity. Although we know certain types of corrective feedback can lead to increased student learning (e.g., Lyster, Saito, & Sato 2013), we may need to look more carefully at effects of peer feedback during small group interaction (Ballinger 2013), especially with diverse proficiency levels and language backgrounds. It will be important in future research to look at ways in which classroom dynamics during interactive tasks facilitate participation for linguistically diverse learners.

Like other studies presented in this volume (e.g., Choi & Iwashita and Sato & Viveros), the analysis summarized in this chapter revealed that other factors interact with language proficiency to mediate peer interaction. Perhaps just as important as, if not more important than, language proficiency are students' perceptions of each other as proficient and capable learners and the types of relationships that form among students during peer interaction.

Limitations

Because this was a classroom-based study, there was a high degree of variability in student participation during group work. Students were at times absent; thus, group dynamics would change, groups were merged, or group members were shifted around, although there was always an effort to maintain the heterogeneous or homogeneous nature of each group as intended. Additionally, the teacher and researchers were circulating around the room during the study and assisted groups from time to time. Such interactions, while typical in actual classrooms, inevitably affected peer interaction.

Conclusion

This study attempted to determine how students with different language proficiency levels interacted with each other during heterogeneous and homogeneous group activities. Findings revealed that when students adopted positions that allowed for a fluid exchange of expert-novice roles, more CD occurred and students participated more equally. Additionally, homogeneous groups tended to facilitate more positive peer interaction patterns for students with similar levels of proficiency *irrespective* of home language background. Although scholars argue (Hamayan, Genesee, & Cloud 2013; Howard, Sugarman, Christian, Lindholm-Leary, & Rogers 2007) and teachers often assume heterogeneous groups will "naturally" lead to scaffolding on the part of more advanced speakers (experts) for the benefit of less proficient speakers (novices), in practice, this may not be the case. Heterogeneous groups, without careful preparation and implementation strategies that lead to increased equal status positioning, may lead to marginalization, excessive languaging (resulting in confusion), and silencing of some students. However, if teachers are able to improve interaction patterns during heterogeneous group work through a variety of scaffolds to support less proficient speakers and collaborative learning strategy training (Ballinger 2013), peer interaction during small group work can provide potential for more and better language development and overall student achievement. If a goal in TWI programs is to encourage students to be language models for each other, it is helpful to better understand how to design instruction that builds on students' mutual linguistic scaffolding.

References

Abdi, K. (2011). "She really only speaks English": Positioning, language ideology, and heritage language learners. *The Canadian Modern Language Review*, 67(2), 161–189. doi:10.3138/cmlr.67.2.161

Angelova, M., Gunawardena, D., & Volk, D. (2006). Peer teaching and learning: Co-constructing language in a dual language first grade. *Language and Education*, 20(3), 173–190. doi:10.1080/09500780608668722

Ballinger, S. (2013). Towards a cross-linguistic pedagogy: Biliteracy and reciprocal learning strategies in French immersion. *Journal of Immersion and Content-Based Language Education*, 1(1), 131–148. doi:10.1075/jicb.1.1.06bal

Ballinger, S., & Lyster, R. (2011). Student and teacher oral language use in a two-way Spanish/English immersion school. *Language Teaching Research*, 15(3), 10–20.

Carrera-Carrillo, L., & Smith, A. R. (2006). *Seven steps to success in dual language immersion: A brief guide for teachers & administrators*. Portsmouth, NH: Heinemann.

Choi, H., & Iwashita, N. (2016). Interactional behaviours of low-proficiency learners in small group work. In M. Sato & S. Ballinger (Eds.), *Peer interaction and second language learning: Pedagogical potential and research agenda* (pp. 113–134). Amsterdam: John Benjamins.

Commins, N. L., & Miramontes, O. B. (2005). *Linguistic diversity and teaching*. Mahwah, NJ: Lawrence Erlbaum Associates.

Corbin, J., & Strauss, A. (2008). *Basics of qualitative research* (3rd ed.). Los Angeles, CA: Sage.

Davies, B., & Harré, R. (1990). Positioning: The discursive production of selves. *Journal for the Theory of Social Behaviour*, 20(1), 43–63. doi:10.1111/j.1468-5914.1990.tb00174.x

de Jong, E. (2002). Effective bilingual education: From theory to academic achievement in a two-way bilingual program. *Bilingual Research Journal*, 26(1), 1–20. doi:10.1080/15235882.2002.10668699

de Jong, E., & Howard, E. (2009). Integration in two-way immersion education: equalising linguistic benefits for all students. *International Journal of Bilingual Education and Bilingualism*, 12(1), 81–99. doi:10.1080/13670050802149531

Fernández Dobao, A. (2016). Peer interaction and learning. A focus on the silent learner. In M. Sato & S. Ballinger (Eds.), *Peer interaction and second language learning: Pedagogical potential and research agenda* (pp. 33–61). Amsterdam: John Benjamins.

Hamayan, E., Genesee, F., & Cloud, N. (2013). *Dual language instruction from A to Z*. Portsmouth, NH: Heinemann.

Howard, E. R., & Christian, D. (2002). *Two-way immersion 101: Designing and implementing a two-way immersion education program at the elementary level*. Berkeley, CA.

Howard, E. R., Sugarman, J., & Christian, D. (2003). *Trends in two-way immersion education: A review of the research*. Baltimore, MD: CRESPAR.

Howard, E. R., Sugarman, J., Christian, D., Lindholm-Leary, K., & Rogers, D. (2007). *Guiding principles for dual language education*. Washington, DC: CAL.

Howard, E., Sugarman, J., Perdomo, M., & Temple Adger, C. (2005). *The two-way immersion toolkit*. Providence, RI: Education Alliance.

Iwashita, N. (2001). The effect of learner proficiency on interactional moves and modified output in nonnative-nonnative interaction in Japanese as a foreign language. *System*, 29, 267–287. doi:10.1016/S0346-251X(01)00015-X

Kim, Y., & McDonough, K. (2008). The effect of interlocutor proficiency on the collaborative dialogue between Korean as a second language learners. *Language Teaching Research*, 12(2), 211–234. doi: 10.1177/1362168807086288

Kowal, M., & Swain, M. (1994). Using collaborative language production tasks to promote students' language awareness. *Language Awareness*, 3(2), 73–96. doi: 10.1080/09658416.1994.9959845

Lindholm-Leary, K. (2001). *Dual language education*. Clevedon, UK: Multilingual Matters.

Lyster, R., Saito, K., & Sato, M. (2013). Oral corrective feedback in second language classrooms. *Language Teaching*, 46(01), 1–40. doi: 10.1017/S0261444812000365

Martin-Beltrán, M. (2010a). The two-way language bridge: Co-constructing bilingual language learning opportunities. *Modern Language Journal*, 94(2), 254–277. doi: 10.1111/j.1540-4781.2010.01020.x

Martin-Beltrán, M. (2010b). Positioning proficiency: How students and teachers (de)construct language proficiency at school. *Linguistics and Education*, 21(4), 257–281. doi: 10.1016/j.linged.2010.09.002

Olmedo, I. M. (2003). Language mediation among emergent bilingual children. *Linguistics and Education*, 14(2), 143–162. doi: 10.1016/S0898-5898(03)00033-0

Padilla, A., & Sung, H. (1999). *The Stanford Foreign Language Oral Skills Evaluation Matrix (FLOSEM): A Rating Scale for Assessing Communicative Proficiency*. ERIC (ED445538).

Parkes, J., Ruth, T., Anberg-Espinoza, M., & de Jong, E. (2009). *Urgent research questions and issues in dual language education*. Santa Fe, NM: Dual Language Education of New Mexico

Patton, M. Q. (2002). *Qualitative research & evaluation methods* (3rd ed.). Thousand Oaks, CA: Sage.

Potowski, K. (2004). Student Spanish use and investment in a dual immersion classroom: Implications for second language acquisition and heritage language maintenance. *The Modern Language Journal*, 88(1), 75–101. doi: 10.1111/j.0026-7902.2004.00219.x

Potowski, K. (2007). Characteristics of the Spanish grammar and sociolinguistic proficiency of dual immersion graduates. *Spanish in Context*, 4(2), 187–216. doi: 10.1075/sic.4.2.04pot

Rogoff, B. (2003). *The cultural nature of human development*. New York, NY: Oxford University Press.

Saldaña, J. (2013). *The coding manual for qualitative researchers*. Los Angeles, CA: Sage.

Sato, M., & Ballinger, S. (2016). Understanding peer interaction: Research synthesis and directions. In M. Sato & S. Ballinger (Eds.), *Peer interaction and second language learning: Pedagogical potential and research agenda* (pp. 1–30). Amsterdam: John Benjamins.

Sato, M., & Viveros, P. (2016). Interaction or collaboration? The proficiency effect on group work in the foreign language classroom. In M. Sato & S. Ballinger (Eds.), *Peer interaction and second language learning: Pedagogical potential and research agenda* (pp. 91–112). Amsterdam: John Benjamins.

Senesac, B. (2002). Two-way bilingual immersion: A portrait of quality schooling. *Bilingual Research Journal*, 26(1), 85–101. doi: 10.1080/15235882.2002.10668700

Swain, M. (2006). Languaging, agency and collaboration in advanced second language proficiency. In H. Byrnes (Ed.), *Advanced language learning: The contributions of Halliday and Vygotsky* (pp. 95–108). London: Continuum.

Swain, M., Brooks, L., & Tocalli-Beller, A. (2002). Peer-peer dialogue as a means of second language learning. *Annual Review of Applied Linguistics*, 22, 171–185. doi: 10.1017/S0267190502000090

Swain, M., & Lapkin, S. (2001). Focus on form through collaborative dialogue: Exploring task effects. In M. Bygate, P. Skehan, & M. Swain (Eds.), *Researching pedagogic tasks: Second language learning, teaching and testing* (pp. 99–118). NJ: Pearson.

Talmy, S. (2004). Forever FOB: The cultural production of ESL in a high school. *Pragmatics*, 14(2–3), 149–172. doi:10.1075/prag.14.2-3.03tal

Tedick, D. J., & Young, A. I. (2014, advance access). Fifth grade two-way immersion students' responses to form-focused instruction. *Applied Linguistics*, 1–25. doi:10.1093/applin/amu066

Thomas, W. P., & Collier, V. P. (2012). *Dual language education for a transformed world*. Albuquerque, NM: Dual Language Education of New Mexico.

Vygotsky, L. S. (1986). *Thought and language* (Rev. ed.). Cambridge, MA: The MIT Press.

Vygotsky, L. S. (1978). *Mind in society*. Cambridge, MA: Harvard University Press.

Watanabe, Y., & Swain, M. (2007). Effects of proficiency differences and patterns of pair interaction on second language learning: collaborative dialogue between adult ESL learners. *Language Teaching Research*, 11(2), 121–142. doi:10.1177/136216880607074599

Wiese, A. M. (2004). Bilingualism and biliteracy for all? Unpacking two-way immersion at second grade. *Language and Education*, 18(1), 69–93. doi:10.1080/09500780408666868

Williams, J. (2001). The effectiveness of spontaneous attention to form. *System*, 29(3), 325–340. doi:10.1016/S0346-251X(01)00022-7

Wood, D., Bruner, J., & Ross, G. (1976). The role of tutoring in problem solving. *Journal of Child Psychology and Psychiatry and Allied Disciplines*, 17, 89–100. doi:10.1111/j.1469-7610.1976.tb00381.x

Wortham, S. (1996). Mapping deictics: A technique for discovering teachers' footing. *Journal of Pragmatics*, 25(3), 331–348. doi:10.1016/0378-2166(94)00100-6

Wortham, S. (2001). Interactionally situated cognition: A classroom example. *Cognitive Science*, 25(1), 37–66. doi:10.1207/s15516709cog2501_3

Appendix

Transcription conventions (adapted from Wortham 2001)

-	Abrupt breaks
?	Rising intonation
.	Falling intonation
___	(underline) stress
(1.0)	Silences, timed to the nearest second
[	Simultaneous talk by two speakers, with one utterance represented on top of the other and the moment of overlap marked by left brackets
=	Interruption with next utterance following immediately represented on separate lines
:	Elongated vowel
°…°	Segment quieter than surrounding talk
,	Pause or breath without marked intonation
(hhh)	Laughter breaking into words

Tasks and interactional modalities

CHAPTER 6

Peer interaction in F2F and CMC contexts

Shawn Loewen and Dominik Wolff

Michigan State University / West Chester University

The current chapter adopts an interactionist perspective to investigate various characteristics of L2 learners' interaction in three different communication modalities: face-to-face, oral synchronous computer-mediated communication, and written synchronous computer-mediated communication. Forty-eight intermediate proficiency L2 learners of English engaged in three different interactive tasks in one of the three communicative contexts. Characteristics of interaction that are considered to be beneficial for L2 development, namely negotiation for meaning, recasts, and language-related episodes, were identified in the discourse and compared across the three modalities. In addition, task effects on interaction were compared. Results indicated that interaction during the face-to-face and oral synchronous computer-mediated communication was similar, but differed from written synchronous computer-mediated communication in terms of a greater number of confirmation checks and language-related episodes. However, no differences in interactional features were found across the three different tasks. These results suggest that different communication modalities may afford different opportunities for learners.

Introduction

The role of interaction in second language acquisition (SLA) has been theorized and researched for a considerable length of time. The interaction hypothesis claims that comprehensible input and interactional feedback (Gass 1997; Long 1996; Pica 1994), pushed output (Swain 1995, 2005), and negotiation for meaning (Long 1991; 1996) support second language (L2) learning. Numerous studies have investigated the characteristics of interaction (e.g., Gass & Varonis 1994; Lyster & Ranta 1997) while others have researched the effectiveness of interaction for inducing noticing of linguistic items (e.g., Mackey, Gass, & McDonough 2000) or the acquisition of linguistic items (see Mackey & Goo 2007). Some studies have also investigated the various contexts in which L2 interaction occurs, and how

DOI 10.1075/lllt.45.07loe

these contexts do or do not affect the characteristics or outcomes of interaction (e.g., Gass, Mackey, & Ross-Feldman 2005).

Meanwhile, technological advancements continue to affect and alter the ways in which people communicate, and these changes make their way into the L2 classroom, for example through hybrid and online classes (Lai, Zhao, & Wang 2011). Consequently, there is a need for SLA theorists and researchers to continue to compare and contrast traditional means of communication with newer modalities, in order to assess and confirm the theoretical relevance of the interaction hypothesis. While there has been some attention to synchronous computer-mediated communication (SCMC), both oral and written, there are only a handful of studies that have compared different types of SCMC with face-to-face (F2F) interaction. Consequently, there is still a need to use SLA theory to understand how recent communication technologies affect the interactive tasks that are used in L2 classrooms and instructed SLA research (Chapelle 1997; Sauro 2011). To that end, the current chapter compares ESL students' performance on three communicative tasks in three different communicative contexts: F2F, oral SCMC, and written SCMC.

Literature review

The interaction hypothesis proposes that negotiating for meaning during communication is beneficial for L2 acquisition, in part because it draws learners' attention to linguistic forms that are problematic for them and because it may help them notice the gap between their own production and target-like norms (Gass 1997; Long 1996; Pica 1994; Schmidt & Frota 1986). Negotiation for meaning may occur in several different ways (Gass et al. 2005; Long 1983; Lyster & Ranta 1997). While engaged in communicative tasks, learners may signal that they do not understand their interlocutor's utterance by means of confirmation checks (e.g., *Do you mean X?*) or clarification requests (e.g., *What do you mean?*). Additionally, individuals may use comprehension checks to verify that their utterances have been understood by their interlocutors (e.g., *Do you know what I mean?*).

In addition to negotiating for meaning, learners may also be involved in focus on form (Long 1996) in which attention is given to linguistic items even though no breakdown in communication has occurred. A frequent type of such focus on form occurs when corrective feedback is given in response to learners' erroneous utterances, with the most common type of feedback being recasts, which reformulate learners' errors without changing the meaning of their utterances (Loewen & Philp 2006; Lyster & Ranta 1997). Another type of focus on form occurs during language-related episodes (LREs) in which learners topicalize linguistic forms during interaction (Swain & Lapkin 1998).

Multiple studies of task-based interaction have investigated the occurrence and characteristics of various types of negotiation for meaning and focus on form when teachers are involved in the interaction (Ellis, Basturkmen, & Loewen 2001; Lyster & Ranta 1997; Sheen 2004). Such studies have found varying rates of focus on form with the instructional context appearing to be an influencing factor; for example, more focus on form has been found to occur in second language classrooms in language schools than in immersion L2 classes (Sheen 2004).

Although many studies have investigated negotiation for meaning and focus on form involving teachers, fewer studies have examined the interactional patterns that occur when learners are involved in peer interaction without the intervention of the teacher (Sato & Ballinger 2016). In one descriptive study of the occurrence of peer corrective feedback, Philp, Walter, and Basturkmen (2010) investigated 12 hours of peer interaction in a French for business course. They found that discussion and role play tasks generated between two and six LREs, accounting for roughly 16 per cent of the turns in the interaction. The overwhelming majority of LREs (80%) focused on vocabulary, with minimal attention to grammar and pronunciation. García Mayo and Azkarai (2016) also investigated the amount and nature of student interaction during a variety of tasks in written and oral modalities. They found more LREs in written interaction; however, task type also influenced the number of LREs, with picture description tasks having the lowest occurrence of LREs.

Studies have also investigated the effects of peer interaction and feedback on L2 development. One such study by Adams (2007) has found that peer feedback during communicative tasks can be beneficial for L2 development. Adams investigated the effects of peer interaction and corrective feedback for 25 ESL learners involved in a series of communicative tasks, and she found that learners had an average accuracy score of 60 per cent on linguistic structures that had received feedback during the tasks. Finally, in another intervention study, Sato and Lyster (2012) trained Japanese university ESL learners to provide corrective feedback, in the form of recasts or prompts, during peer interaction. Sato and Lyster found that the provision of peer feedback resulted in improved accuracy and fluency, while peer interaction alone resulted in improved fluency only. These studies suggest that peer interaction and feedback can be an important context for L2 development.

One issue related to the previous studies is the context in which the interaction occurs, whether a classroom or a laboratory. In particular, Foster (1998) argues that much interaction research is conducted in laboratories and thus does not reflect the realities of what happens inside the classroom. In addition, Gass,

Mackey, and Ross-Feldman (2005) point out that differences between classroom and laboratory contexts, such as less control of classroom interaction and heightened learner awareness in laboratories, may influence the nature of the interaction in these contexts.

In order to investigate this issue further, Gass et al. (2005) conducted three different tasks in both classroom and laboratory contexts, analyzing the interaction for negotiation of meaning and focus on form. In dyads, 74 learners of Spanish performed a picture differences task, a consensus task, and a map task, resulting in approximately one hour of interaction per dyad. Analyses did not find differences in interactional characteristics between the class and lab conditions; however, statistical differences were found among the three tasks. The dyads averaged roughly five confirmation checks for the picture differences and map tasks; however, less than one for the consensus task. Similarly, there was an average of three clarification requests per dyad for the picture differences and map tasks, but less than one for the consensus task. In contrast, comprehension checks averaged close to zero across all three tasks, a non-significant difference. For LREs, the average was low as well, but the statistical differences were similar to the confirmation checks and clarification requests, with LREs being statistically more frequent in the map task and picture differences task, with an average of one and two LREs respectively, than in the consensus task, with an average of .5 LREs. Finally, recasts were also uncommon. On the picture differences task, dyads scored statistically higher with an average of one recast, while the other two tasks were statistically lower with less than .5 recasts on average. In summary, the consensus task generally contained fewer interactional features, although the occurrence of every feature except confirmation checks and clarification requests was very low.

Although considerable information is known about learner interaction in F2F contexts, less is known about interaction in computer-mediated environments. Synchronous computer-mediated communication (SCMC) can be defined as communication that occurs in real time by means of a computer, and it may be either written or oral. An example of written SCMC is a chatroom in which two or more participants are typing and posting messages concurrently, while oral SCMC can take the form of Skype or some other audiovisual computer-mediated communication. SCMC differs from asynchronous CMC, such as discussion boards, in that there is little time lag between messages and interlocutors are present, albeit virtually, at the same time.

Much has been said about the characteristics of written SCMC. Sauro and Smith (2010) state that text chat is different from other types of synchronous communication in that it has multiple overlapping turns, a written record, and greater lag time between turns. Some researchers suggest that SCMC may have advantages over F2F interaction. For example, Pasfield-Neofitou (2012) claims that SCMC will lead to an increase in length and complexity of language production. Another benefit for written SCMC is that learners have more time to monitor and edit their own production, and to change their production in response to incoming messages (Lai & Zhao 2006; Smith & Sauro 2009). For example, Sauro and Smith (2010), examining the overt and covert production of German L2 learners in a text chat context, found that overt chat output showing signs of online planning (through the deletion or altering of text before publishing the message) showed greater linguistic complexity and lexical diversity than did output without evidence of online planning.

Several studies have made comparisons among F2F, oral SCMC and written SCMC interaction. From a sociocultural framework, Rouhshad and Storch (2016) examined patterns of interaction in F2F and written SCMC interaction, finding that F2F contexts contained more collaborative interaction. From an interactionist perspective, Fernández-García and Martínez Arbelaiz (2003) and Lai and Zhao (2006) both found more negotiation in F2F contexts than in written SCMC. Similarly, Hamano-Bunce (2011) conducted a small-scale study comparing required and optional information exchange tasks. He found fewer LREs in the written SCMC than in F2F interaction, which he explained, in part, by suggesting that the typed nature of the text chat made language production difficult. This suggestion may be supported by Yanguas' (2010) findings of equal amounts of negotiation in F2F interaction and oral SCMC. Finally, at least one study has compared different types of SCMC. Jepson (2005) found more repair moves in oral SCMC than in written SCMC, although much of that repair was pronunciation-related.

In addition to modality, other factors may influence online interaction. Some studies have examined task differences. For example, García Mayo and Azkarai (2016) found that task type influenced the number of LREs during peer interaction in both written and oral modalities. Picture description tasks had the lowest occurrence of LREs, while more structured tasks, such as text editing or picture placement, had more LREs. Similarly, both Yilmaz and Granena (2010) and Yilmaz (2011) found significantly more LREs in dictogloss tasks compared to information exchange tasks in approximately 30 minutes of written chat; however, like Gass et al.'s (2005) results, the average was low in all cases. Yilmaz and Granena found a median of 3 LREs in dictogloss tasks and 0 LREs in information exchange tasks, while Yilmaz found an average of 3.6 and 2.4, respectively.

Research questions

As can be seen, research is beginning to identify similarities and differences in interactional features according to modality, as well as task factors; however, there have been calls for additional research to help sort out conflicting claims and findings (Yilmaz 2011). We set out to investigate task-based interaction in three different tasks in three different modalities: F2F, written SCMC and oral SCMC. In examining the interaction patterns, we attempted to partially replicate Gass et al.'s (2005) study by asking the following research questions:

1. How does task-based interaction compare in three modalities: face to face, oral SCMC, and written SCMC?
2. How do the different tasks influence interaction in these three modalities?

Methods

Methodological framework

The current study is observational and non-interventionist, describing the types of interaction that participants engaged in without any specific directions on how to perform the tasks. The data are coded for important discourse characteristics within the interactionist framework, and the types and number of discourse moves are investigated according to modality and task.

Participants

The participants in this study ($N = 48$), 31 males and 17 females, ranged in age from 17 to 35 with an average age of 21. The majority of the participants were enrolled in a level 3 English-as-a-second-language (ESL) class at a large Midwestern university in the United States. This class is considered an intermediate level class in an intensive English program which has four proficiency levels, as well as advanced English for Academic Purposes courses. Participants' first languages were Chinese (31), Arabic (13), and Korean (2). Two participants did not disclose their first language on the questionnaire. Participants' length of English instruction ranged from 0.5 years to 16 years with an average of 8.2 years.

Materials

The participants completed three different tasks, a picture differences task, a consensus task, and a conversation task. Each dyad was randomly assigned to one modality and completed all three tasks in that modality; thus, modality was a between-groups variable while task was a within-groups variable. All three tasks allowed learners to use their own linguistic resources, related to real-world activities, and had non-linguistic outcomes (Ellis 2003).

Picture differences task

In this task, participants had to spot the difference between two similar pictures. The pictures were the same ones used by Gass et al. (2005) and depicted nearly identical park scenes with a number of differences between the pictures. For example, in one version of the picture, a girl is playing with a ball, while in the altered version the ball is missing. Participants had to share information about their respective pictures in order to complete the task.

Consensus task

This task required participants to come to an agreement about the information provided to them, based on a set of criteria. The task was conceptually similar to the consensus task used by Gass et al.; however, the content differed. Instead of deciding where a hypothetical friend should attend college, the dyads had to exchange information about three scholarship candidates and decide which candidate should receive a scholarship to study in the United States. Participants were given a sheet with information about the scholarship requirements which they were told to consider when deciding on the scholarship recipient. Participants also received different pieces of information about each candidate, which they needed to exchange in order to come to a consensus on one candidate.

Conversation task

In an effort to elicit more naturalistic interaction between participants (Nakahama, Tyler, & van Lier 2001), a conversation task was used in which participants asked about their partner's favorite things, in addition to describing their own. Each participant received a list of discussion topics, which contained the same topics but in different orders. Participants were instructed to take turns asking each other about their favorites (e.g., restaurant, film, book, etc.) and to elaborate whenever possible. Furthermore, learners were asked to discuss commonalities and differences between their answers.

Procedure

Dyads were randomly assigned to one of the three modalities, resulting in eight dyads per modality. The order of the tasks was counterbalanced. Before beginning each task, one of the researchers explained the task to the two participants and, because many partners shared a first language, reminded them to use only English during the tasks. After a maximum of twenty minutes on a task, the researcher stopped the participants (if they had not finished earlier) and moved on to the next task. Each session lasted a total of 50 to 60 minutes. For the F2F modality, a camera was used to record the participants who were seated across from each other. In the other two modalities (oral and written SCMC), participants were in separate rooms seated in front of a computer. Skype was used for both the oral and written SCMC groups, but for logistical reasons, only audio was available for the oral SCMC; consequently, the participants did not see each other, a not uncommon occurrence in oral SCMC (Bueno-Alastuey 2013). Audio recordings and chat files were saved for the subsequent analysis. At the end of the three tasks, the participants filled out a background questionnaire and were paid twenty dollars each for their participation.

Coding

Following Gass et al. (2005), we coded for the same interactional features that are widely considered facilitative of L2 development (e.g., Foster 1998; Gass & Varonis 1985; Long 1983, 1996; Swain 1998; Mackey & Philp 1998). These were negotiation for meaning, language-related episodes (LREs), and recasts. Definitions of each term and examples of occurrences in each modality are provided below. When considering written SCMC, Sauro and Smith (2010) and Smith (2009) provide evidence for the usefulness of examining the covert linguistic output of learners in a chat room (i.e., language that is deleted or altered before it is sent). However, the current study investigates only overt output in order to make consistent comparisons across the three contexts.

Negotiation for meaning
Following Long (1983), Foster (1998), and Gass et al. (2005), we operationalized negotiation for meaning in terms of confirmation checks, clarification checks, and comprehension checks. Examples of each category, taken from the data collected for this study, are provided below. Note that there is one example for the oral mode (either F2F or oral SCMC) and one for the written mode (written SCMC).

Confirmation checks. Long (1983) defines confirmation check as "any expressions…immediately following an utterance by the interlocutor which are designed to elicit confirmation that the utterance has been correctly heard or understood by the speaker" (137). Example (1a) comes from the F2F data and Example (1b) was taken from the written SCMC data. Although it is not possible to ensure that there was actual misunderstanding on the part of Learner 2 in each example without some measure of cognition, Learner 2's discourse move in each instance serves the purpose of checking the semantic content of Learner 1's previous statement.

(1) a. Face-to-face, consensus task
          Learner 1:   And, third person in my paper is Julia, is a female, and IQ is 85 and he, she got C grades for subjects.
          Learner 2:   C grades? [confirmation check]
          Learner 1:   C grades. C, A, B, C. C grades for subjects.
          Learner 2:   Ah.
     b. Written SCMC, picture differences task
          Learner 1:   yep I see four flowers
          Learner 2:   just four? [confirmation check]
          Learner 1:   no
          Learner 2:   how many?

Clarification requests. According to Long (1983), a clarification request is "any expression…designed to elicit clarification of the interlocutor's preceding utterance(s)" (137). The following examples illustrate the use of a clarification request where one learner did not initially understand the interlocutor and thus requested clarification.

(2) a. Oral SCMC, consensus task
          Learner 1:   She was sent to a special school for troubled youth.
          Learner 2:   For what? [clarification request]
          Learner 1:   Troubled youth. Like for people who do something, they send them to other school.
          Learner 2:   Ok, she's a criminal.
     b. Written CMC, favorites task
          Learner 1:   what
          Learner 2:   move stars = actors
          Learner 1:   what mean [clarification request]
          Learner 2:   jaky chan steven segan

Comprehension checks. A comprehension check is defined as an interlocutor following their own utterance with an attempt "to…prevent a breakdown in communication" (Long 1983: 136). These two excerpts exemplify such attempts.

(3)   a.   Oral SCMC, picture differences task
          Learner 1:   How many people stand around the table?
                       You can see the table, right? [comprehension check]
          Learner 2:   Yeah.
      b.   Written SCMC, conversation task
          Learner 1:   yes, my best love is COD do you know it? [comprehension
                       check]
          Learner 2:   I'm sorry I don't know
          Learner 1:   It is Call of Duty do yu know it?

Language-related episodes (LREs)

In this study, we defined LREs in accordance with Swain and Lapkin (1998:70) as "any part of a dialogue in which students talk about language they are producing [or] question their language use [or] other- or self-correct"; however, unlike Swain and Lapkin, we did not consider self-corrections in our definition due to our interest solely in peer interaction. The following examples illustrate typical LREs found in the current data set.

(4)   a.   F2F, conversation task
          Learner 1:   The knight. It's not the night (gestures around himself), it's
                       the knight. Who have swords. You know?
          Learner 2:   No.
          Learner 1:   The pronunciation is the same but it's different meaning.
          Learner 2:   Spell it.
          Learner 1:   K-N-I-G-H-T.
      b.   Written SCMC, consensus task
          Learner 1:   she? ALBERT is a man
          Learner 2:   ye, she's a good student
          Learner 1:   Male.
          Learner 2:   oh, sorry

Recasts

The term recast describes the reformulation of an erroneous utterance, i.e. the repetition of an utterance with the error corrected (Lyster & Ranta 1997). In the following examples, the recasts correct a preposition error and spelling mistakes, respectively. Note that both recasts are followed by corrected production on the part of the learner who made the error.

(5)   a.   Oral CMC, picture differences task
          Learner 1:   And the kid between the father.
          Learner 2:   Near the father. [Recast]
          Learner 1:   Yeah, near the father.

    b.   Written SCMC, consensus task
        Learner 1:   what information for fost pople?
        Learner 2:   first people [Recast]
        Learner 1:   people

Occurrences of interaction moves (confirmation checks, clarification requests, comprehension checks, LREs, and recasts) were transcribed and coded by both authors for the F2F and oral SCMC dyads. The chat transcripts for the written SCMC dyads were downloaded and coded by both authors as well. In those cases where there was a disagreement with regards to the coding categories, the researchers engaged in a discussion until a consensus was reached.

Analysis

In addressing our principal research question, "How does task-based interaction compare in the three modalities: F2F, oral SCMC, and written SCMC?" mixed design analyses of variance (ANOVAs) were conducted to investigate the relationships between the modalities and task types. The number of discourse moves served as the dependent variable, with modality as a between-subjects independent variable, and task type as a within-subjects variable. In cases where statistically significant differences were found, Tukey post-hoc tests were carried out to determine the exact nature of the differences.

Results

In order to answer the research questions, the frequencies of each interactional feature in each task were tallied for each dyad in each modality, and the average scores were calculated. As seen in Table 1, the dyads averaged roughly 20 confirmation checks for each of the three tasks in the oral conditions. In contrast, in the written SCMC condition, the dyads averaged two or fewer confirmation checks. For clarification requests, Table 2 shows that all three groups in all three conditions averaged between three and five clarification requests per task, except for the written SCMC group on the consensus task which averaged 1.5 clarification requests. Table 3 indicates that the groups averaged less than one and a half comprehension checks on each of the tasks. In order to test for significant relationships in the data, mixed design ANOVAs were computed. Results showed a main effect for modality for confirmation checks ($F(2, 21) = 12.8, p < .001, \eta^2 = .55$) but not for clarification requests and comprehension checks. In addition, there were no significant effects for task type, nor were there any interaction effects between modality and task type. A Tukey post-hoc test confirmed that there were significantly more instances of confirmation checks in both the F2F and oral CMC group when compared to the written CMC group.

Table 1. Confirmation checks

Task	Modality	Mean	SD
Picture differences	F2F	21.6	14.6
	Oral CMC	15.1	9.2
	Written CMC	2.1	1.4
Consensus	F2F	15.6	8.3
	Oral CMC	15.1	10.4
	Written CMC	.88	1.5
Conversation	F2F	20.8	11.5
	Oral CMC	15.4	7.6
	Written CMC	.88	1.1

Table 2. Clarification requests

Task	Modality	Mean	SD
Picture differences	F2F	5.3	5.4
	Oral CMC	4.0	2.1
	Written CMC	3.8	4.4
Consensus	F2F	3.0	2.3
	Oral CMC	3.5	3.6
	Written CMC	1.5	2.7
Conversation	F2F	2.8	2.4
	Oral CMC	3.4	2.0
	Written CMC	3.3	2.5

Table 3. Comprehension checks

Task	Modality	Mean	SD
Picture differences	F2F	1.5	2.3
	Oral CMC	.88	1.1
	Written CMC	.50	.76
Consensus	F2F	1.0	1.9
	Oral CMC	1.3	1.3
	Written CMC	.13	.15
Conversation	F2F	.75	1.0
	Oral CMC	.63	.74
	Written CMC	1.0	1.4

LREs/Recasts

Similar to clarification requests and comprehension checks, LREs were infrequent in the interaction, as seen in Table 4. For the two oral conditions, dyads averaged between two and three LREs per task; however, the written SCMC dyads had almost no LREs. A mixed-design ANOVA found a significant main effect for modality, $F(2, 21) = 11.6, p < .001, \eta^2 = .527$. Tukey post-hoc tests confirmed more occurrences for the F2F and oral CMC groups than the written CMC group. There was, however, no main effect for task type, nor an interaction effect for modality and task type.

Table 5 shows that the final interaction move, recasts, occurred only rarely across modalities, with no group averaging more than one per task. Although the written SCMC averages were the lowest, there were no statistical differences among the groups.

Table 4. LREs

Task	Modality	Mean	SD
Picture differences	F2F	2.4	1.8
	Oral CMC	2.1	2.0
	Written CMC	.50	1.1
Consensus	F2F	3.0	2.1
	Oral CMC	2.0	2.6
	Written CMC	.13	.35
Conversation	F2F	3.4	2.3
	Oral CMC	2.8	2.1
	Written CMC	.25	.71

Table 5. Recasts

Task	Modality	Mean	SD
Picture differences	F2F	1.1	1.2
	Oral CMC	1.1	1.6
	Written CMC	.25	.46
Consensus	F2F	1.4	1.1
	Oral CMC	1.3	1.0
	Written CMC	.25	.46
Conversation	F2F	1.0	.93
	Oral CMC	.75	1.0
	Written CMC	.38	.74

Figures 1 through 5 illustrate the differences between the three groups for all coding categories.

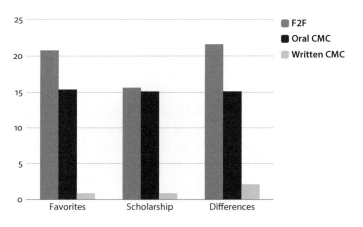

Figure 1. Confirmation checks

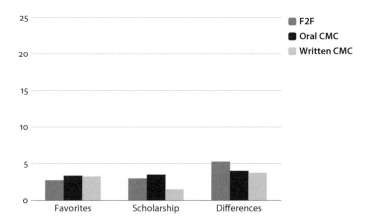

Figure 2. Clarification requests

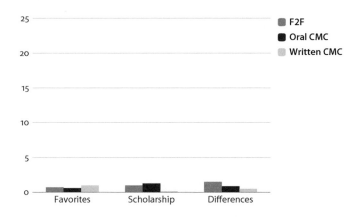

Figure 3. Comprehension checks

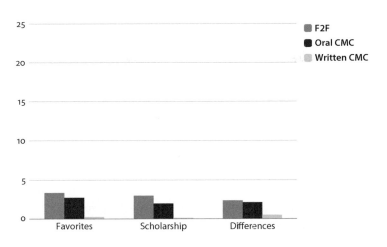

Figure 4. LREs

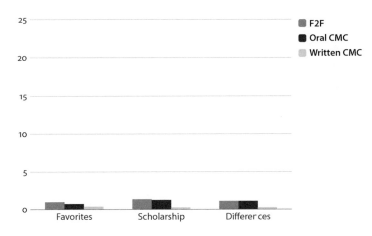

Figure 5. Recasts

Discussion

This study focused on the occurrence of interactional features argued to be beneficial for L2 development. Three different communicative modalities, F2F, oral SCMC, and written SCMC, were investigated with three different tasks performed by L2 English learners. The first research question asked about differences in the occurrence of these interactional moves in the various modalities. Results revealed that there was some effect for modality on the frequency of certain interaction moves, with statistically fewer confirmation checks and LREs occurring in the written SCMC condition. There were no statistical modality effects for clarification requests, comprehension checks or recasts; in addition these interactional moves occurred infrequently in the data.

Because this study was a partial replication of Gass et al. (2005), it is worth comparing the results of the two studies. First, the current study found considerably more confirmation checks in the oral interaction than did Gass et al., a rough average of 20 versus four per task, respectively. However, the average number of clarification requests and confirmation checks was very similar, with fewer than five clarification requests and almost no confirmation checks per task. Both studies found relatively few LREs per task, only between one and three, and almost no recasts in any of the tasks. Since the length of learners' interaction was roughly 60 minutes in both studies, it is unclear why there would be such a difference in the number of confirmation checks between the two studies, particularly when all of the other categories are similar. It may be that the operationalization of confirmation checks differed between the two studies, even though every effort was made to ensure replication of the coding categories.

In terms of modality of interaction, our results support several previous studies. For example, Yanguas (2010) also found that oral interaction was similar in terms of negotiation, regardless of whether it occurred in F2F or in SCMC contexts. Similar to other studies, oral interaction, whether F2F (Fernández-García & Martínez Arbelaiz 2003; García Mayo & Azkarai 2016; Hamano-Bunce 2011) or SCMC (Jepson 2005) contained more interactional features than written SCMC. In part, this latter finding may not be surprising given the slower nature of written SCMC (Hamano-Bunce 2011). Some researchers suggest that the slower pace of discourse may afford greater learning opportunities due to more time to notice linguistic items (e.g., Lai & Zhao 2006; Smith & Sauro 2009). However, the current research indicates that learners may have fewer opportunities to engage in some types of negotiation of meaning or focus on form in written SCMC. Nevertheless, the permanent, visual nature of the chatscripts, as well as the greater opportunity to monitor one's production, may counteract the lower frequency of interaction moves. Thus, it appears that there might be a difference between quantity of interaction versus quality of interaction in written SCMC compared to oral interaction. Future research should investigate these differences in terms of L2 acquisition.

We found clear differences in the nature of interaction between written SCMC on one side and the two verbal types of communication, namely oral CMC and F2F, on the other. The most common interaction moves in the verbal modalities, confirmation checks and LREs, hardly occurred in the written CMC mode at all. The fact that this was a consistent finding for all three tasks may suggest that these tasks, which are traditionally used to elicit verbal interaction, do not work in quite the same way in written CMC even though all dyads, independent of modality, were given the same instructions for each task. In order to better understand the differences in negotiation of meaning and focus on form, a post hoc analysis examined turn-taking in the oral and written modalities. The following excerpt shows a typical information exchange in the verbal modalities. As part of the consensus task, the learners are exchanging information about a scholarship candidate. This excerpt features confirmation checks, clarification requests, and an LRE. Notice also that the negotiation for meaning results in Learner 1 correcting his initial mispronunciation of *intermediate*, a fact which illustrates the beneficial effects of such interaction.

(6) F2F, scholarship task
    Learner 1:   Current level of spoken English, pre-indimediate.
    Learner 2:   (writing) Indimediate. [Confirmation check]
    Learner 1:   Pre-indimediate.
    Learner 2:   What's that mean? [Clarification request]
    Learner 1:   I don't know but I think it's not very good in English.
    Learner 2:   Not very good. [Confirmation check]
    Learner 1:   Maybe.
    Learner 2:   Ok, not very good. Can you say that word again, that sentence? [Clarification request]
    Learner 1:   Current level of spoken English is pre intermediate.
    Learner 2:   Pr, what's a "pr"? [LRE]
    Learner 1:   (spelling) P-R-E. P-R-E intermediate. [LRE]
    Learner 2:   Ok, I see.

It may be that in written SCMC learners did not ask for clarification very frequently because the information they received remained on the screen. Furthermore, in some cases, the participants employed the shortest means of information exchange. Instead of taking turns, learners simply posted all of the information at once. The following examples illustrate this time-saving, but non-interactive technique. In Example (7), Learner 1 presents all of the information about Gina, one post at a time with no comment or interaction from Learner 2. In Example (8), Learner 1 presents all of the candidate information in one post, again with the result that there is very little opportunity for interaction.

(7) Written CMC, scholarship task
    Learner 1:   Gina
    Learner 1:   20 years old
    Learner 1:   sometimes lazy
    Learner 1:   parents killesd in a car crash
    Learner 1:   good at music
    Learner 1:   uncle and aunt live in US
    Learner 1:   current level of spoken English upper intermediate
    Learner 1:   that is all about Gina

(8)   Written CMC, scholarship task
      Learner 1: Gina
      female
      iq of 140
      a grade in school, failed a class because she was partying before the final exam
      difficult childhood stole things at 14
      never been to America
      wants to study paiting and art history

Not all written SCMC employed these non-interactive techniques for exchanging information, nor did all oral groups engage in extensive turn-taking and interaction. However, similar to Rouhshad and Storch's (2016) finding of less collaborative interaction patterns in written SCMC, the current study suggests that modality may affect the way in which learners interact. It may be that the tasks needed to be structured differently in order to encourage more negotiation, particularly in the written modality. Learners may need to be trained how to negotiate and respond to each other's posts (Sato & Ballinger 2012). It may also be the case that written SCMC does not provide as conducive a context for the interactional features that are argued to be beneficial for L2 learning. Again, further research that investigates the effects of these modalities on L2 acquisition is needed.

In terms of our second research question regarding task effects for interactional features, our findings differed from Gass et al. (2005) who found fewer interactional features in their consensus task. In contrast, the consensus task in the current study resulted in similar numbers of interactional features as the picture description and conversation tasks. Upon further inspection, it appears that the consensus task used by Gass et al. did not involve obligatory information exchange; rather, both students in the dyad were given the same information which they used to make their decision. However, in the current study, each student was given only part of the information necessary to reach a decision, thereby requiring an exchange of information to complete the task. These differences in task structure and resulting interaction underscore the importance of ensuring that learners are required to exchange information in order for them to engage in the types of interaction that are beneficial for L2 development.

Pedagogical implications

The current study suggests several implications for the use of technology for L2 interaction in the classroom. First and foremost, teachers may wish to consider the goals that they have for learners engaging in task-based interaction. If the goal is to practice fluent language production, then it may be necessary to engage learners in oral interaction, regardless of modality. Written CMC does not appear to offer the same opportunities for students to engage in large amounts of interaction, nor to produce the features of interaction that are proposed to benefit L2 development (Hamano-Bunce 2011). Nevertheless, the benefits of written CMC may reside in other aspects that were not investigated in the current study, such as increased noticing of linguistic items due to the permanent record of interaction that chatscripts provide.

Second, teachers should consider the nature of the tasks that they provide to their learners. It appears that without obligatory information exchange, learners will be less likely to engage in negotiation for meaning and other types of beneficial interaction. However, even with obligatory information exchange, the amount of negotiation for meaning and focus on form was generally low. Consequently, it may be necessary for teachers to provide learners with instruction regarding how to maximize the effects of interaction, a suggestion that is supported by the low incidences of many interactional features across all tasks (Sato & Ballinger 2012).

Conclusions, limitations, and future research

Some limitations we faced are typically encountered in instructed SLA research. Participants were recruited from intact classrooms and learners often signed up together. Thus, many but not all dyads consisted of learners who were familiar with one another. Many of the dyads were also made up of learners who shared the same L1. Controlling for L1, familiarity, and gender would have been preferred, but was not possible in the current context. Additionally, in the current study it was not possible for learners in the oral SMC condition to have visual contact with each other, even though research suggests that non-verbal information can be useful during interaction (Nakatsukasa 2013).

Subsequent research could also attempt to eliminate some of the other limitations of this study. For the written SCMC condition, we were not able to collect keystroke or scrolling data which would have given us more information about the actions of the participants during the chat sessions (Smith 2009). In addition, it was beyond the scope of this study to simultaneously collect data about the noticing or acquisition of specific linguistic forms. Future studies could employ stimulated recall or other measures of noticing to compare the degree to which differences in noticing occur across modalities. Moreover, research studies that employ pre-test/post-test designs to measure linguistic development across modalities are needed.

In sum, this study provides valuable information into the interaction patterns of learners in different modalities of communication. As the use of hybrid and online L2 instruction increases, teachers will be faced with challenges in how to ensure that learners are able to engage in beneficial and successful interaction. The current study suggests that modality makes a difference in learners' interaction, and teachers need to carefully choose the modalities that will best suit their purposes. While oral interaction, regardless of modality, was more conducive to certain interactional characteristics than was written SCMC, the utility of all methods of L2 interaction should be investigated for the different affordances that they may provide, particularly as the demand for online L2 courses continues to grow.

References

Adams, R. (2007). Do second language learners benefit from interacting with each other? In A. Mackey (Ed.), *Conversational interaction in second language acquisition* (pp. 30–51). Oxford: Oxford University Press.

Bueno-Alastuey, M. C. (2013). Interactional feedback in synchronous voice-based computer mediated communication: Effect of dyad. *System*. 41, 543–559. doi: 10.1016/j.system.2013.05.005

Chapelle, C. (1997). CALL in the year 2000: Still in search of research paradigms? *Language Learning & Technology*, 1, 19–43.

Ellis, R. (2003). *Task-based language learning and teaching*. Oxford: Oxford University Press.

Ellis, R., Basturkmen, H., & Loewen, S. (2001). Learner uptake in communicative ESL. *Language Learning*, 51, 281–318. doi: 10.1111/1467-9922.00156

Fernández-García, M., & Martínez-Arbelaiz, A. (2003). Learners' interactions: A comparison of oral and computer-assisted written conversations. *ReCALL*, 15, 113–136. doi: 10.1017/S0958344003000910

Foster, P. (1998). A classroom perspective on the negotiation of meaning. *Applied Linguistics*, 19, 1–23. doi: 10.1093/applin/19.1.1

García Mayo, M. P., & Azkarai, A. (2016). EFL task-based interaction: Does task modality impact on language related episodes? In M. Sato & S. Ballinger (Eds.), *Peer interaction and second language learning: Pedagogical potential and research agenda* (pp. 241–266). Amsterdam: John Benjamins.

Gass, S. M. (1997). *Input, interaction and the second language learner*. Mahwah, NJ: Lawrence Erlbaum Associates.

Gass, S., Mackey, A., & Ross-Feldman, L. (2005). Task-based interactions in classroom and laboratory setting. *Language Learning*, 55, 575–611. doi: 10.1111/j.0023-8333.2005.00318.x

Gass, S., & Varonis, E. (1985). Variation in native speaker speech modification to nonnative speakers. *Studies in Second Language Acquisition* 7, 35–57. doi: 10.1017/S0272263100005143

Gass, S., & Varonis, E. (1994). Input, interaction and second language production. *Studies in Second Language Acquisition*, 16, 283–302. doi: 10.1017/S0272263100013097

Hamano-Bunce, D. (2011). Talk or chat? Chatroom and spoken interaction in a language classroom. *ELT Journal*, 65, 426–436. doi: 10.1093/elt/ccq084

Jepson, K. (2005). Conversations and negotiated interactions in text and voice chat rooms. *Language Learning and Technology*, 9, 3, 79–98.

Lai, C., & Zhao, Y. (2006). Noticing and text-based chat. *Language Learning and Technology*, 10, 102–120.

Lai, C., Zhao, Y. & Wang, J. (2011). Task-based language teaching in online ab initio foreign language classrooms. *The Modern Language Journal*, 95, 81–103. doi:10.1111/j.1540-4781.2011.01271.x

Loewen, S., & Philp, J. (2006). Recasts in the adult English L2 classroom: Characteristics, explicitness, and effectiveness. *The Modern Language Journal*, 90, 536–556. doi:10.1111/j.1540-4781.2006.00465.x

Long, M. H. (1983). Native speaker/non-native speaker conversation and the negotiation of comprehensible input1. *Applied Linguistics*, 4, 126–141. doi:10.1093/applin/4.2.126

Long, M. H. (1991). Focus on form: a design feature in language teaching methodology. In K. de Bot, R. Ginsberg and C. Kramsch (Eds.), *Foreign language research in cross-cultural perspective* (pp. 39–52). Amsterdam: John Benjamins. doi:10.1075/sibil.2.07lon

Long, M. (1996). The role of the linguistic environment in second language acquisition. In W. Ritchie & T. Bhatia (Eds.), *Handbook of second language acquisition* (pp. 413–468). San Diego: Academic Press.

Lyster, R., & Ranta, L. (1997). Corrective feedback and learner uptake: Negotiation of form in communicative classrooms. *Studies in Second Language Acquisition, Studies in Second Language Acquisition*, 19, 37–66.

Mackey, A., Gass, S., & McDonough, K. (2000). How do learners perceive interactional feedback? *Studies in Second Language Acquisition*, 22, 471–497. doi:10.1017/S0272263100004022

Mackey, A. & Goo, J. (2007). Interaction research in SLA: A meta-analysis and research synthesis. In A. Mackey (Ed.), *Conversational interaction in second language acquisition: A series of empirical studies* (pp. 407–452). Oxford: Oxford University Press.

Mackey, A., & Philp, J. (1998). Conversational interaction and second language development: Recasts, responses, and red herrings? *The Modern Language Journal*, 82, 338–356. doi:10.1111/j.1540-4781.1998.tb01211.x

Nakahama, Y., Tyler, A., & van Lier, L. (2001). Negotiation of meaning in conversational and information gap activities: A comparative discourse analysis. *TESOL Quarterly*, 35, 377–405. doi:10.2307/3588028

Nakatsukasa, K. (2013). *Efficacy of gesture and recasts on the acquisition of L2 grammar.* (Unpublished doctoral dissertation). Michigan State University, East Lansing, MI.

Pasfield-Neofitou, S. (2012). *Online communication in a second language: Social interaction, language use, and learning Japanese.* Bristol, UK: Multilingual Matters.

Philp, J., Walter, S. & Basturkmen, H. (2010). Peer interaction in the foreign language classroom: What factors foster a focus on form? *Language Awareness*, 19, 261–279. doi:10.1080/09658416.2010.516831

Pica, T. (1994). Research on negotiation: What does it reveal about second language learning conditions, processes and outcomes? *Language Learning*, 44, 493–527. doi:10.1111/j.1467-1770.1994.tb01115.x

Rouhshad, A., & Storch, N. (2016). A focus on mode: Patterns of interaction in face-to-face and computer-mediated contexts. In M. Sato & S. Ballinger (Eds.), *Peer interaction and second language learning: Pedagogical potential and research agenda* (pp. 267–289). Amsterdam: John Benjamins.

Sato, M., & Ballinger, S. (2012). Raising language awareness in peer interaction: A cross-context, cross-methodology examination. *Language Awareness*, 21, 157–179. doi: 10.1080/09658416.2011.639884

Sato, M., & Ballinger, S. (2016). Understanding peer interaction: Research synthesis and directions. In M. Sato & S. Ballinger (Eds.), *Peer interaction and second language learning: Pedagogical potential and research agenda* (pp. 1–30). Amsterdam: John Benjamins.

Sato, M., & Lyster, R. (2012). Peer interaction and corrective feedback for accuracy and fluency development: Monitoring, practice, and proceduralization. *Studies in Second Language Acquisition*, 34, 591–626. doi: 10.1017/S0272263112000356

Sauro, S. (2011). SCMC for SLA: A research synthesis. *CALICO Journal*, 28, 1–23. doi: 10.11139/cj.28.2.369-391

Sauro, S., & Smith, B. (2010). Investigating L2 performance in text chat. *Applied Linguistics*, 31, 554–577. doi: 10.1093/applin/amq007

Schmidt, R., & Frota, S. (1986). Developing basic conversation ability in a second language: A case study of an adult learner. In R. Day (Ed.), *Talking to learn: Conversation in second language acquisition* (pp. 237–326). Rowley, MA: Newbury House.

Sheen, Y. (2004). Corrective feedback and learner uptake in communicative classrooms across instructional settings. *Language Teaching Research*, 8(3), 263–300. doi: 10.1191/1362168804lr1460a

Smith, B. (2009). The relationship between scrolling, negotiation, and self-initiated self-repair in a SCMC environment. *CALICO Journal*, 26, 231–45.

Smith, B., & Sauro, S. (2009). Interruptions in chat. *Computer Assisted Language Learning*, 22, 229–247. doi: 10.1080/09588220902920219

Swain, M. (1995). Three functions of output in second language learning. In G. Cook & B. Seidlhofer (Eds.), *Principles and practice in applied linguistics* (pp. 125–144). Oxford: Oxford University Press.

Swain, M. (2005). The output hypothesis: Theory and research. In E. Hinkel (Ed.), *Handbook of research in second language teaching and learning* (pp. 471–483). Mahwah, NJ: Lawrence Erlbaum Associates.

Swain, M., & Lapkin, S. (1998). Interaction and second language learning: Two adolescent French immersion students working together. *The Modern Language Journal*, 82, 320–337. doi: 10.1111/j.1540-4781.1998.tb01209.x

Yanguas, Í. (2010). Oral computer-mediated interaction between L2 learners: It's about time. *Language Learning & Technology*, 14, 72–93.

Yilmaz, Y. (2011). Task effects on focus on form in synchronous computer-mediated communication. *The Modern Language Journal*, 95, 115–132. doi: 10.1111/j.1540-4781.2010.01143.x

Yilmaz, Y., & Granena, G. (2010). The effects of task type in synchronous computer-mediated communication. *ReCALL*, 22, 20–38. doi: 10.1017/S0958344009990176

CHAPTER 7

Thai EFL learners' interaction during collaborative writing tasks and its relationship to text quality

Kim McDonough, William J. Crawford
and Jindarat De Vleeschauwer
Concordia University / Northern Arizona University / Chiang Mai University

Second language (L2) writing research has shown that L2 learners routinely scaffold each other when working together to co-construct written texts. The analysis of peer interaction has focused largely on the occurrence of language-related episodes (LREs), with fewer studies documenting how learners discuss other elements of written texts, such as their content or organization (Elola & Oskoz 2010; Storch 2005; Storch & Wigglesworth 2007; Wigglesworth & Storch 2009), or establishing a link between student interaction and text quality. This chapter describes the interaction that occurred when Thai EFL students worked in pairs to write summary and problem/solution paragraphs and explores whether their discussions were related to text quality in the form of analytic ratings. The results indicated that problem/solution collaborative writing tasks showed a positive relationship between student talk and text quality and elicited significantly more discussion of content, organization, and language than summary tasks. Implications are discussed in terms of pedagogical considerations for the use of collaborative writing tasks in EFL contexts.

Literature review

Numerous studies have shown that second language (L2) learners scaffold each other during a variety of pair and small group activities in L2 classrooms, ranging from dictogloss tasks (e.g., Basterrechea & García Mayo 2013; Kuiken & Vedder 2002; Leeser 2004; Swain 1998) to decision-making and information-exchange tasks (e.g., Kim & McDonough 2011), consciousness-raising activities (e.g., Wagner & Toth 2013), jigsaw tasks (e.g., Alegria de la Colina & Garcia Mayo 2007; Swain & Lapkin 1998), and picture narration tasks (Fernández Dobao 2012; Fernández Dobao & Blum 2013). In L2 writing classes more specifically, pair and

DOI 10.1075/lllt.45.08mcd
© 2016 John Benjamins Publishing Company

small group activities frequently occur in the form of prewriting brainstorming tasks (Neumann & McDonough 2014a, 2014b; Shi 1998), peer review of written texts (Hu & Lam 2010; Liu & Sadler 2003; Lundstrum & Baker 2009; Min 2006), and collaborative writing, which Storch (2013) defined recently as a task in which two or more writers interact throughout the writing process to co-construct a single text. As opposed to collaborative activities such as peer editing and co-authoring (i.e., individually writing sections of a text and then combining them into a single paper), collaborative writing involves a sustained pattern of oral inter-action between writers and shared responsibility for the co-construction of texts.

Given this definition, it is not surprising that collaborative writing tasks find support from both interactionist (Gass 2003; Long 1996; Mackey 2012) and socio-cultural (Donato 1994; Lantolf 2011; Swain 2010) perspectives to L2 development. From an interactionist standpoint, collaborative writing elicits communication between students, thereby creating opportunities for interactional adjustments, such as negotiation of meaning, feedback, and modified output, which can facili-tate L2 development. From a sociocultural perspective, collaborative writing provides the social contexts necessary to promote "languaging," which Swain (2006: 98) defined as "the process of making meaning and shaping knowledge and experience through language." Complementing these theoretical perspectives on L2 development, contemporary approaches to writing instruction highlight the importance of collaboration for students' writing skill development and their preparation for team writing tasks in workplace settings (Storch 2013).

Collaborative writing research has generally investigated two main issues: (1) whether co-constructed texts differ in their complexity, accuracy, fluency or overall quality from individual texts (e.g., Fernández Dobao 2012; Shehadeh 2011; Storch & Wigglesworth 2007; Wigglesworth & Storch 2009); and (2) what aspects of writing and language L2 speakers discuss during the process of col-laborative writing (Alegría de la Colina & García Mayo 2007; Fernández Dobao 2012; Fortune 2005; Kuiken & Vedder 2002; Malmquist 2005; Niu 2009; Storch & Aldosari 2010, 2013; Wigglesworth & Storch 2009). Whereas the comparative research of individual and collaborative writing explores how the process of co-construction leads to differences in the linguistic features or overall quality of students' written texts, the student interaction research focuses more narrowly on the language forms that students discuss and incorporate into their written texts. Situated within the second body of research, the present chapter similarly focuses on the nature of student interaction during collaborative writing tasks, but also explores whether their interactions are related to overall text quality. Establishing a link between the nature of students' interaction while co-constructing texts and the overall quality of their texts would provide further evidence that students ben-efit from collaborative writing tasks. Although the majority of the collaborative dialogue research has focused on the different aspects of language (e.g., form, meaning, word choice) that students discuss, some studies, highlighted below, have considered other aspects of writing, such as content and organization, which also impact text quality.

In a series of studies, Storch and colleagues (Storch 2005; Storch & Wigglesworth 2007; Wigglesworth & Storch 2009) analyzed the interaction between ESL students enrolled in university degree programs in Australia who carried out collaborative writing tasks involving two text types: data commentary (i.e., describing information illustrated in a figure) and an argumentative essay. In Storch (2005), students taking a required, credit-bearing ESL writing class worked collaboratively on a data commentary task. Analysis of their interaction indicated that they spent most of their time composing, followed by planning and revising, and that they discussed content most often, followed by language, and organization. Follow-up experimental studies (Storch & Wigglesworth 2007; Wigglesworth & Storch 2009) further investigated students' interaction during a data commentary task and also included a collaborative argumentative essay task. Similar to the classroom study, the students spent most of their time on the composing process, followed by planning and revision for both text types; the most frequent topics they discussed during both tasks were content and language. In sum, regardless of text type, these ESL university students spent the majority of their time composing their texts and talked about content more often than other aspects of writing.

L2 students' orientation to content during collaborative writing tasks was also reported by Elola and Oskoz (2010), who analyzed the chat scripts that occurred when students of Spanish composed wiki essays. They classified the students' talk into episodes based on the categories used by Storch and colleagues (e.g., content, organization, grammar, and vocabulary) and also identified specific interactional moves, such as asking for opinions, planning task performance, and showing agreement/disagreement. The results indicated that the students focused on content most frequently, followed by a combination of organization and structure, sources of information used as support, grammar and organization, with very little discussion of vocabulary. In terms of interactional moves, the collaborative writers most frequently showed agreement and disagreement followed by planning, providing opinions, providing feedback and dividing the work. The prevalence of talk about sharing the work may indicate that the learners chose to complete specific parts of the task individually, which Storch (2013) refers to as co-authoring as opposed to collaborative writing.

Taken together, the findings of these studies indicated that L2 students spend the majority of their time on the composing process regardless of text type (data commentary, argumentative essay) or target language (English or Spanish), and focus on content most often. This finding falls in line with findings from studies that used think-aloud protocols to identify how individual writers construct texts (Bosher 1998; Cumming 1989; Raimes 1987; Sasaki 2000) and suggests that composing processes are the main concern of both individual and collaborative writers. For text types that require source materials, such as the data commentary task in Storch's research and the wiki essay in Elola and Oskitz's study (2010), students spend time discussing the sources during the collaborative writing process, most likely to ensure that they have comprehended the materials correctly. It is not clear whether the students' interaction has any relationship to the overall quality of their written texts because that analysis was beyond the scope of the previous studies.

Although the relationship between students' interaction and text quality has been investigated in the collaborative planning literature (Neumann & McDonough 2014, 2015; Shi 1998; Sweigart 1991), collaborative writing studies have yet to investigate this relationship. Collaborative writing studies that focused on language-related episodes have shown that students incorporate linguistic forms that they discussed into their written texts (e.g., Brooks & Swain 2009; Watanabe & Swain 2007) and are able to remember linguistic forms when taking tailor-made post-tests (e.g., Adams 2007; Swain & Lapkin 2001). Previous collaborative writing studies have assessed text quality by using analytic rubrics or linguistic measures of accuracy, fluency, or complexity to compare the collaborative and individual texts (e.g., Kuiken & Vedder 2002; Shehadeh 2011; Storch 2005), but have not explored whether these features are related to the students' interaction. A relevant and unexplored issue for collaborative writing research is the extent to which students' talk about different aspects of their writing, such as its content, organization, and language, is related to global assessments of text quality.

Thus, this chapter aims to contribute to the collaborative writing research by examining the nature of student talk while composing two different text types (summary and problem/solution paragraphs) and exploring whether their interaction has any relationship to text quality. Whereas text types have been shown to elicit similar types of interaction (i.e., students focus on composing and discuss content), it is possible that the relationship between their interaction and text quality may differ by text type. For example, tasks that require discussion of source materials may result in more interaction to facilitate comprehension, as opposed to discussion of the content, organization, or language of the text. Furthermore, the prevalence of interaction to facilitate comprehension may be reflected in global text ratings. Therefore, our first research question asked whether the interaction between Thai EFL students during collaborative writing tasks differed by text type (summary or problem/solution). Because neither text type has been previously targeted in collaborative writing research, we did not formulate a directional hypothesis or prediction about which text type would elicit different categories of student talk. The second research question asked whether there was a relationship between Thai EFL students' interaction during collaborative writing tasks and text quality. Because previous collaborative writing studies have not investigated whether different amounts or types of student talk are associated with text quality, we did not hypothesize about the direction of any potential correlation.

Method

Methodological framework

A quantitative, mixed design was used to investigate Thai EFL students' interaction during collaborative writing tasks and its relationship to text quality. Because it was carried out in a Thai university EFL class where collaborative writing tasks are used as part of the normal instructional practices, the study has high ecological validity, i.e., it closely resembles what happens in real life, which allows for generalization to actual educational practices (see Sato & Ballinger this volume). However, high ecological validity comes with a trade-off in the form of reduced experimental control over other variables, such as text types, topics, timing, or order of the writing tasks, which can complicate the identification of relationships between variables.

In terms of the specific research questions, a within-groups comparison was carried out to determine if the students' interaction differed when they wrote summary or problem/solution paragraphs. In other words, rather than compare one pair of students who wrote a summary paragraph to a different pair of students who wrote a problem/solution paragraph (e.g., a between-groups design), each pair wrote both text types. The advantage of the within-groups design type is that personality, proficiency, and other individual variables are controlled by comparing students to themselves. Because students selected their own partners and worked with the same partner for both tasks, there was also some control over potentially intervening variables, such as learners' willingness to work with specific classmates, pair dynamics, and proficiency, which have been shown to affect peer interaction (Kim & McDonough 2008; Leeser 2004; Sato 2013; Sato & Ballinger this volume; Storch 2002a, 2002b; Storch & Aldosari 2013; Watanabe & Swain 2007). However, because the writing tasks were a normal part of the instructional routine, there was no opportunity to counterbalance the tasks. For the second research question, a correlational design was used to determine whether the students' interaction (what the students talked about) was related to text quality (ratings of the content, organization, and language for each text). While correlations can indicate the existence and strength of a relationship, they do not provide insight into causal relationships. This means that it is not possible to determine whether quality conversations cause quality writing.

Participants

The initial participant pool consisted of 70 second-year undergraduate students in the Faculty of Medicine at a university in northern Thailand who were enrolled in a required EFL class. Eight students were excluded from the study because they withdrew from the EFL class before completing the second collaborative writing task ($n = 4$) or switched partners between the first and second writing tasks ($n = 4$). The final participant pool consisted of 62 students (32 women and 30 men) who ranged in age from 17 to 20 years, with a mean of 18.6 years ($SD = .6$). They reported studying English previously from 10 to 18 years ($M = 13.5$ years, $SD = 1.9$), but the majority of the students (41/62) had never traveled to a place that required English for communication. Of those that had, 17 used English for communication during trips outside Thailand that lasted from three to 30 days, while only four reported longer stays, ranging from over one month to one year. Most of the participants did not know any additional languages besides Thai and English, but a few students reported knowledge of Chinese (6), French (1), German (1), Japanese (1), and Korean (1). In terms of their exposure to English outside class, most participants (49/62) reported spending at least three hours per week studying English, and at least two hours per week listening to English music, TV programs, or movies, and using English online. However, the majority of the participants (43/62) indicated that they never spoke English outside class, and the remainder reported spending only one to two hours per week speaking English. The students had never taken any standardized proficiency tests or in-house placement exams, but they were considered intermediate proficiency level by the English department. The researchers agreed that their written English texts indicated that most of the students were at the A2 (basic user) level, with a few participants reaching the B1 (proficient user) level in the Common European Framework of Reference for Languages.

Instructional context

The students were enrolled in two sections of a required, critical reading and writing EFL class taught by the third author. The class met for thirty, 90-minute class periods over an 18-week semester (including holidays and a midterm examinations week). In the semester when the data was collected, the department offered a total of 130 sections of the reading and writing class, which were taught by 83 teachers and which enrolled over four thousand students. The class was designed to develop students' critical thinking and reading abilities and foster paragraph-level writing skill, and used a textbook created by faculty members in the English Department of the university. The textbook included reading passages in the form of jokes, headlines, advertisements, and news reports, most of which were adapted from *Reader's Digest* and had Flesch-Kincaid grade levels ranging from 1.1 to 8.4. The writing portion of the textbook focused on sentence-level writing in the first two chapters, and then emphasized short (80–120 word) paragraph writing in the remaining four chapters, with each chapter introducing a different text type (summary, compare/contrast, cause/effect, problem/solution). Course grades were based on attendance (10%), four collaborative in-class writing tasks (30%), a midterm examination (30%) and a final examination (30%). Both exams included vocabulary and reading comprehension items along with paragraph writing.

Materials

As part of a larger dataset (McDonough, Crawford, & De Vleeschauwer 2013), this study examined the interaction that occurred when students carried out a collaborative writing task in week 7 (summary paragraph) and week 17 (problem/ solution paragraph) of their EFL class. In an effort to minimize cheating during examinations, the department created multiple versions of each task that were randomly assigned across the 130 sections of the writing class. The summary task consisted of a short reading passage that described three potential problems with the internet, such as virus attacks, pornography, social isolation, and lack of privacy. Each version of the task presented a different combination of problems and listed them in a different order, but the reading passages across task versions were similar in the length (174–204 words), Flesch reading ease (43% to 51%), and Flesch-Kincaid grade level (9.9 to 10.9). Half of the participants received version A that presented the problems of lack of control, privacy, and social isolation, while the other participants received version B, which focused on virus attacks, privacy, and pornography. Below the reading passage, an outline of the reading passage was provided (72–76 words) which listed the topic, main idea, three main points, and a conclusion. The main idea and conclusion were complete sentences, but the main points were phrases and clauses in a bullet point list. The instructions stated that the students should work together to write a summary paragraph of the source text. The problem/solution task presented a problem statement about current events in Thailand or issues faced by Thai university students. Multiple versions of the problem/solution task were created and randomly assigned across the 130 sections of the class, with representative problem statements including the shortage of English teachers in Thailand, the level of English proficiency in Thailand, video game addiction among university students, protecting national parks, and drug use by teenagers. All of the participants received the same problem statement, which was video game addiction among university students. The instructions stated that the students should work together to write a paragraph to propose solutions to the problem.

Procedure

The collaborative writing tasks were administered by the instructor, who was the third author, following the standardized departmental procedures for collaborative writing assignments. The collaborative writing assignments were summative assessments administered at the end of two instructional units to determine to what extent the students had acquired the ability to write summary and problem/solution paragraphs. The students were not provided with models or given training in how to collaborate because the purpose in administering the collaborative writing tasks was to assess the students' written texts. Put simply, the tasks were used to assess the product created through the students' collaboration, rather than guide or evaluate their writing process. The students self-selected a partner, were given the task instructions, and had the entire class period (75 minutes) to write their collaborative paragraphs by hand. The students were allowed to talk to their partner, but discussion across pairs was not allowed. The departmental procedure did not specify what language should be spoken during the collaborative writing tasks, so the students were free to choose which language(s) to speak when interacting with each other. Students were permitted to consult a paper-based dictionary while writing the paragraphs, but no electronic dictionaries or other electronic devices (phones, tablets, or laptops) were allowed. Their performance was monitored to ensure that no additional resources were being consulted and that no conversation across other pairs of students occurred. When each pair finished writing and submitted their paragraphs, they were required to leave the classroom. The only deviation from the standard procedure was that each pair was given a digital audio-recorder at the beginning of the class. The students were instructed to place the audio-recorder wherever was most convenient for them and were told that they could move the recorder while they were working as needed.

Analysis

The audio-recordings were transcribed and verified by three research assistants who spoke Thai as their first language (L1). To facilitate comparison with prior research (Storch 2005; Storch & Wigglesworth 2007; Wigglesworth & Storch 2009), the transcripts first were analyzed in terms of the amount of time students spent planning, composing, and revising their paragraphs. The transcripts were segmented into episodes based on the focus of student talk (content, organization, language, reading and re-reading, task clarification and management, and off-task talk), which were adapted from the coding categories used in previous studies (Storch 2005; Storch & Wigglesworth 2007; Wigglesworth & Storch 2009). Definitions and examples of the episodes are provided in Table 1. Because the students spoke Thai extensively when they were collaborating, the examples have been translated to English by the first author and checked by the third author. Any words or phrases that the students spoke in English, as opposed to Thai, are indicated in italics.

Table 1. Episode definitions and examples

Episode type	Definition	Example
Content	Generating, discussing, and evaluating ideas; agreeing, disagreeing, and proposing alternative ideas; talking about source text meaning (for summary writing)	[Discussing a solution to the problem of video game addiction] A: and they should use their free time productively B: *in sport* like this, use in sport, in playing A: in something better than a game B: and then *such as sport* or something like this
Organization	Discussing the structure of the paragraphs; ordering ideas; moving sentences to a different place in the paragraph; deciding to cut information from sections of the paragraphs	[Discussing solutions to the problem of video game addition] A: *who*. Write *who* first B: yes *who* A: *who* first B: then there's *what* then there's *why* A: then the *game addict* and how to solve the problem
Language	Discussing or questioning the meaning, spelling, or pronunciation of individual words, phrases or grammatical forms; correcting errors; discussing how to manipulate language when paraphrasing (for summary writing)	A: with the word *friendship*, we use *get new friendship*? B: *know new friend, new friend* A: know new friend? We use *met*? Or *meet*? meet new friend? B: *meet new friend, know new friend* Look in the dictionary. Look at the word *know*.
Task management	Talking about what they are supposed to do; assigning task roles; clarifying task requirements; monitoring time	A: three [disadvantages] is enough. We're wasting time B: but are we writing too little? A: it's okay B: but the paragraph is almost done A: it's okay. We shouldn't write longer than the example. We should have finished by now.
Reading and re-reading	Reading sentences out loud from their paragraphs; reading sentences from the source text out loud (for summary writing)	A: [reading their paragraph] *Become deeply involved and drifting apart. Last, internet is the one reason that separate us and our family.* Like this? B: yeah

Table 1. (*continued*)

Episode type	Definition	Example
Off task	Talking about topics that are unrelated to the writing task	A: are you going to wear a mask to the party? B: yeah A: did you buy one yet? B: not yet A: where are you going to get one? Behind the university? I've looked already. They're not very good. B: I'm not surprised because they were so cheap A: yeah only 29 or 39 baht

Following training with the first author, which involved (a) discussion of the coding categories and examples, (b) collaborative coding of one transcript, and (c) independent coding of one transcript followed by discussion, one of the Thai L1 research assistants coded all transcripts. A subset of the transcripts (16/62 transcripts or 26%) was randomly selected and coded by the third author, who followed the same training as the research assistant. Interrater reliability was calculated as Cronbach's alpha for each coding category using a two-way random model. The intraclass correlation coefficients were as follows: task management (.97), reading and re-reading (.92), content (.94), language (.92), organization (.91), and off task talk (.92). Disagreements were resolved by the first author and included in the dataset.

To facilitate data exchange among the researchers, the students' hand-written summary and problem/solution paragraphs were converted into Microsoft Word documents by three English L1 research assistants. No changes were made to the formatting, spelling, punctuation, or language use in the students' texts during the conversion process, with the exception of ignoring words and sentences that the students had crossed out in their texts. The electronic texts were independently rated by two English L1 research assistants who had not participated in the data conversion process, and had experience using analytic rubrics to evaluate paragraphs written by English L2 students (Neumann & McDonough 2014, 2015). To rate the texts, analytical rating scales were created by the researchers based on the grading criteria for the summary and problem/solution paragraphs used in the students' EFL reading and writing class (see Appendices A and B). The EFL class grading criteria had been articulated by a curriculum committee, pilot tested, revised, and approved by the English department, and had been in use for three years at the time the study was carried out.

The researchers converted the format of the grading criteria into a rubric, equalized the points in the content, organization, and language categories (10 points each), and assigned descriptors to four bands of performance: above standard, standard, approaching standard, and below standard. The raters were trained by the first author using texts written by students who were not included in the study. After rating and discussing several texts, both raters independently coded all the paragraphs. To evaluate the reliability of their ratings, interrater reliability was assessed using a two-way mixed average-measures intraclass correlation coefficient, which was .87 for the summary paragraphs and .84 for the problem/solution paragraphs. The means for each subscore and the total score assigned by the two raters for each text were calculated, and these means were used for subsequent analyses. Because no directional hypotheses or predictions had been formulated, two-tailed tests of significance were used. Alpha was set at .05.

Results

The first research question asked whether the interaction between Thai EFL students during collaborative writing tasks differed by text type. To address this research question, we first considered the students' total time on task and the amount of time they spent on each phase of the writing process: planning, composing, and revising. In terms of the descriptive statistics (provided in Table 2), the students interacted for a mean of 55.2 minutes while writing the summary paragraphs and a mean of 58.7 minutes during the problem/solution paragraphs. In terms of the three phases, they spent more time planning and revising during the problem/solution task, but more time composing during the summary task. Using an adjusted alpha level of .012 (.05/4 comparisons), paired-samples t-tests indicated that there were no statistically significant differences between the summary and problem/solution tasks in terms of the students' total time on task or the amount of time they spent in each phase of the writing process. The effect sizes (Cohen's d) failed to reach the level considered small (.60) based on benchmarks for within-groups comparisons in applied linguistics research (Plonsky & Oswald 2014).

Table 2. Time by phase and task

	Summary		Problem/solution		Statistics		
	M	SD	M	SD	t(30)	p	d
Total time	55.2	9.5	58.7	14.5	1.41	.158	.29
Planning	5.3	6.5	8.3	6.4	1.96	.059	.47
Composing	44.6	13.3	40.3	13.1	1.36	.183	.33
Revising	4.5	6.4	10.0	11.6	2.42	.022	.58

To further investigate the potential impact of text type on the students' interaction, we compared the types of episodes that occurred during each task, regardless of the specific process (planning, writing, or revising) that the students were engaged in at the time the episodes occurred. Because total time on task was not a factor, we reported the frequency counts for each episode type. As shown in Table 3, the students produced more episodes about content, organization, language, and off-task talk while writing their problem/solution paragraphs, but produced more episodes about task management and reading/re-reading during the summary task. Paired-samples t-tests for each episode type, with an adjusted alpha level of .008 (.05/6 comparisons), indicated that the differences were statistically significant with the exception of task management and off-task talk. The effect sizes for the significant episode types ranged from approaching small (.60) to medium (1.00) (Plonsky & Oswald 2014).

Table 3. Episodes by type and task

	Summary			Problem/solution			Statistics		
	Sum	M	SD	Sum	M	SD	t(30)	p	d
Content	334	10.77	6.41	475	15.45	7.84	2.76	.008	.65
Organization	145	4.68	2.96	244	7.87	2.99	4.57	.001	1.07
Language	419	13.52	7.28	538	17.35	8.08	3.03	.005	.50
Task management	177	5.71	3.70	153	4.94	2.67	1.18	.246	.24
Reading/re-reading	62	2.00	2.42	23	.74	1.24	3.22	.003	.66
Off-task	47	1.52	2.13	89	2.87	4.64	1.74	.092	.37

The second research question asked whether there was a relationship between the students' interaction and text quality. In order to reduce the number of correlations, the number of content, organization, and language episodes per pair were summed and divided by the total number of episodes to obtain a proportion score. While it would be possible to address this research question by simply summing the content, organization, and language episodes, such an approach would not provide insight into students' orientation to these aspects of writing relative to the total number of episodes they engaged in. For example, a pair of students that produces five content episodes out of 10 total episodes (50%) shows a different orientation to content than a pair that produced five content episodes out of 30 total episodes (17%).

To determine whether there was a relationship between the students' interaction and text quality, the proportion of content, organization, and language episodes were correlated with the students' paragraph ratings. As shown in Table 4, the students produced more content, organization, and language episodes in the problem/solution task than in the summary task in terms of both raw frequency (as previously illustrated in Table 3), as well as the proportion of content, organization, and language episodes to total episodes. The mean ratings for summary and problem/solution paragraphs were similar, 23.39 and 23.44, respectively. There was a statistically significant relationship between the proportion of content, organization, and language episodes and the text ratings for the problem/solution paragraphs, with a small effect size ($rho^2 = .14$), but not for the summary paragraphs.

Table 4. Correlation between episodes and ratings

	Content, organization & language episodes			Text ratings		Statistics	
	Sum	M prop	SD	M	SD	rho	p
Summary paragraphs	898	.76	.11	23.39	1.73	.011	.955
Problem/solution paragraphs	1257	.83	.08	23.44	1.95	.374	.038

Discussion

The current study explored the nature of student interaction during collaborative writing tasks and its relationship to text quality. In terms of the students' interaction, they spent the majority of their time on the composing process, as opposed to planning or revising, for both text types, which confirms the findings of previous L2 studies involving a data commentary task and an argumentative essay (Storch 2005; Storch & Wigglesworth 2007; Wigglesworth & Storch 2009). However, unlike the ESL students investigated in those studies, who had achieved the required proficiency scores to be admitted to degree programs at an Australian university, these Thai EFL students discussed language most frequently for both text types. Their greater orientation to language, rather than content, may be due to differences in the text types targeted in previous studies (i.e., essays and data commentary), which may have required greater attention to content than the paragraph writing tasks used here. Text length may also be an important reason for the EFL students' orientation to language. Their paragraph-level texts required less content and had simpler rhetorical structures than the longer texts written in previous studies. Since their texts did not involve extended discourse to show relationships across paragraphs, the students may have focused more on word and sentence level aspects of language.

The divergent findings may also be due to differences in the students' proficiency (degree-seeking student versus basic users), learning context (ESL versus EFL) or perhaps even some combination of text type, proficiency, and learning context. In other words, for paragraph-level writing in this EFL setting with students at this proficiency level, the instructional focus is on writing to learn language, which emphasizes the role of writing in promoting the acquisition of linguistic knowledge and skills (Cumming 1990; Manchón 2011), which may have been reflected in the students' focus on language rather than content. This contrasts with the instructional focus in ESL settings, particularly for matriculated university students, which emphasizes the acquisition of "good" writing and focuses on the cognitive processes involved in writing (e.g., planning, integrating, synthesizing, revising), the development of rhetorical voice (i.e., author interpretation), and the social demands imposed by the context for writing and the intended audience (Hyland 2011; Manchón 2011). In such contexts, students may be more oriented toward content, due to the emphasis on text-responsible writing in their academic classes, whereas students in general EFL courses may be more oriented toward language.

Although both text types elicited a similar distribution of episodes across categories of student talk, the students produced more content, organization, and language episodes while writing problem/solution paragraphs and engaged in more reading and re-reading episodes while writing summary paragraphs. Because the students had to write problem/solution paragraphs without any reference to a source text, which was not the case for the summary paragraphs, the problem/solution task required that they generate all the content themselves, which included proposing three solutions to the stated problem, providing supporting details for each solution, and evaluating their potential effectiveness. For summary writing, the content of the students' paragraphs was determined by the source text information, so there was no need to generate new ideas. Problem/solution paragraphs also elicited greater talk about organization, which is likely due to the need to decide the order in which the three solutions should be presented. This contrasts with summary paragraphs, where the order of information typically follows that of the source text. In addition, students in this EFL context have been shown to incorporate explicit instruction about the rhetorical organization of summary paragraphs into their own writing (McDonough, Crawford, & De Vleeschauwer 2014), which may reduce their need to discuss the organization of summary paragraphs. And finally, summary writing naturally lends itself to reading and re-reading episodes as students not only have to read and comprehend the source text, but also have to read their own paragraphs to ensure that they have paraphrased source text information appropriately.

In terms of the second research question, which asked about the relationship between interaction and text quality, the correlation analysis indicated that there was a significant positive relationship for problem/solution paragraphs. The findings extend those of previous collaborative writing studies which demonstrated that students subsequently remember and use the linguistic forms that they discussed during collaborative tasks (Adams 2007; Brooks & Swain 2009; Swain &

Lapkin 2001). The current data provides evidence that the quantity of student talk about content, organization, and language is positively associated with text quality as assessed through paragraph ratings based on content, organization, and language subscores. In sum, besides promoting attention to language form, collaborative writing tasks also help L2 students discuss other aspects of writing, and their discussions are positively linked to text quality.

However, there was a positive correlation between the students' talk about content, language, and organization episodes and text quality for the problem/solution paragraphs only. Studies that investigated the relationship between students' interaction during collaborative prewriting tasks and writing quality (Neumann & McDonough 2015) also found that the relationship varied by topic and paragraph type. For example, Neumann and McDonough found a positive correlation between the students' reflective content episodes (i.e., evaluating ideas, consideration of alternatives, and justifying) and text quality (i.e., content subscores) for only two out of six paragraphs, both of which required students to state and justify their opinions. An interesting question then, is why there was no relationship between the students' interaction and text quality for their summary paragraphs.

One potential explanation may be that writing summary paragraphs required students to focus on source text comprehension, as reflected by the significantly greater number of reading and re-reading episodes. Previous collaborative writing studies that involved the use of sources also reported that students' interaction included episodes to interpret a graph or table (1–13% of total task time in Storch 2013) and to discuss source texts (mean of nearly 15% of total episodes in Elola & Oskoz 2010). In other words, because the summary task required source text comprehension, the students' reading/re-reading, content, and language episodes may have focused on the meaning of what they were reading, as opposed to the meaning of what they were writing. Because the texts were written in a single class period under examination conditions, it may be that the time the students spent discussing text comprehension reduced the time available to focus on the content, organization or language of their own paragraphs. It is possible that students would focus on these aspects of writing if they were given more time to complete the writing task.

As mentioned in the literature review, one benefit of collaborative writing tasks is that they encourage learners to interact in the target language, thereby creating opportunities for interactional feedback, attention to form, and modified output. However, our findings suggest that in this EFL setting, the students rarely used the target language while carrying out the collaborative writing tasks. Nevertheless, they were engaged in 'on-task' conversation, with off-task episodes accounting for only 4% of the summary episodes and 6% of the problem/solution episodes. Similar to previous studies of L1 use during collaborative tasks (e.g., Scott & de la Fuente 2008; Storch & Aldosari 2010; Swain & Lapkin 2000; Wagner & Toth 2013), these students used their L1 purposefully to develop content, organize ideas, and use language appropriately and accurately, although they spoke their L1 at rates higher than reported in the previous studies. In short, although collaborative writing may not always elicit oral L2 production, it still creates opportunities for students to co-construct written L2 texts while using their L1 as a tool to support the writing process.

One factor that may have contributed to the students' extensive use of the L1 is the fact that the collaborative writing tasks were used for assessment purposes, with each text worth 8% of the students' final class grade. Although numerous studies of peer interaction have been carried out in L2 classrooms, the collaborative tasks (e.g., dictogloss, text reconstruction, text editing, etc.) are frequently implemented as 'one-shot' research activities, as opposed to being a regular part of instructional routine. For the few previous studies in which collaborative writing tasks were integrated into the curriculum (Elola & Oskoz 2010; Storch 2005; Shehadeh 2011), it is not clear whether the tasks were used as formative assessments to provide opportunities for L2 use and writing development, or as a summative assessment task to evaluate the students' writing abilities as part of their class grade. In the context reported here, the collaborative writing tasks were used as summative assessments that contributed to the students' class grades. The department's evaluation criteria awarded points for the content, organization, language use, and mechanics of the students' texts. There were no assessment criteria related to the process of text co-construction, and the instructions did not specify which language the students should use when talking to their partner. Because the students knew that they would be evaluated based on the quality of their written product exclusively, they may have believed that speaking their L1, rather than their L2, would help them write better texts and get higher grades.

Pedagogical implications

The findings of the current study may help inform instructors' decisions about the design and implementation of collaborative writing tasks in their writing classes. If, for example, instructors have identified text comprehension as a skill that their students require additional practice with, then asking students to collaboratively write a summary may promote discussion about text comprehension. On the other hand, asking students to collaboratively write a problem/solution argument may promote more discussion of content, organization and language. It is possible that other text types, such as comparison or process description, may also elicit student talk about content, organization and language. In other words, collaborative writing tasks that require students to generate and organize their own ideas may promote discussion of content, organization and language to a greater extent than tasks which require comprehension of source texts, at least when time constraints are present.

An important factor for instructors to consider when implementing collaborative writing tasks in their L2 classrooms is their pedagogical objective. If an EFL instructor's objective is to promote the use of the target language, then it may be necessary to include explicit instructions and assessment criteria related to language use during task performance. In addition, if students are not accustomed to interacting with their classmates in their L2, an instructor may find it useful to provide them with models of collaborative task performance (Kim & McDonough 2011; Swain 1998; Swain & Lapkin 2001) or interactional strategies for successful communication (Fujii et al. this volume; Sato & Lyster 2012). This may be particularly useful if the goal is to encourage students to equally participate in the collaborative writing process. As mentioned previously, the collaborative writing tasks in the current study were used for summative assessment based exclusively on the students' written texts. As a result, the instructor did not monitor or evaluate the amount and type of the students' interaction while they were writing other than to discourage talk across pairs per the departmental guidelines.

However, if the objective is to evaluate the students' written text, then it may not be as important to specify which languages students speak while collaborating. Using the L1 during collaborative writing tasks, which may be particularly prevalent in EFL contexts with lower proficiency students, may help students comprehend source texts and discuss the content, organization, or language features of their written texts in ways that they may not be equipped to do in their L2. Studies documenting the use of the L1 in collaborative writing tasks are generally in agreement that the L1 can serve important functions during collaborative writing, such as word choice in the L2 (Storch & Aldossari 2010; Swain & Lapkin 2000). Furthermore, studies of individual writers have shown that the relationship between L1 use and text quality varies depending on its cognitive function. For example, van Weijen and colleagues (van Weijen, van den Bergh, Rijlaarsdam, Sanders 2009) found that L1 use to generate ideas and plan had no relationship with text quality, but L1 use to manage the writing process had a negative relationship with text quality. However, using the L2 to manage the writing process also had a negative relationship with text quality, which suggests that the underlying cognitive function may be more important than the language spoken. Finally, if the goal is to ensure that each student equally contributes to task performance (both process and product), it may be useful to incorporate evaluation criteria, self-assessment opportunities, and peer-assessment components into the task evaluation procedures.

Limitations and future research

As pointed out in the methodological orientation section, the current study bears close resemblance to how collaborative writing tasks are used in 'the real world' of this Thai university (i.e., ecological validity), which comes with the trade-off of reduced experimental control. Consequently, there are several limitations that should be addressed through future research. First, the text types (summary and problem/solution) and their order of presentation were determined by the course textbook and could not be changed for research purposes. Ideally, in a laboratory-based experiment, the order of text types would have been counterbalanced so that some students wrote the summary tasks first, while other students wrote the problem/solution paragraphs first. This would serve as a check against development, because the students' performance on the second task could differ simply because they have had more instruction and have done previous collaborative writing tasks. In other words, the differences between the summary and problem/solution tasks documented here could be due to the students' development, rather than the text type. While this is a possible interpretation of the findings, the students' text quality scores were nearly identical for the two tasks, which suggests there was little change in the students' writing development over time. However, future studies with greater experimental control would be necessary to confirm that text type, rather than development or practice, accounted for the divergent findings for summary and problem/solution texts.

Because the collaborative writing tasks were used for assessment purposes, it is possible that students felt pressure to produce texts that would receive high grades, which influenced their interaction. As a result of the assessment context, it is not clear whether similar amounts and types of episodes would occur when students carry out collaborative writing tasks under no stakes conditions, such as for research purposes, or in low stakes settings, such as ungraded learning or practice activities for formative assessment. Furthermore, because the collaborative writing tasks were administered under test conditions, students were not asked to compose multiple drafts of the same text, as they would have if they were working together to revise their paragraphs after receiving instructor or peer feedback. The nature of students' interaction and its relationship to text quality may be very different when students engage in collaboration throughout the writing process. Future research should compare student interaction during collaborative writing tasks that were carried out under a variety of authentic classroom conditions.

The present study focused on what learners talk about while collaboratively writing two paragraph types that had very different purposes. Summary paragraphs are a type of source-based writing with a strong emphasis on text comprehension and the expectation that the summary will reliably convey the source information without imposing the writer's own opinion. In contrast, the problem/

solution paragraphs required that the students propose a novel set of solutions without the use of any source materials. Future studies should explore a wider variety of collaborative writing tasks, as many previous studies have examined a fairly narrow range of tasks, such as dictogloss, text reconstruction, and text editing. Including a wider range of text types, with a more elaborated writing process (i.e., multiple drafts), and the use of source materials will help future studies identify whether these factors potentially result in different types of interaction and have varying relationships to text quality.

Finally, the participants in this study were at the lower-intermediate level studying in an EFL setting. Collaborative dialogue studies that compared students from different proficiency levels (Leeser 2004; Storch & Aldosari 2013) found that higher proficiency L2 students produce more language-related episodes than lower-proficiency students. Their findings indicate that proficiency plays a role in the types of episodes that occur during collaborative tasks, at least for language episodes (see Choi & Iwashita 2016; Sato & Viveros 2016). Further research is needed to determine whether proficiency differences also impact content and organization episodes during a wider range of collaborative writing tasks, and whether certain proficiency pairings lead to different types of episodes or show varying relationships to text quality. Although the impact of L1 use on L2 text quality has been widely studied with individual writing tasks (for overview see van Weijen et al. 2009), future research is needed to determine how L1 and L2 use during collaborative writing tasks contribute to text quality. Our future studies aim to address these issues through classroom-based research that can contribute to on-going investigations into the benefits of peer interaction for L2 writing development, and provide L2 writing instructors with information that can help inform their decisions about how to use collaborative writing tasks in ways that maximize learning outcomes.

References

Adams, R. (2007). Do second language learners benefit from interacting with each other? In A. Mackey (Ed.), *Conversational interaction in second language acquisition* (pp. 29–51). Oxford: Oxford University Press.

Alegría de la Colina, A., & García Mayo, M. P. (2007). Attention to form across collaborative tasks by low-proficiency learners in an EFL setting. In M. P. García Mayo (Ed.), *Investigating tasks in formal language learning* (pp. 91–116). Clevedon, UK: Multilingual Matters.

Basterrechea, M. & García Mayo, M. P. (2013). Language-related episodes during collaborative tasks: A comparison of CLIL and EFL learners. In K. McDonough & A. Mackey (Eds.), *Second language interaction in diverse educational contexts* (pp. 25–43). Amsterdam: John Benjamins. doi:10.1075/lllt.34.05ch2

Bosher, S. (1998). The composing processes of three Southeast Asian writers at the post-secondary level: An exploratory study. *Journal of Second Language Writing* 7, 205–241. doi:10.1016/S1060-3743(98)90013-3

Brooks, L., & Swain, M. (2009). Languaging in collaborative writing: Creation of and response to expertise. In A. Mackey & C. Polio (Eds.), *Multiple perspectives on interaction: Second language research in honor of Susan M. Gass* (pp. 58–89). New York, NY: Routledge.

Cumming, A. (1989). Writing expertise and second-language proficiency. *Language Learning* 39, 81–141. doi: 10.1111/j.1467-1770.1989.tb00592.x

Cumming, A. (1990). Metalinguistic and ideational thinking in second language composing. *Written Communication*, 7, 482–511. doi: 10.1177/0741088390007004003

Donato, R. (1994). Collective scaffolding in second language learning. In J. P. Lantolf & G. Appel (Eds.), *Vygotskian approaches to second language research* (pp. 33–56). Norwood, NJ: Ablex.

Elola, I., & Oskoz, A. (2010). Collaborative writing: Fostering foreign language and writing conventions development. *Language Learning and Technology*, 14(3), 51–71.

Fernández Dobao, A. (2012). Collaborative writing tasks in the L2 classroom: Comparing group, pair, and individual work. *Journal of Second Language Writing*, 21, 40–58. doi: 10.1016/j.jslw.2011.12.002

Fernández Dobao, A., & Blum, A. (2013). Collaborative writing in pairs and small groups: Learners' attitudes and perceptions. *System*, 41, 365–378. doi: 10.1016/j.system.2013.02.002

Fortune, A. (2005). Learners' use of metalanguage in collaborative form-focused L2 output tasks. *Language Awareness*, 14, 21–38. doi: 10.1080/09658410508668818

Fujii, A., Zeigler, N., & Mackey, A. (2016). Learner-learner interaction and metacognitive instruction in the EFL classroom. In M. Sato & S. Ballinger (Eds.), *Peer interaction and second language learning: Pedagogical potential and research agenda* (pp. 63–89). Amsterdam: John Benjamins.

Gass, S. (2003). Input and interaction. In C. Doughty & M. Long (Eds.), *Handbook of second language acquisition* (pp. 224–255). Oxford: Blackwell. doi: 10.1002/9780470756492.ch9

Hu, G., & Lam, S. (2010). Issues of cultural appropriateness and pedagogical efficacy: exploring peer review in a second language writing class. *Instructional Science*, 38, 371–394. doi: 10.1007/s11251-008-9086-1

Hyland, K. (2011). Learning to write: Issues in theory, research, and pedagogy. In R. Manchón (Ed.), *Learning-to-write and writing-to-learn in an additional language* (pp. 17–35). Amsterdam: John Benjamins. doi: 10.1075/lllt.31.05hyl

Kim, Y., & McDonough, K. (2008). The effect of interlocutor proficiency on the collaborative dialogue between Korean as a second language learners. *Language Teaching Research*, 12, 211–234. doi: 10.1177/1362168807086288

Kim, Y., & McDonough, K. (2011). Using pretask modelling to encourage collaborative learning opportunities. *Language Teaching Research*, 15(2), 183–199. doi: 10.1177/1362168810388711

Kuiken, F., & Vedder, I. (2002). Collaborative writing in L2: The effect of group interaction on text quality. In S. Randsdell & M.-L. Barbier (Eds.), *New directions for research in L2 writing* (pp. 169–188). Dordrecht: Kluwer. doi: 10.1007/978-94-010-0363-6_9

Lantolf, J. (2011). The sociocultural approach to second language acquisition: Sociocultural theory, second language acquisition, and artificial L2 development. In D. Atkinson (Ed.), *Alternative approaches to second language acquisition* (pp. 24–47). London: Routledge.

Leeser, M. J. (2004). Learner proficiency and focus on form during collaborative dialogue. *Language Teaching Research*, 8, 55–81. doi: 10.1191/1362168804lr134oa

Liu, J., & Sadler, R. (2003). The effect and affect of peer review in electronic versus traditional modes on L2 writing. *Journal of English for Academic Purposes*, 2, 193–227. doi: 10.1016/S1475-1585(03)00025-0

Long, M. (1996). The role of the linguistic environment in second language acquisition. In W. Ritchie & T. K. Bhatia (Eds.), *Handbook of language acquisition: Vol. 2. Second language acquisition* (pp. 413–468). San Diego, CA: Academic Press.

Lundstrum, K., & Baker, W. (2009). To give is better than to receive: The benefits of peer review to the reviewer's own writing. *Journal of Second Language Writing*, 18, 30–43. doi:10.1016/j.jslw.2008.06.002

Mackey, A. (2012). *Input, interaction, and corrective feedback in L2 learning*. Oxford: Oxford University Press.

Malmquist, A. (2005). How does group discussion in reconstruction tasks affect written language output? *Language Awareness*, 14, 128–141. doi:10.1080/09658410508668829

Manchón, R. (2011). Writing to learn the language: Issues in theory and research. In R. Manchón (Ed.), *Learning-to-write and writing-to-learn in an additional language* (pp. 61–82). Amsterdam: John Benjamins. doi:10.1075/lllt.31.07man

McDonough, K., Crawford, W., De Vleeschauwer, J. (2013). *Collaborative and individual writing in a Thai university context*. Paper presented at *the 24th European Second Language Association conference*, Amsterdam, the Netherlands.

McDonough, K., Crawford, W., De Vleeschauwer, J. (2014). Summary writing in a Thai EFL university context. *Journal of Second Language Writing*, 24, 20–32. doi:10.1016/j.jslw.2014.03.001

Min, H. (2006). The effects of trained peer review on EFL students' revision types and writing quality. *Journal of Second Language Writing*, 15, 118–141. doi:10.1016/j.jslw.2006.01.003

Neumann, H., & McDonough, K. (2014). Exploring the relationships among student preferences, prewriting tasks, and text quality in an EAP context. *Journal of English for Academic Purposes*, 15, 14–26. doi:10.1016/j.jeap.2014.05.002

Neumann, H., & McDonough, K. (2015). Exploring student interaction during collaborative prewriting discussions and its relationship to L2 writing. *Journal of Second Language Writing*, 27, 84–104. doi:10.1016/j.jslw.2014.09.009

Niu, R. (2009). Effect of task-inherent production modes on EFL learners' focus on form. *Language Awareness*, 18, 384–402. doi:10.1080/09658410903197256

Plonsky, L., & Oswald, F. (2014). How big is "big"? Interpreting effect sizes in L2 research. *Language Learning*, 64, 878–912. doi:10.1111/lang.12079

Raimes, A. (1987). Language proficiency, writing ability, and composing strategies: A study of ESL college student writers. *Language Learning* 37, 439–469. doi:10.1111/j.1467-1770.1987.tb00579.x

Sasaki, M. (2000). Toward an empirical model of EFL writing processes: An exploratory study. *Journal of Second Language Writing* 9, 259–291. doi:10.1016/S1060-3743(00)00028-X

Sato, M. (2013). Beliefs about peer interaction and peer corrective feedback: Efficacy of classroom intervention. *The Modern Language Journal*, 97, 611–633. doi:10.1111/j.1540-4781.2013.12035.x

Sato, M., & Ballinger, S. (2016). Understanding peer interaction: Research synthesis and directions. In M. Sato & S. Ballinger (Eds.), *Peer interaction and second language learning: Pedagogical potential and research agenda* (pp. 1–30). Amsterdam: John Benjamins.

Sato, M., & Lyster, R. (2012). Peer interaction and corrective feedback for accuracy and fluency development: Monitoring, practice, and proceduralization. *Studies in Second Language Acquisition*, 34, 591–626. doi:10.1017/S0272263112000356

Sato, M. Viveros, P. (2016). Interaction of collaboration? Group dynamics in the foreign language classroom. In M. Sato & Ballinger (Eds.), *Peer interaction and second language learning: Pedagogical potential and research agenda* (pp. 91–112). Amsterdam: John Benjamins.

Scott, V. M., & de la Fuente, M. J. (2008). What's the problem? L2 learners' use of the L1 during consciousness-raising form-focused tasks. *The Modern Language Journal*, 92, 100–113. doi:10.1111/j.1540-4781.2008.00689.x

Shehadeh, A. (2011). Effects and student perceptions of collaborative writing in L2. *Journal of Second Language Writing*, 20, 286–305. doi:10.1016/j.jslw.2011.05.010

Shi, L. (1998). Effects of prewriting discussions on adult ESL students' compositions. *Journal of Second Language Writing*, 7(3), 319–345. doi:10.1016/S1060-3743(98)90020-0

Storch, N. (2002a). Patterns of interaction in ESL pair work. *Language Learning*, 52, 119–158. doi:10.1111/1467-9922.00179

Storch, N. (2002b). Relationships formed in dyadic interaction and opportunity for learning. *International Journal of Educational Research*, 37, 305–322. doi:10.1016/S0883-0355(03)00007-7

Storch, N. (2005). Collaborative writing: Product, process, and students' reflections. *Journal of Second Language Writing*, 14(3), 153–173. doi:10.1016/j.jslw.2005.05.002

Storch, N. (2013). *Collaborative writing in L2 classrooms*. Bristol, UK: Multilingual Matters.

Storch, N., & Aldosari, A. (2010). Learners' use of first language (Arabic) in pair work in an EFL class. *Language Teaching Research*, 14, 355–375. doi:10.1177/1362168810375362

Storch, N., & Aldosari, A. (2013). Pairing learners in pair work activity. *Language Teaching Research*, 17, 31–48. doi:10.1177/1362168812457530

Storch, N., & Wigglesworth, G. (2007). Writing tasks: The effects of collaboration. In M. P. García Mayo (Ed.), *Investigating tasks in formal language learning* (pp. 157–177). Clevedon, UK; Multilingual Matters.

Swain, M. (1998). Focus on form through conscious reflection. In C. Doughty, & J. Williams (Eds.), *Focus on form in classroom second language acquisition* (pp. 64–81). Cambridge: Cambridge University Press.

Swain, M. (2006). Languaging, agency, and collaboration in advanced second language proficiency. In H. Byrnes (Ed.), *Advanced language learning: The contributions of Halliday and Vygotsky* (pp. 95–108). London: Continuum.

Swain, (2010). Talking-it-through: Languaging as a source of learning. In R. Batstone (Ed.), *Sociocognitive perspectives on language use and language learning* (pp. 112–130). Oxford: Oxford University Press.

Swain, M., & Lapkin, S. (1998). Interaction and second language learning: Two adolescent French immersion students working together. *Modern Language Journal*, 82, 320–337. doi:10.1111/j.1540-4781.1998.tb01209.x

Swain, M., & Lapkin, S. (2000). Task-based second language learning: The uses of the first language. *Language Teaching Research* 4, 251–274. doi:10.1177/136216880000400304

Swain, M., & Lapkin, S. (2001). Focus on form through collaborative dialogue: Exploring task effects. In M. Bygate, P. Skehan, & M. Swain (Eds.), *Researching pedagogic tasks* (pp. 99–118). Harlow, UK: Longman.

Sweigart, W. (1991). Classroom talk, knowledge development, and writing. *Research in the Teaching of English*, 25, 469–496.

Van Weijen, D., van den Bergh, H., Rijlaarsam, G., & Sanders, T. (2009). L1 use during L2 writing: An empirical study of a complex phenomenon. *Journal of Second Language Writing*, 18, 235–250. doi:10.1016/j.jslw.2009.06.003

Wagner, E., & Toth, P. (2013). Building explicit L2 Spanish knowledge through guided induction in small group and whole class interaction. In K. McDonough, & A. Mackey (Eds.), *Second language interaction in diverse educational contexts* (pp. 89–108). Amsterdam: John Benjamins. doi:10.1075/lllt.34.08ch5

Watanabe, Y., & Swain, M. (2007). Effects of proficiency differences and patterns of pair interaction on second language learning: Collaborative dialogue between adult ESL learners. *Language Teaching Research*, 11, 121–142. doi:10.1177/1362168806074599

Wigglesworth, G., & Storch, N. (2009). Pair versus individual writing: Effects on fluency, complexity and accuracy. *Language Testing*, 26, 445–466. doi:10.1177/0265532209104670

Appendix A

Summary paragraph rubric

		Content	Organization	Language use
10 9	Above standard	– Main idea is correct – All three main points are correct – Conclusion is correct – No additional details or personal opinions are included	Summary includes all three of the following parts: – introductory sentence stating source and the main idea – three main points presented in an effective order – concluding sentence	– Almost no errors in grammar and/or mechanics – Errors do not interfere with meaning – Acceptable amount and type of paraphrasing
8 7	Standard	– Part of the main idea is missing or incorrect – One of the main points is missing or incorrect – Part of the conclusion is missing or incorrect – No additional details or personal opinions are included	– Summary is missing one of the three parts – A few ideas are not presented in an effective order	– Few errors in grammar and/or mechanics – Some errors interfere with meaning – Insufficient amount or type of paraphrasing
6 5 4	Approaching standard	– Most of the main idea is missing or incorrect – Two of the main points are missing or incorrect – Most of the conclusion is missing or incorrect – Some additional details or personal opinions are included	– Summary is missing two of the three parts – Some ideas are not presented in an effective order	– Many errors in grammar and/or mechanics – Most errors interfere with meaning – Extensive copying with little paraphrasing
3 2 1 0	Below standard	– Main idea is completely incorrect or missing – All three main points were missing or incorrect – Conclusion is completely missing or incorrect – Many additional details or personal opinions are included – Not enough language to evaluate	– Summary is missing all three parts – Most ideas are not presented in an effective order – Not enough language to evaluate	– Extensive errors – Meaning is unclear – Exclusive copying – Not enough language to evaluate

Appendix B

Problem/solution paragraph rubric

		Content	Organization	Language use
10 9	Above standard	– Problem is clearly stated – Solution 1 is supported with logical, relevant, and sufficient supporting details – Solution 2 is supported with logical, relevant, and sufficient supporting details – Conclusion is an accurate restatement of the topic sentence.	Problem/solution paragraph contains all three parts – Topic sentence that clearly states the problem – Two solutions with supporting details – An effective concluding sentence	– Almost no errors in grammar and/or mechanics – Errors do not interfere with meaning
8 7	Standard	– Problem isn't clearly stated, but can be inferred from the title or solutions – One of the solutions is not clearly stated or lacks logical, relevant, and sufficient supporting details – Conclusion attempts to restate the topic sentence, but it is too narrow or broad	– Problem/solution paragraph is missing one of the three parts.	– Few errors in grammar and/or mechanics – Some errors interfere with meaning
6 5 4	Approaching standard	– Problem isn't clearly stated, but can be inferred from the title or solutions – Both of the solutions are not clearly stated or lacks logical, relevant, and sufficient supporting details – Conclusion is a verbatim copy of the topic sentence.	– Problem/solution paragraph is missing two of the three parts.	– Many errors in grammar and/or mechanics – Most errors interfere with meaning
3 2 1 0	Below standard	– Problem isn't stated and is difficult to infer – Solutions aren't stated or lack supporting details – Conclusion is completely missing or incorrect – Not enough language to evaluate	– Problem/solution paragraph is missing all three parts – Not enough language to evaluate	– Extensive errors – Meaning is unclear – Not enough language to evaluate

CHAPTER 8

Engagement with the language

How examining learners' affective and social engagement explains successful learner-generated attention to form

Melissa Baralt, Laura Gurzynski-Weiss and YouJin Kim
Florida International University / Indiana University / Georgia State University

Interactive tasks that have successfully promoted attention to form and language learning in face-to-face (FTF) can be ineffective when performed online (Baralt 2013, 2014). This research is concerning, given the push for online language classes in higher education (Leow, Cerezo, & Baralt 2015). One reason that interactive language tasks do not translate to online settings may be the diminished affect and socialization present in online settings (Baralt 2014). Despite this hypothesis, researchers continue to explore learners' attention to form from exclusively the cognitive perspective. Recently, Svalberg (2009; 2012) proposed a new model for exploring how learners achieve awareness of forms: a threefold construct including cognitive as well as social and affective engagement. The present chapter is the first to empirically operationalize Svalberg's model for analyzing learners' attention (or not) to forms during task-based peer interaction. Forty intermediate-level learners of Spanish performed either cognitively simple or complex interactive dyadic tasks in person or online. Learners' interaction and post-task questionnaires were then coded for the three types of engagement. Results showed more cognitive engagement (e.g., attention to language forms, reflection), social engagement (e.g., supportive interaction) and affective engagement (e.g., positive feelings) in FTF, particularly during the more complex task. All three types of engagement were diminished or were entirely absent in the online interactions. We argue that the lack of social and affective engagement is what deterred cognitive engagement with language forms. The chapter concludes with a discussion on why researchers must consider social and affective engagement to understand how language awareness can be differentially experienced online.

DOI 10.1075/lllt.45.09bar
© 2016 John Benjamins Publishing Company

Introduction

In the field of instructed second language (L2) acquisition, both cognitivist and social theories alike posit a crucial role for learners attending to and interacting with the target language. Whether it be via the construct of noticing (Schmidt 1990, 2001), opportunities for negotiation of meaning (Long 1996), evidence of self-scaffolding and meta-talk (Knouzi, Swain, Lapkin, & Brooks 2010), or production of output and hypothesis testing (Swain 1995, 2005), research – irrespective of theoretical paradigm – consistently shows that learners' awareness of linguistic form leads to L2 learning. What's more, research has shown that some tasks are more effective than others at encouraging learners to attend to forms (Kim 2009; Yilmaz 2011). This research has significant implication as it can inform the ways we as researchers and teachers design tasks.

With over 70% of universities reporting online learning as a critical component of their long-term strategic plans (Allen & Seaman 2015), what we know about how to promote language learning awareness cannot preclude the extension of this research to the online environment. Opportunely, peer interaction in synchronous computer-mediated chat (SCMC) has been shown to assist learners to attend to and become aware of forms (see discussion in Sato & Ballinger 2016; as well as Payne & Whitney 2002; Yilmaz & Yuksel 2011). However, not all tasks that effectively encourage attention to form in the FTF environment translate directly to the online environment (Baralt 2013, 2014). For example, in exploring task-based interaction in SCMC, Baralt (2014) found that learners did not achieve awareness of forms (operationalized as language-related episodes, or LREs) as much as they did during face-to-face (FTF) interaction.

Baralt's (2014) surprising result may be due to the limited way in which she explored learners' achieved awareness (LREs). The construct of LREs is exclusively cognitive, as it only examines learners' attention to linguistic forms. Svalberg (2009, 2012) has recently challenged researchers to go beyond cognitive engagement with forms, and explore language awareness more holistically. Svalberg claims that language awareness is a process that occurs as a result of *Engagement With the Language* (EWL), a construct that includes cognitive, social, and affective engagement. Svalberg argues that this construct is a richer means with which we can research awareness, because it examines *why* certain language-related behaviors and even attitudes lead to learning more than others. To date, no study has used her construct to examine how learners become aware of forms during peer interaction. The goal of this chapter is to "push beyond established units of analysis" (Sato & Ballinger 2016) by examining learners' attention to form as more than simply LREs.

The present chapter operationalizes Svalberg's threefold construct of EWL to qualitatively explore how and why interaction-generated awareness is different in

FTF as compared to SCMC. We examine two types of interactive tasks, one that is cognitively simple, and one that is cognitively complex (the latter theoretically posed to promote more attention to form), and compare learners' task performance in the FTF versus SCMC environments. We also utilize a questionnaire to triangulate learners' EWL. The overarching aim of this exploratory study is to understand how we can promote the best types of peer interaction in FTF and SCMC that result in learning.

Literature review

Role of learner-initiated language awareness in interaction and L2 learning

Learners' attendance to the target language is largely held to be facilitative of language development, though not all agree at what level learners need to attend to input in order for it to be available for conversion to intake. For example, terminology to discuss how learners attend to forms differs widely (e.g., attention, noticing, awareness, orientation, alertness, detection; see Leow's (1997, 1998, 2001, 2010) work on operationalizing levels of noticing and depth of processing). We adopt the definition of language awareness as "explicit knowledge about language, and conscious perception and sensitivity in language learning, language teaching, and language use" (from the Association for Language Awareness[1], cited in Svalberg 2012: 376). Thus, it is akin to Schmidt's rendition of noticing (1990, 2001), which ascribes an explicit, conscious component defined as attention plus awareness. In this chapter, we explore language awareness that emerges as an outcome of EWL, following Svalberg (2012). We assume a facilitative role for language awareness in language learning and learners' ability to explicitly discuss language without claiming that learning is necessarily predicated by this awareness.

Learner-initiated language awareness is hypothesized to be more facilitative of learning than instructor/researcher-initiated language awareness for several reasons. While negotiation of meaning is considered to be beneficial due to the presumption that learners are paying attention to meaning, are vested in the exchange, and therefore are more likely to attend to form (Long 1996), the extent of this benefit may be dependent in part on the individual who draws learners' attention to form. For example, if a researcher or instructor interlocutor attempts to draw learners' attention to form, the interlocutor is demonstrating their own attendance to form within the meaning-based interaction. Learner-initiated focus on form, on the other hand, may be argued to be demonstrative of and predicated

---

1.   <www.languageawareness.org>

on learner attendance; the learner is deliberately addressing a particular gap in knowledge. While exchanges for negotiation of meaning are often introduced by the more advanced interlocutor who identifies a gap between what the learner does and should know, learner-initiated focus on form verifies that the learner herself has identified a gap in knowledge and, importantly, that the learner is interested in addressing this gap herself.

Researching learner-initiated language awareness during peer interaction

There are multiple methods to research how learners attend to form during peer interaction (see Rouhshad & Storch 2016). By far, the most common way to operationalize learner-initiated focus on form has been language-related episodes (LREs); some researchers also refer to these as 'focus on form episodes' or 'languaging' (e.g., Baralt 2014; Ellis, Basturkmen, & Loewen 2001; García Mayo & Azharai 2016; Kim 2012; Kowal & Swain 1994; Loewen & Wolff 2016; Révész 2011; Ross-Feldmen 2007; Rouhshad & Storch 2016; Swain & Lapkin 1998, 2002; Tocalli-Beller & Swain 2007; Williams 2001; see also Gagné & Parks 2013). LREs occur when, in the context of interaction, learners stop to focus on the linguistic aspect of their interaction. They are "any part of a dialogue where the students talk about the language they are producing, question their language use, or correct themselves or others" (Swain & Lapkin 1998: 326). LREs have been found to relate to L2 development. For example, Williams (2001) found that learners retained many of the forms they had discussed in LREs during peer interaction. Tocalli-Beller and Swain (2007) operationalized 'languaging' by coding for Meaning-focused LREs, Form LREs, and Metatalk LREs. They found that all LRE types mediated learners' ability to construct new knowledge around humor. Storch's work in particular (e.g., Storch 2008; Storch & Wigglesworth 2010) has improved the robustness of how we research the quality of LRE metatalk. For example, Storch (2008) examined LREs that involved limited engagement (e.g., simply stating the linguistic item) versus elaborate engagement (e.g., deliberating over linguistic items, seeking an explanation, etc.). She found that LREs with elaborate engagement was what most facilitated language learning. García Mayo and Azkarai (2016) applied Storch's operationalization, and examined elaborate (both learners in a dyad are engaged in the LRE), limited (one learner only engaged in the LRE), and limited + limited (both learners did not discuss the linguistic form) outcomes. Like Storch, García Mayo and Azkarai found that elaborate LREs were more facilitative of learning, but also, that task mode can influence the outcomes of LREs.

Svalberg's proposed construct of EWL (Engagement With the Language) is different than Storch's level of engagement in LRE metatalk. The former is a construct to study how learners construct language awareness, while the latter is a means of coding LRE outcome quality. A fundamental difference of Svalberg's (2007, 2009, 2012) work on EWL as compared to LREs is her inclusion of other aspects of interaction besides cognitive noticing of forms. For Svalberg, research that examines how language awareness happens must include consideration for affective and social phenomena that occur during the interaction. Svalberg defines EWL as a "cognitive, and/or affective, and/or social state and a process in which the learner is the agent and language is the object (and sometimes vehicle)" (2009: 247). *Cognitive engagement* refers to focused attention to form, direction of cognitive resources and problem solving (e.g., does the learner compare, ask questions and draw conclusions or inferences with the target language?). *Affective engagement* refers to learners' attitudes towards the task, the interlocutor, and to participating in the task (e.g., is the learner withdrawn or eager to participate? Is there anxiety?). Finally, *social engagement* refers to learners' initiation and maintenance of interactional behavior (e.g., is the learner interactive? Does she engage in scaffolding?). In Svalberg's view, social and affective engagement can drive cognitive engagement, which mediates language awareness during peer interaction (the reader is reminded that Svalberg defines language awareness as explicit knowledge about, conscious perception of, and sensitivity to language; all three aspects of engagement lead to language awareness in her view). Given that Baralt (2014) found no LRE production in SCMC for the same tasks that were successful in FTF, EWL as a construct may be a potentially richer way to explore why learners did or did not attend to form.

Task design factors as mediating language awareness

In light of the posited and indeed empirically corroborated facilitative role of learners' language awareness on learning, a fascinating line of research has focused on ways to encourage learners' awareness to aspects of language. One of the most successful research areas has been on tasks, and how manipulating task design factors can increase learners' awareness. To date, almost all of these approaches have been exclusively from the cognitive perspective. For example, learners' awareness can be directed via the degree of specificity of the instructions given, via consciousness-raising techniques such as textual enhancement or task-essentialness, via the cognitive resources required to complete a task (task complexity), or via task complexity sequences. In this latter category, much work has been undertaken examining the possibility of maximizing learner noticing of form by increasing the cognitive complexity of a task (Robinson 2010; Robinson & Gilabert 2007). More specifically, by requiring a communicative need and increasing the cognitive effort involved (synonymous with making the task more complex), learners' attentional resources can be directed to specific linguistic features, and this may help them to internalize and learn those forms more effectively.

Indeed, research within this framework has largely found support for this idea. Studies have found that cognitively complex tasks can encourage learners' awareness of task-induced structures in the FTF mode (Baralt 2010, 2014; Kim 2012; Révész 2009, 2011; Kim &Tracy-Ventura 2011; but see Nuevo 2006). The majority of studies examining learner awareness in relation to task complexity have found a relationship between awareness, complexity, and learning outcomes. For example, Baralt (2014), Kim (2012) and Révész (2011), who all examined LREs as a means of generating language awareness, found that learners produced more LREs in more complex tasks; these studies also found a link between increased learner awareness in complex tasks and learning outcomes. Baralt (2014) asked learners to complete a story re-tell task, manipulating whether or not the learner had to hypothesize why a character acted a certain way (+intentional reasoning). Kim (2012) had learners complete several series of tasks, the most complex of which asked learners to make suggestions for the best choice (+intentional reasoning and −few elements). In Révész (2011), learners completed decision-making tasks, with the more complex task operationalized as −few elements and +reasoning. Nuevo, Adams, and Ross-Feldman (2011), who examined learner self-repair as evidence of attendance to form, found that cognitively complex tasks encouraged more self-repair and learning in a decision-making task; however, they did not find that cognitive complexity was related to more self-repair and subsequent learning when learners completed a narration task. Importantly, all of these studies were done within the interactionist framework and, not including Baralt's (2014) SCMC group, took place in FTF environment.

Task interaction environment as mediating language awareness

In light of the fact that more than 25% of university-level language classes are now offered online (Blake 2011), researchers are examining how learning opportunities, including features of interaction that can promote language awareness, may differ online (additional discussions in this volume can be seen in Sato & Ballinger as well as Loewen & Wolff). Much of this work has been undertaken via task-based interactional comparisons using FTF and written SCMC to provide the necessary controls for interpreting initial findings. Theoretically, the two environments are believed to offer unique learning affordances according to the availability and saliency of input provided to learners. For example, in SCMC, learners have more time to focus their attention to language forms (Gurzynski-Weiss & Baralt 2014; Lai & Zhao 2006), forms that are also more permanently available to them for additional consultation. Learners in SCMC settings also have and often take advantage of the opportunity to return to their interlocutor's feedback on the target structure (Gurzynski-Weiss & Baralt 2014). SCMC is therefore hypothesized to promote opportunities for language awareness (Ortega 2009). These hypotheses have not always been borne out, however, in empirical research. When it comes to comparing learners' interpretation of the linguistic target of feedback, studies have found mixed results. For example, while Lai and Zhao (2006) found that English L2 learners' awareness of negotiation for meaning was heightened in SCMC, and that learners' self-corrections were greater in SCMC, there were no FTF or SCMC differences according to the noticing of recasts or modified output. Contrarily, Gurzynski-Weiss and Baralt (2014) examined Spanish learners' interpretation and use of feedback in SCMC and FTF and found learners' perception to be equally accurate regardless of mode in which feedback was provided. They also found significantly more opportunities to work with feedback in the FTF mode, and learners took advantage of these opportunities significantly more in FTF as well.

Possible relationships between task complexity and interaction environment

Two recent studies (Baralt 2013, 2014) have examined possible relationships between task type and interaction environment, finding that the theorized facilitative effects of increased task complexity do not translate from FTF to SCMC. In her 2013 study, Baralt examined the efficacy of recasts in more or less complex tasks in FTF and SCMC. Task complexity was operationalized as +/− intentional reasoning, with learners in the less complex group simply reporting what had occurred to their interlocutor via a story retell (−intentional reasoning). Learners in the more complex group had to express a hypothesis as to why someone in a story did a certain action (+ intentional reasoning). In this study, learning was measured via differences from three pre- to post-tests: (a) an interactive task in FTF, (b) an interactive task in CMC; and (c) a multiple-choice receptive test administered via a computer. Baralt found that the more complex tasks led to more learning in FTF, while the less complex tasks led to more learning in SCMC.

Building on this research agenda, Baralt (2014) examined the effects of different task sequencing orders (such as simple to complex, complex to simple, and u-shape complexity sequences), with task complexity once again operationalized as +/− intentional reasoning. The study compared the relationship between the presence of LREs produced by students who interacted together, and their language development (acquisition of the Spanish past subjunctive), testing for task complexity/sequencing effects as well as mode effects (a traditional, FTF classroom versus an online classroom). Baralt found that students who completed sequences with more complex task opportunities produced significantly more LREs and attempted to use the target structure more than the sequences with less complex task opportunities. However, like the earlier study, this result only held in FTF. In SCMC, regardless of task sequence (more simple or more complex task opportunities), learners did not produce a single LRE. Additionally, while the more complex task sequences in FTF led to the most learning (e.g., pre- to post-test gains in use of the target structure in paired oral and written tasks), it was the more simple task sequences that facilitated learning of Spanish past subjunctives in SCMC. In light of the results from these initial two comparisons of task complexity in FTF and SCMC, Baralt called for further research examining learners' use of language in the two environments, and how this may or may not be mediated by task type or sequence. She also highlighted the need for research examining learner language use via operationalizations other than LREs to attempt a more thorough understanding of what appears to be so different about task interaction in FTF and SCMC.

Summary and justification for current study

Looking at features of interaction from only a cognitive perspective limits our understanding of how learners construct language awareness. Svalberg argues that language awareness as an outcome of peer interaction involves much more than focusing strictly on noticing linguistic forms (e.g., LREs). Despite the increase in the use of online language learning contexts, we still do not have a thorough understanding of how FTF and SCMC environments differentially mediate opportunities for learners to become aware of forms. Additionally, we are only beginning to understand how or why task complexity, which has been found to heighten learners' attention to the target language in FTF, does not yield the same benefits in SCMC.

Given that language awareness is theoretically and empirically held as important for language development, and given the increase in considering online language learning and evidence from studies that FTF and SCMC encourage learner attention differentially, more research is needed examining how language awareness is mediated by different types of tasks and interaction environments. The construct of EWL (Svalberg 2012) may more robustly elucidate why and how peer interaction generates awareness of forms, especially given the findings of tasks that work in FTF but not in SCMC. In order to address the aforementioned research gaps, the following research question was posed: Can examining learners' engagement with the language (EWL) shed light on why different task types (cognitively simple vs. complex) and interaction environments (FTF vs. SCMC) differentially affect how learners attend to linguistic form?

Methodology

Participants

Participants were 40 learners of Spanish as a foreign language from two intermediate Spanish II classes. Twenty were taking the course in a traditional classroom, while the other 20 took the course online. All were monolingual native speakers of English except for one student in the traditional class, who was bilingual in English and Haitian Creole. Eighteen of the students were male, 22 female, with an average age of 22 years old. All participants reported having extensive experience with SCMC on a daily basis through social media such as Gchat or Facebook.

Task complexity and target structure

The tasks used in the current study come from Baralt (2013, 2014). One task was cognitively simple, while the other was cognitively complex. Following Robinson's (2010) Cognition Hypothesis and Triadic Componential Framework for increasing the complexity of tasks, the resource-directing variable [+/− intentional reasoning] was operationalized to manipulate cognitive complexity. [−Intentional reasoning], or the cognitively simple task version, required learners only retell events that happened; they did not have to reflect on the intentional reasons of others that caused their actions. In the more complex version [+Intentional reasoning], learners were required to reflect on and communicate the reasons for which people did certain events in addition to retelling events that happened. According to Robinson, this task design requirement prompts learners to reflect on the mental and emotional states that causes peoples' actions, in conjunction with complex syntactic embedding (e.g., "John did X because ... John <u>was envious</u> that Mary ...). Communicating intentional reasoning naturally induces the task-essential linguistic forms needed in order to successfully perform the task. In the Spanish language, reflecting on the mental and emotional states of people in the primary clause necessitates a grammatical mood marking on the verb in the dependent clause position. This led to the targeted linguistic item in the study, the Spanish past subjunctive, given its intrinsic relationship to the functional demands of [+/− intentional reasoning]. In the present study, all participants had formally studied the subjunctive in the present tense, and had carried out tasks that required its use. Two days before the project, they had received instruction on the past subjunctive in class, but they had not done any communicative practice with the form (see Baralt 2013, 2014 for additional discussions on this task as well as independent measures employed to confirm the way in which cognitive complexity was operationalized).

Materials

Interactive tasks

The interactive tasks were a dialogic story retell, for which there was a cognitively simple [−intentional reasoning] and a cognitively complex [+intentional reasoning] version. To facilitate participants' memory of the story events, the story was divided into six sections, with each section presented on a card. Participants first read a card silently to themselves, then worked with their partner to retell the content of that card before moving on to the next card in the sequence. A comic picture strip followed each of the story sections, which served to assist participants in retelling the story. The story cards and accompanying comic strips served as the means by which [+/−intentional reasoning] was incorporated into the task. For example, in the cognitively simple task, characters' mental states and emotions that caused them to do certain things were already provided for participants in the story card strip and in the comic card. As is demonstrated in Figure 1 below, the emotional state is written in the story and is also provided in a thought bubble in the comic:

> When they got to the city stadium, they saw a sign that said "*INVITADOS* ENTER HERE". There was a line of about 15 men. Some soccer players laughed when they saw Alejandro and Luís go to the line. "Alejandro … are .. are you sure about this?" Luís stopped walking. "I don't know about this man." He doubted that they could do this. "Luís, what's wrong with you!? This is our chance! And this is *my dream*!" "I don't want to do this" said Luís. Alejandro grabbed Luís shirt and rolled his eyes. He hated that Luís give up his dreams like this.

Figure 1. Cognitively simple task: Example of L1 story section with accompanying comic

In the cognitively complex task, the mental states and emotional reasoning behind the story's characters were not provided; only the story events were detailed. Thought bubbles in this group's comic strips were empty, requiring participants to come up with the intentional reasoning behind that character's action in order to retell the story. This is depicted below in Figure 2:

When they got to the city stadium, they saw a sign that said "*INVITADOS* ENTER HERE". There was a line of about 15 men. Some soccer players laughed when they saw Alejandro and Luís go to the line. "Alejandro … are .. are you sure about this?" Luís stopped walking. "I don't know about this man." 𝒫 "Luís, what's wrong with you!? This is our chance! And this is *my dream!*" "I don't want to do this" said Luís. Alejandro grabbed Luís shirt and rolled his eyes. 𝒫

Figure 2. Cognitively complex task: Example of L1 story section with accompanying comic

Thus, all participants in both versions of the task had to produce the past subjunctive in the dependent clause position while retelling the story. The only difference was the absence or provision of intentional reasoning demands: the complex task group had to think of the characters' intentional reasoning themselves, while the simple task group was already provided with this information (see Figure 3 below). The tasks satisfied Ellis's (2009) design criteria to count as a task, as well as his suggestions for interactive tasks that promote grammatical development: two-way in nature, collaborative information exchange requirement, human ethical topics as well as topics that were familiar to participants, and a closed outcome (Ellis 2003: 96). The tasks had also been successful in eliciting the Spanish subjunctive form during FTF and SCMC task-based interaction in past studies (Baralt 2010, 2013, 2014).

Study Design

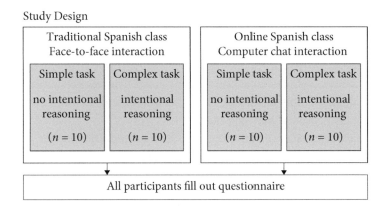

Figure 3. Study design

Questionnaire

The post-task questionnaire, which can be seen in the Appendix, contained eight questions regarding participants' views on peer interaction in their class, their overall perceptions and attitudes about the task, how they took to the task, and what they thought the purpose of the task might be. Two items on the questionnaire targeted each component of EWL: cognitive, affective, and social engagement. Students' written comments on the survey were collected in order to understand their perspectives on task performance, which allowed for a comparison between the engagement patterns during their interactions and the self-reported data from the questionnaires.

Procedure

This study followed a one-shot design that was completed in two parts: a practice session and a data collection session. Learners from the traditional classroom made up the FTF group. For this group, participant interaction took place amongst students at desks in a classroom and was recorded using audio digital recorders. Learners from the online class made up the SCMC group. In this group, participant interaction took place amongst students connected via computers in a computer lab. Their chat-based interaction was recorded via Genesis™ software.

The data collection session occurred during the regular class meeting time following the practice session. The researchers were not present for this session; rather, the participants' teachers implemented the task for the study[2]. The teachers began by splitting their classes in half so that they could give different directions to the two groups. Teachers began with the simple task [−intentional reasoning] group first, while the complex task [+intentional reasoning] group was given a brief, unrelated vocabulary exercise to do. The teachers paired participants in the simple task group and gave them the task story cards with accompanying comic strips. Students were instructed to retell the story together as best as they could in Spanish and in the past tense. They were told to read the story strip (provided to them in English) to themselves first, and then use the comic strip to work together with their partner, saying what happened in Spanish. The teachers modeled a similar task for them, reading a story blurb to themselves and then retelling the story in Spanish based on what they had read.

Once participants in the simple group had started, the teacher went to the other half of the class (those who would perform the complex task), collected

---

2.   Teachers were trained on how to implement the task in their classrooms beforehand in order to ensure consistency across the two classes.

their vocabulary exercise sheets, and paired them into dyads. These dyads were given nearly the same instructions as the simple group, with the exception that they were also told they would have to reflect together on why the characters in the story did a certain action (i.e., reflect on the intentional reasons of the story characters via the empty thought bubbles). The teacher modeled a similar task for this group as well.

The same instructional procedure was followed for the SCMC group, the only difference being the fact that participants completed the tasks in the computer lab via chat. Once the tasks were completed, learners in both groups were given a post-task questionnaire to fill out individually. On average, participants took 25 minutes for the simple task and 30 minutes for the complex task in FTF. For the SCMC group, the average time was 36 and 40 minutes for the simple and complex task, respectively.

Data sources, coding, and analysis

The data sources collected for this study were (1) transcriptions of the audio recordings of the FTF group's interaction; (2) saved chat logs of the SCMC group's interaction; and (3) participants' post-task questionnaires. The independent variables in this study were task complexity [+/− intentional reasoning] and task interaction environment (FTF or SCMC), while the dependent variable was participants' EWL (Engagement With the Language). Following Svalberg (2009, 2012), we devised a coding scheme to operationalize EWL, provided in Figure 4 below.

As depicted in Figure 4, all participants' transcripts were coded for the three dimensions that comprise EWL: cognitive, affective, and social. All of Svalberg's proposed criteria were included in the scheme to assist the researchers in identifying types of engagement, with a space for writing down and tallying those examples. The coding scheme also included space for learners' questionnaire comments. Given the paucity of studies that have examined how learners construct language awareness through EWL, an exploratory–interpretive paradigm (e.g., Grotjahn 1987) was employed to analyze the data. We sought to explore an additional understanding of how learners engage, as opposed to validating one specific theory. Comparing, inducing, and synthesizing how each participant took to the task, as well as their self-reported perceptions of the task, allowed us to gain insight into the factors behind the cognitive, affective, and social engagement that Svalberg discusses. The first analytical iteration involved coding each participant's task performance transcription using the scheme developed (Figure 4), as well as their post-task questionnaire. Both *in vivo* comments and researcher-induced themes from the questionnaires were included. For example, a student comment

Criterion	Coder comments	Data / tallies
Cognitive engagement	Noticing of language and/or interaction features?	
	Attention on the language as an object or as a medium?	
	Critical / analytic reflection during the task? (Reasoning induction or memory/imitation-based reflection?) Hypothesis formation?	
	Data triangulation: comments from questionnaire	
Affective engagement	Willingness to engage? (Eagerness or withdrawal?)	
	Learner's purposefulness (Focused on task or bored?)	
	Autonomy: dependent or independent behavior?	
	Data triangulation: comments from questionnaire	
Social engagement	How interactive with partner to learn?	
	Socially supportive? Negotiates and scaffolds?	
	Leader or follower? (Reactive or initiating types of interactions?)	
	Data triangulation: comments from questionnaire	

Figure 4. Scheme for coding learners' Engagement With the Language (based off of Svalberg 2012)

such as "wait, I wonder if that has to be in the subjunctive" was coded under cognitive engagement, because it demonstrated critical reflection of form. A student's comment on the questionnaire, "I felt kind of anxious during this task," was coded under affective engagement, since it addressed the psychological/affective state of that learner, which could have affected her willingness to participate (Svalberg 2012). One student's comment, "I felt my partner didn't really involve me in completing this task," as well as evidence of students encouraging each other to contribute (or not), were coded under social engagement, as they addressed how interactive learners were with each other to learn, and how or whether they supported each other.

Coding was first done for each group individually (simple task in FTF, complex task in FTF, simple task SCMC, complex task SCMC), and was then followed by a second iteration where all schemes were compared within each group to draw out general patterns. Two additional iterations were conducted that compared and contrasted the four different groups' engagement. In correspondence with this interpretive, discovery-oriented approach (e.g., Grotjahn 1987), the data are presented in a way that reflects an inductive analysis. In our results, participants' task- and environment-specific performance are discussed under each of the three components of EWL.

Results

The goal of this exploratory study was to examine learners' EWL during peer interaction in hopes of better understanding how and why language awareness is differentially mediated by task complexity and interaction environment (FTF and SCMC). To provide a general picture of learners' task-based interaction, learners' turn-taking data is provided in Table 1.

Table 1. Learners' turn-taking according to task type and mode

FTF Mode			
Simple task [−intentional reasoning]		Complex task [+intentional reasoning]	
	Total number of turns		Total number of turns
Dyad 1	38	Dyad 6	147
Dyad 2	25	Dyad 7	141
Dyad 3	40	Dyad 8	178
Dyad 4	18	Dyad 9	104
Dyad 5	20	Dyad 10	120
Group average:	28	Group average:	138
SCMC Mode			
Simple task [−intentional reasoning]		Complex task [+intentional reasoning]	
	Total number of turns		Total number of turns
Dyad 11	39	Dyad 16	52
Dyad 12	35	Dyad 17	99
Dyad 13	20	Dyad 18	35
Dyad 14	35	Dyad 19	32
Dyad 15	45	Dyad 20	15
Group average:	35	Group average:	47

Overall, the complex tasks in both FTF and SCMC modes elicited more turns than the simple version of tasks, with the complex task in FTF eliciting the largest number of turns ($M = 138$).

A synthesis as well as examples of each aspect of engagement – cognitive, affective, and social – are presented below.

Cognitive engagement

The primary data utilized to analyze cognitive engagement were the interactions, either transcribed from FTF, or via the SCMC written chat logs. The secondary data utilized for cognitive engagement analysis was the questionnaires.

Simple versus complex tasks in the FTF environment
All 20 participants in the FTF group took to the task as a goal that was accomplishable by use of the language. There was noticing of language and interaction features during both the simple and complex tasks. This involved stopping to talk about the language and asking questions about how to say something accurately; such noticing occurred in Spanish and also in participants' L1, English. All 20 of the FTF dyads evidenced cognitive engagement for lexical items (e.g., *How do you think you say 'try outs' in Spanish?*), for transition phrases (e.g., *We should use* entonces or siguiente [then or next]), and for past tense forms (e.g., *It would be* quería *right?*). Attention to the language as an object most often occurred in analyzing whether past tense forms should be in the preterit or the imperfect tense. An example from a dyad that performed the cognitively simple task is given in (1) below:

(1) 1.   Learner A: Sí pero Luís dormió (*Yes but Luis slept*)
     2.   Learner B: I think durmió isn't that like irregular?
     3.   Learner A: Or wait maybe it should be imperfect?
     4.   Learner B: Aaaahh sí sí sí acción en progreso (*Aaaaahh yes yes yes action in progress*)
     5.   Learner A: Entonces Luís dormir …dormía… dormía. (*So Luis to sleep… was sleeping…was sleeping*)

As can be seen in (1), learners A and B use functional language (e.g., asking for help) to reflect on the accuracy of the past tense form. In fact, all participants in the FTF class stopped to reflect on accurate past tense forms to complete their task. It was also observed that those who were performing the cognitively complex task (which required intentional reasoning) reflected together on the past subjunctive as a concept. Specifically, all five dyads in the complex task group reflected on and inferred about the subjunctive at least four times. Only three of the five dyads in the simple group did this. Additionally, all five of the complex group dyads tried to draw conclusions together about accurate subjunctive *morphology* marking on the past tense forms. An example of this is shown in the following exchange in the complex task group:

(2) 1. Learner C: Hmm. Alejandro no … how do you say *couldn't believe?*
     2. Learner D: No creía I think.
     3. Learner C: Alejandro no creía que … que Luis estaba dormiendo [sic]
         (*Alejandro could not believe that Luis was sleeping.*)
     4. Learner D: No creía wait I think we have to use the subjunctive. Because
         no creer? Dudar? Those take the subjunctive.
     5. Learner C: No creía que Luis dorma? Duerma? Can we ask [the teacher]
         what it is?
     6. Learner D: No I think we have to do it ourselves. So Alejandro no creía
         que Luis duerma. Duermaba. (*Alejandro could not believe that Luis sleeps-
         SUB. Was sleeping -SUB*).
     7. Learner C: I think Alejandro no creía que Luis duerma. (*…Alejandro could
         not believe that Luis sleeps-SUB*).
     8. Learner C: Go us!
     9. Learner D: Vamos nosotros! (*Go us* [sic]!) (laughter)

In lines 4–7, learners C and D are collaboratively hypothesizing on what the past tense subjunctive form might be. They ask each other questions, work out and propose different form possibilities, and eventually come to a conclusion together on what they believe is the accurate form. As all participants in the FTF complex group did this, it appeared that performing the complex task resulted in more cognitive engagement with the form. Data from the questionnaires corroborated this interaction coding. Nine out of the ten participants in the FTF complex group explicitly cited "the subjunctive" as "language features that you noticed or needed" during the task. Only two of the ten participants in the simple task FTF group cited the form as noticed or as necessary.

Simple versus complex tasks in the SCMC environment
During the SCMC interaction, participants in both the simple and the complex task groups were not as focused on the task as a collaborative activity when critical reflection on forms took place. One of Svalberg's criteria for cognitive engagement asks if participants "seem focused" or if they "seem to wander" during their engagement with the language, and indeed, 19 out of the 20 participants in this group also used their time-on-task to check email and look at other websites[3].

---

3. This observation was captured by the Genesis software, which shows (on the teacher's computer) what all students in the lab are doing on their individual computers. What's more, this behavior had nothing to do with task (e.g., looking up words) nor was it done while waiting for a partner to respond. The teachers were asked not to intervene during the task at the onset of the study, so as to best capture what students actually do when asked to interact online.

While there was cognitive engagement of language forms in SCMC, it was almost exclusively targeted to lexical items. Sometimes one participant's attention to a word would be noticed by their partner and other times, it was skipped over. For example, in line one of exchange (3) below, participant E indicates lack of knowledge of a word by using the L1 in parentheses. His partner provides him with the form, which he then reuses in the next turn:

(3)   1.   Learner E: Todos los ninos (said) "no" (sic; *All of the children said "no"*)
2.   Learner F: dijeron: decir (*they said: to say*)
3.   Learner E: dijeron (*they said*)

There were instances however where a partner's feedback on form was not recognized or was simply ignored by a participant, as shown in lines 3–5 in Example (4):

(4)   1.   Learner G: Senorita Gomez ayuda a senorita Martinez para encontrar sus joyas (sic; *Ms. Gomez helps Ms. Martinez to find her jewelry*)
2.   Learner H: No Patricia! Senor Martinez ayudo a Senora Martinez (sic; *No Patricia! Mr. Martinez helped Mrs. Martinez*)
3.   Learner G: Senorita Martinez piensaba que no puede ser Senorita Gomez que robo (sic; *Ms. Martinez thought [sic] that it can't be Mrs. Gomez who robbed them*)
4.   Learner G: Senorita Martinez corrio al cuarto (sic; *Ms. Martinez ran to the room*)
5.   Learner G: Senorita Martinez penso, Donde esta Senorita Gomez? (sic; *Ms. Martinez thought, where is Ms. Gomez?*)

Here, learner G is carrying out the task in an autonomous fashion and not including her partner in the construction of the story line. At one point (line 2), her partner, learner H, says to her, *No Patricia!* and gives her two corrections: first with the correct name of the character in the story (focusing on content), and second, with the correct past tense form, *helped* instead of *help* (focus on form). Learner G ignores learner H's other-correction and continues on telling the story. While this was an extreme example, overall, there were few instances of analysis or reflection on forms that resulted from collaboration in SCMC. In the simple task group, a total of 13 instances of reflective questioning on correct past tense forms occurred in the SCMC environment. In the complex group, this type of reflection on past tense forms happened only four times. The majority of interaction in this environment was for the purpose of turn-taking or task procedure management (e.g., "Do you want to start this one?" "Should I go next?" "K now it's you"). Notably, there was no overt reflection or hypothesis testing on possible subjunctive morphological forms in SCMC, regardless of task type. Overall, there was not the same amount of cognitive engagement with the language as there was in the FTF environment. Comments from the questionnaires corroborated this finding from the interaction data. For example, not a single participant (out of 20) wrote "the subjunctive" as a possible goal of the task that they had to do.

Affective engagement

The primary data utilized to analyze affective engagement were learners' questionnaires. The interaction data was utilized to corroborate themes found in the questionnaires. This was done to ensure that learners' own perception data was the primary source for understanding their affective engagement and reduce potential researcher bias. Unlike cognitive or social engagement, affective engagement refers to learners' attitudes, which are more difficult to uncover from the interaction data.

Simple versus complex tasks in the FTF environment

Learners' questionnaire data indicated that overall there was positive orientation towards the language, the tasks, and interaction with a partner in FTF: all 20 participants in the FTF group reported on their questionnaire that the task was positive, and provided descriptions such as *enjoyable, great practice,* and *interesting; *every single participant wrote *fun.* They also viewed working with their partner as important, and all 20 also expressed that their partner helped them in many ways, both as a source of language assistance and as a friend. Affective engagement was therefore positive, purposeful, and dependent upon working with and co-constructing with a partner. Based on participants' comments, affective engagement was positive in this environment when learners reported that their partner was focused and highly willing to accomplish the task. Five participants in the simple task group described the task as "good practice" in the questionnaire. Nine of the ten participants in the complex task group referred to the task as an "intellectual challenge". Examples of their descriptions are:

> a good challenge, I want more tasks like this to make me really think, I had to work hard but my partner helped me, this task pushed me to really use Spanish like I never have before, this was fun!

Simple versus complex tasks in the SCMC environment

Contrary to the FTF participants, those in the SCMC group displayed an overall negative orientation towards the task and task performance in SCMC. In both the simple and complex SCMC task, there was not as much willingness to affectively engage. The SCMC participants were not as eager, not as purposeful, and many reported not enjoying the experience. Autonomy was one theme in particular that came out of affective engagement in the SCMC environment: most of the participants' behavior in this group was independent, e.g., not needing – or necessarily wanting to – work with a partner to complete the task. This was corroborated by the interaction data. For example, some of the SCMC chat transcripts showed that a few participants retold the story and then, even retold the same information that their partner had just retold. This implied that they were not at all vested in their partner's contribution to the task or did not pay attention to their partners' participation. In fact, there were twice as many turns taken in the FTF dataset than the SCMC set, and three times as many turns in FTF than in SCMC for the complex task. While this difference could be due to the SCMC environment itself (as opposed to being entirely indicative of affective engagement), number of turns and length of on-task talk are facets of active participation, which Svalberg (2012) argues is a component of affective engagement. Comments from the questionnaire were in line with these observations. Sentiments indicating a frustration and a lack of willingness to interact were common, especially in the complex task group (e.g., "It was hard to get my partner to respond in the right way"). Thirteen participants in the SCMC group wrote "anxious" and "tense" to describe their task experience. Only five participants completing the simple task viewed working with their partner as important or necessary; no one in the complex task group reported feeling this way. The overall low affective engagement in this environment is summarized by the following questionnaire quote from a SCMC participant in the simple task group:

> No, I don't think my partner and I were both equally willing to contribute in retelling the story. This experience felt like tension in a quiet room.

Social engagement

The primary data utilized to analyze social engagement were the interactions, either transcribed from FTF, or via the SCMC written chat logs. The secondary data utilized for social engagement analysis was the questionnaires.

Simple versus complex tasks in the FTF environment

There was a great deal of social engagement in the FTF group. Participants in both simple and complex task groups responded positively to the interaction and were interactionally supportive of each other. This was demonstrated via: suggestions to each other for words or accurate forms, praise (e.g., "muy bien!", "yes!" "good job"), questions that encouraged the partner's involvement (e.g., "… but what do you think?"). As noted on the questionnaires, there was a notable, mutual sense of social inclusion in the FTF group because all participants enjoying interacting with 'friend(s)' from their traditional language class (as compared to the SCMC group who regularly met online and only saw each other on exam days). This sense of friendship and belonging in the FTF group appeared to foster the social inter-actional processes that contributed to awareness of forms. The following example (captured from the audio recording) demonstrates this:

(5) 1. Learner J: "...but yeah it was really fun! You should come out with us next time!"
    2. Learner I: "I'd love to. You know what else –
    3. – [comment in background from another classmate, jokingly telling students to get to work and "stop talking about guys"] –
    4. (simultaneous laughter from both students)
    5. Learner I: Ok let's do this LOL. I'm excited for our plans. Ok, *Luis y Alejandro*. We can do this!
    6. Learner J: Go *amiga* you got the first card!
    7. Learner I: (laughs), *Alejandro y Luis son, eran?* (Alejandro and Luis are, were?)
    8. Learner J: Yep *eran*. (Were).
    9. Learner I: *Sí, gracias. Alejandro y Luis eran mejores amigos y ...*"

The brief peer assistance in lines 7–8, where learner I stops to ask her partner if the correct form should be *son* or *eran*, is prefaced with excitement talking about social plans outside of the classroom. Friendship, playful banter from a classmate, and laughter are visible. Learner J encourages her by letting her tackle the first comic strip card "...you got the first card!" and calls her friend (*amiga*) in Spanish. The task was highly interactive, socially supported, where friendships and social-izing were established first, followed by working together (in an encouraging way) to then solve a linguistic problem. Remarks on the questionnaire also underpin this observation: *I liked that I could work with my friend on this task, my partner really helped me, this was super fun*. It was noted that more social scaffolding took place in the complex task group in FTF. For example, there were more amounts of initiation and helpful responses to initiation in the complex task. This was often done (with an average of three times per dyad) by asking one another how they thought they could say something (e.g., "*How do you say* He felt nervous that?"). Those in the simple task group did not do this, presumably because characters' intentional reasons were already provided in the story for them. Simple task par-ticipants did use social scaffolding to reflect together on accuracy of other forms such as the indicative past tense, however. In sum, all participants in the FTF group viewed the task as a way to use and learn language with each other socially, and the complex task in this mode generated higher instances of social scaffold-ing, in other words, helping each other socially to use the language in order to successfully perform a task.

Simple versus complex tasks in the SCMC environment

In contrast, the hallmarks of social engagement – initiation of ideas, of turns, and of scaffolding with positive responses to those initiations – were rarely observed in the SCMC group. There was not much social "leading" or "following" in this environment (Svalberg 2012: 378), because most participants performed the task autonomously and did not interact with their partner for help. Many did not see the task as a process where they could get language support, and SCMC learners rarely each other asked for it (contrary to those in FTF). Story sections were often repeated by learners, which implied they were not socially vested in what their partner had to say. Typing out story content with no consideration of what the partner had already contributed implied an overall lack of simultaneous attention to "relational space," where the other person's contribution – and even the notion of face – were taken into account (Svalberg 2012: 379; see also Foster & Ohta 2005). What's more, unlike the FTF group, SCMC peer interaction did not include any discussion, agreement, or disagreement about proposals on how to complete the task. Comments that refer to social engagement from the questionnaires included *working with my partner was not necessary to complete this task,* and *I would have preferred to do this [task] alone.* One participant even wrote that an aspect of online language learning that she liked was the fact that she could do tasks by herself. Learners used words to describe the SCMC task such as "uncomfortable" and "unfamiliar". Another issue that emerged in the SCMC was lack of turn-taking management. For example, one student would send a message and completely miss his or her partner's utterance from before (whether due to typing at the same time or not considering their partner's contribution). This resulted in missed opportunities to reflect on the characters' intentional reasons in the story by some participants in the complex group.

Results summary

A visual summary of learners' EWL according to task type (simple versus complex) and interaction environment (FTF versus SCMC) is provided in Table 2.

Table 2. Results summary

Language engagement	FTF class	SCMC class
Cognitive	5/5 dyads in complex task group reflected and inferred on the target form (subjunctive); 3/5 dyads in the simple task group did this	Participants in both complex and simple groups focused on lexis or accuracy; not one participant in SCMC reflected on subjunctive morphology

Language engagement	FTF class	SCMC class
Affective	Positive outlook to completing the task, willingness to engage, especially in complex task group. View of task as purposeful, fun, enjoyable	Negative outlook to completing task; most negative in +complex task group; learners were bored, anxious, tense
Social	Presence of encouragement, support, and praise. Socializing that facilitated linguistic scaffolding, particularly in complex task group. Friendships an important theme when reporting task outcome and fun	No observable socialization or any establishment of relationship before beginning task. Problematic turn-taking also led to high autonomy in the complex task group. Reports of feeling that story re-tell contributions were disregarded by a partner that they did not know

Discussion

The current study examined learners' EWL to better understand why different task types (cognitively simple vs. complex) and interaction environments (FTF vs. SCMC) differentially affect how learners achieve awareness of forms. To date, learners' attention to form in task-based interaction has principally been addressed through constructs such as LREs or interpretation and/or use of corrective feedback. These operationalizations of attention to form may be limiting our understanding of what leads to successful language awareness. In the current study, we have expanded upon existing research and explored learner's EWL in terms of its affective and social dimensions, in addition to the more traditional cognitive/linguistic dimensions, operationalizing Svalberg's model (2009, 2012). As Duff (2013), Long and Norris (2015), and Van den Branden (2015) have stated, task-based research needs to investigate not only how tasks affect learners' task performance, but also how and why (or why not) learners engage during task-based peer interaction. By triangulating both cognitive as well as learner affective and social engagement during the task, the findings of the current exploratory study provide useful insights into what leads students to attend (or not attend) to language forms.

Cognitive engagement

It is worth noting that the findings of the current study are in line with previous LRE studies, in that learners who performed more complex tasks in FTF tended to show a higher level of cognitive engagement with task-induced language (e.g.,

Baralt 2010, 2014; Kim 2012; Kim & Tracy-Ventura 2011; Révész 2009, 2011; see also Loewen & Wolff 2016). Table 3 shows four sample excerpts around the same point in the story from each group, which represents task performance of each interaction context. All excerpts were based on the same part of task performance.

Table 3. Examples of each group's engagement with the language

Simple FTF	Complex FTF	Simple SCMC	Complex SCMC
"Alejandro no pudo creer que Luís dormía." (Alejandro could not believe that Luis was sleeping-IND).	"Alejandro … no … how do you say was in disbelief? Or was shocked?"	"Alejandro no pudo creer que Luís dormió." (Alejandro could not believe that Luís slept-IND, preterit form).	"Alejandro no (believe) (that) Luís dormía." (Alejandro no (believe) (that) Luís dormía. [Participant wrote word the English version of the word he did not know in Spanish].
"Sí. (yes) Wait should that be subjunctive?"	"No creer maybe? (to not believe maybe?) You know what, I think this is what we've been talking about in class, the subjunctive.	"durmió." (slept) [next line] "irregular."	"Do you want me to go next? I thought I was supposed to do this one."

As shown above, FTF interaction seemed to promote cognitive engagement, i.e., learners paying attention to forms while carrying out tasks. In particular, learners in the complex task groups experimented with language forms through communicating and collaborating with their partner, and the FTF environment fostered this. On the other hand, the learners in the online setting in the current study showed a limited amount of evidence for cognitive engagement. This finding also supports past studies that showed that increased task complexity, theorized to be beneficial in the FTF mode, is not as effective in SCMC (Baralt 2010, 2013, 2014).

Affective engagement

Our findings on affective engagement support the need to take into account affective factors when implementing task design features theorized to promote cognitive engagement. For example, participants who carried out the task in FTF demonstrated greater affective engagement via the expression of more positive attitudes towards having to work with their partner in order to complete the task. They viewed it as helpful, enjoyable, and fun. This type of engagement helps to explain why in FTF, more cognitive engagement took place. FTF participants reported that their task performance was dependent on working with their partner, for which there was more willingness to participate and a shared focus on performing the task together (aspects of affective engagement). Contrarily, students who were in the SCMC demonstrated low affective engagement via reported anxiety and tension while carrying out tasks online, mainly due to their unfamiliarity with their partners. This appeared to be related to the trust component that Svalberg describes: because their class was online and they rarely had one-on-one personal interaction, several of the participants (in both simple and complex SCMC task groups) wrote that they did not know their partner and did not like how their partner engaged in the task; in other words, participants' affective engagement in this group was more independent and autonomous from needing to interact. For example, one participant in the SCMC complex task wrote:

> To be honest I hated this task. I didn't really know the person I was chatting with, and I don't think he really cared about working with me. He just wanted to get the task done and didn't really talk to me at all. It was weird, we didn't even really take turns. I tried but he just kept going so finally I just let him retell the story and mentally checked out.

This participant's comment shows that the SCMC group was not accustomed to interactive tasks with peers and that her partner did not perceive (or care to perceive) her as capable of contributing to what he perceived as his own task. This impacted her emotions during the task; she felt bad and so stopped performing the task altogether. Her not feeling included therefore precluded her from noticing forms. In sum, learners' affective engagement, e.g., their attitudes towards task performance as well as towards their partner, affected their cognitive engagement with form.

Social engagement

Social engagement was found to be just as capable of mediating learners' cognitive engagement of the targeted form in this study. For example, those who reported feeling happy, having fun, and who saw their partners as friends engaged in more social scaffolding that led to greater instances of cognitive engagement. Participants in SCMC group did not know each other personally, and so there was not the shared sense of a social network than there was in the FTF group. Our finding that there was no reference to "friend" in these participants' questionnaires, as well as zero socialization activity around the task, underscores this notion. This lack of social engagement in SCMC may explain why there was so little cognitive engagement and, subsequently, no indications of noticing of the subjunctive form. The complex task in SCMC appeared to be the most problematic, with participants not working together towards the task outcome. While this finding reiterates Baralt's (2013, 2014) previous finding that increased task complexity is not effective in SCMC, the findings in this current study show that lack of trust and friendships may be precisely what exacerbated a lack of cognitive engagement with forms in SCMC.

In sum, our findings suggest that the three types of engagement (i.e., cognitive engagement, affective engagement, and social engagement) are closely related and mediate each other. To date, interaction-driven learning opportunities have been examined by focusing mainly on cognitive attention to forms (e.g., LREs). However, the findings of the current study suggest that in fact, cognitive attention to form can very much be moderated by learners' affective and social engagement during peer interaction. When learners had positive attitudes, viewed the task as fun, demonstrated willingness to engage and felt that their partner did as well, and felt socially included and supported, they cognitively engaged more. Furthermore, task type and interaction environment mediated learners' EWL.

Pedagogical implications

In addition to their theoretical value of the nature of attention in language development, these findings are pedagogically important given the increased emphasis for more online language classes in university contexts. Although online language classes may address economic concerns and students might find them useful for their own schedule, they might not provide satisfying learning conditions from theoretical points of view (e.g., Sociocultural Theory, Interaction Hypothesis, Noticing Hypothesis). In order to increase the benefits of online language courses, we need to train language learners how to constructively interact in SCMC (see Kim 2013; Sato & Lyster 2012 for the benefits of peer interaction training). In order to do so, however, it is imperative to (1) encourage learners' sense of belonging to a community, (2) to facilitate friendships, and (3) to build on the additional affective and social components in online language learning. In the present study, the lack of these components in the SCMC environment appeared to be the main reason for which there was not the same level of beneficial attention to language forms as compared to the FTF interaction.

It has been empirically and theoretically suggested that task complexity plays an important role in facilitating learners' cognitive engagement, and particularly in facilitating language awareness in FTF contexts. This notion is fundamentally different, however, in SCMC environments. When designing tasks, teachers need to consider the appropriate level of task complexity that can generate cognitive, affective *and* social engagement during task performance. It seems that cognitively simple tasks work best in SCMC. In order to facilitate language learning in SCMC contexts, opportunities to get to know classmates and achieve a sense of belonging to the class community are essential. Simple tasks in chat could be prefaced with activities where students get to know each other, share about their personal lives, and establish friendships and trust before beginning the task. How to best accomplish this goal is certainly warranted in future research, as is the development of training materials for teachers precisely for this purpose.

Limitations

This study does not go without limitations. First, the SCMC interactions were conducted in a lab because of the practicality of data collection, and this was unnatural for the online students who were not as used to in-person interaction (with the exception of exam days, which did take place in the lab space). This design issue undoubtedly has consequences for the ecological validity of the study. Additionally, the current study examined Svalberg's EWL construct with interaction and questionnaire data only. In order to examine affective and social engagement and explore the direct relationships between the three types of engagement, various data sources such as stimulated recall data, interviews, and learning journals could shed more light on learners' EWL. Finally, the current study did not address the long-term effects of task-based learning. Future studies would benefit from longitudinal investigations of learners' cognitive, social, and affective EWL during task performance, and how it affects their language learning over time. As the first to operationalize EWL, this study was exploratory in nature, and future studies could continue to modify and better our initial attempt at researching the construct.

Conclusion

This exploratory study operationalized, for the first time, Svalberg's (2009, 2012) *Engagement With the Language* (EWL) by examining the cognitive, affective, and social dimensions of learners' engagement during task-based peer interaction in FTF and SCMC. We also examined task type (simple or cognitively complex) as well as interaction environment (FTF or SCMC), and how these independent variables might affect learners' EWL. The findings from this study showed that learners' cognitive engagement is influenced by their social and affective engagement, and that this is mediated by both the complexity of the task and interaction environment. In all four groups, learners' social and affective engagement influenced their cognitive engagement: the more affective and social engagement, the more cognitive engagement learners demonstrated.

References

Allen, I. E., & Seaman, J. (2015). Grade level: Tracking online education in the United States. Retrieved April 13, 2015 from: <http://www.onlinelearningsurvey.com/reports/gradelevel. pdf.>

Baralt, M. (2010). *Task complexity, the Cognition Hypothesis, and interaction in CMC and FTF environments* (Unpublished doctoral dissertation). Georgetown University, Washington, DC.

Baralt, M. (2013). The impact of cognitive complexity on feedback efficacy during online versus face-to-face interactive tasks. *Studies in Second Language Acquisition*, 35, 689–725. doi:10.1017/S0272263113000429

Baralt, M. (2014). Task sequencing and task complexity in traditional versus online classes. In M. Baralt, R. Gilabert, & P. Robinson (Eds.), *Task sequencing and instructed second language learning* (pp. 95–122). London: Bloomsbury.

Blake, R. J. (2011). Current trends in online language learning. *Annual Review of Applied Linguistics*, 31, 19–35. doi:10.1017/S026719051100002X

Duff, P. A. (2013). *Sociocultural and discursive approaches to task-based language learning, teaching, and research*. Plenary talk given at the *5th Biennial International Conference on Task-Based Language Teaching*. Banff, Canada.

Ellis, R. (2003). *Task-based language learning and teaching*. Oxford: Oxford University Press.

Ellis, R. (2009). Task-based language teaching: Sorting out the misunderstandings. *International Journal of Applied Linguistics* 19(3): 221–246. doi:10.1111/j.1473-4192.2009.00231.x

Ellis, R., Basturkmen, H., & Loewen, S. (2001). Learner uptake in communicative ESL lessons. *Language Learning*, 51(2), 281–318. doi:10.1111/1467-9922.00156

Foster, P., & Ohta, A. (2005). Negotiation for meaning and peer assistance in second language classrooms. *Applied Linguistics*, 26, 402–30. doi:10.1093/applin/ami014

Gagné, N., & Parks, S. (2013). Cooperative learning tasks in a Grade 6 intensive ESL class: Role of scaffolding. *Language Teaching Research*, 17, 188–209. doi:10.1177/1362168812460818

García Mayo, M. & Azharai, A. (2016). EFL task-based interaction: Does task modality impact on language-related episodes? In M. Sato & S. Ballinger (Eds.), *Peer interaction and second language learning: Pedagogical potential and research agenda* (pp. 241–266). Amsterdam: John Benjamins.

Grotjahn, R. (1987). On the methodological basis of introspective methods. In C. Faerch & G. Kasper (Eds.), *Introspection in second language research* (pp. 54–81). Clevedon, UK: Multilingual Matters.

Gurzynski-Weiss, L., & Baralt, M. (2014). Exploring learner perception and use of task-based interactional feedback in FTF and CMC modes. *Studies in Second Language Acquisition*, 36, 1–37. doi:10.1017/S0272263113000363

Hama, M., & Leow, R. P. (2010). Learning without awareness revisited: Extending Williams (2005). *Studies in Second Language Acquisition*, 32, 465–491. doi:10.1017/S0272263110000045

Kim, Y. (2009). The effects of task complexity on learner-learner interaction. *System*, 37, 254–268. doi:10.1016/j.system.2009.02.003

Kim, Y. (2012). Task complexity, learning opportunities and Korean EFL learners' question development. *Studies in Second Language Acquisition*, 34, 627–658. doi:10.1017/S0272263112000368

Kim, Y. (2013). Effects of pretask modelling on attention to form and question development. *TESOL Quarterly* 47, 8–35. doi:10.1002/tesq.52

Kim, Y., & Tracy-Ventura, N. (2011). Task complexity, language anxiety and the development of past tense. In P. Robinson (Ed.), *Task complexity: Researching the Cognition Hypothesis of language learning and performance* (pp. 287–306). Amsterdam: John Benjamins. doi:10.1075/tblt.2.18ch11

Kowal, M., & Swain, M. (1994). Using collaborative language production tasks to promote students' language awareness. *Language Awareness*, 3, 73–93. doi:10.1080/09658416.1994.9959845

Knouzi, I., Swain, M., Lapkin, S., & Brooks, L. (2010). Self-scaffolding mediated by languaging: Microgenetic analysis of high and low performers. *International Journal of Applied Linguistics* 20(1), 23–49. doi:10.1111/j.1473-4192.2009.00227.x

Lai, C., & Zhao, Y. (2006). Noticing and text-based chat. *Language Learning & Technology*, 10, 102–120.

Leow, R. P. (1997). Attention, awareness, and foreign language behavior. *Language Learning*, 47, 467–506. doi:10.1111/0023-8333.00017

Leow, R. P. (1998). Toward operationalizing the process of attention in SLA: Evidence for Tomlin and Villa's (1994) fine-grained analysis of attention. *Applied Psycholinguistics*, 19, 133–59. doi:10.1017/S0142716400010626

Leow, R. P. (2001). Attention, awareness and foreign language behavior. *Language Learning*, 51, 113–55. doi:10.1111/j.1467-1770.2001.tb00016.x

Leow, R., Cerezo, L., & Baralt, M. (2015). *A psycholinguistic approach to technology and language learning*. Berlin: De Gruyter. doi:10.1515/9781614513674

Loewen, S., & Wolff, D. (2016). Peer interaction in F2F and CMC contexts. In M. Sato & S. Ballinger (Eds.), *Peer interaction and second language learning: Pedagogical potential and research agenda* (pp. 163–184). Amsterdam: John Benjamins.

Long, M. H. (1996). The role of the linguistic environment in second language acquisition. In W. C. Ritchie & T. K. Bhatia (Eds.), *Handbook of second language acquisition* (pp. 413–68). New York: Academic Press.

Long, M. H., & Norris, J. M. (2015). *An international collaborative research network on task complexity. Colloquium presented at the Task-Based Language Teaching Conference*. University of Leuven.

Nuevo, A.-M. (2006). Task complexity and interaction: L2 learning opportunities and interaction (Unpublished doctoral dissertation). Georgetown University, Washington, DC.

Nuevo, A.-M., Adams, R., & Ross-Feldman, L. (2011). Task complexity, modified output, and L2 development in learner–learner interaction In P. Robinson (Ed.), *Second language task complexity: Researching the Cognition Hypothesis of language learning and performance* (pp. 175–202). Amsterdam: John Benjamins. doi:10.107/tblt.2.13ch7

Ortega, L. (2009). Interaction and attention to form in L2 text-based computer-mediated communication. In A. Mackey & C. Polio (Eds.), *Multiple perspectives on interaction* (pp. 226–253). New York, NY: Routledge.

Payne, J. S. & Whitney, P. J. (2002). Developing L2 oral proficiency through sychronous CMC: Output, working memory, and interlanguage development. *CALICO Journal*, 20, 7–32.

Révész, A. (2009). Task complexity, focus on form, and second language development. *Studies in Second Language Acquisition*, 31, 437–70. doi:10.1017/S0272263109090366

Révész, A. (2011). Task complexity, focus on L2 constructions, and individual differences: A classroom-based study. *Modern Language Journal*, 95, 162–181. doi:10.1111/j.1540-4781.2011.01241.x

Robinson, P. (2010). Situating and distributing cognition across task demands: TheSSARC model of pedagogic task sequencing. In M. Putz & L. Sicola (Eds.), *Cognitive processing in second language acquisition: Inside the learner's mind.* (pp. 243–68). Amsterdam: John Benjamins. doi:10.1075/celcr.13.17rob

Robinson, P., & Gilabert, R. (2007). Task complexity, the Cognition Hypothesis and second language learning and performance. *International Review of Applied Linguistics in Language Teaching*, 45, 161–76.

Ross-Feldmen, L. (2007). Interaction in the L2 classroom: Does gender influence learning opportunities? In A. Mackey (Ed.), *Conversational interaction in second language acquisition* (pp. 53–78). Oxford: Oxford University Press.

Rouhshad, A., & Storch, N. (2016). A focus on mode: Patterns of interaction in face-to-face and computer-mediated contexts. In M. Sato & S. Ballinger (Eds.), *Peer interaction and second language learning: Pedagogical potential and research agenda* (pp. 267–289). Amsterdam: John Benjamins.

Sato, M., & Ballinger, S. (2016). Understanding peer interaction: Research synthesis and directions. In M. Sato & S. Ballinger (Eds.), *Peer interaction and second language learning: Pedagogical potential and research agenda* (pp. 1–30). Amsterdam: John Benjamins.

Sato, M., & Lyster, R. (2012). Peer interaction and corrective feedback for accuracy and fluency development: Monitoring, practice, and proceduralization. *Studies in Second Language Acquisition* 34(4), 591–626. doi:10.1017/S0272263112000356

Schmidt, R. W. (1990). The role of consciousness in second language learning. *Applied Linguistics*, 11(2), 129–58. doi:10.1093/applin/11.2.129

Schmidt, R. (2001). Attention. In P. Robinson (Ed.), *Cognition and second language instruction* (pp. 3–32). Cambridge: Cambridge University Press. doi:10.1017/CBO9781139524780.003

Storch, N. (2008). Metatalk in a pair work activity: Level of engagement and implications for language development. *Language Awareness*, 17, 95–114. doi:10.2167/la431.0

Storch, N., & Wigglesworth, G. (2010). Learners' processing, uptake and retention of corrective feedback on writing: Case studies. *Studies in Second Language Acquisition*, 32, 303–334. doi:10.1017/S0272263109990532

Svalberg, A. M.-L. (2007). Language awareness and language learning. *Language Teaching*, 40, 287–308. doi:10.1017/S0261444807004491

Svalberg, A. M.-L. (2009). Engagement With Language: Developing a construct. *Language Awareness*, 18, 242–258. doi:10.1080/09658410903197264

Svalberg, A. M-L. (2012). Thinking allowed: Language awareness in language learning and teaching: A research agenda. *Language Teaching* 45(3), 376–388. doi:10.1017/S0261444812000079

Swain, M. (1995). Three functions of output in second language learning. In G. Cook & B. Seidlhofer (eds.), *Principle and practice in applied linguistics: Studies in honour of H. G. Widdowson*, pp. 125–144. Oxford: Oxford University Press.

Swain, M. (2005). The output hypothesis: Theory and research. In E. Hinkel (ed.), *Handbook of research in second language teaching and learning*, pp. 471–484. Mahwah, NJ: Lawrence Erlbaum.

Swain, M., & Lapkin, S. (1998). Interaction and second language learning: Two adolescent French immersion students working together. *Modern Language Journal*, 82, 320–337. doi:10.1111/j.1540-4781.1998.tb01209.x

Swain, M., & Lapkin, S. (2002). Talking it through: Two French immersion learners' response to reformulation. *International Journal of Educational Research*, 37, 285–304. doi:10.1016/S0883-0355(03)00006-5

Tocalli-Beller, A., & Swain, M. (2007). Riddles and puns in the ESL classroom: Adults talk to learn. In A. Mackey (Ed.), *Conversational interaction in second language acquisition* (pp. 143–167). Oxford: Oxford University Press.

Van den Branden, K. (2015). Tasks for real! Hold on, how real is 'real'? Plenary paper presented at *the Task-Based Language Teaching Conference*. University of Leuven.

Williams, J. (2001). The effectiveness of spontaneous attention to form. *System*, 29, 325–340. doi: 10.1016/S0346-251X(01)00022-7

Yilmaz, Y. (2011). Task effects on focus on form in synchronous computer-mediated communication. *The Modern Language Journal*, 95, 115–132. doi: 10.1111/j.1540-4781.2010.01143.x

Yilmaz, Y., & Yuksel, D. (2011). Effects of communication mode and salience on recasts: A first exposure study. *Language Teaching Research*, 15, 457–477. doi: 10.1177/1362168811412873

Appendix

Post-task questionnaire

Name: _____

Teacher: _____

Class: _____

1. What was your overall perception of the task that you just did with your partner?

2. Do you think there was a specific goal to this task?

3. What features of language did you notice or need during the task?

4. How important and/or helpful was working with your partner in order to finish telling the story?

5. Did your partner help you? If so, how?

6. Provide three adjectives to describe the task.

7. Now provide three adjectives to describe how you felt during the task.

8. Do you think that you and your partner were both equally willing to contribute in re-telling the story?

CHAPTER 9

EFL task-based interaction

Does task modality impact
on language-related episodes?

María del Pilar García Mayo and Agurtzane Azkarai
University of the Basque Country

Research on L2 interaction has shown that task modality (written vs. oral) influences language learning opportunities. However, most research has been carried out in ESL settings and few studies have investigated task modality differences in EFL contexts, where both quantity and quality of exposure to the target language differ considerably. In addition, most research has only focused on how task modality impacts on the incidence, nature and outcome of language-related episodes (LREs), but has not considered the relationship between task modality and learners' level of engagement. This chapter examines the impact of task modality on the LREs and level of engagement in the oral interaction of 44 Spanish-Basque EFL learners while completing four communicative tasks. The findings point to a significant impact of task modality on the incidence, nature and outcome of LREs but a minor impact on learners' level of engagement.

Introduction

Research on second language (L2) task-based interaction has shown that different tasks offer different language learning opportunities. Thus, collaborative writing tasks usually elicit more attention to form than speaking tasks, which do not require the production of written output and seem to focus learners' attention more on meaning (Adams 2006; Adams & Ross-Feldman 2008; Niu 2009). In order to identify language learning opportunities that occur during interaction and collaborative work, researchers have employed language-related episodes (LREs), defined as "[…] any part of the dialogue in which students talk about the language they are producing, question their language use, or other- or self-correct" (Swain 1998: 70). LREs include conversational turns in which learners may question the meaning of a word and/or its form (spelling, pronunciation, grammatical status), and they have been claimed to represent L2 learning in progress (Gass &

DOI 10.1075/lllt.45.10gar

Mackey 2007). Throughout this chapter, such language learning opportunities will be operationalized as LREs.

Many studies have examined LREs, including those considering learners' proficiency (Leeser 2004; Storch & Aldosari 2013; Williams 2001), task type (Adams 2006; Adams & Ross-Feldman 2008; Niu 2009), context (Basterrechea & García Mayo 2013), and the relationship between LREs and L2 development (Kim 2008; McDonough & Sunitham 2009; Swain & Lapkin 1998). Storch (2008) examined the impact of learners' level of engagement in LREs during collaborative work. She used the term 'engagement' to describe the quality of the learners' metatalk (Storch 2008:98) and found that the higher the learners' engagement, the more opportunities they have to develop their L2.

The studies mentioned above have shown the benefits of collaborative work and LREs during task-based interaction. However, most have been carried out in English as a second language (ESL) settings, where the quality and quantity of exposure to the target language differ considerably from English as a foreign language (EFL) settings or foreign language settings in general (García Mayo & García Lecumberri 2003; Muñoz 2006). In most foreign language settings, teachers have less class time contact with their students and L2 input opportunities are limited, both inside and outside the classroom in comparison to most ESL settings (García Mayo & Pica 2000; Philp & Tognini 2009). These opportunities are limited inside the classroom because some teachers do not have the expected English proficiency level and classroom management skills, and outside the classroom because English is a foreign language and is not on TV (in Spain films are dubbed), or even in the linguistic landscape. Therefore, it is important for EFL teachers to have information about the types of tasks that would be more beneficial for their students. The goal of this chapter is to explore the impact of task modality on the production, nature and outcome of LREs and on the engagement that EFL learners show when an LRE is generated in conversational interaction. Its ultimate aim is to consider the kinds of tasks that are more likely to foster language learning opportunities.

Interaction and language learning opportunities

This chapter is framed within the interactionist approach, which is based on the Interaction Hypothesis (Long 1996). The Interaction Hypothesis states that conversational interaction facilitates L2 learning because learners receive comprehensible input and feedback from their interlocutors and they also have the opportunity to produce modified output (Gass 1997, 2003; Long 1996; Pica 1994; Sato & Ballinger 2016; Swain 2005). Interaction provides learners with opportunities to negotiate meaning and form and to 'notice the gap' (Schmidt & Frota 1986) between their production and the target language. The benefits of interaction have been reported in numerous studies (see Keck, Iberri-Shea, Tracy-Ventura & Wa-Mbaleka 2006 and Mackey & Goo 2007 for meta-analyses; García Mayo & Alcón Soler 2013 for a recent review), which have shown a strong link between learners' participation in conversational interaction and L2 learning. Many of these studies have used collaborative, form-focused tasks, as they have been claimed to trigger learners' attention to their own interlanguage and to lead to the production of LREs. Drawing learners' attention to formal aspects of language is of crucial importance in an otherwise communicative-based teaching approach as a large body of research has shown that explicit attention to form facilitates L2 acquisition (Norris & Ortega 2000; Spada & Tomita 2010). In addition, attention to form has also been claimed to enhance "[…] cognitive mapping among forms, meaning and use" (Doughty 2001:211).

As mentioned above, the LRE is a unit of analysis used to identify whether learners consciously reflect on their own language use. LREs have been mainly classified on the basis of their focus (lexis or grammar) and outcome (resolved [target-like or non target-like] or not resolved) (Alegría de la Colina & García Mayo 2007; Leeser 2004; Ross-Feldman 2007; Williams 2001) – see Examples (1) to (5) below. During an LRE, when a learner raises an issue about the target language, the other learner has the option to either join in the discussion or move on with the task at hand. It is precisely this aspect that Storch (2008) considered in detail when she analyzed engagement in LREs. Thus, she distinguished between LREs showing elaborate engagement (E LREs), when both learners deliberated over language items seeking and providing confirmation and explanations, and LREs showing limited engagement, when participants mentioned a linguistic item without deliberating about it. When analyzing the latter, Storch realized that there was a need to further distinguish between LREs showing limited engagement by only one participant (L LREs), and LREs showing limited engagement by both participants (L+L LREs) – see examples below.

Storch (2008) tested 22 ESL learners who worked in pairs on a text reconstruction task. She examined the nature of their engagement with the items they discussed and whether engagement affected language development or not. Her findings showed that participants focused more on grammar than on lexis or mechanics and that the majority of LREs were correctly resolved and of the E LRE type. Those learners who showed an elaborate engagement in their grammar choices learned the target structures. Elaborate engagement triggered more deliberations, questions and explanations than limited engagement.

Storch and Wigglesworth (2010) analyzed the relationship between level of engagement and feedback in a group of ESL students with different first languages (L1s) while they carried out a text composition task. They found that a high level of engagement in feedback episodes led these students to high levels of uptake (immediate revision). In a subsequent study, Wigglesworth and Storch (2012) examined the written texts produced by ESL students with different L1s. When analyzing LREs, they distinguished between LREs consisting of one turn, which showed little engagement and LREs consisting of more turns, which led to more discussion and engagement. Their findings showed that, overall, the level of engagement was high, although the researchers could not establish whether a higher engagement led to greater accuracy.

As a whole, the studies by Storch and Wigglesworth found that during collaborative work learners' engagement tends to be elaborate or high and that this higher level of engagement is more likely to lead to L2 learning. However, to the best of our knowledge, there is no study that has considered learners' level of engagement in EFL settings, nor the impact of task modality on that engagement. This chapter tries to address this gap in task modality research.

Task modality: Speaking vs. writing tasks

The impact of task-modality on L2 interaction has been the subject of recent research, although it is yet to be explored in depth (Rouhshad & Storch 2016; Kuiken & Vedder 2012: 364). Tasks that encourage speaking, such as information-gap tasks (Pica, Kanagy, & Falodun 1993) have been claimed to focus learners' attention more on meaning, whereas writing tasks, such as dictogloss or text editing, focus learners' attention more on form (García Mayo 2002a, 2002b). Although both speaking and writing are essential for language learning, the process of writing is:

> [...] five to eight times slower than speaking, since more time is needed for the verbalization of content [...]. As a consequence, cognitive resources can be used for a longer period of time, from which information retrieval from long-term memory, as well as planning time, should benefit.   (Kuiken & Vedder 2012: 366)

Writing encourages learners to attend to both form and meaning (Cumming 1989) in the sense that, once meaning is understood, learners can pay more attention to the form of the message. Previous research has suggested that tasks that incorporate a writing component are more likely to provide learners with more language learning opportunities, operationalized as LREs, than speaking tasks (see Adams & Ross-Feldman 2008; Williams 2008). Learners are likely to use structures in writing that they do not use when speaking and they might also use a form first in their writing and then in their speech (Williams 2008). Further, writing requires higher levels of accuracy because people tend not to tolerate as many errors in written language as they do in spoken language (Schoonen, Snellings, Stevenson, & van Gelderen 2009).

Adams (2006) examined the impact of task modality when ESL learners with different L1s worked on two tasks that elicited two target forms: locative prepositions and past tense. Each task required an oral and a written component and for the data analysis Adams considered the amount of LREs, self-repairs, and use of target structures in both the writing and speaking parts of the tasks. Her findings showed that the writing part of the task led these students to initiate more LREs, self-repair and use the target structures more often. Ross-Feldman (2007) analyzed the incidence and outcome of LREs in Spanish ESL dyads who worked on a picture placement, a picture differences, and a picture story task. Her findings showed that these learners initiated and resolved more LREs in the picture story task, which incorporated a writing component, than the other two tasks with only a speaking component. More recently, Adams and Ross-Feldman (2008) examined the production of LREs by ESL learners with different L1s when they completed different collaborative writing and speaking tasks. The two target structures were locative prepositions and past tense morphology. They reported that the majority of LREs in both tasks focused on form and that their participants produced more LREs when they had to write than when they only engaged in speaking, although the differences were not statistically significant.

In an EFL context, Niu (2009) also compared the production of LREs when EFL Chinese learners worked on a text reconstruction task. Four pairs completed the task as a collaborative oral output task and another four pairs did it as a collaborative written output task. Her findings showed that those pairs that completed the task as a collaborative written output task initiated more LREs that focused on lexis, form, and discourse than collaborative oral output pairs. Niu concluded that collaborative writing might promote more language learning than only oral communicative tasks.

Azkarai and García Mayo (2012) explored the production and outcome of LREs generated by 12 EFL Basque-Spanish learners when they worked in pairs on a picture placement, a picture differences, a picture story and a dictogloss task. They found that these learners generated more LREs in the picture story and dictogloss tasks, which required them to produce a final written text, than in the other two tasks, which only required them to reach a solution by interacting orally.

The studies reviewed above support the use of collaborative writing tasks, as they provide L2 learners with the opportunity to generate more LREs than speaking tasks. However, in EFL settings only a few studies have focused on the impact of task modality on LREs and there is clearly a need for further research on this topic. As mentioned above, EFL learners generally receive fewer hours of classroom exposure than ESL learners and outside L2 input is also limited (García Mayo & García Lecumberri 2003; Muñoz 2006). It is, therefore, important for teachers to know which tasks could provide their learners with more learning opportunities so that they can obtain the maximum benefit.

The study

The main goal of the present chapter is to investigate the extent to which task modality (writing vs. oral) has an impact on the occurrence of LREs during EFL task-based interaction and on learners' level of engagement while completing collaborative tasks. The following research questions guided this chapter:

a. Is there a task modality (writing vs. oral) effect on the incidence, nature, and outcome of LREs?
b. Is the level of engagement different depending on task modality?

In line with previous findings (Adams 2006; Adams & Ross-Feldman 2008; Azkarai & García Mayo 2012; Niu 2009; Ross-Feldman 2007), we expected a clear impact of task modality on LREs. Specifically, collaborative writing tasks should generate more LREs overall, which would mainly focus on form, than oral communicative tasks, where it is expected that more LREs would focus on meaning. The majority of LREs should also be resolved correctly, but the amount of correctly resolved LREs would be higher in the written tasks. No studies have considered the relationship between level of engagement and task modality. However, one could speculate that, as collaborative writing tasks have been claimed to provide L2 learners with more language learning opportunities, this task modality might also generate a higher level of engagement among learners.

Participants

Forty-four Spanish-Basque bilinguals (22 females and 22 males) took part in this study. Participants were all EFL learners and were enrolled in different degree courses at a major Spanish university. Their English level was assessed by means of a standardized test, the Quick Oxford Placement Test (OPT) (Syndicate U.C.L.E. 2001). Table 1 provides a detailed description of the participants' profile:

Table 1. Participants' profile

	Age	Years studying English	English proficiency		
			Elementary	Lower intermediate	Upper intermediate
Average	24	11	6	26	12
Mean	24.22	11.59			
Range	20–31	8–15			

Materials

The materials used in this study were four collaborative tasks (see Appendix). Two required the production of oral and written output (henceforth, writing tasks), a dictogloss and a text editing task, and the other two required just the production of oral output (henceforth, oral tasks), a picture placement and a picture differences task.

The writing tasks were taken from the New English File Elementary, Pre-Intermediate and Upper Intermediate Text Books (Oxenden, Latham-Koenig, & Seligson 1997a, 1997b, 1997c). Dictogloss and text editing are tasks that have been extensively used in studies framed within the Interaction Hypothesis and they have demonstrated the benefits of writing during interaction (García Mayo 2002a, 2002b).

Dictogloss (Wajnryb 1990) has been found to favor collaborative work and encourage learners to reflect on their own output (Kowal & Swain 1994; Swain 1998; Swain & Lapkin 2001). Both participants work together to reconstruct the original text and in doing so they refine their understanding of the language being used (Basterrechea & García Mayo 2013; García Mayo 2002a, 2002b). Studies have shown that during dictogloss, students notice gaps in their grammatical knowledge and work together to resolve those gaps when attempting to co-produce the text (Nassaji 2000). This task has been shown to promote participation for both partners, to activate the cognitive processes necessary for the acquisition of an L2, and to draw learners' attention to form.

During the text editing task, participants insert function words that have been deleted from the text and correct errors such as omitted subjects, verb tense and agreement, and missing prepositions. This task has also been claimed to be an effective form-focused task, since learners work together collaboratively and peer feedback is available (Alegría de la Colina & García Mayo 2007; García Mayo 2002a, 2002b; Storch 1998a, 1998b).

The oral tasks (picture placement and picture differences) chosen for this study are considered information-gap tasks (Pica et al. 1993). Both tasks engage learners in functional, meaning-focused use of the target language and allow them to gain access to input for learning (Pica, Kang, & Sauro 2006). These tasks also provide L2 learners with opportunities for negotiation of meaning and output modification, since both participants have part of the information they need to exchange in order to complete the task (Sato & Lyster 2007).

All these tasks, very similar to those available in commercial ESL/EFL textbooks, were chosen for the present study because they represented the two task modalities and previous research has shown their effectiveness.

Table 2, describes the average time in minutes taken to complete each task and shows that the four tasks were comparable in terms of the amount of time devoted to each by this group of learners.

Table 2. Time employed by participants in each task

	Writing tasks		Oral tasks	
	Dictogloss	Text editing	Picture placement	Picture differences
Mean	06:30	06:30	06:31	05:45
Range	03:28–11:15	03:09–12:55	04:08–10:27	03:03–12:11

Procedure

This study took place in a laboratory setting and was part of a larger study investigating the role of gender in task-based interaction. As stated earlier, students completed the OPT to assess their proficiency in English and were paired on the basis of their score. Different versions of the four tasks were prepared to avoid task repetition effects, but the tasks were not counterbalanced, which we acknowledge as a weakness.

After task completion, the participants were asked to fill in a post-questionnaire regarding their feelings and thoughts about the tasks. Most participants (34 [77%]) liked the tasks, 24 participants (54%) indicated that they found them difficult and 42 participants (95%) indicated that they had the impression that these tasks helped them learn English. When they were asked about their favorite and least favorite task, most participants (32 [73%]) indicated that the picture differences task was their favorite task and the dictogloss (12 [25%]) and text editing (20 [45%]) tasks were identified as the least favorite. Table 3 provides more details:

Table 3. Participants' opinions on tasks (44 participants)

	Dictogloss	Text editing	Picture placement	Picture differences	No answer
Favorite task	4	2	5	32	1
Least favorite task	12	20	10	1	1

Data analysis and codification

All conversational interactions, consisting of a total of 17 hours and 16 minutes of talk, were transcribed verbatim, and the total number of turns and LREs in each task were tallied. A turn began when a learner started talking and finished when his/her partner began a new utterance. An LRE started when a participant raised a concern about language and finished when they had moved on to a new conversational topic or when the participants moved on with the task at hand, thus resolving the initial concern (see examples below for more details). The incidence of LREs was analyzed considering proportions of the total number of turns in each LRE to the total number of turns in each task.

As the types of LREs and the level of engagement recorded in this study were similar to those reported in Ross-Feldman (2007) and Storch (2008), respectively, we used the same categorizations that were used in those studies. The nature of LREs was coded on the basis of form and meaning-focused LREs and the outcome of LREs on the basis of resolved and not resolved LREs. We further distinguished two types of "not resolved" LREs, namely addressed and ignored LREs, as we thought a more detailed categorization might shed more light on the data. In the categorization of the level of engagement in LREs, we distinguished between E LREs, when the two members of the dyad were engaged in addressing an issue; L LREs, when only that member of the dyad who initiated the LRE was engaged in the linguistic issue and his/her partner did not join in or deliberate about it; and L+L LREs, when the two members of the dyad did not deliberate/discuss the linguistic issue at hand. Figure 1 illustrates this information:

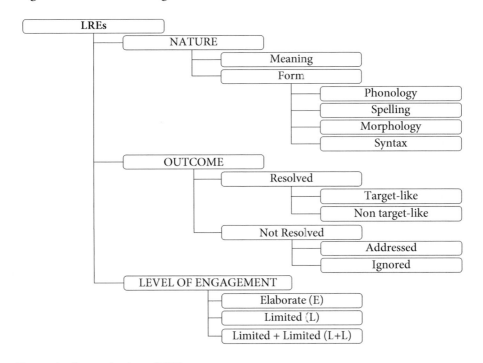

Figure 1. Categorization of LREs

The following examples, all of them from our database, illustrate different types of LREs and the level of engagement in each. In Example (1), Miguel and Susana are completing the picture placement task. Miguel asks Susana where the 'oven glove' is (turn 1), but Susana does not know the correct answer. However, she lets him know that she has understood what he meant (turn 2). In turn 3 Miguel provides more details about the object he refers to and initiates another LRE, as he does not know how to say the word 'oven'. Susana provides him with the correct answer for 'oven' in turn 4 (meaning-focused, target-like resolved and elaborate LRE), and still seems to be thinking about the correct word for 'oven glove'. The first LRE, referring to 'oven glove' was left unresolved, but addressed as both participants deliberated about it and tried to find a solution, for this reason it was also coded as an E LRE:

(1) 1. Miguel: Where is the the thing that we use to put with hand inside?
     2. Susana: Oh, yes! To take something?
     3. Miguel: For the *horno* [oven]. Cook? In the *horno* [oven].
     4. Susana: Yeah, oven.
     5. Miguel: Oven. Yes.
     6. Susana: Ok. Er…

Example (2) shows a form-focused phonology LRE. When completing the picture differences task, Iria mispronounces the word 'hat' (/hæt/) (turn 3) and Sergio immediately provides her with the correct pronunciation of the word in turn 4. As Sergio's answer is correct, this LRE was coded as a target-like resolved LRE and as an E LRE as both members are actively engaged.

(2) 1. Iria: He has a carrot in his nose.
     2. Sergio: Yes.
     3. Iria: Han /hæn/? A green han /hæn/? Han /hæn/?
     4. Sergio: Hat /hæt/!
     5. Iria: *O sea* [I mean], hat /hæt/!

Example (3) took place during the dictogloss. David misspells the word 'T-H-R-U-S-D-A-Y' (turn 3), but later in turn 5 he spells it correctly. This seems to confuse Raúl, who repeats the correct word in turn 6. In turn 7, David tells Raúl that he is wrong and that he should spell it as in turn 3 (Thrusday), with an 'R' (turn 9). Raúl is confused and repeats the word (turn 8) and, finally, in turn 10 he realizes that the correct spelling is 'Thursday' and not 'T-H-R-U-S-D-A-Y' as his partner was suggesting. In turn 11 David realizes that he was wrong and apologizes for his mistake. This spelling-focused LRE was coded as a target-like resolved LRE because the participants finally provided the right answer, and as an E LRE because both participants were engaged in trying to get the correct spelling of 'Thursday' and deliberated about it.

(3) 1. David: My favorite day, my favorite day of the week.
     2. Raúl: Of the week.
     3. David: It's T-H-R-U-S-D-A-Y.
     4. Raúl: Is?
     5. David: T-H-R-U-S-D-A-Y.
     6. Raúl: Thursday.
     7. David: Thru! Thru!
     8. Raúl: Thursday.
     9. David: With R.
    10. Raúl: Thursday!
    11. David: Ok, ok. Yes. Excuse me! Excuse me!
    12. Raúl: Thursday.

Example (4) shows a morphology-focused LRE. In the text editing, Candela asks whether the correct form of the verb is 'being' instead of 'be' in the sentence 'Despite be the most famous Englishman…' (turn 2). Paz ignores her, and for this reason it was coded as an ignored LRE, and Candela goes on with the task and both learners focus on the following sentence. As they do not try to provide an answer, both seem not to be engaged with this LRE and for this reason it was coded as an L+L LRE.

(4) 1. Paz: He is the most…
     2. Candela: Yes. Or being *igual, ¿no?* [maybe, don't you think? Despite be the most famous Englishman in the world, little is know for certain about Shakespeare's…
     3. Paz: Shakespeare's private life.

Example (5) took place during the text editing. Rebeca is discussing whether to insert the pronoun 'it' in the sentence or not. At the beginning, she is convinced that they have to insert the pronoun in the sentence (turn 2), but later she changes her mind (in turns 4 and 6). Note that the original sentence was "Whatever food you are looking for, you can find it in San Francisco". Rebeca refers to 'restaurants' instead of 'food' and that is the reason why she thinks that inserting the pronoun would only refer to one restaurant and not to food. She deliberates about it, seeking Marcos' confirmation in turns 4 and 6, but he only answers 'Yes' and does not help her, thus showing little engagement. At the end, Rebeca decides to omit the pronoun. The LRE was coded as a syntax-focused non target-like LRE. As she was engaged in trying to get the correct answer and Marcos was not, the LRE was also coded as an L LRE.

(5) 1. Marcos: You find it.
    2. Rebeca: You can find it.
    3. Marcos: Oh! You can find it in San Francisco.
    4. Rebeca: And why not "you can find in San Francisco"? You can find it?
    5. Marcos: Yes.
    6. Rebeca: It is more than one. You can find.
    7. Marcos: Yes.
    8. Rebeca: In San Francisco.

After all LREs were identified and categorized on the basis of their nature, outcome and the learners' level of engagement, the data were submitted to statistical
analysis. A bilateral two sample binomial test for independent samples ($\alpha = 0.05$)
was used to determine significance.

Results

This section presents the findings on the basis of the two research questions posited above. The significant findings have been summarized into three different
graphs which are presented at the end of the section.

   Our first research question asked whether there was a task modality effect on
the incidence, nature, and outcome of LREs. Regarding the incidence of LREs,
participants initiated significantly more LREs in the writing tasks (467) than in the
oral tasks (357) ($z = 31.72$, $p < 0.0001$). There were also differences between same-
modality tasks: participants initiated significantly more LREs in the text editing
task than in the dictogloss ($z = 30.83$, $p < 0.0001$) and significantly more LREs in
the picture placement than in the picture differences task ($z = 17.26$, $p < 0.0001$).
These findings are detailed in Table 4 below.

Table 4. Incidence of LREs in the two task modalities and in each task

Tasks	Turns	Turns comprising LREs	Number of LREs	Mean	SD
Writing tasks	4991	2200 (44.08%)	467	10.61	4.211
Dictogloss	2227	444 (19.94%)	107	2.43	2.774
Text editing	2764	1756 (63.53%)	360	8.18	3.082
Oral tasks	7579	1365 (18.01%)	357	8.11	3.610
P. placement	3171	856 (27%)	221	5.02	2.565
P. differences	4408	509 (11.55%)	136	3.09	1.736

Note. The percentages are calculated considering the total number of turns comprising LREs to the total
amount of turns initiated in each task

The analysis of the nature of LREs showed that participants initiated significantly
more form-focused LREs in the writing tasks (344 [73.66%]) and significantly

more meaning-focused LREs in the oral tasks (326 [91.32%]) ($z = 18.56$, $p <$ 0.0001). Specifically, form-focused LREs were significantly more common in the text editing task (274 [76.11%]) than in the dictogloss ($z = 2.20$, $p = 0.0276$), and meaning-focused LREs were significantly more common in the picture placement task (208 [94.12%]) than in the picture differences task ($z = 2.40$, $p = 0.0166$). These findings are detailed in Table 5 below.

Table 5. Nature of LREs in both task modalities and in each task

Tasks	Form-focused			Meaning-focused		
	LREs	Mean	SD	LREs	Mean	SD
Writing tasks	344 (73.66%)	7.82	3.432	123 (26.34%)	2.80	1.850
Dictogloss	70 (65.42%)	1.59	2.171	37 (34.58%)	.84	1.077
Text editing	274 (76.11%)	6.23	2.532	86 (23.89%)	1.95	1.493
Oral tasks	31 (8.68%)	.70	.904	326 (91.32%)	7.41	3.350
P. placement	13 (5.88%)	.30	.509	208 (94.12%)	4.73	2.395
P. differences	18 (13.23%)	.41	.583	118 (86.77%)	2.68	1.581

Note. The percentages are calculated considering the number of LREs initiated in each condition (form or meaning) to the total number of LREs initiated in each task

Regarding the outcome of LREs, in terms of percentages, resolved LREs occurred significantly more in the writing tasks (376 [80.51%]) than in the oral tasks ($z = 6.73$, $p < 0.0001$), and addressed LREs were significantly more frequent in the oral tasks (123 [84.25%]) than in the writing tasks ($z = 4.45$, $p < 0.0001$). LREs were also resolved in a target-like manner more often in the oral tasks than in the writing tasks, but this difference was not significant.

The comparison between same-modality tasks was only significant in the case of the amount of target-like/non target-like resolved LREs: participants correctly resolved significantly more LREs in the dictogloss (70 [76.92%]) ($z = 2.76$, $p = 0.0058$) and the picture differences (72 [82.76%]) ($z = 3.46$, $p = 0.0006$) tasks than in their modality counterparts. These findings are detailed in Table 6 below.

Our second research question asked whether task modality could impact the level of engagement in LREs. The results indicated that, overall, the level of engagement in LREs was elaborate in all the tasks and no major difference was found between task modalities or same-modality tasks. Overall, E LREs occurred more frequently in the oral tasks, but the task that proportionally generated more E LREs was the dictogloss (76 [71.03%]). In addition, when comparing the amount of E LREs initiated in the dictogloss and the text editing, the results showed a significant difference ($z = 2.02$, $p = 0.043$). Significant differences were also found in the amount of L LREs, as these LREs were more frequent in the writing tasks (86 [18.42%]) than in oral tasks ($z = 3.21$, $p = 0.001$). No differences were found for the rest of the comparisons. These findings are detailed in Table 7 below.

Table 6. Outcome of LREs in both task modalities and in each task

Tasks	Resolved			Target-like (resolved)			Addressed (not resolved)		
	LREs	Mean	SD	LREs	Mean	SD	LREs	Mean	SD
Writing tasks	376 (80.51%)	8.55	3.688	244 (64.89%)	5.55	2.905	53 (58.24%)	1.20	1.304
Dictogloss	91 (85.05%)	2.07	2.245	70 (76.92%)	1.59	1.909	10 (62.5%)	.23	.642
Text editing	285 (79.17%)	6.48	2.921	174 (61.05%)	3.95	2.188	43 (57.33%)	.98	.976
Oral tasks	211 (59.10%)	4.80	2.455	147 (69.67%)	3.34	1.976	123 (84.25%)	2.80	2.075
P. placement	124 (56.11%)	2.82	1.896	75 (60.48%)	1.70	1.488	83 (85.57%)	1.89	1.528
P. differences	87 (63.97%)	1.98	1.320	72 (82.76%)	1.64	1.222	40 (81.63%)	.91	1.007

Note. The percentages are calculated considering the number of LREs initiated in each condition (resolved [target-like/non target-like] or not resolved [addressed/ignored]) to the total number of LREs initiated in each task

Table 7. Level of engagement in LREs in both task modalities and in each task

Tasks	Elaborate			Limited			Limited+limited		
	LREs	Mean	SD	LREs	Mean	SD	LREs	Mean	SD
Writing tasks	293 (62.74%)	6.66	3.154	86 (18.42%)	2.07	1.897	88 (18.84%)	1.89	1.646
Dictogloss	76 (71.03%)	1.73	1.757	17 (15.89%)	.39	.895	14 (13.08%)	.32	.639
Text editing	217 (60.28%)	4.93	2.671	69 (19.16%)	1.68	1.667	74 (20.56%)	1.57	1.576
Oral tasks	245 (68.63%)	5.57	2.897	37 (10.36%)	.84	.939	75 (21.01%)	1.70	1.773
P. placement	150 (67.87%)	3.41	2.171	24 (10.86%)	.55	.697	47 (21.27%)	1.07	1.404
P. differences	95 (69.85%)	2.16	1.413	13 (9.56%)	.30	.553	28 (20.59%)	.64	.865

Note. The percentages are calculated considering the number of LREs initiated in each condition (elaborate, limited or limited+limited) to the total number of LREs initiated in each task

As indicated at the beginning of this section, the following graphs summarize the significant findings of the study:

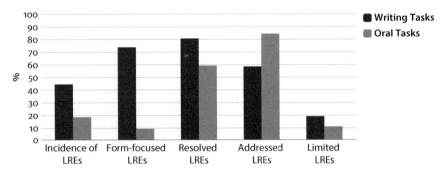

Graph 1. Significant differences in the incidence, nature, outcome and level of engagement in LREs between writing and oral tasks

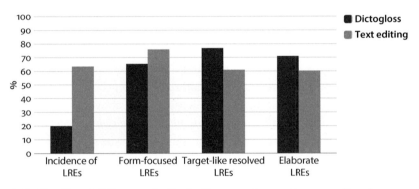

Graph 2. Significant differences in the incidence, nature, outcome and level of engagement in LREs between the dictogloss and the text editing

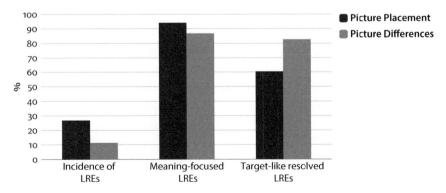

Graph 3. Significant differences in the incidence, nature and outcome of LREs between the picture placement and the picture differences tasks

Discussion

The main goal of this study was to investigate the impact of task modality (writing vs. oral tasks) on LREs during EFL task-based interaction and on the learners' level of engagement in those LREs. There is a clear gap in the research on this topic in EFL settings, where the learners receive fewer hours of exposure to the target language than in most ESL settings and do not have many opportunities to practice their target language outside the classroom. Our findings reflect previous research in ESL settings on the impact of task modality, as participants initiated more LREs in the writing tasks, mainly focusing on form, than in the oral tasks, where LREs mainly focused on meaning. The EFL participants also solved more LREs in the writing tasks than in the oral tasks. Although previous research had not considered the relationship between task modality and engagement, we expected to find a more elaborate level of engagement in the LREs generated in the writing tasks than in oral tasks because learners seemed to be more concerned with formal issues while completing the writing tasks. However, this prediction was not borne out.

In line with previous studies (Adams & Ross-Feldman 2008; Azkarai & García Mayo 2012; Niu 2009; Ross-Feldman 2007), these participants initiated significantly more LREs in the writing tasks than in the oral tasks, specifically in the text editing task. As participants had to submit a final written product, they may have felt more concerned about making errors. As mentioned above, writing demands higher levels of accuracy and errors are less likely to be overlooked (Schoonen et al. 2009). It is perhaps for this reason that raising an issue about language was more common in the writing tasks.

However, we also found differences in the incidence of LREs between same-modality tasks. In line with García Mayo (2001, 2002a, 2002b) and Storch (1998a), participants in this study generated significantly more LREs in the text editing task than in the dictogloss task, a finding that would be expected considering that discussing language issues is a requirement in a collaborative text editing task. García Mayo (2002b) attributed her findings to the nature of the stimulus of the dictogloss (aural) and also to the learners' lack of familiarity with the procedure. Some studies have also reported that dictogloss is not a "successful" activity. For example, Dunn (1993) and Lukin (1994) found that their students produced texts that were less grammatically accurate than those they usually produced in writing classes. However, Swain and Lapkin (2000, 2001) have used dictogloss tasks successfully in several of their studies.

Similarly to Ross-Feldman (2007), the present study also showed that participants produced significantly more LREs in the picture placement than in the picture differences task. In the picture placement task, the objects on which participants had to focus were related to a specific semantic field. If they were not familiar with the vocabulary associated with that semantic field, they would encounter difficulties completing the activity. In the picture differences task, the items that appeared in their pictures were more numerous than in the picture placement task and not related to any specific semantic field. Therefore, when participants could not refer to one object, they would just refer to another one with which they were familiar.

To sum up, the findings from the present study indicate that including a writing component in interactive tasks leads learners to produce more LREs and that there is a clear task modality effect: more structured tasks (text editing or picture placement) seem to elicit more attention to language than their modality counterparts.

Nature of LREs

The nature of LREs was task-modality dependent and there were significantly more form-focused LREs in the writing tasks and significantly more meaning-focused LREs in the oral tasks. When working on the former, participants appeared to pay more attention not only to the content, but also to the form and structure of the output they generated. In this way, our study supports previous research in ESL settings and provides more evidence for the scarce database existing in EFL contexts from learners with different L1s.

There were also differences regarding the nature of LREs in same-modality tasks: form-focused LREs occurred significantly more often in the text editing task than in the dictogloss. In line with previous studies (García Mayo 2001, 2002a, 2002b), dictogloss was the least efficient in this sense. Although both tasks require oral and written output, text editing seems to be a more effective task for stimulating a focus on form (Storch 1998a). As argued by García Mayo (2002a, 2002b) it could be that those tasks that offer a written stimulus (text editing) prompt more attention to form because participants have been provided with a written version of the activity. However, the stimulus received from the dictogloss is aural and participants need to understand the text before starting to write it so they might be more focused on trying to understand the text than on producing error-free writing. In addition, during dictogloss learners not only have to understand the text that they have just heard, but they also have to remember it. The extra listening, comprehension and memory component involved may increase the cognitive demand of the task for learners.

Differences were also found between the two oral tasks: the picture placement task generated more meaning-focused LREs than the picture differences task, but no differences were found between these two tasks in the amount of form-focused LREs. As indicated above, the picture placement task contained more specific items than the picture differences task, and for this reason participants may have encountered more difficulties.

Overall, the analysis of the nature of LREs showed that the writing tasks led these learners to focus on formal aspects of language while oral tasks focused learners' attention more on meaning. In addition, more structured tasks, such as text editing or picture placement tasks, led these learners to focus more on form and meaning, respectively, than their modality counterparts.

Outcome of LREs

There were no major task-related differences regarding the outcome of LREs. However, in line with previous findings (Adams & Ross-Feldman 2008; Azkarai & García Mayo 2012; Ross-Feldman 2007), participants resolved more LREs in the writing tasks than they did in the oral tasks, specifically in the dictogloss; however, they addressed significantly more LREs in the oral tasks than in the writing tasks.

The majority of LREs in oral tasks were related to vocabulary issues. If participants did not know how to say a specific word in English, they were not able to help their partner resolve his/her doubt and, therefore, the LRE was left unresolved. However, most made an attempt to resolve the problems they encountered and they did try to reach a consensus (consider Example (1)).

In the writing tasks, participants may have felt unable to deal with some of the grammar-related issues that arose during interaction and they simply ignored them (consider Example (4) above). However, possibly due to the emphasis on formal grammatical aspects in foreign language classrooms, when they felt they could provide a correct answer, they deliberated about it until they could find common ground, even if it was non target-like.

In same-modality tasks, significant differences were only found in the case of target-like resolved LREs, as participants correctly resolved significantly more LREs in the dictogloss and the picture differences tasks than in their modality counterparts. Possible explanations for why this might be so would be merely speculative. More detailed research on differences between same-modality tasks is needed.

To sum up, the analysis of the outcome of LREs in this study showed that the writing tasks led these learners to resolve more LREs than in the oral tasks. However, although participants left more LREs unresolved in the oral tasks, they at least addressed their linguistic concerns significantly more when working in these tasks than in the writing tasks. No major differences were found between same-modality tasks, but dictogloss and picture differences led to significantly more target-like resolved LREs than their modality counterparts.

Level of engagement in LREs

The analysis of the level of engagement in LREs showed that, overall, participants' engagement was elaborate and very similar in both task-modalities. These findings support the benefits of collaborative work and are similar to those reported above in ESL settings (Storch 2008; Storch & Wigglesworth 2010; Wigglesworth & Storch 2012). Our findings suggest that despite the few hours of exposure and opportunities to practice English outside the classroom, EFL learners are as engaged as ESL learners when completing these types of task. However, our findings also showed that L LREs were significantly more frequent in the writing tasks than in the oral tasks, which suggests that in the writing tasks at least one member of the dyad was not as engaged as the one that raised an issue about language.

Regarding same-modality tasks, the results indicated differences only when comparing the amount of E LREs between the dictogloss and text editing: E LREs were more frequent in the dictogloss probably because, as indicated above, text editing is a more structured task and participants may have felt unable to resolve some of the linguistic issues that arose during interaction. This might have led them to a more limited engagement (consider Examples (4) and (5)). No differences were found regarding level of engagement in the picture placement and the picture differences tasks.

Overall, these results suggest that engagement in LREs is similar in both task modalities and that the participants deliberated over language items, looking for answers and sharing them with their partners. There was a difference regarding the limited engagement of one of the participants in the writing tasks (L LREs). As the writing tasks were more structured than the oral tasks, these participants could have felt that the linguistic concerns of their partners were too complex to deal with and instead of trying, they just ignored them. In addition, as reported in the post-questionnaire, the writing tasks were their least favorite tasks and the picture differences (oral task) the most popular. This could also have influenced their engagement in the LREs generated in those tasks.

Conclusion and pedagogical implications

The present study set out to investigate the impact of task modality on the production, nature, and outcome of LREs and on the learners' level of engagement while completing four collaborative tasks in an EFL setting. Research on these topics is clearly needed in this context because the learners' quality and quantity of exposure to the target language differs from that in ESL settings. Our findings have shown that the participants generated more LREs in the writing tasks, which also focused their attention more on form, than in oral tasks, which focused their attention more on meaning. The participants also resolved more LREs in the writing tasks. These findings support previous research in ESL settings. Regarding the impact of task modality on learners' level of engagement, the findings pointed to a high learner involvement in all tasks while discussing LREs.

These findings are encouraging considering the specific characteristics of foreign language settings, where teachers do not have many hours of classroom contact with the learners and where learners have barely any chance of using the target language outside the classroom. Foreign language teachers therefore might want to consider the use of communicative tasks that include a writing component because these tasks seem to provide learners with many language learning opportunities (operationalized as LREs in this study) and help them focus their attention on formal language issues. During task completion, the learners discuss language choices, help each other and provide appropriate answers to their common concerns. Our findings seem to indicate that in EFL collaborative pair work learners can profit from each other's knowledge, work together to move the task along and co-construct meaning. In this sense, "[…] students act as language users with the explicit analysis of language structures and forms emerging from difficulties experienced during the completion of tasks" (Ogilvie & Dunn 2010: 162).

Although this study has provided evidence about the role of task modality in EFL learner-learner interaction, there are limitations that should be addressed in future studies. For example, further research should consider a larger sample of participants to obtain more robust conclusions. Our study was experimental and took place in an EFL laboratory setting; future research should consider using classroom settings in order to have more ecological validity. Different instructional settings should also be analyzed in detail, such as Content and Language Integrated Learning (CLIL), as little experimental research has been conducted in this context known from the extra amount of input provided to learners in foreign language settings and a more interactive methodology (Basterrechea & García Mayo 2013; Dalton-Puffer 2011). Further studies should also consider learners' proficiency and its impact on level of engagement, as well as the relationship between task-modality and task complexity (Robinson 2011) since this study has reported differences between same-modality tasks that might be related to task difficulty.

References

Adams, R. (2006). L2 tasks and orientation to form: A role for modality? *ITL: International Journal of Applied Linguistics*, 152, 7–34. doi:10.2143/ITL.152.0.2017861

Adams, R., & Ross-Feldman, L. (2008). Does writing influence learner attention to form? In D. Belcher & A. Hirvela (Eds.), *The oral-literate connection. Perspectives on L2 speaking, writing, and other media interactions* (pp. 243–265). Ann Arbor, MI: The University of Michigan Press.

Alegría de la Colina, A., & García Mayo, M. P. (2007). Attention to form across collaborative tasks by low-proficiency learners in an EFL setting. In M. P. García Mayo (Ed.), *Investigating tasks in formal language learning* (pp. 91–116). Clevedon, UK: Multilingual Matters.

Azkarai, A., & García Mayo, M. P. (2012). Does gender influence task performance in EFL? Interactive tasks and language related episodes. In E. Alcón Soler & M. P. Safont Jordá (Eds.), *Discourse and learning across L2 instructional contexts* (pp. 249–278). Amsterdam: Rodopi.

Basterrechea, M., & García Mayo, M. P. (2013). Language-related episodes during collaborative tasks: A comparison of CLIL and EFL learners. In K. McDonough & A. Mackey (Eds.), *Interaction in diverse educational settings* (pp. 25–43). Amsterdam: John Benjamins. doi:10.1075/lllt.34.05ch2

Cumming, A. (1989). Writing expertise and second language proficiency. *Language Learning*, 39, 81–141. doi:10.1111/j.1467-1770.1989.tb00592.x

Dalton-Puffer, C. (2011). Content-and-language integrated learning: From practice to principles? *Annual Review of Applied Linguistics*, 31, 182–204. doi:10.1017/S0267190511000092

Doughty, C. (2001). Cognitive underpinnings of focus on form. In P. Robinson (Ed.), *Cognition and second language instruction* (pp. 206–257). Cambridge: Cambridge University Press. doi:10.1017/CBO9781139524780.010

Dunn, A. (1993). Dictogloss – When the words get in the way. *TESOL in Context*, 3(2), 21–23.

García Mayo, M. P. (2001). Focus on form tasks in EFL grammar pedagogy. In D. Lasagabaster & J. M. Sierra (Eds.), *Language awareness in the foreign language classroom* (pp. 221–236). Bilbao: University of the Basque Country Press Service.

García Mayo, M. P. (2002a). The effectiveness of two form-focused tasks in advanced EFL pedagogy. *International Journal of Applied Linguistics*, 12(2), 156–175. doi:10.1111/1473-4192.t01-1-00029

García Mayo, M. P. (2002b). Interaction in advanced EFL pedagogy: A comparison of form-focused activities. *International Journal of Educational Research*, 37, 323–341. doi:10.1016/S0883-0355(03)00008-9

García Mayo, M. P., & Alcón Soler, E. (2013). Negotiated input and output interaction. In J. Herschensohn & M. Young-Scholten (Eds.), *The Cambridge handbook of second language acquisition* (pp. 209–229). Cambridge: Cambridge University Press. doi:10.1017/CBO9781139051729.014

García Mayo, M. P., & García Lecumberri, M. L. (Eds.). (2003). *Age and the acquisition of English as a foreign language*. Clevedon, UK: Multilingual Matters.

García Mayo, M. P., & Pica, T. 2000. L2 interaction in a foreign language setting: Are learning needs addressed. *International Review of Applied Linguistics*, 38, 35–58.

Gass, S. (1997). *Input, interaction and the second language learner*. Mahwah, NJ: Lawrence Erlbaum Associates.

Gass, S. (2003). Input and interaction. In C. Doughty & M. Long (Eds.), *Handbook of second language acquisition* (pp. 224–255). Oxford: Blackwell. doi:10.1002/9780470756492.ch9

Gass, S., & Mackey, A. (2007). Input, interaction and output in second language acquisition. In B. VanPatten & J. Williams (Eds.), *Theories in second language acquisition. An introduction* (175–199). Mahwah, NJ: Lawrence Erlbaum Associates.

Keck, C. M., Iberri-Shea, G., Tracy-Ventura, N., & Wa-Mbaleka, S. (2006). Investigating the empirical link between task-based interaction and acquisition: A quantitative meta-analysis. In J. M. Norris & L. Ortega (Eds.), *Synthesizing research on language learning and teaching* (pp. 91–131). Amsterdam: John Benjamins. doi:10.1075/lllt.13.08kec

Kim, Y. (2008). The contribution of collaborative and individual tasks to the acquisition of L2 vocabulary. *The Modern Language Journal*, 92, 114–130. doi:10.1111/j.1540-4781.2008.00690.x

Kowal, M., & Swain, M. (1994). Using collaborative language production tasks to promote students' language awareness. *Language Awareness*, 3(2), 73–93. doi:10.1080/09658416.1994.9959845

Kuiken, F., & Vedder, I. (2012). Speaking and writing tasks and their effects on second language performance. In A. Mackey & S. Gass (Eds.), *The Routledge handbook of second language acquisition* (pp. 364–377). New York, NY: Routledge.

Leeser, M. J. (2004). Learner proficiency and focus on form during collaborative dialogue. *Language Teaching Research*, 8, 55–81. doi:10.1191/1362168804lr134oa

Long, M. H. (1996). The role of the linguistic environment in second language acquisition. In W. C. Ritchie & T. K. Bhatia (Eds.), *Handbook of second language acquisition* (pp. 413–468). New York, NY: Academic Press.

Lukin, A. (1994). Functional grammar and dictogloss: What does 'Good Grammar' really mean? *TESOL in Context*, 4(2), 49–51.

Mackey, A., & Goo, J. (2007). Interaction research in SLA: A meta-analysis and research synthesis. In A. Mackey (Ed.), *Conversational interaction in second language acquisition* (pp. 407–472). Oxford: Oxford University Press.

McDonough, K., & Sunitham, W. (2009). Collaborative dialogue between Thai EFL learners during self-access computer activities. *TESOL Quarterly*, 43, 2321–254. doi:10.1002/j.1545-7249.2009.tb00166.x

Muñoz, C. (Ed.). (2006). *Age and the rate of foreign language learning*. Clevedon, UK: Multilingual Matters.

Nassaji, H. (2000). Towards integrating form-focused instruction and communicative interaction in the second language classroom: some pedagogical possibilities. *The Modern Language Journal*, 84(2), 241–250. doi:10.1111/0026-7902.00065

Norris, J., & Ortega, L. (2000). Effectiveness of L2 instruction: A research synthesis and quantitative meta-analysis. *Language Learning*, 50, 417–428. doi:10.1111/0023-8333.00136

Niu, R. (2009). Effect of task-inherent production modes on EFL learners' focus on form. *Language Awareness*, 18(3-4), 384–402. doi:10.1080/09658410903197256

Ogilvie, G., & Dunn, W. (2010). Taking teacher education to task: Exploring the role of teacher education in promoting the utilization of task-based language teaching. *Language Teaching Research*, 14(2), 161–181. doi:10.1177/1362168809353875

Oxenden, C., Latham-Koenig, C., & Seligson, P. (1997a). *New English file. Elementary student's book*. Oxford: Oxford University Press.

Oxenden, C., Latham-Koenig, C., & Seligson, P. (1997b). *New English file. Pre intermediate student's book*. Oxford: Oxford University Press.

Oxenden, C., Latham-Koenig, C., & Seligson, P. (1997c). *New English file. Upper intermediate. student's book*. Oxford: Oxford University Press.

Philp, J., & Tognini, R. (2009). Language acquisition in foreign language contexts and the differential benefits of interaction. *International Review of Applied Linguistics*, 47, 245–266. doi:10.1515/iral.2009.011

Pica, T. (1994). Research on negotiation: What does it reveal about second-language learning conditions, processes, and outcomes? *Language Learning*, 44, 493–527. doi:10.1111/j.1467-1770.1994.tb01115.x

Pica, T., Kanagy, R., & Falodun, J. (1993). Choosing and using communication tasks for second language instruction and research. In G. Crookes & S. M. Gass (Eds.), *Tasks and language learning* (pp. 9–34). Clevedon, UK: Multilingual Matters.

Pica, T., Kang, H., & Sauro, S. (2006). Information gap tasks. Their multiple roles and contributions to interaction research methodology. *Studies in Second Language Acquisition*, 28(2), 301–338. doi:10.1017/S027226310606013X

Robinson, P. (Ed.). (2011). *Second language task complexity: Researching the Cognition Hypothesis of language learning and performance*. Amsterdam: John Benjamins. doi:10.1075/tblt.2

Ross-Feldman, L. (2007). Interaction in the L2 classroom: Does gender influence learning opportunities? In A. Mackey (Ed.), *Conversational interaction in second language acquisition: A collection of empirical studies* (pp. 52–77). Oxford: Oxford University Press.

Rouhshad, A., & Storch, N. (2016). A focus on mode: Patterns of interaction in face-to-face and computer-mediated contexts In M. Sato & S. Ballinger (Eds.), *Peer interaction and second language learning: Pedagogical potential and research agenda* (pp. 267–289). Amsterdam: John Benjamins.

Sato, M., & Ballinger, S. (2016). Understanding peer interaction: Research synthesis and directions. In M. Sato & S. Ballinger (Eds.), *Peer interaction and second language learning: Pedagogical potential and research agenda* (pp. 1–30). Amsterdam: John Benjamins.

Sato, M., & Lyster, R. (2007). Modified output of Japanese EFL learners: Variable effects of interlocutor vs. feedback types. In A. Mackey (Ed.), *Conversational interaction in second language acquisition: A collection of empirical studies* (pp. 123–142). Oxford: Oxford University Press.

Schmidt, R., & Frota, S. (1986). Developing basic conversational ability in a second language. A case study of an adult learner of Portuguese. In R. R. Day (Ed.), *Talking to learn: Conversation in second language acquisition* (pp. 237–326). Rowley, MA: Newbury House.

Schoonen, R., Snellings, P., Stevenson, M., & van Gelderen, A. (2009). Towards a blueprint of the foreign language writer: The linguistic and cognitive demands of foreign language writing. In R. M. Manchón (Ed.), *Writing in foreign language contexts: Learning, teaching, and research* (pp. 77–101). Bristol, UK: Multilingual Matters.

Spada, N., & Tomita, Y. (2010). Interaction between type of instruction and type of language feature: A meta-analysis. *Language Learning*, 60, 1–46. doi:10.1111/j.1467-9922.2010.00562.x

Storch, N. (1998a). Comparing second language learners' attention to form across tasks. *Language Awareness*, 7, 176–191. doi:10.1080/09658419808667108

Storch, N. (1998b). A classroom-based study: Insights from a collaborative, text reconstruction task. *ELT Journal*, 52(4), 291–300. doi:10.1093/elt/52.4.291

Storch, N. (2008). Metatalk in a pair work activity: Level of engagement and implications for language development. *Language Awareness*, 17(2), 95–114. doi:10.2167/la431.0

Storch, N., & Aldosari, A. (2013). Pairing learners in pair-work activity. *Language Teaching Research*, 17(1), 31–48 doi:10.1177/1362168812457530

Storch, N., & Wigglesworth, G. (2010). Learners' processing, uptake and retention of corrective feedback on writing: Case studies. *Studies in Second Language Acquisition*, 32(2), 303–334. doi: 10.1017/S0272263109990532

Swain, M. (1998). Focus on form through conscious reflection. In C. Doughty & J. Williams (Eds.), *Focus on form in classroom second language acquisition* (pp. 64–81). Cambridge: Cambridge University Press.

Swain, M. (2005). The Output Hypothesis: Theory and research. In E. Hinkel (Ed.), *Handbook on research in second language teaching and learning* (pp. 471–484). Mahwah, NJ: Lawrence Erlbaum Associates.

Swain, M., & Lapkin, S. (1998). Interaction and second language learning: Two adolescent French immersion students working together. *Modern Language Journal*, 82, 320–337. doi: 10.1111/j.1540-4781.1998.tb01209.x

Swain, M., & Lapkin, S. (2000). Task-based second language learning: The uses of the first language. *Language Teaching Research* 4(3), 251–274. doi: 10.1177/136216880000400304

Swain, M., & Lapkin, S. (2001). Focus on form through collaborative dialogue: Exploring task effects. In M. Bygate, P. Skehan, & M. Swain (Eds.), *Researching pedagogic tasks: Second language learning, teaching and assessment* (pp. 99–118). London: Pearson Education.

Syndicate, U.C.L.E. (2001). *Quick placement test*. Oxford: Oxford University Press.

Wajnryb, R. (1990). *Grammar dictation*. Oxford: Oxford University Press.

Wigglesworth, G., & Storch, N. (2012). Feedback and writing development through collaboration: A sociocultural approach. In R. Manchón (Ed.), *L2 writing development: Multiple perspectives* (pp. 69–100). Berlin: Mouton De Gruyter.

Williams, J. (2001). The effectiveness of spontaneous attention to form. *System*, 29, 325–340. doi: 10.1016/S0346-251X(01)00022-7

Williams, J. (2008). The speaking-writing connection in second language and academic literacy development. In D. Belcher & A. Hirvela (Eds.), *The oral-literate connection. Perspectives on L2 speaking, writing, and other media interactions* (pp. 10–25). Ann Arbor, MI: The University of Michigan Press.

Appendix

Some examples of tasks employed in the present study:

Dictogloss (lower-intermediate level version)

Instructions: You will be listening to a text that will be read twice at normal speed. Your task will be to reproduce the original text as faithfully as possible and in a grammatically accurate form. The first time you listen to the text you should not write down anything; the second time your partner and you are allowed to write down some key words that you feel will help you to reproduce the original text. Together, you have to reproduce the original text and one of you will write the final version, which I will collect once you finish. Please, make sure you explain your choices.

Text: I was very optimistic when I went to meet Claire. My first impression was that she was very friendly and very extrovert. Physically she was my type: she was quite slim and not very tall with long dark hair, very pretty! And she was very funny too! She had a great sense of humor, we laughed a lot. But the only problem was that Claire was very talkative.

Text editing (upper-intermediate level version)

Instructions: Read the following text. Work with your partner to insert the missing words and make whatever changes necessary to produce a meaningful and grammatically correct paragraph. Explain why you make those changes.

Original text: Louise Woodward was the 18-year old nanny convicted in 1998 by a court in the United States of murdering the infant Matthew Eappen. Recently she spoke about her experience of a televised court case at the Edinburg Television Festival.

Louise criticized the televising of trials. 'It should never be the case of looking into a defendant's eyes and making a decision on their guilt or innocence', she told the Edinburg Television Festival. 'It should be the law that decides on a person's guilt, but television, with its human and emotional interest, takes the attention away from this.'

Although she thought it was an inevitable development, she added: 'Television turns everything into entertainment. We should remember that in the end courtrooms are serious places. It is people's lives and future lives that you are dealing with. It is not a soap opera and people should not see it like that. Serious issues should not be trivialized.' […]

Modified text: Louise Woodward was the 18-year nanny convicted in 1998 by a court in the United States of murder the infant Matthew Eappen. Recently she speak her experience of a televised court case the Edinburg Television Festival.

Louise criticize the televising of trials. 'It should never be the case of looking into a defendant's eyes and making a decision their guilt or innocence', she told the Edinburg Television Festival. 'It should be the law decides on a person's guilt, but television, with its human and emotional interest, takes the attention from this.'

Although she thought it was an inevitable development, she add: 'Television turn everything in entertainment. We should remember that in end courtrooms are serious places. It is people lives and future lives you are dealing with. It is not a soap opera and people should not see it like that. Serious things should not be trivialized.' […]

Picture placement (in color in the original task)

Instructions: You and your partner each have a picture of the same bathroom with some bathroom items in it. The names of half of the items are in your bathroom and the other half of the names are in your partner's bathroom. DO NOT LOOK AT YOUR PARTNER'S PICTURE! You want to make your pictures look the same. You need to learn where the items are in your partner's bathroom so that you can put them in the correct place in your bathroom. For example, your partner does not know where the towel is. You know that it is hanging on the wall between the window and the bathtub.

Version A   *Version B*

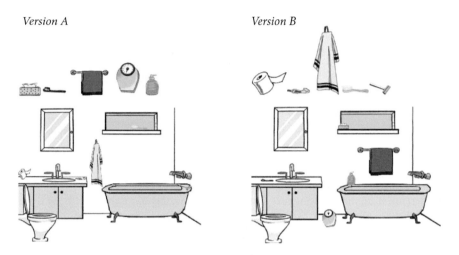

Picture differences (in color in the original task)
Instructions: You and your partner each have a picture. Do not show your picture to your partner. Your pictures are very similar, but there are some differences. Ask your partner questions to find the differences between your pictures.

Version A   *Version B*

Note. Pictures retrieved from http://commons.wikimedia.org/wiki/File:Spot_the_difference.png

CHAPTER 10

A focus on mode

Patterns of interaction in face-to-face and computer-mediated contexts

Amir Rouhshad and Neomy Storch
University of Melbourne

Research on pair and small group work has shown that collaborative writing tasks generally encourage learners to focus on language. However, some studies (e.g., Storch 2002) have also shown that patterns of interaction during collaborative writing tasks affect the quantity and quality of learners' attention to language and ultimately language learning. The study reported in this chapter compared patterns of interaction of the same pairs of intermediate ESL learners completing a collaborative writing task in a face-to-face and a computer-mediated mode (Google Docs). The study found that mode had an impact on patterns of interaction and attention to language. Learners were more likely to collaborate in the face-to-face mode and to cooperate in the computer-mediated mode. It was only when learners collaborated, that they engaged extensively in deliberations about language.

Introduction

There is consensus amongst second language (L2) researchers that interaction in the L2 is necessary for successful L2 learning (see Sato & Ballinger 2016). For example, researchers informed by cognitive theories of L2 acquisition, such as Long's (1996) interaction hypothesis, regard interactions as opportunities to negotiate meaning and form (e.g., Fujii & Mackey 2009; Gass, Mackey & Ross-Feldman 2011; Mackey 2007; McDonough & Mackey 2008). These negotiations are said to provide learners with comprehensible input, corrective feedback and prime them to notice certain language forms in subsequent input. Researchers informed by Vygotsky's (1978, 1981) sociocultural theoretical perspective view interactions as opportunities for learners to verbalize their deliberations about the L2 and in the process co-construct new knowledge or consolidate existing L2 knowledge (e.g., Ohta 2001; Storch 2002, 2013; Swain 2000, 2006, 2010). Thus these two leading

DOI 10.1075/lllt.45.11rou

theoretical perspectives in the field of second language acquisition (SLA) provide a solid rationale for the use of pair and small group work in the L2 classroom, where learners are provided with opportunities to interact in the L2.

Research has also shown that when pairs or small groups interact on tasks that require the production of a written text rather than only speaking there is a greater focus on form (see Adams & Ross-Feldman 2008; Niu 2009; Rouhshad 2014). These findings are not surprising. As a number of scholars (e.g., Cumming 1989; Williams 2008, 2012) have pointed out, writing, being less ephemeral than speaking, is more likely to encourage a focus on language choice and grammatical accuracy than speaking. Thus Storch (2011, 2013) promotes the use of collaborative writing tasks, tasks that combine interaction and writing, in L2 classes.

Collaborative writing is defined by Storch (2013: 3) as "an activity where there is a shared and negotiated decision making process and a shared responsibility for the production of a single text." The distinguishing traits of collaborative writing are co-construction and co-ownership. These traits encourage learners to deliberate about how best to express their ideas and to contribute to the resolutions of these deliberations. Deliberations about language form occur throughout the process of creating a meaningful text. Thus, collaborative writing may provide the optimal conditions for L2 learning.

Research on collaborative writing has identified a number of variables that may affect the quantity and quality of interaction on language form, including the type of writing task (e.g., Alegría de La Colina & Garcia Mayo 2007), the L2 proficiency of learners assigned to work together (e.g., Leeser 2004; Storch & Aldosari 2013), and the size of the small group (e.g., Fernández Dobao 2012). One other important variable that has been investigated in a small number of studies is the pattern of interactions; that is, the relationships that learners form when engaging in collaborative writing.

Patterns of interaction in collaborative writing

Research conducted by Storch (2001, 2002, 2013) showed that learners form distinct types of relationships when completing collaborative writing tasks. Four patterns of interactions (collaborative, dominant/dominant, dominant/passive, and expert/novice) were identified, based on the degree of mutuality (engagement with each other's contribution) and equality (degree of control over the task). Figure 1 illustrates how these patterns can be mapped onto a diagram composed of mutuality and equality as two intersecting continua.

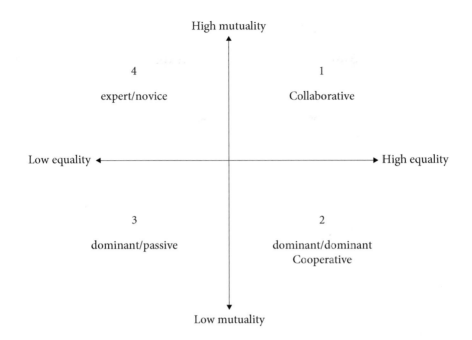

Figure 1. A model of pair interaction (Storch 2002, 2009, 2013)

A collaborative pattern (Quadrant 1) is one where the pair displays a medium to high degree of mutuality and equality. In this pattern both participants contribute to the joint text and engage with each other's contribution. A pattern labelled as dominant/dominant or cooperative (Quadrant 2) is one where the pair displays medium to high degree of equality but medium to low mutuality. In such pairs, both participants contribute to the completion of the task but do not engage very much with each other's contribution. A distinctive trait of the cooperative pattern is a clear division of labour in which neither of the participants attempts to take control of the task, as is the case with dominant/dominant pairs (see Tan, Wigglesworth, & Storch 2010). A dominant/passive pattern (Quadrant 3) is one where both mutuality and equality are medium to low. In this pattern, one participant takes over control of the task and there is little contribution forthcoming from the other participant, nor is there much engagement with each other's suggestions. Finally, an expert/novice pattern (Quadrant 4) is one where mutuality is medium to high but equality is medium to low. In this pattern, one learner takes a leading role but attempts to encourage the passive participant to contribute to the task.

Storch (2002, 2009) found that these patterns of interaction impact on the quantity and quality of learners' focus on language as well as on language learning. Pairs that collaborated were more likely to pay attention to and deliberate

about language choice, to pool their linguistic resources to resolve their deliberations, and to retain the linguistic knowledge that was co-constructed during their
deliberations than pairs who formed other patterns of interaction. Subsequent
research, conducted in a range of L2 learning contexts (e.g., Kim & McDonough
2008; Storch & Aldosari 2013; Watanabe & Swain 2007) confirmed that assigning
learners to work in pairs does not necessarily mean that the learners will work collaboratively. This research has also shown that the extent of collaboration affects
the level of learners' engagement with language form (e.g., Storch & Aldosari
2013) and ultimately language learning (e.g., Kim & McDonough 2008; Moranski
& Toth 2016; Watanabe & Swain 2007). Most of this research has been conducted
with learners working in pairs in a face-to-face (FTF) mode.

Recently, researchers have begun investigating the nature of learners' interaction in the computer-mediated environment when completing collaborative
writing tasks. This environment is receiving increasing attention given the rapid
changes in technology and the growth in long distance learning programs. To date,
the focus of research on computer-mediated collaborative writing has been on
wikis. Wikis enable learners to co-author a text in pairs or larger groups outside
the physical confines of the classroom. They are relatively easy to use and provide
learners with dedicated spaces for composing a text and for interacting about the
texts. To date there has been relatively little research on the pattern of interactions
in this mode. The existing research does suggest that, as in the face-to-face mode,
learners form very distinct patterns of interaction when composing on wikis (e.g.,
Bradley, Lindström, & Rystedt 2010; Kost 2011; Li & Zhu 2011). For example,
Bradley et al. (2010) conducted a study with 54 learners of EFL in Sweden working on different wiki projects in pairs or small groups. The researchers analysed
the nature of the learners' interaction and contributions to the creation of the
wiki pages. They reported that of the 25 groups formed, 15 groups showed a collaborative approach, five a cooperative approach and another five did not interact
at all. It is not clear, however, whether it was the mode that affected the pattern of
interaction and contributions since the same groups were not asked to complete
the collaborative writing assignment in a FTF mode.

Tan et al. (2010) is the only study that compared patterns of interaction
formed when the same seven pairs of learners completed a range of writing tasks
in the face-to-face and then in a computer-mediated mode. The study with begin-
ner learners of Chinese found that the mode affected the pattern of interaction.
Most pairs displayed a different pattern of interaction in each mode. Furthermore,
although there was evidence of collaboration in both modes, instances of a cooperative pattern of interaction were only found in the computer-mediated mode.
When working cooperatively, the joint text was an amalgam of individually composed sentences in which there was little input or feedback from the peer. Thus

there were far fewer deliberations about language in the computer-mediated mode than in the FTF mode. However, it should be noted that this study used MSN messenger and not a collaborative writing platform. Thus the findings could be attributed to the tool used.

Attention to language

As mentioned above, research (e.g., Storch 2002; Watanabe & Swain 2007) suggests that patterns of interaction may influence the quantity of the attention to language generated during task interaction. The unit used to measure attention to language in these studies is the Language Related Episode (LRE), defined as instances in the learners' dialogues where the learners talk about their language use, other or self correct (Swain & Lapkin 1995, 1998, 2001). These LREs may be occasions for language learning. Some studies (e.g., Kim 2008; LaPierre 1994; Storch 2002, 2008) have shown that learners retain the language point that was negotiated during the LREs. That is, LREs result in language learning and/or consolidation of existing language knowledge.

However, the quality of deliberations about language in LREs is an important factor. As a number of studies have shown (e.g., Qi & Lapkin 2001; Storch 2008; Swain et al. 2009), learning is more likely to take place when there is extensive attention paid to language form rather than perfunctory attention. To date, studies that have investigated both the quantity and quality of learners' attention to form have been conducted using think-aloud protocols (e.g., Qi & Lapkin 2001) or face-to-face pair interaction (e.g., Storch 2008). Although a number of studies (Kaneko 2009; Loewen & Reissner 2009; Rouhshad 2014) have compared opportunities for language learning in dyadic and small group interaction between face-to-face and computer-mediated mode (using speaking tasks), the unit of analysis employed was negotiation for meaning in most cases. Such units do not take into consideration the quality of attention to language and may omit other aspects of interaction that may be equally important for language learning (see Foster & Ohta 2005; Sato & Ballinger 2012).

Taken together, our review of the literature suggests that the effect of mode on the patterns of interaction and on attention to language requires additional investigation. Thus, our study set out to compare the performance of the same pairs on similar collaborative writing tasks in two modes: face-to-face and in a synchronous text-based computer-mediated environment. In our analysis, we focused on the patterns of interaction and on the quantity and quality of attention to language in each mode.

The study

This study formed part of a larger study (Rouhshad 2014) on pair interaction and was conducted in a college in Australia. The college offers intensive ESL courses, primarily preparing students to meet the English language proficiency requirements at English-medium universities. Students participating in these courses attend classes on five days a week, for four hours per day. They have two, two-hour classes per day, separated by a two-hour break. During the two-hour break, the students are encouraged to take advantage of the college's independent learning centre.

Participants

Data for this study was collected from 24 adult intermediate ESL learners. According to the college's documents, these learners' proficiency was considered intermediate. It was equivalent to an overall score of 5.5 on the International English Language Testing System (IELTS). Most had spent an average of 12 years learning English in their home countries. Although the students came from a range of first language (L1) backgrounds, the majority were speakers of Chinese or other South East Asian languages such as Thai or Vietnamese. Their mean age was 26. Participants' length of stay in Australia at the time of data collection ranged between two to six months. Pseudonyms are used to refer to the participants in the study.

Tasks

Two similar collaborative writing tasks were employed. One task (Task 1) was completed in the face-to-face (FTF) mode; the other (Task 2) using Google Docs. The tasks opened with a hypothetical situation in which prison managers have decided to release some prisoners due to overcrowded conditions in their prison. In each task, the profiles of two fictitious prisoners were provided and participants were invited to help the managers decide which of the two prisoners to release. The profiles included paragraph-long information about the prisoners' age, job, reason for being in prison, behaviour in prison, and their plans for the future. Participants were asked to make a decision and then produce a joint report of 150 words. In this study, we focus our analysis on the part of the task in which students were writing this report jointly.

As mentioned previously, collaborative writing in the computer-mediated environment was performed using Google Docs. Google Docs is a free online software program that allows one to create a document and share it with others who are signed in to Google Docs. The program provides co-writers with two windows, as shown in the screenshot from the current study (Figure 2). In the small window, shown on the right side of the screen shot, participants can exchange their opinions about any aspects of their report. The report is written collaboratively in the large window.

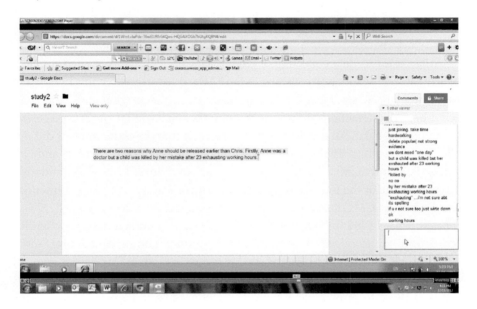

Figure 2. A screen shot of Google Docs

Google Docs, unlike wiki, is a synchronous form of computer-mediated communication (SCMC). Words typed in the large window are immediately visible to all participants. However, it should be noted that in our study the setting of the document in Google Docs was set so that, throughout the performance of the task, only one member of the pair could type the report in the large window. This decision was made to make it similar to the collaborative writing in the FTF mode. In the small window, both participants can type and communicate instantly through text-based communication but the words are not visible until the enter button is hit. Additionally, SCREEN2EXE,[1] a free online software program, was employed to video record the participants' computer screens when working on Google Docs. This software was employed to make data coding easier.

---

1. http://www.screen-record.com/screen2exe.htm

Data collection

Data was collected in a private room in the college outside class time. Data collection commenced in the second week of the term. Participants were asked to attend a data collection session in self-selected pairs. Our motivation to allow students to self-select their partners was based on research which has shown that acquaintanceship can affect the quality of joint texts (O'Sullivan 2002). Of the 12 pairs, nine were of the same-gender and three shared the same first language. The majority of participants (87%) were familiar with online chatting.

A day prior to data collection, a Google Docs account was opened for each participant. The collaborative writing in the FTF mode was written in a designated notebook. In the SCMC mode, participants sat at two different computers away from each other. All interactions were done through the small window in Google Docs.

A counter-balanced design was used to ensure that the order of tasks did not influence the results. The use of two versions of the task (Task 1 and 2) and two modes (FTF and SCMC) created a total of four conditions. Pairs were randomly assigned to one of the four conditions. For example, Pairs 1, 5 and 9 commenced with Task 1 in SCMC and proceeded with Task 2 in FTF whereas Pairs 2, 6, and 10 began with Task 2 in FTF and Task 1 in SCMC. FTF interactions were audio-recorded and transcribed following the transcription symbols adapted from Storch (2002). SCMC interactions (i.e., the small window in Google Docs) were saved in MS Word documents. In light of the findings of previous studies that L2 learners seem unwilling to provide peer corrective feedback (e.g., Fujii & Mackey 2009; Iwasaki & Oliver 2003; Philp, Walter & Basturkmen 2010; Rouhshad 2013), participants in the current study were explicitly encouraged to provide their peers with corrective feedback. Before starting the tasks in both modes, participants were told, "Please correct your peers throughout the task. For example, if they use "goed" instead of "went", you are encouraged to correct you peer." Data collection was concluded with questionnaires that elicited some background information about the participants.

Theoretical framework informing data analysis

Data consisted of the dyadic interactions in FTF and SCMC modes during the performance of collaborative writing. Analysis of this data was informed by Vygotsky's sociocultural theory.

The underlying premise of sociocultural theory is that learning has its inception in social interaction (Vygotsky 1981). Learning occurs in interaction between humans where a more able interlocutor (parent or peer) provides carefully attuned assistance to the novice, assistance that is eventually internalized and used by the novice independently. The term commonly used to describe this form of assistance is scaffolding (Wood, Bruner, & Ross 1976). Thus researchers informed by this theoretical perspective focus on the nature of the assistance provided during interaction.

Language plays a key role in learning. During interaction, language is vocalised and other directed, enabling the interactants to communicate and coordinate their actions (Wells 1999). On an individual level, language is used to help structure one's thinking when performing a task, it is self-directed and sub-vocal. This self-directed language is used to make sense of complex information or resolve a difficult problem. It is the articulation of thinking. Swain (2006, 2010) uses the term languaging to describe these uses of language.

During peer interaction, languaging can have two forms: other-directed speech or collaborative dialogue (Swain 2000) and self-directed speech. However, in the presence of a peer, self-directed speech may be vocalised. When it is vocalised, it can elicit a response from the peer and in this way initiate collaborative dialogue. When interacting about a language task, both forms of languaging are potentially conducive for language learning: they provide learners opportunities to deliberate about language, to seek assistance overtly (via collaborative dialogue) or implicitly (via self-directed talk), and to receive timely assistance.

Research conducted with L2 learners has shown that peers of similar L2 proficiency can pool their available knowledge of the L2 and co-construct assistance. The term used to describe this assistance is collective scaffolding (see Donato 1994; Storch 2002, 2009). However, both Donato (1994) and Storch (2002, 2009) found that such collective scaffolding was found mainly in groups and pairs that engaged in collaborative interaction patterns.

Thus, in our study, we first analysed the data for patterns of interaction in each mode. Our analysis was informed by the model and categories developed by Storch (2001, 2002, 2009) discussed earlier. In the current study, the main patterns found were: collaborative, cooperative, and dominant/passive. The following excerpts in the examples illustrate these three patterns.

The excerpt in Example (1) comes from the FTF interaction between Jan and Nima and was coded as collaborative. As can be seen, Jan and Nima engage with each other's contribution (turns 28, 32, 34) as they are co-constructing the paragraph. They contribute equally to the task, and the length of their turns is roughly similar. Co-construction takes the form of repeating each other's suggested ideas and then extending the ideas (e.g., turns 23–24, 26–27). There are also instances of assistance being requested and provided. For example, Jan's request for assistance (turn 37) was responded to and led to extensive engagement (turns 38–45) over form, with the learners pooling their knowledge of language.

(1)   Collaborative pattern (Pair 11, FTF)

23	Jan:	hard-working and popular doctor, doctor. And and at that time, at that time, [she
24	Nima:	[she she work for twenty three hours
25	Jan:	she was working
26	Nima:	she was working
27	Jan:	working for twenty three hours
28	Nima:	hours, yes
29	Jan:	maybe maybe this is their mistake, of
30	Nima:	of
31	Jan:	[hospital
32	Nima:	[hospital yeah, because
33	Jan:	maybe hospital can't allowed her continued work for so so long
34	Nima:	so, yeah
35	Jan:	[a long time
36	Nima:	[too much
37	Jan:	maybe hospital, "shouldn't", right? Shouldn't
38	Nima:	maybe XXX should not, yeah.
39	Jan:	shouldn't allowed
40	Nima:	allow
41	Jan:	allow … allow somebody to do something
42	Nima:	allow allowed the doctor or
43	Jan:	allowed allowed to or allow?
44	Nima:	allow
45	Jan:	allow, allow doctor
46	Nima:	allow, yeah. Allow doctor to [to allow doctor to

A collaborative pattern of interaction was also found in the SCMC mode, as shown in the excerpt of SCMC interaction between Saber and Naka (Pair 1) in Example (2). Notable in their interaction was the frequent engagement with each other's suggestions (see turns 31, 37, 42), and the expression of gratitude by Saber (who took on the role of the scribe) following Naka's suggestions (see turn 34). Worth mentioning is that their exchanges were not limited to editing aspects of grammar and lexis but extended to discussion over content (see turns 43, 44).

(2)   Collaborative pattern (Pair 1, SCMC)

28	Saber:	Write again I could not find it ..
29	Naka:	After both
30	Saber:	No .. I mean they killed In the past

31	Naka:	I know,,, but its better to cheang
		And mistake not mistaken
32	Saber:	Ok
		You are write
		But in the past\
		You are right
		Not write sorry
		Ok??
33	Naka:	ok
34	Saber:	thank you
35	Naka:	are killers
36	Saber:	You say that both of them are killers by mistaken????
		You write all sentence I will fix it.
37	Naka:	Both of them are killers by mistake.
38	Saber:	Ok
		Have we finished?
39	Naka:	that is why
		Not the why
40	Saber:	Ok
		Anything else
		???
41	Naka:	Have already …. this sentence not clear
42	Saber:	It is clear
		They have one more year at jail
		I want to state this situation
		in this sentence
43	Naka:	We need to clearfy it more
44	Saber:	I want to support our decision
		Maybe it is ok
		Naka
		After this sentence look at the last sentence

Example (3) is of a cooperative pattern taken from the data of Pair 2 in the SCMC mode. Here we see a clear division of labour. Feri was the scribe and wrote most of the text independently in the large window. Tina took on the role of the language editor and provided feedback on what Feri wrote in the small window (shown in turn 36). In most instances, Feri did not respond to Tina's suggested amendments in the small window (see turn 37) but implemented most of them in their paragraph. Thus, although both contributed to the activity, there was limited engagement with each other's suggestions.

(3)   Cooperative pattern (Pair 2, SCMC)

    36 Tina: I think the 3rd sentence is more clearly
                        ok keep going
                        and
                        will
                        continue
                        her job
                        once she is free
                        delete "so she keep uo to dat"
    37 Feri: I start to talk 2nd reason

The next pattern of interaction depicted in Example (4) is dominant/passive taken from Pair 4 in the SCMC mode. Here too there is a division of labour, but different to that in Example (3). In this pair, Fiona took on the role of the scribe but she did not generate any ideas. Jill generated and wrote the content in the small window and Fiona just copied it into the large window. Although Jill asked Fiona to improve the ideas before copying them into the large window (see the last sentence in turn 1), Fiona declined and argued that Jill was a better writer (see turn 2).

(4)   Dominant/passive (Pair 4, SCMC)

    1 Jill: because she protects herself from the crime scene and
                    because she scared and ran out of her apartment but she
                    has reported to the police and returned the crime scene
                    with the pollice
                    after she hits the thief, she do not knows thief is alive or
                    death. it is because she just hits the thief's head once and
                    do not know will cause the thief to daeth.
                    haha…you can write ur idea also….
    2 Fiona: i try .. 55
                    but i read that u write it better

We then coded pair interactions for language-related episodes (LREs). Informed by previous research, which has also utilised these units of learner talk (e.g., Storch 2002, 2008; Swain & Lapkin 1995, 1998, 2001), we defined LREs in our study as excerpts in which learners deliberate about their language use and other-correct. Because our focus was on pair interaction, we omitted LREs where the learners self-corrected.

LREs were coded for focus, distinguishing between three types of LREs: Form-LREs (F-LREs) dealing with syntax and morphology; Lexis-LREs (L-LREs) dealing with word meaning and choice; and Mechanics-LREs (M-LREs) dealing with punctuation, spelling and pronunciation. We also coded these LREs for their resolution (correctly resolved, incorrectly resolved or left unresolved). The following examples demonstrate the different types of LREs.

Example (5) is of an F-LRE dealing with verb tense/aspect and coded as resolved correctly. It comes from pair 5 completing the task in the FTF mode. The LRE is initiated by Peter (turn 2), who suggests that the verb "decide" should be in the present perfect instead of the simple past. Shawn (turn 3) notes that Peter's suggestion is not target-like and provides a correction. Although Peter seems uncertain (turn 4), Shawn repeats the correction (turn 5) and eventually the suggested correction is accepted. This LRE was coded as resolved correctly.

(5) F-LRE resolved correctly (Pair 5, FTF)
    1   Shawn: according to the reasons mentioned in the paragraphs we can decide that
    2   Peter: or, we have decide
    3   Shawn: we have decided
    4   Peter: uhm
    5   Shawn: we have to decide, decided
    6   Peter: we have decided to to release
    7   Shawn: yeah

Example (6) comes from Pair 9 in SCMC and illustrates an L-LRE dealing with meaning. In turn 16 Sue seeks confirmation of the meaning of the phrase "lost his mind", and Wick confirms by providing a definition and examples (turn 17). This LRE was also coded as resolved correctly.

(6) L-LRE resolved correctly (Pair 9, SCMC)
    15   Wick: whose name is Chris or Prisoner B, Christ,
                      he tried to stop fighting at the bar. For a moment he lost his mind, he hit one of footbal player in the head. after that the man was died.
                      do u agree?
    16   Sue: lost his my it means he does not intend to do something wrong right?
    17   Wick: lost his mind = he cant control himself, coz he was angry he hit some guess.
                      Chris has served 4 years in prison. While he is imprisoning, he feel very upset.

Example (7) is of an M-LRE dealing with the correct spelling of "sacrificing". Aki notes that the spelling of the word is incorrect but is not sure how to spell it and seeks assistance. However Betty does not respond but instead focuses on content (see turn 33). In turn 38, Aki brings it again to Betty's attention and they eventually decide to use a different word after extensive discussion, as they could not work out the accurate spelling of "sacrificing". This LRE was coded as unresolved.

(7)   M-LRE unresolved (Pair 8, SCMC)

    31 Betty: as well as being useful for others by sacrifying herself for studying phycology

    32 Aki: "sacrifying" is wrong
               do u remember how to spell this

    33 Betty: Clearly, there would be a counselor who can help people from their problem by providing counselling if prisoner C can be freed earlier
               I think that is enough
               What do you think

    34 Aki   Ok
    35 Betty   Do you want to add anything?
               that's all
    36 Aki   Finish?
    37 Betty   yeap
    38 Aki   How about the word "scarifying"

LREs were also coded for the nature of the learners' engagements. Here, following Storch (2008), we distinguished between LREs that showed extensive engagement (E) and those that showed limited engagement (L). LREs where participants deliberated over language use and provided explanations to their peer were coded as extensive. Examples (5) and (6) were coded as showing extensive engagement. This analysis in a sense helped to verify our global coding for patterns of interaction. A large proportion of LREs resolved with extensive engagement in the data of a pair confirmed that the pair formed a collaborative pattern of interaction.

To check for inter-rater reliability, four transcripts of pair interactions, two from each mode (comprising 17% of data) were double rated for patterns of interaction and LREs by both authors. The inter-rate reliability scores, measured through simple percentage agreement, were 100% for patterns of interaction and 87% for LREs. Further discussion between the authors resolved disagreements about LRE coding.

Findings

Our first aim was to code and compare patterns of interaction across the two modes. As shown in Table 1, collaboration (Collab) was the predominant pattern of interaction in the FTF mode. Eight out of the 12 pairs formed this pattern, co-constructing the joint text. In the SCMC mode, only one pair collaborated. The predominant pattern in SCMC was cooperation (Coop), where the participants divided the labour between them. Seven pairs formed such a pattern. It should be noted that, when these seven pairs interacted in the FTF mode, they collaborated (six of the seven pairs). Also, whereas when interacting in FTF, only two pairs formed a dominant/passive (D/P) pattern, in the SCMC mode four pairs formed such a pattern, including a pair which collaborated (Pair 4) and a pair which cooperated (Pair 9) when writing in the FTF mode. Altogether, only four pairs (Pairs 1, 3, 8 and 10) exhibited the same pattern of interaction across the two modes. These findings suggest that mode of interaction may influence the pattern of interaction.

Table 1. Patterns of interaction across the modes

	FTF	SCMC	Change
Pair 1	Collab	Collab	No
Pair 2	Collab	Coop	Yes
Pair 3	D/P	D/P	No
Pair 4	Collab	D/P	Yes
Pair 5	Collab	Coop	Yes
Pair 6	Collab	Coop	Yes
Pair 7	Collab	Coop	Yes
Pair 8	D/P	D/P	No
Pair 9	Coop	D/P	Yes
Pair 10	Coop	Coop	No
Pair 11	Collab	Coop	Yes
Pair 12	Collab	Coop	Yes

Findings for the number of LREs found in the data are shown in Table 2. As the table shows, there were substantially more LREs in FTF than in SCMC (177 vs. 71). This, indeed, is an interesting finding given that pairs spent substantially more time on the writing task in the SCMC mode than the FTF mode (356 min. vs. 222 min.). As shown in Table 2, F-LREs predominated in both modes (over 40% of all LREs), followed by L-LRE (over 30%) and finally M-LREs (over 20%). These findings suggest that mode of interaction does not influence the type of LREs as there was no substantial difference in the percentage of LRE types across the modes. For example, F-LREs accounted for 42% and 48% of total LREs in FTF and SCMC modes respectively.

Table 2. LREs across the modes (frequency and %)

	Total	F-LRE	L-LRE	M-LRE
FTF	177 (100%)	75 (42%)	62 (35%)	40 (23%)
SCMC	71 (100%)	34 (48%)	22 (31%)	15 (21%)
Total	248 (100%)	109 (44%)	84 (34%)	55 (22%)

Additionally, mode of interaction did not influence the resolution of LREs (see Table 3). The majority of LREs in both the FTF and SCMC modes were resolved correctly. In the FTF mode, 142/177 of LREs (i.e., around 80%) were resolved correctly and in the SCMC mode 53/71 (i.e., just over 74%) were resolved correctly. The same proportion (around 14%) of all LREs was resolved incorrectly in both modes.

Table 3. Resolution of LREs across the modes (frequency and %)

	Total	Correct	Incorrect	Unresolved
FTF	177	142 (80.22%)	25 (14.71%)	10 (5.65%)
SCMC	71	53 (74.65%)	10 (14.08%)	8 (11.27%)
Total	248	195	35	18

However, a different picture emerges when we compare level of engagement in resolving LREs across the modes (see Table 4). While in the SCMC mode the majority of LREs showed limited engagement (57/71 i.e., around 80%), in the FTF mode the majority showed extensive engagement (129/177 i.e., around 73%). In other words, participants were more likely to engage with each other's contribution and provide explanation for their suggestions in the FTF mode.

Table 4. The nature of engagement across the modes (frequency and %)

	Total	Extensive	Limited
FTF	177	129 (72.88%)	48 (27.12%)
SCMC	71	14 (19.71%)	57 (80.29%)
Total	248	139 (56.10%)	109 (43.95%)

Given that the type of LREs was similar across modes and that in both modes LREs were in the majority of instances resolved correctly, we next considered whether patterns of interaction affected the number of LREs generated and the level of engagement in LRE resolution. Table 5 shows the pattern each pair formed in FTF and SCMC, the number of LREs and the proportion of LREs showing extensive level of engagement. What the table shows is that in FTF, pairs who formed collaborative patterns, tended to generate more LREs (e.g., Pair 1, 2, 6, 7,

12) than those who formed cooperative patterns (e.g., Pairs 9, 10). Collaborative pairs also tended to resolve LREs with extensive levels of engagement (see for example Pair 1, 7, 11, 12). In the SCMC mode, pairs who formed cooperative patterns generated more LREs (ranging from 4–9) than those who formed dominant/passive patterns (ranging from 0–6). However, as the table shows quite clearly, regardless of patterns formed in SCMC, few LREs were resolved with extensive levels of engagement.

Table 5. Pattern of interaction across modes, LREs & level of engagement

	FTF			SCMC		
	Pattern	No. LREs	Extensive engagement	Pattern	No. LREs	Extensive engagement
Pair 1	Collab	21	18 (86%)	Collab	9	2 (22%)
Pair 2	Collab	29	18 (62%)	Coop	11	3 (27%)
Pair 3	D/P	4	2 (50%)	D/P	0	0
Pair 4	Collab	10	6 (60%)	D/P	6	0
Pair 5	Collab	12	9 (75%)	Coop	4	0
Pair 6	Collab	19	13 (68%)	Coop	6	1 (16%)
Pair 7	Collab	17	15 (88%)	Coop	4	0
Pair 8	D/P	23	16 (70%)	D/P	2	0
Pair 9	Coop	5	4 (80%)	D/P	6	0
Pair 10	Coop	5	3 (60%)	Coop	9	3 (33%)
Pair 11	Collab	13	10 (77%)	Coop	9	0
Pair 12	Collab	19	15 (79%)	Coop	5	1 (20%)

Discussion

Our study set out to investigate the impact of mode of interaction on patterns of interaction and on attention to language during collaborative writing tasks. Our findings suggest that mode of interaction does affect the pattern of interaction. In the FTF mode, most of the pairs formed a collaborative relationship. When collaborating in FTF, learners co-constructed the text, each contributing and building on each other's suggestions. In this process of co-construction, they deliberated extensively about language, seeking and providing each other with assistance and corrective feedback.

Collaboration was rare in SCMC. The predominant pattern in SCMC was cooperation or dominant/passive. These findings are similar to those reported in Tan et al. (2010), but the nature of cooperation was different in this study. Rather than composing sentences in turn, as was the case in cooperative pairs in the Tan et al. study, in this study the division of labour was in terms of roles.

One participant took on the role of the scribe and composed the text in the large window; the other learner took on the role of the language editor, making editing suggestions to the written text in the small window but contributing very little to the content of the text. In most instances there was limited engagement with the suggestions made. In the dominant/passive pattern, there was a similar division of labour, but in this pattern, one member of the pair composed and edited the entire text in the small window; the other member simply copied the text into the larger window. Here there was generally little interaction about language form.

The findings also suggest that it is the mode more so than the relationships learners form which affect focus on language in SCMC. What is striking about our findings is the relatively small number of LREs generated in the SCMC mode, despite the longer time the learners spent on the task in this mode and despite the encouragement to provide corrective feedback given in the instructions. These findings are consistent with the findings of previous studies which also compared opportunities for language learning in face-to-face and computer-mediated modes (e.g., Loewen & Reissner 2009; Loewen & Wolff 2016; Rouhshad 2014; Rouhshad, Wigglesworth & Storch forthcoming). Overall, those pairs that cooperated generated only slightly more LREs than those who formed a dominant/passive pattern. The mode of interaction did not, however, impact the target of the LREs, or the nature of their resolution. The vast majority of LREs were resolved correctly. This indicates that peer interaction is a reliable resource for language learning.

However, what is perhaps even more striking in our data is the limited engagement in resolving LREs in the SCMC mode, even in the one pair (Pair 1) who collaborated in this mode. These findings accord with the findings of a number of studies that have been conducted using wikis (for a more extensive discussion, see Storch 2013). These studies have reported on learners' reluctance to amend the contributions of others posted on the wiki (e.g., Kessler & Bikowski 2010; Lund 2008). Oskoz and Elola (2012), who examined their learners' wiki discussion spaces, also reported little evidence of deliberations in these spaces on language use. In interviews conducted with the learners (Elola & Oskoz 2010), it was revealed that the learners saw these discussion spaces as being suitable mainly for content-related discussions rather than for deliberations about language. Kessler, Bikowski and Boggs (2012), who used Google Docs with their ESL students, found that even when the learners deliberated and provided corrective feedback to their peers, it was mainly on fairly superficial language features (spelling and punctuation).

Thus, despite the ease of composing and editing on these collaborative online platforms, the dedicated discussion space and synchronicity in the case of Google Docs (unlike wikis), learners seem averse to collaborate in the creation of the text and even more averse to deliberate about language form. These findings suggest a need to consider very carefully how we implement online collaborative writing tasks in L2 classrooms.

Pedagogical implications

Collaborative writing tasks combine oral interaction and writing and as such seem to provide an ideal context for L2 learning. In our study, this was found to be the case only if these tasks are implemented in the FTF mode. In the FTF mode, the majority of pairs collaborated and when they collaborated, they engaged extensively in deliberations about language. Storch's (2009) longitudinal classroom based study also found that collaborative patterns of interaction prevailed during FTF collaborative writing task. Collaboration and a focus on language seems less likely when collaborative writing activities are implemented in the computer-mediated mode.

Kim and McDonough (2011) reported that prior modelling of collaborative discourse encouraged their paired learners to adopt a collaborative pattern of interaction in the FTF mode. Perhaps such modelling may be even more pertinent when implementing collaborative writing in the online mode. One possible reason for the lack of collaboration in the computer-mediated mode, and the higher incidence of cooperative patterns, is the cumbersome nature of interaction in this environment. It is logistically more complicated to type texts in the large frame of Google Docs whilst communicating and editing in the small window compared to the FTF mode where it is possible to simultaneously discuss and write a text. Thus, some researchers suggest using a blended approach. A blended approach combines an online platform such as Google Docs (or wikis) with more immediate and familiar forms of interaction such as face-to-face meetings or email communication. Zorko (2009) found that a combination of wikis and FTF interaction encouraged a focus on language among her L2 learners. Oskoz and Elola (2011) suggested supplementing wikis with synchronous web-based voice applications, thus combining as in FTF interaction, oral and written language output. More research is needed to verify whether these blended approaches encourage learners to deliberate about language.

Collaborative writing is likely to increase given the rapid developments in technology. Ortega (2009) argues that in our technologically driven world, the inclusion of computer-mediated activities in language classes is no longer a choice but an imperative. The findings of this study suggest that in order to make computer-mediated collaborative writing activities optimal sites for language learning, such activities need to be very carefully designed and monitored.

References

Adams, R., & Ross-Feldman, L. (2008). Does writing influence learner attention to form? In D. Belcher & A. Hirvela (Eds.), *The oral-literate connection. Perspectives on L2 speaking, writing, and other media interactions* (pp. 243–266). Ann Arbor MI: The University of Michigan Press.

Alegría de la Colina, A., & García Mayo, M. P. (2007). Attention to form across collaborative tasks by low-proficiency learners in an EFL setting. In M. P. García Mayo (Ed.), *Investigating tasks in foreign language learning* (pp. 91–116). Clevedon, UK: Multilingual Matters.

Bradley, L., Lindström, B., & Rystedt, H. (2010). Rationalities of collaboration for language learning in a wiki. *ReCALL* 22(2), 247–265. doi:10.1017/S0958344010000108

Cumming, A. (1989). Writing expertise and second language proficiency. *Language Learning*, 39, 81–141. doi:10.1111/j.1467-1770.1989.tb00592.x

Donato, R. (1994). Collective scaffolding in second language learning. In J. P. Lantolf & G. Appel (Eds.), *Vygotskian approaches to second language research* (pp. 33–56). Norwood, NJ: Ablex.

Elola, I., & Oskoz, A. (2010). Collaborative writing: Fostering foreign language and writing conventions development. *Language Learning and Technology*, 14, 51–71.

Fernández Dobao, A. (2012). Collaborative writing tasks in the L2 classroom: Comparing group, pair, and individual work. *Journal of Second Language Writing*, 2, 40–58. doi:10.1016/j.jslw.2011.12.002

Foster, P., & Ohta, A. (2005). Negotiation for meaning and peer assistance in second language classrooms. *Applied Linguistics*, 26, 402–430. doi:10.1093/applin/ami014

Fujii, A., & Mackey, A. (2009). Interactional feedback in learner-learner interactions in a task-based EFL classroom. *International Review of Applied Linguistics*, 47, 267–302. doi:10.1515/iral.2009.012

Gass, S., Mackey, A., & Ross-Feldman, L. (2011). Task-based interactions in classroom and laboratory settings. *Language Learning*, 61(Suppl. 1), 189–220. doi:10.1111/j.1467-9922.2011.00646.x

Iwasaki, J., & Oliver, R. (2003). Chat-line interaction and negative feedback. *Australian Review of Applied Linguistics*, 17, 60–73.

Kaneko, A. (2009). Comparing computer-mediated communication (CMC) and face-to-face (FTF) communication for the development of Japanese as a foreign language (Doctoral dissertation). Retrieved from: <http://www.uwa.edu.au/research/theses> (10 November, 2013).

Kessler, G., & Bikowski, D. (2010). Developing collaborative autonomous learning abilities in computer-mediated language learning: Attention to meaning among students in wiki space. *Computer Assisted Language Learning*, 23, 41–58. doi:10.1080/09588220903467335

Kessler, G., Bikowski, D., & Boggs, J. (2012). Collaborative writing among second language learners in academic web-based projects. *Language Learning and Technology*,16, 91–109.

Kim, Y. (2008). The contribution of collaborative and individual tasks to the acquisition of L2 vocabulary. *The Modern Language Journal*, 92, 114–130. doi:10.1111/j.1540-4781.2008.00690.x

Kim, Y., & McDonough, K. (2008). The effect of interlocutor proficiency on the collaborative dialogue between Korean as a second language learners. *Language Teaching Research*, 12, 211–234. doi:10.1177/1362168807086288

Kim, Y., & McDonough, K. (2011). Using pretask modelling to encourage collaborative language learning opportunities. *Language Teaching Research*, 15, 183–199. doi:10.1177/1362168810388711

Kost, C. (2011). Investigating writing strategies and revision behaviour in collaborative writing projects. *CALICO Journal*, 28(3), 606–620. doi:10.11139/cj.28.3.606-620

LaPierre, D. (1994). Language output in a cooperative learning setting: Determining its effects on second language learning (Unpublished master's thesis). University of Toronto.

Leeser, M. J. (2004). Learner proficiency and focus on form during collaborative dialogue. *Language Teaching Research*, 8, 55–81. doi:10.1191/1362168804lr134oa

Li, M., & Zhu, W. (2011). Patterns of computer-mediated interaction in small writing groups using wikis. *Computer Assisted Language Learning*, 24, 1–22. doi:10.1080/09588221.2010.520674

Loewen, S., & Reissner, S. (2009). A comparison of incidental focus on form in the second language classroom and chat room. *Computer Assisted Language Learning*, 22(2), 101–114. doi:10.1080/09588220902778211

Loewen, S., & Wolff, D. (2016). Peer interaction in F2F and CMC contexts. In M. Sato & S. Ballinger (Eds.), *Peer interaction and second language learning: Pedagogical potential and research agenda* (pp. 163–184). Amsterdam: John Benjamins.

Long, M. H. (1996). The role of the linguistic environment in second language acquisition. In W. C. Ritchie & T. K. Bhatia (Eds.), *Handbook of language acquisition. Vol. 2: Second language acquisition* (pp. 413–468). New York, NY: Academic Press.

Lund, A. (2008). Wikis: A collective approach to language production. *ReCALL*, 20(1), 35–54. doi:10.1017/S0958344008000414

Mackey, A. (2007). Interaction as practice. In R. DeKeyser (Ed.), *Practice in a second language: Perspectives from applied linguistics and cognitive psychology* (pp. 85–110). Cambridge: Cambridge University Press.

McDonough, K., & Mackey, A. (2008). Syntactic priming and ESL question development. *Studies in Second Language Acquisition*, 30, 31–47. doi:10.1017/S0272263108080029

Moranski, K., & Toth, P. (2016). Small-group meta-analytic talk and Spanish L2 development. In M. Sato & S. Ballinger (Eds.), *Peer interaction and second language learning: Pedagogical potential and research agenda* (pp. 291–316). Amsterdam: John Benjamins.

Niu, R. (2009). Effect of task-inherent production modes on EFL learners' focus on form. *Language Awareness*, 18(3-4), 384–402. doi:10.1080/09658410903197256

Ohta, A. S. (2001). *Second language acquisition processes in the classroom. Learning Japanese.* Mahwah, NJ: Lawrence Erlbaum Associates.

Ortega, L. (2009). Interaction and attention to form in L2 text-based computer-mediated communication. In A. Mackey & C. Polio (Eds.), *Multiple perspectives on interaction. Second language research in honour of Susan Gass* (pp. 226–253). New York, NY: Routledge.

Oskoz, A., & Elola, I. (2011). Meeting at the wiki: The new arena for collaborative writing in foreign language courses. In M. Lee & C. McLaughlin (Eds.), *Web 2.0-based e-learning: Applying social informatics for tertiary teaching* (pp. 209–227). Hershey, PA: IGI Global. doi:10.4018/978-1-60566-294-7.ch011

Oskoz, A., & Elola, I. (2012). Understanding the impact of social tools in the FL writing classroom: Activity theory at work. In G. Kessler, A. Oskoz & I. Elola (Eds.), *Technology across writing contexts and tasks* (pp. 131–153). San Marcos, TX: CALICO.

O'Sullivan, B. (2002). Learner acquaintanceship and oral proficiency test pair-task performance. *Language Testing*, 19, 277–295. doi:10.1191/0265532202lt2050a

Philp, J., Walter, S., & Basturkmen, H. (2010). Peer interaction in the foreign language classroom: what factors foster a focus on form? *Language Awareness*, 19, 261–279. doi:10.1080/09658416.2010.516831

Qi, D.S., & Lapkin, S. (2001). Exploring the role of noticing in a three-stage second language writing task. *Journal of Second Language Writing*, 10, 277–303. doi:10.1016/S1060-3743(01)00046-7

Rouhshad, A. (2013). Nature of negotiations in face-to-face and computer-mediate communication, paper presented at *American Association of Applied Linguistics (AAAL) conference*, Dallas, TX, March.

Rouhshad, A. (2014). *The nature of negotiations in computer-mediated and face-to-face modes with/without writing modality* (Unpublished doctoral dissertation). Retrieved from: <http://repository.unimelb.edu.au/10187/18441> (19 April 2014).

Rouhshad, A., Wigglesworth, G., & Storch, N. (forthcoming). The nature of negotiations in face-to-face versus computer mediated communication in pair interaction. *Language Teaching Research*. doi:10.1177/1362168815584455

Sato, M., & Ballinger, S. (2012). Raising language awareness in peer interaction: A cross-context, cross-method examination. *Language Awareness*, 21(1–2), 157–179. doi:10.1080/09658416.2011.639884

Sato, M., & Ballinger, S. (2016). Understanding peer interaction: Research synthesis and directions. In M. Sato & S. Ballinger (Eds.), *Peer interaction and second language learning: Pedagogical potential and research agenda* (pp. 1–30). Amsterdam: John Benjamins.

Storch, N. (2001). How collaborative is pair work? ESL tertiary students composing in pairs. *Language Teaching Research*, 5, 29–53. doi:10.1177/136216880100500103

Storch, N. (2002). Patterns of interaction in ESL pair work. *Language Learning*, 52, 119–158. doi:10.1111/1467-9922.00179

Storch, N. (2008). Metatalk in pair work activity: Level of engagement and implications for language development. *Language Awareness*, 17, 95–114. doi:10.2167/la431.0

Storch, N. (2009). *The nature of pair interaction. Learners' interaction in an ESL class: its nature and impact on grammatical development*. Saarbrücken, Germany: VDM Verlag.

Storch, N. (2011). Collaborative writing in L2 contexts: Processes, outcomes, and future directions. *Annual Review of Applied Linguistics*, 31, 275–288. doi:10.1017/S0267190511000079

Storch, N. (2013). *Collaborative writing in L2 classrooms*. Bristol, UK: Multilingual Matters.

Storch, N., & Aldosari, A. (2013). Pairing learners in pair work activity. *Language Teaching Research*, 17, 31–48. doi:10.1177/1362168812457530

Swain, M. (2000). The output hypothesis and beyond: Mediating acquisition through collaborative dialogue. In J. Lantolf (Ed.), *Sociocultural theory and second language learning* (pp. 97–114). Oxford: Oxford University Press.

Swain, M. (2006). Languaging, agency and collaboration in advanced second language learning. In H. Byrnes (Ed.), *Advanced language learning: The contributions of Halliday and Vygotsky* (pp. 95–108). London: Continuum.

Swain, M. (2010). Talking-it-through: Languaging as a source of learning. In R. Batestone (Ed.), *Sociocognitive perspectives on language use and language learning* (pp. 112–130). Oxford: Oxford University Press.

Swain, M., & Lapkin, S. (1995). Problems in output and the cognitive processes they generate: A step towards second language learning. *Applied Linguistics*, 16, 371–391. doi:10.1093/applin/16.3.371

Swain, M., & Lapkin, S. (1998). Interaction and second language learning: Two adolescent French immersion students working together. *Modern Language Review*, 58, 44–63. doi:10.3138/cmlr.58.1.44

Swain, M., & Lapkin, S. (2001). Focus on form through collaborative dialogue: exploring task effects. In M. Bygate, P. Skehan, M. Swain, (Eds.), *Researching Pedagogic Tasks: Second Language Learning, Teaching and Testing* (pp. 99–118). London: Longman.

Swain, M., Lapkin, S., Knouzi, I., Suzuki, W., & Brooks, L. (2009). Languaging: University students learn the grammatical concept of voice in French. *The Modern Language Journal*, 93, 5–29. doi:10.1111/j.1540-4781.2009.00825.x

Tan, L., Wigglesworth G., & Storch N. (2010). Pair interactions and mode of communication: Comparing face-to-face and computer-mediated communication. *Australian Review of Applied Linguistics*, 33, 1–24. doi:10.2104/aral1027

Vygotsky, L.S. (1978). *Mind in society. The development of higher psychological processes.* Cambridge, MA: Harvard University Press.

Vygotsky, L.S. (1981). The genesis of higher mental functions. In J.V. Wertsch (Ed.), *The concept of activity in Soviet psychology* (pp. 144–188). Armonk, NY: M.E. Sharpe.

Watanabe, Y., & Swain, M. (2007). Effects of proficiency differences and patterns of pair interaction on second language learning: Collaborative dialogue between adult ESL learners. *Language Teaching Research*, 11, 121–142. doi:10.1177/136216880607074599

Wells, G. (1999). *Dialogic inquiry. Towards a sociocultural practice and theory of education.* Cambridge: Cambridge University Press. doi:10.1017/CBO9780511605895

Williams, J. (2008). The speaking-writing connection in second language and academic literacy development. In D. Belcher & A. Hirvela (Eds.), *The oral-literate connection. Perspectives on L2 speaking, writing, and other media interactions* (pp. 10–25). Ann Arbor, MI: University of Michigan Press.

Williams, J. (2012). The potential role(s) of writing in second language development. *Journal of Second Language Writing*, 21, 321–333. doi:10.1016/j.jslw.2012.09.007

Wood, D., Bruner, J.S., & Ross, G. (1976). The role of tutoring in problem-solving. *Journal of Child Psychology and Psychiatry*, 17(2), 89–100. doi:10.1111/j.1469-7610.1976.tb00381.x

Zorko, V. (2009). Factors affecting the way students collaborate in a wiki for English language learning. *Australasian Journal of Educational Technology*, 25(5), 645–665.

CHAPTER 11

Small-group meta-analytic talk
and Spanish L2 development

Kara Moranski and Paul D. Toth
University of Pennsylvania / Temple University

In this chapter, we examine the meta-analytic talk of nine adolescent L2 Spanish learners and their subsequent accuracy on a grammaticality judgment task, with the pronoun *se* as an instructional target. Data come from a U.S. high school during three 90-minute lessons, where learners "co-constructed" rules for *se* in groups based on its use in reading passages. We coded learners' analytic talk as belonging to higher or lower *levels of analytical abstraction* (LAAs) to distinguish labeling L2 forms and categories from identifying broader patterns and rules. The amount of individual and group analytic talk, as well as talk at higher LAAs, was compared to individual grammaticality judgment scores before and six weeks after instruction. Results show that learners in groups with greater mutuality improved their scores even when their overall individual participation was only low or moderate. Implications for theory and practice are discussed.

Introduction

This chapter investigates nine adolescent second-language (L2) Spanish learners as they engage in a small-group task requiring them to formulate grammatical rules for a target structure based on a narrative text. Social interaction within four learner groups is analyzed for its impact on target-structure accuracy. The two main sections of the literature review address social interaction and the processing of L2 form-function relationships as key components of the learners' experience. The first section considers the impact of interactional patterns on social and linguistic outcomes. Next, we present learners' orientation to L2 form and function within Craik and Lockhart's (1972) depth of processing (DOP) framework, in which deeper conceptual processing is associated with heightened long-term retention.

DOI 10.1075/lllt.45.12mor
© 2016 John Benjamins Publishing Company

The data for this study comes from three lessons in a third-year, high school Spanish class that used Adair-Hauck and Donato's (2010) "PACE" lesson sequence for instruction on the pronoun *se*. After presenting target structures within a narrative text, PACE includes a guided, inductive *co-construction* phase in which learners collaborate to discern L2 grammar rules based on the text. This activity is supported within L2 sociocultural theory in that learners progress from object- and other-regulation (i.e., charts, texts, and peers) toward internalization and self-regulation in their understanding of the target structure.

Following Toth, Wagner, and Moranski (2013), the analytic talk in four groups was transcribed and coded within four *levels of analytical abstraction* (LAA) to indicate the depth of conceptual processing. Learners were then categorized according to both the amount and level of their analytic talk. Results from the quantitative data indicated a positive relationship between an individual's overall amount of analytic talk and target structure accuracy as measured by a delayed grammaticality judgment posttest. Subsequent transcript analyses then revealed two predominant and opposing interactional patterns: *analytic mutuality* and *analytic isolation*. For learners with lower levels of participation in analytic talk, there was a relationship between their long-term grammatical accuracy and their group's predominant interactional pattern. Building on Sato and Ballinger's (2016) depiction of interpersonal relationships as key in shaping learning outcomes for peer interaction, we discuss pedagogical implications of explicit knowledge as a mutually constructed, socio-cognitive phenomenon.

Literature review

Social in-group interactional patterns

Dramatically different patterns of interaction are often present when learners complete collaborative tasks in small groups (Sato & Viveros 2016; Storch 2002; Toth, Wagner & Moranski 2013; Young & Tedick 2016). A metaphor for the variety of learner behaviors during small-group tasks can be found in marathoners running together in a pace or time group. All group members must "train" together with warm-up activities prepared by their coach (i.e., the instructor), and all share the common goal of completing their task. Although the athletes know that they should run in tandem, some may deviate from the pace and pull ahead or fall behind. Conversely, a runner that is slightly ahead of another may help bring the other runner up to pace. The role of leader can also be fluid in such groups, as individuals take turns guiding others (Ohta 1995; Kowal & Swain 1994; Sato & Viveros

2016). However, when L2 learners work in small groups, there are some who never leave the starting line, sitting quietly as their peers progress (Rouhshad & Storch 2016; Young & Tedick 2016). Others may run on a parallel course, focusing on language issues that are only tangentially related to the target task (Seedhouse 2004; Toth 2008; Toth, Wagner & Moranski 2013), while still others may walk off the course entirely and engage in unrelated off-task behavior.

Variation in learners' small-group behavior has been shown to have differing implications for task completion and L2 development. For example, Donato (1994) found that learners in small groups often engaged in *collective scaffolding*, where they pooled their individual knowledge to successfully complete a dialogue-writing task. Meanwhile, Storch (2002) investigated interactions during a semester's dyadic writing tasks as a function of *equality* and *mutuality*, where equality referred to "the degree of control over the direction of a task," and mutuality reflected the "the level engagement with each other's contributions" (127). In her study, dyads in which learners exhibited high degrees of both mutuality and equality were categorized as collaborative/collaborative, and those with high mutuality but not equality were expert/novice. Dyads with low mutuality but high equality were labeled dominant/dominant, and those with both low mutuality and equality were dominant/passive. In the end, the groups with higher mutuality (collaborative/collaborative and expert/novice) showed more evidence of knowledge transfer from one writing-related context to another than those with low levels of mutuality. Studies within the present volume, including Sato and Viveros (2016), Rouhshad & Storch (2016), and Young & Tedick (2016), likewise underscore the importance of mutuality in creating optimal conditions for peer interaction. Thus, variation in the amount of on-task participation and the degree of engagement with peers may yield observable consequences for learning outcomes.

Depth of processing and cognitive levels in SLA

In addition to the various ways that L2 learners orient themselves socially to group work, there is variation in how learners cognitively process the material they discuss. The degree to which a learner assimilates new information is often called *depth of processing* (DOP), where *depth* represents the "amount of attention devoted to the stimulus, its compatibility with the analyzing structures, and the processing time available" (Craik & Lockhart 1972:676). Craik and Lockhart first introduced this concept to counter conceptualizations of memory as three "box-like" categories of sensory, short-term, and long-term storage. They posited that the key to understanding an item's *trace*, or persistence, in memory lay in *how* – and not *where* – it was stored. According to their DOP framework, there was a "series or hierarchy of processing stages," and greater depth implied a greater degree of cognitive, conceptual analysis (675). They distinguished *Type I* from *Type II* processing, where Type I included the repetition of "analyses already carried out," while Type II described deeper conceptual processing through "pattern recognition and the extraction of meaning" associated with greater retention (675).

An early application of the DOP concept to adult L2 learning was Schmidt's (1990) *noticing hypothesis,* which proposed that the conscious detection of L2 grammatical forms was "the necessary and sufficient condition for converting input to intake" (1990: 129). To explain instances where learners might fail to incorporate teacher-corrected errors in later speech, Schmidt (1990), citing Craik and Lockhart (1972), proposed that such corrected forms would only have been noticed "momentarily," without being processed "sufficiently deeply to ensure retention" (Schmidt 1990: 141). More recently, DOP has been applied to other aspects of L2 learning, including vocabulary acquisition (Brown & Perry 1991; Joe 1998) and text comprehension (Oded & Walters 2001). These studies have corroborated L1 research suggesting that deeper levels of conceptual processing are associated with better retention (Oded & Walters 2001). Meanwhile, Ellis (1999) has applied the concept of DOP to both justify the cognitive theoretical claim that negotiated interaction facilitates L2 learning and also to support the sociocultural view that learners' private speech promotes a "deep processing of input" that eventually helps them "achieve self-regulation" (29). Ellis later calls for further L2 research to investigate DOP within interactional contexts.

To date, however, only a modest number of L2 studies have addressed DOP within sociocultural or interactional contexts. In one, Borer (2007) distinguishes between three processing depths – repetition, manipulation, and generation – and investigates their relationship to vocabulary retention under individual and collaborative conditions. Although she reports that both conditions promoted retention similarly overall, processing at the lowest level, repetition, correlated with weaker retention in the collaborative setting. Borer found that "other repetition" (i.e. listening to a peer) had a less positive effect on retention than manipulation or generation and referenced follow-up interviews in which learners mentioned that aspects of their partner's pronunciation distracted them during repetitions (286). However, a qualitative analysis of transcripts suggested that deeper processing strategies such as creating mnemonics or formulating opinions coincided with better vocabulary retention on a written posttest.

Swain, Lapkin, Knouzi, Suzuki, and Brooks (2009) consider distinct processing categories from a sociocultural framework in their investigation of how self-directed talk during an individual think-aloud task benefited nine L2 French learners in mastering the passive voice. Sociocultural theory holds that

self-directed language, whether in the L1 or the L2, mediates cognition and facilitates the transformation of thought into externalized activity (Lantolf & Thorne
2006; Vygotsky 1981, 1987), which in the Swain et al. (2009) study involved use
of the French passive. The authors explicitly identified *languaging* units as "cognitively complex on-task talk" and distinguished the categories of paraphrasing,
inferencing, and analyzing. Within inferencing, the subcategories of integration,
elaboration, and hypothesis formation were further delineated. The analysis of
learners' self-directed talk showed high variability in both the quantity and quality of languaging. In terms of quantity, individuals were easily classified as high,
middle, or low languagers. Regarding quality however, the "high languagers used
a balance of languaging types" relative to other learners, with notably higher rates
of self-assessment and inferencing (21–22). Later, results from a delayed posttest
demonstrated that "a more accurate and a greater depth of understanding of the
concept of voice" was mostly found among the high languagers (20).

In a previous study (Toth, Wagner & Moranski 2013), we documented how L2
Spanish learners engaged in four increasingly complex levels of L1 meta-analytic
talk (to be defined in detail later) while co-constructing L2 grammar rules in small
groups and whole-class discussions. The lower levels, *labeling* and *categorizing*
represented a lesser DOP while the higher levels of *patterning* and *rule formulation* corresponded with greater DOP. When engaged in analytic talk, learners
"moved iteratively between higher and lower inductive levels, with broader proposals often preceded or followed by 'talking through' more narrowly-focused,
supportive exemplars" (297). This study extends our previous work as we investigate how learners' overall analytic talk time and talk time at higher levels of
analysis related to their L2 target-structure accuracy within the contexts of various
group dynamics.

The present study

As a learner engages in group-work tasks, she is simultaneously negotiating both
social interactions and her own depth of processing of L2 concepts and content.
Although social and cognitive components of language learning have been studied
extensively in their own right, they are seldom investigated together (Ellis 1999;
Borer 2007). The goal of the present study is to take preliminary steps toward
understanding the interplay of group social dynamics and individual depth of
processing. Of particular interest is the possibility that the higher or lower levels
of conceptual processing from certain learners could impact those of others, given
the social context in which they collaborate. Our research questions are as follows:

1. How is a learner's overall collaborative analytic talk and talk at higher levels of analysis distributed during an L2 metalinguistic task?
2. Is there a relationship between the total amount of individual and group analytic talk and an individual's target-structure accuracy?
3. Is there a relationship between the total amount of individual and group higher-level analytic talk and an individual's L2 target structure accuracy?

Methodological framework

Because not all instructional contexts equally promote a range of processing levels among language learners (Rouhshad & Storch 2016; Leow, Moreno, & Hsieh 2014), we chose Adair-Hauck and Donato's (2010) "PACE" lesson sequence for this study, as it is designed to facilitate the deeper processing of L2 grammatical concepts through a carefully-managed balance between instructional support and learner autonomy. In proposing PACE, Adair-Hauck and Donato noted that whereas top-down, teacher-led explanations often exclude learners from constructing grammatical knowledge, unstructured, bottom-up exposure to L2 input leaves many learners ill-equipped to build such knowledge independently. Hence, PACE involves a dialogic process of guided, inductive rule formulation where learners "co-construct" an understanding of L2 grammar with instructional assistance, based on the use of target forms in culturally authentic texts. Specifically, a PACE lesson first involves "presenting" target forms within a short narrative text and then drawing learners' "attention" to their use. In groups, learners then "co-construct" proposals for grammar rules based on the patterns they find, with the teacher later guiding the class toward a consensus as the groups share their analyses. Learners then apply their grammar rules to language use during communicative "extension" tasks.

This proposal to achieve the deeper processing of L2 grammar fits within sociocultural theory in that instructionally-mediated verbal reasoning is used to build conceptual knowledge that can in turn be used to regulate oneself and others (Vygotsky 1987). Hence, as learners collaboratively identify patterns in L2 form-function relationships, they are necessarily pushed to reconcile observations of the target structure with their pooled background knowledge to derive a solution to the grammar problem. Although such verbal activity is often carried out in the learners' L1, the cognitive value of "talking through" metalinguistic understandings of the L2 has indeed been advocated not only by Adair-Hauck and Donato (2010) for the co-construction in PACE, but also by other Vygotskyan L2 scholars (Brooks & Donato 1994; Brooks, Donato, & McGlone 1997; Swain & Lapkin 2000; Swain 2010).

Methodology

Participants and instructional context

The data for this study were collected in a public, suburban U.S. high school from an intact, third-year L2 Spanish class that met every other school day for 90 minutes. The total enrollment in the class was 17 learners, all European-Americans between ages 15 and 18. During co-construction activities, the class worked in eight small groups, and a total of nine learners in four of these groups (seven males and two females) volunteered to record their interactions with portable digital recorders. The interactions of these nine learners during co-construction are the focus of this study. To prepare learners for this project, the teacher taught PACE lessons for 2 weeks before data gathering began. The lessons in this study were designed jointly by this article's second author, the teacher, and a research assistant.

PACE lessons and instructional target

The goal of the instructional unit was to introduce learners to uses of the Spanish pronoun *se* in "non-agentive" constructions, which results in an impersonal or passive meaning, as in (1), or may yield an inchoative meaning with some verbs, as shown in (2). *Se* is difficult for English-speaking learners because similar constructions with *se*, a verb, and a noun phrase correspond to various English equivalents (Toth & Guijarro-Fuentes 2013). Learners had explicitly studied the reflexive uses of *se*, shown in (3), one year earlier in the Spanish curriculum, but they had no previous instruction on its non-agentive functions. The unit consisted of 3 consecutive 90-minute lessons, each one a complete PACE sequence focusing on different aspects of non-agentive *se*.

(1) *Se preparó la comida.*
   "The food **was** prepared / **One** prepared food."
(2) *La comida se cocinó.*
   "The food [Ø] cooked / The food **was** cooked / **One** cooked food"
(3) *Los niños se prepararon.*
   "The children washed **themselves / each other**."

During the presentation phase of each lesson, learners listened twice to a recording of that day's focus text while reading along (see Appendix). A different meaning-based comprehension task followed each listening round. Then, the attention phase had learners working in groups of two or three to sort selected sentences from the text into those representing a specific cause and effect (i.e., sentences without *se*) versus "general" events with an unspecified "doer" (i.e., *se*-derived impersonal passives). These sentences are underlined in the Appendix; the result was a chart like Table 1. Then, for the co-construction phase, learners first worked for 5–10 minutes in groups of two or three to derive a rule for *se* based on the differences between the two columns. The teacher then led a 5–10 minute whole-class discussion where volunteers shared their analyses while she guided them toward a consensus. Unlike the rest of the lesson, English was used in the co-construction phase so that learners could focus on their analyses without facing proficiency limitations (Adair-Hauck & Donato 2010). The remaining 40 minutes then consisted of whole-class and small-group extension tasks where rules for *se* could be applied to the communicative functions exemplified in the focus text. For Lesson 1, this involved using impersonal *se* in a restaurant review; for Lesson 2, it meant using passive *se* in a recipe; and for Lesson 3, it involved using inchoative *se* to narrate an accident.

Table 1. Comparing sentences with and without *se* in Lesson 1's co-construction

La experiencia de la autora	*Los restaurantes en general*
1. *No lo encontré así.*	1. *Se dice que los dos restaurantes son iguales.*
2. *Me gustó mucho la comida.*	2. *Se come bien en los dos lugares.*
3. *Encontré problemas con la cuenta.*	3. *Se llega en carro o autobús.*
4. *Me dijo que costaba 3,000 colones.*	4. *Se sirve comida tradicional.*
5. *Me sentaron inmediatamente.*	5. *Se necesita una reservación.*

English gloss (did not appear in lesson materials):

The author's experience	The restaurants in general
1. I didn't find it that way.	1. They* say the restaurants are the same.
2. I liked the food a lot.	2. One eats well in both places.
3. I found problems with the check.	3. You arrive by car or bus.
4. He told me it cost 3,000 *colones*.	4. They* serve traditional food.
5. They seated me immediately.	5. You need a reservation.

* This English "they" is meant to correspond with Spanish impersonal *se*.

Data gathering and analysis

Audio and video recordings

The qualitative data to be presented here came from audio recordings of the small-group portion of co-construction. Across the three 90-minute lessons, this consisted of 17 minutes 22 seconds of total class time. During these collaborative analyses of the target structure, the nine focal learners remained in the same groups and recorded their interactions while a digital camcorder at the back of the room also recorded each lesson to help inform transcription and coding. The present data set thus consist of 12 total recordings: four small-group interactions in each of three lessons. All learners were given Spanish aliases in the transcripts.

Levels of analytical abstraction (LAA)

The co-construction interactions were transcribed, coded, and analyzed using Transana 2.42 software (Fassnacht & Woods 2009), which links recorded data to transcripts and measures the time of coded segments. The learners' aggregate analytic talk during the co-construction task was coded as described in Toth, Wagner, and Moranski (2013), with instances of "analytic talk" defined as any clause overtly referencing L2 form or meaning. The second author and an independent coder separately identified 188 total instances of analytic talk and sorted them into four levels of analytical abstraction (LAAs), defined as follows:

1. *Labeling*: Observations limited to naming individual morphosyntactic forms in the source text, e.g., "What's *sentaron* mean?"
2. *Categorizing*: Observations linking linguistic properties of two or more tokens, e.g., "these are all like *él ella Usted* form."
3. *Patterning*: Observations that linked two categories, including categories of form and meaning, e.g., "They have *me* if it's her experience, *se* if it's the restaurant's."
4. *Rule formulation*: Comments that extended beyond the source text and attempted to describe a Spanish grammatical norm, e.g., "You use *se* if the subject is the same as the direct object."

With an 87% overlap, Cohen's kappa showed satisfactory overall inter-coder reliability between the two coders ($\kappa = 0.82$), who then reconciled their discrepancies to reach 100% agreement.

In order to streamline the categories of learner analyses in the present study, labeling and categorizing were collapsed into *low LAAs*, while patterning and rule formulation were considered *high LAAs*. These categories reflect Craik and Lockhart's (1972) original dichotomy in which "pattern recognition and the extraction of meaning" represent deeper conceptual processing rather than mere item detection (675). Learners who had 67%–100% of their total analytic talk at high LAAs were classified as high-level analyzers; those with 34%–66% of their analytic talk at high LAAs were considered balanced analyzers; and those with only 0%–33% of their analytic talk at high LAAs were categorized as low-level analyzers.

In-group participation
A learners' participation in analytic talk over the three lessons was measured as the proportion of total analytic talk time within the group occupied by that learner (at all LAAs). Learners whose total analytic talk comprised 67%–100% of the group's total were considered high-level participators; those whose analytic talk comprised 34%–66% of the group total were mid-level participators; those whose analytic talk comprised 0%-33% of the group total were low-level participators. Measured in this way, an individual learner's analytic participation reflected Storch's (2002) concept of equality in that it indicated each individual's proportional presence within task-relevant talk.

Grammaticality judgment task
The primary assessment consisted of an auditory, picture-based grammaticality judgment (GJ) task, where learners rated pre-recorded sentences within a fixed time interval for how well they represented corresponding pictures. A 4-second gap was used between each sentence based on pilot testing of 2- through 8-second intervals with another third-year L2 Spanish class. Following Juffs's (2001) suggestions, learners responded on an answer sheet using a 6-point Likert scale, as shown in Figure 1, with "6" indicating total acceptability, "1" indicating total unacceptability, and intermediate values between. Learners were told to respond intuitively about how well the sentence described the picture, and to select "Don't Know" if they were unsure.

Recorded sentences:

"*La ventana se cerró*"

"*Las flores se crecen.*"

Visuals appearing in the test book:

Corresponding items on student answer sheet:

CIRCLE YOUR ANSWER:

How well does the sentence describe the picture?

      (worst)   (best)

1.   1 2 3 4 5 6   Don't Know

2.   1 2 3 4 5 6   Don't Know

1.   2.

Figure 1. Items from the auditory picture-based grammaticality judgment task ("The window closed," "The flowers (*se) are growing")

Learners took the test three times: first as a pre-test immediately before instruction, then as a posttest immediately following, and finally as a delayed post-test six weeks later. The instructor confirmed that prior to the delayed posttest, *se* occurred only incidentally in classroom discourse and was never the focus of instruction. Thus, the delayed posttest could assess the retention of learning gains from the PACE lessons with reasonable validity. For each test administration, pre-recorded instructions took participants through three examples before starting. Then, 88 randomly-ordered items presented grammatical and ungrammatical sentences involving the use and omission of *se* as well as a wide range of distractors. The data to be considered here are the learners' ratings for the nine grammatical sentences with non-agentive *se* that represented the instructional target. The task took about 25 minutes to complete.

The second author of this study worked with the teacher and an assistant to design three versions of the GJ task based on third-year Spanish vocabulary. Near-final drafts of each version were given to three native Spanish speakers to check for validity, and adjustments were made accordingly. During data gathering, final drafts of each version were administered in a split-block design to control for test-learning effects, so that each version was evenly and randomly distributed to learners as their pretest, and then each person cycled through the remaining versions for the two posttests (i.e., ABC, BCA, or CAB). The equivalency of the test versions was confirmed by piloting them in two other third-year L2 Spanish classes in the same high school (N = 35; Version A, $n = 13$; Version B, $n = 11$; Version C, $n = 11$). A univariate ANOVA on the scores of the nine target items revealed no significant differences for test version.

Results

Of the 17 minutes and 22 seconds (1,042 sec) total time available for small-group co-construction, the far right two columns of Table 2 show that analytic talk in each group ranged from a low of 113.8 sec (11%) in Group 3 to a high of 320.5 sec (31%) in Group 2. The audio and video recordings reveal that learners used the rest of the available time either to orient themselves to the task or to engage in off-task conversations once they considered themselves finished.

To address Research Question 1, we first determined how much each group member contributed to the group's total analytic talk, and to talk at high LAAs. The middle two sets of columns in Table 2 show the percentage of analytic participation and the proportion of high LAAs for each of the nine learners. Group 1 was the most balanced in these two categories, although Diego's level of participation and level of high LAAs were both lower than those of his partner, Raquel. In Group 2, Pepe demonstrated an extremely strong presence in that group's analytic talk, which resulted a total analytic talk time for his group that was almost twice that of the other three groups. In Group 3, José and Alberto had very high LAAs but their social interaction was marked by an imbalance in analytic participation, with José making more than two-thirds of the contributions. Finally, in Group 4, Lucas also accounted for more than two-thirds of the analytic talk time, but he and Clara maintained relatively balanced proportions of high LAAs.

Table 2. Levels of participation and high analytic abstraction over three lessons

Group	Learner	Level of analytic participation			Level of high-level analytical abstraction		Total analytic talk time* (in seconds)			
		Low	Mid	High	Low to balanced	High	Individual LAAs		Group LAAs	
							All	High	All	High
1	Raquel		56%		52%		86.0	44.7	152.7	65.8
	Diego		40%		35%		60.7	21.1		
2	Luis	1%				100%	1.2	1.2		
	Jesús	21%			61%		67.7	41.3	320.5	216.4
	Pepe			74%		70%	238.3	166.7		
3	José			68%		98%	77.4	75.8	113.8	112.2
	Alberto	32%				100%	36.4	36.4		
4	Lucas			68%	55%		110.3	61.2	162.2	86.0
	Clara	32%			48%		51.9	24.8		

* Individual talk time may not add up to the total talk time for all groups due to a small amount of interjections from the teacher or classmates from other groups.

Table 3 shows how learners were categorized according to their analytic participation and the amount of high LAAs over the three lessons. Meanwhile, the three columns to the right indicate each learner's pretest and delayed posttest scores for the GJ task as well as the net change in those scores. We list the delayed rather than immediate posttest scores here because we believe they better represent the retention that is claimed to accompany deeper conceptual processing.

   To address the second and third research questions, correlations were calculated for each learner's GJ score and his or her aggregate amount of: (1) time in analytic talk; and (2) time at the higher LAAs. Since this was a small sample size and some variables did not have normal underlying distributions, the

Table 3. Amounts of participation and high LAAs with GJ test results

Group	Learner	Amount of analytic participation	Amount of high-level analytical abstraction	GJ scores (on a scale of 1–6)		
				Pretest	Delayed posttest	Change
1	Raquel	Mid	Balanced	4.28	4.22	−0.06
	Diego	Mid	Balanced	4.33	4.78	0.44
2	Luis	Low	High	3.33	2.78	−0.56
	Jesús	Low	Balanced	3.22	3.44	0.22
	Pepe	High	High	3.89	4.78	0.89
3	José	High	High	4.06	3.22	−0.83
	Alberto	Low	High	3.78	3.72	−0.56
4	Lucas	High	Balanced	4.11	4.56	0.44
	Clara	Low	Balanced	3.33	4.22	0.89

nonparametric correlation coefficient Kendall's tau was used. As shown in Table 4, there was a significant correlation at the $p < .1$ level between the learners' individual analytic talk at all LAAs and their delayed GJ post-test scores, $\tau(9) = .457$, $p = .092$, meaning that greater analytic participation coincided with higher scores. The lack of a significant correlation between the pretest and individual analytic talk further suggests a positive treatment effect. Finally, at the $p < .01$ level, there was a significant correlation between total analytic talk at all levels and total analytic talk at high LAAs, $\tau(9) = .722$, $p = .007$. This means that the more analytic talk a learner produced, the more likely that he or she would also produce high LAAs, and vice-versa.

Regarding Research Question 3, neither the correlation between individual talk at high LAAs and delayed GJ scores, nor between group analytic talk and delayed GJ scores were significant. Thus, one's individual analytic talk at all levels more strongly predicted one's delayed posttest score than did analysis at high LAAs or the amounts of analytic talk that one was exposed to in-group. There was, however, a statistically significant inverse correlation for group analytic talk at higher LAAs and GJ *pretest* scores, $\tau(9) = −.648$, $p = .011$. This indicated that individuals with lower scores on the pre-test happened to be in groups that ultimately had more analytic talk at the higher LAAs, whereas those with higher pretest scores were in groups with less talk at high LAAs. In the discussion section, we will consider how this could have affected the correlation between high-level analytic talk and subsequent L2 accuracy as measured by the delayed GJ posttest.

Table 4. Kendall's tau correlation coefficients between analytic talk variables and GJ test scores ($n = 9$)

	1. Individual GJ pretest score	2. Individual GJ delayed posttest score	3. Individual analytic talk at all LAAs	4. Individual analytic talk at high LAAs	5. Group analytic talk at all LAAs
1. Individual GJ pretest score					
2. Individual GJ delayed posttest score	.435*				
3. Individual analytic talk at all LAAs	.254	.457*			
4. Individual analytic talk at high LAAs	.085	.171	.722***		
5. Group analytic talk at all LAAs	−.401	.063	.122	−.061	
6. Group analytic talk at high LAAs	−.648**	−.438	−.122	.183	.467

* $p < .1$ (2-tailed)

** $p < .05$ (2-tailed)

*** $p < .01$ (2-tailed)

Given the possibility that many unforeseen individual variables could have affected the learners' performance, we turned to the transcripts to shed light on patterns in the quantitative data. In particular, we focused on the lower-level participators and analyzers that maintained gains in the GJ test: Diego, Jesús, and Clara. These learners were of particular interest because their gains came despite producing either less analytic talk overall (Jesús, Clara) or less talk at higher LAAs (Diego) than the other members of their respective groups. The transcripts revealed that these learners belonged to groups whose interactions often showed mutuality in the LAAs that they were addressing. These differed markedly from the interaction patterns where lower-level learners did not make gains, which were often characterized by a single learner dominating analytic talk.

In-group interactional patterns

Analytic mutuality

We have labeled the first interactional pattern in analytic talk as "analytic mutuality," meaning that learners' contributions in at least three of the four levels during a particular lesson were distributed relatively evenly between the participants. Figures 2 and 3 illustrate this mutuality in Groups 1 and 2 during Lesson 1, where for the first three LAAs, a less-productive learner provided no less than one third of the total analytic talk.

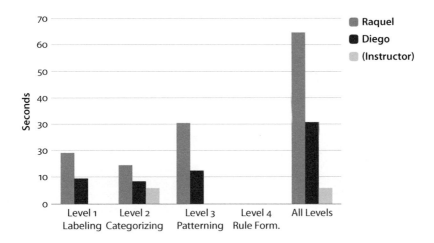

Figure 2. Analytic mutuality in Group 1 for Lesson 1

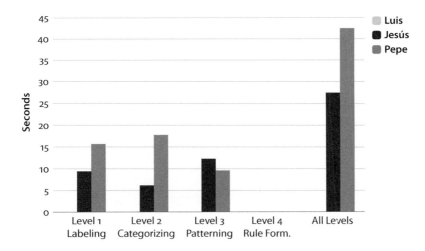

Figure 3. Analytic mutuality in Group 2 for Lesson 1

Our choice of the term "analytic mutuality" was also meant to reflect Storch's (2002) definition of mutuality as the degree of engagement between learners. In her study, such engagement existed when learners reached similarly high levels of target structure comprehension or when an "expert" and "novice" interacted extensively. A review of our transcripts suggested a similar mutuality in groups where periods of balance in both the quantity and analytic level of participants' contributions occurred frequently during one or more of the lessons. On such days, learners did not appear to distribute analytic talk randomly among the levels, but rather spent time progressing through the analytic levels together, as Table 5 shows.

Table 5. Excerpt of transcript from co-construction for Group 1 in Lesson 1

Transcript coded for level of analytic talk			Commentary
10	Diego:	This is like, stuff that's like, basically	*White text shaded in* dark grey
11		this is kind of indirect. So like things	*represents the higher LAA of*
12		happen to her.	*patterning. They are examining*
13	Raquel:	Yeah that's what [reflexive	*the occurrences of the pronouns*
14	Diego:	umm]	*"se" and "me" in the chart*
15	Raquel:	=is. Something that you do to yourself.	*that they have made and are*
16	Diego:	No that's not re (.) [no	*attempting to agree upon a*
17	Raquel:	That's] the [things with the SE ME =	*form-meaning pattern to explain*
18	Diego:	Well kind of]	*them. Diego proposes that they*
19	Raquel:	=at the ends.	*are indirect objects, but Raquel*
20	Diego:	Yeah.	*asserts that they are reflexive. The*
21	Raquel:	Yeah↑ Which is reflexive, right?↑	*learners are mutually engaged in*
22	Diego:	Well it's just (.) 'member, you know,	*this exchange, and Raquel makes*
23		it's kind of like indirect where it's (.)	*an attempt to define the concept of*
24		(they) did it to her like	*reflexivity to Diego.*
25	Raquel:	it's that's [present=	
26	Diego:	it's like]	
27	Raquel:	=dijo's present, [isn't it?↑	*Dark text shaded in* light grey
28	Diego:	No it's not.	*represents the lower LAA of*
29	Raquel:	What is it?	*labeling.*
30	Diego:	[Preterit.	*Raquel begins by labeling the verb*
33	Raquel:	[Past tense?↑] What's "sentaron?"	*tenses of two individual verbs*
34		Preterit?↑	*from their chart, and Diego tells*
35	Diego:	Yeah.	*her the correct tense.*
36	Raquel:	Why's it "me sentaron"? It doesn't it	
37		[mean Ustedes (form)?	
38	Diego:	Cuz they sat her down.] And she was	
39		saying it (.) like they did it to me.	

Table 5 demonstrates this analytic mutuality in an excerpt from Group 1's Lesson 1 co-construction, which corresponds with Figure 2. When Raquel shifts from the higher LAA of categorizing to the lower LAA of labeling at line 25, Diego follows along. The roles of expert and novice are taken up by both learners at different points in this excerpt: Raquel attempts to show Diego forms that she believes to be reflexive in lines 13 through 21, and Diego helps Raquel label the correct verb tense in lines 28 through 35. The learners' mutuality is further evidenced by the equality in the number and length of the turns taken by each.

Although there were slight variations in the cohesiveness with which different groups shifted from one LAA to another, all of the transcripts with frequent episodes of analytic mutuality evidenced high degrees of engagement among two or more learners. Analytic mutuality was the predominant pattern for five of the twelve co-construction transcripts.

Episodes of isolation at the higher LAAs
The second interactional pattern identified during co-construction suggested the opposite of mutuality. Here, one learner often generated talk at one or more of the LAAs and occupied well over two-thirds of that group's total analytic talk. As Figures 4 and 5 show, these episodes of "analytic isolation" generally occurred at the higher LAAs of patterning and rule formulation. Table 6 shows an excerpt of the transcript that corresponds with Figure 4, showing co-construction between Alberto and José for Lesson 3. Here, José begins the task by stating a version of the rule that he has developed independently (lines 1–8) and ends by asking his partner, leadingly, if he agrees. In line 15, Alberto makes an attempt to meet the task requirements by proposing a rule that starts with, "when the subject is defined," but is quickly contradicted when Alberto changes the grammatical context to "when the subject is *not* defined" (line 16).

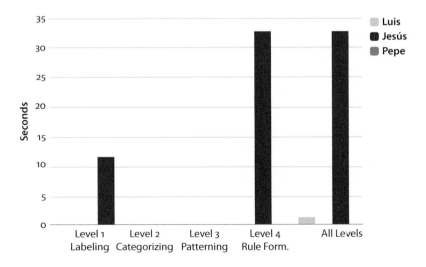

Figure 4. Analytic isolation in Group 2 for Lesson 3

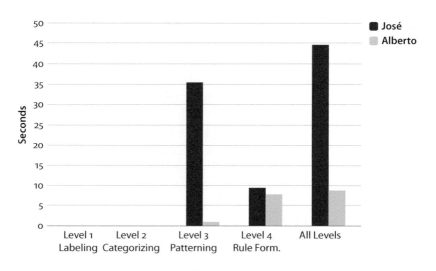

Figure 5. Analytic isolation in Group 3 for Lesson 2

Table 6. Excerpt of transcript from co-construction for Group 3 during Lesson 2

Transcript coded for level of analytic talk		Commentary
01	José:	OK so in: la narración ah, la, the	*White text shaded in dark grey*
02		subject is president, is present and the	*represents the higher LAA of*
03		verb seems to follow whether or not the	*patterning. Here, José begins*
04		subject is (.) singular or plural (.) but	*the co-construction activity by*
05		like in la receta (.) the (.) verb–or the	*stating what he believes to be*
06		subject, isn´t um, specified and the	*the grammar rule. He does not*
07		verb seems to follow whether or not the	*include his partner, Alberto, in*
08		direct object is plural. Would you agree	*the construction of this rule. He*
09		Alberto?	*ends this long turn with a leading*
10	Alberto:	I would agree	*question to which Alberto readily*
11	José:	That's good that's good	*agrees.*
12	Alberto:	Yeah. So now what was the straight up	
13		rule? [#2] Should we have=	*White text shaded in black*
14	José:	Say=	*denotes the highest LAA*
15	Alberto:	=like when the subject is defined?	*of rule formulation. Here,*
16	José:	Say like when the subject is not defined	*Alberto proposes a rule but is*
17		the verb follows–the verb conjugates	*contradicted by José. José does*
18		according to the direct object	*not tell Alberto the reason for this*
19	Alberto:	That's good.	*reformulation of the rule.*

This interaction between Alberto and José exemplifies Storch's (2002) dominant/ passive category, in which the dominant learner (José) maintains a "higher degree of control" over the task (lack of equality) with low mutuality. José's influence in this interaction is illustrated by the length and number of his turns as well as the leading nature of his contributions. Although the expert/novice patterns in Diego and Raquel's co-construction also show that one learner is often guiding their conversation (Table 5), the high level of mutuality allows the other learner to remain active in the task.

Summary of interactional patterns

Table 7 shows the predominant interactional patterns during co-construction for all four groups over the three lessons. For Groups 1 and 4, analytic mutuality was predominant in two of the three lessons. The lower-level learners that had the greatest sustained gains on the GJ posttest, Diego and Clara (see Table 4), belonged to these two groups. Analytic mutuality was also predominant during Lesson 1 in Group 2, but Lessons 2 and 3 were then characterized by episodes of analytic isolation dominated by Pepe. However, the lower-level learner from this group who did participate, Jesús, maintained very modest gains on his GJ scores. Lastly, analytic isolation was predominant in Group 3 for all three lessons. Both the high- and low-level learners from this group, Alberto and José, regressed on their GJ scores from pre- to delayed posttest.

Regarding the first research question on how overall and higher-level analytic talk would be distributed among participants, Table 7 suggests that the social quality of their collaboration influenced the outcome. The two dominant interactional patterns were analytic mutuality and isolation and the higher LAAs: Groups 1, 2, and 4 illustrated both patterns to varying degrees, while Group 3 showed only the latter.

Table 7. Predominant interactional patterns for co-construction activities

Group	Dominant analytic pattern		
	Lesson 1	Lesson 2	Lesson 3
1	Mutuality	Mutuality	Isolation*
2	Mutuality	Isolation (Pepe)	Isolation (Pepe)
3	Isolation (Alberto)	Isolation (José)	Isolation (José)
4	Mutuality	Isolation (Lucas)	Mutuality

* An interaction in which each learner contributed less than 10 seconds of analytic talk

The second research question asked if there was a relationship between the proportion of time spent in individual or group analytic talk and target structure accuracy. A statistically significant correlation was found between learners' delayed posttest scores and their individual amounts of analytic talk, but not the group's total analytic talk. There was also a significant correlation between individual overall analytic talk and individual analytic talk at higher LAAs. A qualitative analysis of the transcripts showed that the low-level participators whose group transcripts showed evidence of mutuality (Jesús and Clara) made modest gains on the GJ task. The low-level participator whose group had no instances of mutuality (Alberto) did not improve, however.

Similarly, the third research question sought to investigate any relationship between time spent at higher analytic levels and L2 target structure accuracy. No statistically significant correlation was found between the GJ test scores and amounts of higher LAAs, either at the group or individual level. This could be partially due to the significant inverse correlation between individual GJ pretest scores and group analytic talk at the higher LAAs, in that learners with lower pretest scores might have affected the quality of the analytic talk at the high LAAs. However, the transcripts showed that the learner with lower LAAs who was in a group with high levels of mutuality (Diego) did make modest gains. In short, learners had to contribute to analytic talk to affect their delayed posttest score, but it need not have been talk at a high LAA.

Discussion

Quantitative results

The quantitative results showed that individual analytic talk, even when conducted in the L1, was positively associated with target structure accuracy. In addition, the strong positive correlation between individuals' overall analytic talk and their analytic talk at high LAAs indicated that learners who produced more overall analytic talk also produced more talk at high LAAs, and vice-versa. However, only overall analytic talk correlated with higher GJ delayed posttest scores, not talk at higher LAAs.

A potential explanation for the lack of a relationship between high LAAs and delayed posttest scores can be found in the significant inverse correlation between an individual's GJ pretest scores and the overall amount of high-level analytic talk in his or her group. This indicated that individuals with lower initial GJ scores were members of groups with greater amounts of high-level analytic talk. It was therefore possible that learners with lower pretest scores shared misconceptions about the target structure with peers when articulating high-level patterns and rules. An examination of the transcripts showed that for groups with high analytic mutuality, these misconceptions at times manifested themselves as inaccurate grammatical rules that were discussed and in some cases accepted by the other group members, as Table 8 demonstrates.

This exchange is from one of the two groups where analytic mutuality was the predominant pattern. Clara is a lower-level participator in that she contributes

Table 8. Misconceptions of grammar rules at high LAAs (Group 4, Lesson 3)

Transcript coded for level of analytic talk		Commentary
52	Clara:	And for the other one just say pers	*Dark text shaded in light grey represents*
53		subject is a person. Except for the	*the lowest LAA of labeling.*
54		rain, that's not a person. So mojar	*Dark text shaded in medium grey repre-*
55		is just weird	*sents the lower LAA of categorizing.*
56	Lucas:	Yeah. We'll say it works except for	*White text shaded in dark grey represents*
57		mojar	*the higher LAA of patterning.*
58	Clara:	Maybe it's cuz it's like a "jar" verb	*White text shaded in black denotes the*
59		er	*highest LAA of rule formulation.*
60	Lucas:	°There we go, yeah.	
61	Clara:	and so it's like mo-ho.	
62	Clara:	Err. (Done)	

less than one third of the group's total analytic talk time. She also had a relatively low GJ pretest score (Tables 3 and 4). Although she also contributed to fewer of the dyad's high LAAs (29%), this group's high mutuality allowed for her high-LAA contributions to be prevalent during the interaction. In this portion of Lesson 3 co-construction, she and Lucas are formulating a rule for inchoative *se*, and they have accounted for verbs that take *se*, but they cannot explain those that do not. In lines 52–54, Clara proposes that *se* is used when the "subject is a person" but notes that one of the verbs, *mojar* (to wet, to soak) does not correspond to this rule. In line 58 she incorrectly proposes that a phonological property of the verb itself makes it an exception to her rule. Her partner agrees, and the two conclude the task.

These instances of incorrect rules that are proposed and accepted at the high LAAs could account for the lack of a relationship between total individual or group analytic talk at the higher LAAs and accuracy on the delayed GJ posttest. However, it should be noted that even with these occurrences of learners that proposed and accepted incorrect higher-level analyses, a significant positive relationship was still found between total individual analytic talk and GJ posttest scores. In other words, the incorrect hypotheses at the higher LAAs did not negate the overall benefit of L1 analytic talk. Indeed, Clara improved nearly one point on her pre- to delayed posttest scores.

Qualitative results and interactional patterns

The qualitative transcript analysis underscored the role of mutuality in small-group settings, especially for the lower-level participators and analyzers. The two lower-level learners whose groups had the highest degree of analytic mutuality, Diego and Clara, also had the highest sustained gains on the GJ posttest. The lower-level learner whose group showed analytic mutuality for only one of the three lessons, Jesús, showed very modest gains. Thus, it appeared that for these lower-level learners, analytic mutuality was necessary for them to benefit from the analytic talk of their peers. Although the learners' attempts at rule formulation at the higher LAAs were not always accurate, the results suggest that learners' DOP during the co-construction interactions in the groups with high analytic mutuality may have been sufficient for the lower-level learners to establish a deeper memory trace.

However, not all of the learners in groups where analytic mutuality was the predominant pattern had sustained gains on the GJ test. The high-level participator from Group 1, Raquel, had almost no net change between the pre- and delayed post GJ test. This could be due to the fact that much of her analytic talk was not in relation to the target *se* structure, as evidenced in the exchange in Table 5 in which she asks her partner about rules for reflexivity and verb inflection. In addition, the very low participator from Group 2, Luis, regressed on the delayed posttest, suggesting that there is a minimum threshold for participation in order for lower-level learners to benefit from analytically mutual interactions.

Areas for further analysis

The analyses presented in this chapter are by no means exhaustive for in-group analytic talk, either for this study or in general. Additional variables, such as certain aspects of learners' personal histories could have affected in-group interactions due to the power dynamics associated with gender roles or socioeconomic and cultural differences (Young & Tedick 2016). Recent research in the area of learners' personal histories has thus underscored the potential role of the "baggage" or "backpack" that each learner brings to small-group interactions (Young & Astarita 2013), and these affective variables remain an area for future analysis for this data corpus.

Also excluded from this analysis are the whole-class discussions following the co-construction phases of each lesson. The decision to focus on the small-group interactions was due to two main factors. First, all students heard the same teacher-led, follow-up discussion and therefore had equal opportunity to benefit from it. Second, none of the students' participation behaviors differed substantially between the small-group and whole-class interactions. As reported in Toth, Wagner, and Moranski (2013), a statistically significant correlation was found between the amount of a learner's analytic talk in the small-group and whole-class settings, indicating that learners who were low-level participators during small-group co-construction were similarly low contributors to the whole-class follow-up. However, further qualitative analysis in the form of stimulated recall or follow-up interviews could have provided more information on potential effects of the follow-up discussions.

A final consideration for further analysis is that of the relationship between self-directed speech and subsequent L2 accuracy. Our analysis did not measure self-directed, private speech during or following the co-construction activity, which might have provided further insights into the in-group interactional patterns described in this study.

Pedagogical implications

The main pedagogical implications of this work relate to gains made by the lower-level participators and analyzers in this study. Specifically, the four lower-level learners improved in L2 accuracy in proportion with the amount of analytic mutuality displayed by their respective groups. This implies that when assigning learners to small groups, instructors should be mindful not only of the proficiency level of each learner but also of the group's social dynamic. Very advanced or independent learners may require encouragement to actively engage other members in group discussion. Conversely, lower-level or quieter learners may need more reassurance in order to better connect with peers. Instructors could use videos or sample conversations to model high levels of analytic mutuality to learners before they embark upon group work. Given that learners may be of diverse cultural backgrounds, it should not be assumed that highly mutual in-group interactional patterns will be standard or comfortable for all learners. Lastly, it should be emphasized that, for the lower-level learners in this study, analytic mutuality was more influential on L2 accuracy than correctness of their contributions. Thus, learners should be encouraged to contribute *while* they are arriving at a rule instead of waiting until *after* they have done so.

Summary

This study supported the notion of meta-analytic talk as a facilitator of developing L2 accuracy; a positive correlation was found between an individual's overall amount of L1 meta-analytic talk during a small-group co-construction task and his or her subsequent performance on a delayed posttest. There was no significant benefit found for greater amounts of individual or whole group analytic talk at the higher LAAs (indicating higher DOP), but the correlation data suggest that that could have been a function of several lower-level learners with grammatical misconceptions that were in groups with greater amounts of high-level analytic talk. A strong positive correlation was found between an individual's overall amount of meta-analytic talk and his or her talk at the higher LAAs, showing the learners that produced greater amounts of L1 meta-analytic talk tended to do so at the higher LAAs.

A qualitative review of the transcripts supported previous research that holds *mutuality* to be an integral component of successful group work for collaborative L2 tasks (Storch 2002), particularly for the lower-level learners in this study. Lower-level learners whose groups' predominant interactional pattern was *analytic mutuality* had sustained gains in L2 accuracy as measured by a delayed GJ posttest. Conversely, the lower-level learner whose group lacked mutuality but rather had a dominant interactional pattern of *analytic isolation* did not make similar gains. These results suggest that lower-level learners can benefit from the analytic talk of their group members, provided that there is a high degree of mutuality present in the interaction. Indeed, other studies in this volume such as Young and Tedick (2016), and Sato and Viveros (2016) support this conclusion as one that may have generalizability to a variety of instructional contexts.

References

Adair-Hauck, B., & Donato, R., (2010). Using a story-based approach to teach grammar. In J. L. Shrum & E. W. Glisan (Eds.), *Teacher's handbook: Contextualized foreign language instruction* (4th ed., pp. 216–244). Boston, MA: Heinle Cengage Learning.

American Council on the Teaching of Foreign Languages. (2012). *ACTFL proficiency guidelines.* Alexandria, VA: ACTFL.

Brooks, F. B., & Donato, R. (1994). Vygotskyan approaches to understanding foreign language discourse during communicative tasks. *Hispania*, 77(2), 262–274. doi:10.2307/344508

Brooks, F. B., Donato, R., & McGlone, J. V. (1997). When are they going to say "it" right? Understanding learner talk during pair-work activity. *Foreign Language Annals*, 30(4), 524–541. doi:10.1111/j.1944-9720.1997.tb00860.x

Brown, T. S., & Perry, F. L. (1991). A comparison of three learning strategies for ESL vocabulary acquisition. *TESOL Quarterly*, 25, 655–670. doi:10.2307/3587081

Borer, L. (2007). Depth of processing in private and social speech: Its role in the retention of word knowledge by adult EAP learners. *The Canadian Modern Language Review/La Revue Canadienne des Langues Vivantes*, 64(2), 273–300. doi:10.3138/cmlr.64.2.269

Craik, F. I., & Lockhart, R. S. (1972). Levels of processing: A framework for memory research. *Journal of Verbal Learning and Verbal Behavior*, 11, 671–684. doi:10.1016/S0022-5371(72)80001-X

Donato, R. (1994). Collective scaffolding in second language learning. In J. P. Lantolf & G. Appel (Eds.), *Vygotskian approaches to second language research* (pp. 33–56). Norwood, NJ: Ablex.

Ellis, R. (1999). Theoretical perspectives on interaction and language learning. In R. Ellis (Ed.), *Learning a second language through interaction* (pp. 3–31). Amsterdam: John Benjamins. doi:10.1075/sibil.17.04ell

Fassnacht, C., & Woods, D. K. (2009). *Transana (Version 2.42).* Madison, WI: Wisconsin Center for Education Research, School of Education, University of Wisconsin-Madison.

Joe, A. (1998). What effects do text-based task promoting generation have on incidental vocabulary acquisition? *Applied Linguistics*, 19(3), 357–377. doi:10.1093/applin/19.3.357

Juffs, A. (2001). Discussion: Verb classes, event structure, and second language learners' knowledge of semantics-syntax correspondences. *Studies in Second Language Acquisition*, 23(2), 305–314. doi:10.1017/S027226310100208X

Kowal, M., & Swain, M. (1994). Using collaborative language production tasks to promote students' awareness. *Language Awareness*, 3, 73–93. doi:10.1080/09658416.1994.9959845

Lantolf, J. P., & Thorne, S. L. (2006). *Sociocultural theory and the genesis of second language development*. Oxford: Oxford University Press.

Leow, R., Moreno, N., & Hsieh, H. (2014). *Awareness, type of medium, and L2 development*. Paper presented at *the annual Georgetown University Roundtable on linguistics*, Washington, DC, March.

Oded, B., & Walters, J. Deeper processing for better EFL reading comprehension. *System*, 29, 357–370. doi:10.1016/S0346-251X(01)00023-9

Ohta, A. S. (1995). Applying sociocultural theory to an analysis of learner discourse: Learner-learner collaborative interaction in the Zone of Proximal Development. *Issues in Applied Linguistics*, 6(2), 93–121.

Rouhshad, A., & Storch, N. (2016). A focus on mode: Patterns of interaction in face-to-face and computer-mediated contexts. In M. Sato & S. Ballinger (Eds.), *Peer interaction and second language learning: Pedagogical potential and research agenda* (pp. 267–289). Amsterdam: John Benjamins

Sato, M., & Ballinger, S. (2016). Understanding peer interaction: Research synthesis and directions. In M. Sato & S. Ballinger (Eds.), *Peer interaction and second language learning: Pedagogical potential and research agenda* (pp. 1–30). Amsterdam: John Benjamins.

Sato, M., & Viveros, P. (2016). Interaction or collaboration? The proficiency effect on group work in the foreign language classroom. In M. Sato & S. Ballinger (Eds.), *Peer interaction and second language learning: Pedagogical potential and research agenda* (pp. 91–112). Amsterdam: John Benjamins.

Schmidt, R. W. (1990). The role of consciousness in second language learning. *Applied Linguistics*, 11(2), 129–158. doi:10.1093/applin/11.2.129

Seedhouse, P. (2004). *The interactional architecture of the language classroom: A conversation analysis perspective*. Malden, MA: Blackwell.

Storch, N. (2002). Patterns of interaction in ESL pair work. *Language Learning*, 52(1), 119–158. doi:10.1111/1467-9922.00179

Swain, M., Lapkin, S., Knouzi, I., Suzuki, W., & Brooks, L. (2009). Languaging: University students learn the grammatical concept of voice in French. *Modern Language Journal*, 93(1), 5–29. doi:10.1111/j.1540-4781.2009.00825.x

Swain, M. (2010). 'Talking-it-through': Languaging as a source of learning. In R. Batstone (Ed.), *Sociocognitive perspectives on language use and language learning* (pp. 112–130). Oxford: Oxford University Press.

Swain, M., & Lapkin, S. (2000). Task-based second language learning: The uses of the first language. *Language Teaching Research*, 4(3), 251–274. doi:10.1177/136216880000400304

Toth, P. D. (2008). Teacher- and learner-led discourse in task-based grammar instruction: Providing procedural assistance for L2 morphosyntactic development. *Language Learning*, 58(2), 237–283. doi:10.1111/j.1467-9922.2008.00441.x

Toth, P. D., & Guijarro-Fuentes, P. (2013). The impact of instruction on second-language implicit knowledge: Evidence against encapsulation. *Applied Psycholinguistics*, 34(6), 1163–1193. doi: 10.1017/S0142716412000197

Toth, P. D., Wagner, E., & Moranski, K. (2013). 'Co-constructing' explicit L2 knowledge with high school Spanish learners through guided induction. *Applied Linguistics*, 34(3), 255–278. doi: 10.1093/applin/ams049

Vygotsky, L. S. (1981). The genesis of higher mental functions (J. V. Wertsch, Trans.). In J. V. Wertsch (Ed.), *The concept of activity in Soviet psychology* (pp. 144–188). Armonk, NY: M. E. Sharpe.

Vygotsky, L. S. (1987). Thinking and speech. In R. W. Reiber & A. S. Carton (Eds.), *The collected works of L. S. Vygotsky, Volume 1, Problems in general psychology* (pp. 39–288). New York, NY: Plenum Press.

Young, A., & Tedick, D. J. (2016). Collaborative dialogue in a two-way Spanish/English immersion classroom: Does heterogeneous grouping promote peer linguistic scaffolding? In M. Sato & S. Ballinger (Eds.), *Peer interaction and second language learning: Pedagogical potential and research agenda* (pp. 135–160). Amsterdam: John Benjamins

Young, R. F., & Astarita, A. C. (2013). Practice theory in language learning. *Language Learning*, 63(Supplement 1), 171–189. doi: 10.1111/j.1467-9922.2012.00743.x

Appendix

LA CRÍTICA DE COMIDA: Un cuento de dos restaurantes

SAN JOSÉ, COSTA RICA. En las guías turísticas, se dice que los dos restaurantes son más o menos iguales, y que se come muy bien en los dos lugares, pero no lo encontré así. Es verdad que los dos restaurantes ofrecen vistas excelentes de la ciudad. Están encima de montañas, y se llega en carro o autobús subiendo por un camino largo con muchas curvas. Desde los dos restaurantes, se ve todo el valle central y, cuando no está nublado, el Golfo de Nicoya. Pero mientras ofrecen comida muy buena en los dos lugares, el servicio no es igual.

El primer restaurante es muy elegante y tiene bailes tradicionales una vez por semana. Se sirve comida tradicional del país y platos internacionales. Durante los bailes, se come al estilo «buffet» y se dice que el precio es un poco menos de 15,000 colones. Visité este restaurante durante la noche del baile y buffet, y aunque me gustó mucho la comida, encontré problemas con la cuenta. Durante la cena, pedí una botella de vino chileno, y el mesero me dijo que costaba 3,000 colones. Pero cuando me trajo la cuenta al final, tuve que pagar 10,000 colones por el vino. El mesero insistió en que no hizo ningún error, y me dijo que no él podía cambiar la cuenta. Evidentemente, se debe llevar mucho más de 15,000 colones a este restaurante si se quiere vino.

El segundo restaurante sirve una variedad de platos europeos, pero se entiende que su especialización es la comida francesa. Se necesita hacer una reservación antes de llegar, pero el servicio es excelente. Cuando entré en la puerta, me sentaron inmediatamente en una mesa con una vista excelente y me ofrecieron una copa de vino. La comida estuvo deliciosa, y no me dieron problemas con la cuenta. Se dice que se necesitan 23,000 colones para cenar allí, pero sólo pagué 20,000 con el vino incluido. Se dice que los restaurantes son más o menos iguales, pero yo digo que si se quiere una buena cena sin complicaciones, se debe comer en el segundo.

Learning settings

CHAPTER 12

How adolescents use social discourse to open space for language learning during peer interactions

Melinda Martin-Beltrán, Pei-Jie Chen, Natalia Guzman
and Kayra Merrills
University of Maryland

This chapter investigates how adolescents learning English and Spanish mediated two-way language learning opportunities during their interactions in a language exchange program in one high school. Drawing upon sociocultural theory and interactional ethnography, we examined moment-to-moment discourse to identify language-related episodes (LREs) and discursive moves of *social inquiry, solidarity*, and *support*. Findings revealed how adolescent peers mediated each other's learning using relationship-building discourse. This chapter contributes to interactional research in SLA by revealing how students construct *comity* in their interactions with peers, and how their discourse may afford opportunities for co-construction of knowledge and second language learning. We consider the pedagogical implications of recognizing social discourse as a tool to expand language learning among peers.

Introduction

Although second language acquisition (SLA) research has documented the benefits of interaction for second language (L2) development (García Mayo 2005; Gass & Selinker 2008; Long 1996; Mackey 2012; Mackey & Goo 2007), many unanswered questions remain regarding the *nature* of interaction which shapes the learning-in-process (see Philp, Walter, & Basturkmen 2010; Storch 2008). Research has found that peer interaction may lead to language learning through negotiation of meaning, interactional adjustments, selective attention, comprehensible input, and opportunities for learners to produce language and test new output hypotheses (Gass 1985; Hatch 1992; Long 1996; Long & Porter 1985; Mackey, Gass, & McDonough 2000; Pica 1994; Swain 1985; Swain & Lapkin 1998). Language learning in peer interaction may vary due to learner characteristics, tasks, interactional

DOI 10.1075/lllt.45.13mar
© 2016 John Benjamins Publishing Company

patterns, learners' perceptions and learning settings (Ballinger & Lyster 2011; Sato 2013; see others in this volume). However, less research has given attention to social factors and learners' relationship with their sociocultural context (Block 2003; Firth & Wagner 2007; Swain & Deters 2007).

Recent research has begun to give attention to social factors that are central to peer interaction. In the introductory chapter of this book, Sato and Ballinger (2016) review studies that have found that comfort level between peers positively affects L2 learning, yet we need more research to reveal *how* this comfort level is established and relationships are built in interactions. This chapter highlights the importance of social relationships in peer interaction, which is also echoed throughout several chapters in this volume (see chapters by Baralt, Gurzynski-Weiss, & Kim; Bigelow & King; Choi & Iwashita; García Mayo & Azkarai; Moranski & Toth; Sato & Viveros; Rouhshad & Storch; Young & Tedick). Storch's research (2002a, 2002b; Rouhshad & Storch 2016) demonstrates how learning opportunities are influenced by patterns of peer interaction, which she defines in terms of *equality* (authority over task) and *mutuality* (level of engagement with each other's contribution). Building upon Storch's definition of collaborative inter-actional styles, Ballinger (2013) investigated collaboration patterns, and correc-tive feedback among immersion students and she found that corrective feedback was more effective when peers shared what she called a collaborative mindset. Ballinger's (2013: 144) qualitative analysis of language related episodes (LREs) and corrective feedback (CF) between partners showed that the "fine-tuned interactional moves that accompanied the provision and acceptance of CF", such as discourse of approval, confirmation, and appreciation of partners' input, are key to reciprocal learning in peer interaction. Sato and Ballinger's (2012) study also argued that effective peer feedback depends on the collaborative mindset learners share, which they described as mutual trust and respect for peers. Philp, Walter, and Basturkmen's (2010) study also revealed that peers' social relationships (e.g., face-saving), task related discourse and perceived proficiency (see Martin-Beltrán 2010) influenced the likelihood of peers to offer corrective feedback in their interactions. Our chapter builds upon this body of research that calls atten-tion to the importance of collaborative relationships among peers by investigating the discursive processes peers use to engage in relationship-building during their interactions.

Drawing upon Aston's (1993) work in socio-pragmatics, Dalton-Puffer (2005: 1291) focused on teacher-student interactions and argued that communication is "equally about creating community or 'comity.'" Aston (1993: 226) argued that, "much everyday speech use instead has as its primary goals the *negotiation of interpersonal relationships*" (emphasis added). Aston uses the term *comity* (Leech 1983) to refer to the establishment and maintenance of friendly relationships

(Aston 1993:226). The notion of *comity* has been largely neglected in peer inter-action research; yet examining this negotiation of interpersonal relationships in discourse has the potential to reveal important factors that impact language learn-ing opportunities.

Breen (2001) argues that "social relationships in the classroom orchestrate what is made available for learning, how learning is done, and what we achieve" (Breen 2001:131). Our research also responds to Naughton's (2006) study, which demonstrated the importance of creating an environment of collaboration to pro-mote language learning opportunities during peer interactions. We argue that our chapter can offer a more nuanced understanding of how teachers and students can create this environment. Learning languages involves "personal relationships that affect learners' engagement with opportunities to learn, including whether they engage at all" (Atkinson 2010:610). If such social relationships are paramount in language learning and especially relevant in peer interactions as a social activity, research is needed to understand *how* relationships are constructed in moment-to-moment talk and how this may afford or constrain language learning.

Research questions

The overarching purpose of our larger research project (in which the data from this chapter was situated) was to understand how language learning is mediated through peer interaction among English learners and Spanish learners (who we also call multilingual language-users; see Martin-Beltrán 2013). These adolescent learners were of "complementary language backgrounds" which Ballinger (2013) described as students who were "both learning language from and teaching lan-guage to a classmate" (Ballinger 2013:134). As we analyzed our data, social aspects of this mediation became salient as youth created a context for *languaging* (Swain 2006); thus, we sought to better understand the discursive construction of social relationships among adolescents during their interactions as they were composing bilingual text together.

For the purposes of this chapter, we focus on the following research questions:

1. How do adolescents use discourse in their interactions with peers (from com-plementary language backgrounds) to negotiate *comity* and language learning opportunities?
2. More specifically, how do peers use discursive moves of *solidarity*, *support* and *social inquiry*, and how do these discursive moves relate to opportunities to engage in languaging?

Conceptual and methodological framework

This study employs a sociocultural theoretical framework, which conceptualizes learning as a cultural-historical practice, mediated through social interaction and cultural tools such as language (Cole 1996; Engeström 1987; Moll 2010; Rogoff 1990; Vygotsky 1978). Vygotsky (1978:90) explained "an essential feature of learning is that it creates the zone of proximal development; that is, learning awakens a variety of internal development processes that are able to operate only when the child is interacting with people in this environment in cooperation with her peers." Through interaction with others, learners extend, dialogically co-construct and transform their knowledge (Vygotsky 1978; Wertsch 1985). When students talk together and jointly contribute to create an utterance or build an idea, sociocultural research in SLA has identified this as "co-construction" of knowledge (Foster & Ohta 2005).

Our conceptualization of student dialogue is also informed by research examining *languaging* or "the use of speaking and writing to mediate cognitively complex activities" (Swain & Deters 2007:821). Swain and Lapkin (2013:105) explained how learners use language to "focus attention, solve problems and create affect." Thus, we seek to understand how language learning occurs during an interaction, not simply as a result of it (Foster & Ohta 2005; Lantolf 2000; Swain 2006; Swain & Lapkin 1998; 2002; van Lier 2000). In this study, we conceptualize the language-related episode (LRE) (Foster & Ohta 2005; Mackey 2007; Swain & Lapkin 1998) as a unit of analysis to examine languaging (defined as mediation of language learning, questioning and hypothesizing about language use and co-construction of linguistic knowledge). We conceptualize the LRE as both product and process. As a product, an LRE is an identifiable group of utterances, such as questions about language, feedback or hypotheses about language, which can become an object for analysis. "Through languaging – a crucial mediating psychological and cultural activity – learners articulate and transform their thinking into an artifactual form, and in doing so, make it available as a source of further reflection" (Swain & Deters 2007:822). We also conceptualize LREs as evidence of languaging or "thinking in progress" (Swain 2006:89). Examining languaging in this peer interactional context will help us to better understand how learners can create further language learning affordances (van Lier 2000).

Although sociocultural theory attends to the mediation of learning, scholars working with this framework have rarely disentangled how socio-emotional relationships between participants affect learning opportunities. As we analyzed our data, relationship-building and socio-emotional aspects of the adolescents' interactions became salient; thus we sought to better understand the discursive construction of adolescent social relationships and how they were linked to language learning. In order to examine this discursive construction in context, we draw upon interactional ethnography as a methodological framework (Castanheira, Crawford, Dixon, & Green 2001; Castanheira, Green, Dixon, & Yeagerb 2007) to analyze discourse and contexts as socially and locally constructed by participants and "intersubjectively ratified" (Titscher, Meyer, Wodak, & Vetter 2000: 106). We also draw upon the work of Aston (1993) and Goffman (1971) by applying their notion of *comity*, which conceptualizes communication as more than the exchange of information but also negotiation of interpersonal relationships. Specifically, our study builds upon Aston's (1993) concepts of *comity, solidarity* and *support*. We explain our operational definition of these concepts in the data analysis section below.

Methods

Context

This study examines an alternative program in Southwoods High[1] school in which linguistically diverse students, who would otherwise be in separate language classes, were brought together to learn languages from each other. The Language Ambassadors (LA) program, which is the focus of our research over three years, brought together students of complementary language backgrounds (English learners and Spanish learners) to participate in collaborative literacy activities culminating in a final co-constructed multimodal literacy project.

During the first year of this research project, the LA program occurred over fifteen weekly sessions during a 45-minute lunch period and four monthly two-hour sessions after school. Within an institutional context (a public high school in the U.S.) that privileges a standard variety of English, the LA program aspired to create a Third Space (Gutiérrez 2008; Moje, Ciechanowski, Kramer, Ellis, Carrillo & Collazo 2004) in which students' wider linguistic repertoires became tools for participating and meaning-making in multilingual literacy activities. The LA program occupied "extra spaces" (Kirkland 2009) for language learning beyond the boundaries of the state-sanctioned English Language Arts or World Languages curriculum. Within this extra space, our research team[2] acted as participant-observers and auxiliary teachers. Our roles as teachers/researchers inevitably

1. We use pseudonyms throughout.

2. Our research team included the author and graduate students Kayra Alvarado Merrills, Pei-Jie Chen, Eliza Hughes, and Alexandra Ralph who brought their experience as bilingual, ESOL and world language teachers.

shaped the interpretation of our data as we formed close relationships with the students. Our research team (which included a Spanish teacher from the high school who became a doctoral student research assistant) initiated the project in collaboration with Spanish and ESOL teachers in the high school. Our team led the final design and implementation of lessons and activities. Depending on availability, one to four adults were with the students guiding and facilitating student participation and collaboration.

Language ambassador program design

At each session, students participated in a community building activity (to guide collaborative learning) and a literacy activity (involving writing, reading, listening, speaking, and the use of technology in dyads or small groups). The sessions usually began with a "write, pair, share" activity, in which students were asked to respond to questions in writing and then to share with a partner orally and to offer feedback on language form and function. These pair-share questions were related to their culminating project, which was to create a bilingual (Spanish/English) multimodal presentation that described their high school to new students. The students created narrated power points using photos, text, music and video, which they presented to their classmates in the final session.

Each student was told to speak and write in their target language[3], but they were allowed to draw upon all of their linguistic resources as they consulted with their peers. Students worked simultaneously in Spanish and English in the same shared space and were grouped with peers from "complementary language backgrounds" (Ballinger 2013: 134) who brought distinct linguistic expertise The most common grouping in the LA program was an "English-expert[4]" student paired with a "Spanish-expert" student. Another common grouping included a

---

3.   Students taking ESOL courses wrote in English. Students taking Spanish courses (and not enrolled in ESOL courses) wrote in Spanish (this included bilingual students). They were allowed to use either language during the composition process.

4.   English experts were English-dominant speakers who were enrolled in levels 2–4 (of 5) of high school Spanish. This group included 4 African American, 6 White and 2 students of mixed race/ethnicity. Spanish experts were from Central and South American countries and had been in the U.S. for less than 5 years and who were enrolled in levels 1–3 (of 5) of ESOL. Bilingual students grew up bilingually in families that predominately used a language other than English. These students had exited ESOL services in elementary school. The age range of the participating students was 14–17. Attendance ranged from 10–24 students at each session, with an average of 16 students present per session.

"bilingual-expert," "an English-expert" and a "Spanish-expert." Student grouping configurations varied throughout the semester since student attendance to the program fluctuated during the year. Teachers acted as facilitators to offer guidelines for peer interactions and created a context where feedback was necessary and constructive. Teachers established the following guidelines for peer interaction in the LA program: (1) ask peers questions about ideas and language; (2) share expertise (offer help and feedback); (3) play language detective (notice differences and similarities across languages or use meta-talk to discuss language form and function). During the peer-led interactions, teachers/researchers roved around the room to observe different groups and offered help with questions the students could not solve on their own. The teachers often re-directed questions to their peers and encouraged students to offer feedback as well as to ask more questions. At the end of each session, the students completed self-evaluation rubrics to reflect on their collaboration.

The dataset analyzed for this chapter is from the first year of the study when we recruited 24 students from ESOL and Spanish language classes: twelve "English experts", four "bilingual experts," and eight "Spanish experts." In the findings section, we provide background about each student highlighted in the excerpts. Data collection included more than 2000 minutes of audio recordings, which were the primary data analysis source. Other supporting data sources include observational field notes, students' handwritten work and power point presentations, pre- and post-surveys, and interviews with eight focal students and their teachers.

Data analysis

We analyzed discourse in multiple phases and data analysis was a recursive process influenced by interactional ethnography (Castanheira et al. 2007). Interactional ethnography begins with ethnographic questions to explore what participants are doing and how they make sense of their context. In our initial stage of analysis, we listened to audio interactions accompanied by transcripts and field notes, and we created event maps (Castanheira et al. 2001) of the activities occurring in each session to reveal patterns across the data. At this initial stage, we were guided by our broad research question "how is language learning mediated through peer interaction among English learners and Spanish learners in the LA program?" We used event maps to map out student interactions across 12 sessions in broad strokes, and we dedicated one column to delineate theoretical/analytical notes (guided by Cosaro 1981) and initial coding of LREs.

We identified language-related episodes (LREs) as utterances in which participants were engaged in talking about the language they were producing, including
questioning and correcting language, as well as requesting feedback about language usage (Foster & Ohta 2005; Mackey 2007; Swain & Lapkin 1998). An LRE
could be one or many turns of speech related to one question or comment about
language and included all turns of speech until the question/problem was resolved
or dropped. We identified 539 LREs in our data set and categorized these LREs to
understand the kinds of language questions students discussed. In this study, we
do not focus on the types of language questions (or LRE typology) posed by participants, rather we foreground the context and specifically the social discursive
tools that triggered LREs. In this second stage of coding, social discourse became
salient. We refined the questions guiding our analysis to examine the following:
How do students use social discourse moves in their interactions? What kinds of
social discourse do they use? What does this look like and when does this occur in
their interactions? How do peers' social discourse moves relate to opportunities to
engage in LREs/languaging? We analyzed what we called social discourse moves
to highlight the ways that students use language as a social tool to negotiate interpersonal relationships. We explain our framework for identifying and analyzing
these different kinds of discursive moves below.

Developing an analytical framework for social discourse

We developed a coding framework to capture the different social discursive moves
that commonly occurred throughout the interactions, which appeared to facilitate or co-occur with LREs. First, we found students frequently engaged in what
we term *social inquiry* discursive moves when they asked their peers about their
academic and social identities – seeking to situate their interlocutors in a larger
social context in order to gauge their language use. For example, students often
asked questions (unprompted by the assignment) to find out more about their
peers' family heritage or cultural experiences to determine shared speech styles or
translanguaging practices (Canagarajah 2011; García 2009). Students also inquired
to compare academic standing and to discover common experiences they shared
as high school students with similar concerns and common interests.

   Our analysis of student discourse also revealed evidence of negotiating for *support* (Aston 1998, 1993; Goffman 1971), which has been defined as "sympathizing,
feeling for the other, or showing appreciation" (Aston 1993: 231; see also Goffman
1971). We adapted and expanded this definition to include utterances when students encouraged their peers to talk, opened a new space for peers to participate,

co-constructed utterances, and when they recognized each other's expertise. We also included utterances that were examples of co-constructing language (Foster & Ohta 2005) when students finished their partners' sentence and/or repaired syntax and word choice to rephrase and then allowed their partners to continue.

We also found that the students frequently used discursive moves to negotiate for *solidarity* (Aston 1993). We expanded Aston's definition of *solidarity* "sharing attitudes toward features of common experience" (Aston 1993:237) to also include utterances in which students acknowledged shared experiences and struggles. Although discursive moves of *solidarity* were similar to discursive moves of *support,* negotiation for *solidarity* was distinct in the way that students foregrounded shared experiences. We found students' used solidarity discourse moves to recognize their common experiences as members of the school community, as members of families, as children of immigrants and as language learners who made mistakes. In addition, we coded as solidarity cases in which participants sought to "even out" differences together (e.g., participant A acknowledges that participant B is older, participant B reacts by answering that A is taller).

Finally, we coded the data for contrasting cases or interactions where students used discourse that was the opposite of *solidarity* and *support*. We coded these moments in discourse as "impatience, lack of support, and ridicule," a category that captures social discourse moves in which a student expressed a lack of awareness of partner's contribution, including derision or disrespect for peer's linguistic resources. Our definition of this code draws upon Sato and Ballinger's (2012:169) study when they discussed how students used "an emphatically derisive or argumentative tone of voice."

In Table 1 below we offer more examples and operational definitions of our codes. For coding purposes, we considered the beginning of a social discourse episode to be when a speaker: (a) asked a question about a partner's academic and social identity, (b) affirmed or recognized common feelings/experiences, or (c) appreciated or encouraged the partner's contribution. We marked the end of this episode as being when the participants moved on to the next topic. We coded data using Dedoose[5], a mixed-method research software, which allowed our research team to code collaboratively. We selected samples of the data to code together in order to reach consensus about the definitions of codes, and we flagged unclear codes to discuss at weekly research meetings to ensure reliability.

---

5.   See: www.dedoose.com

Table 1. Coding social discourse

Code	Definition	Examples of episodes
Social inquiry	Questions about interlocutors' experiences and identities to situate peer in institutional (school) and social context (beyond school)	S1:* So, um, what grade are you in? Like grade… are you a senior? S2: I' m…9th? S1: How old are you?
	Asking about age, graduating class, family, ethnicity, heritage, membership or affinity with academic or extra-curricular activities or favorite past times often to seek common experiences	S3: Where are you from? S4: My mom, she's from West Africa and my dad is from Illinois. Where are you from? S3: I'm from El Salvador S4: Oh, okay, I always wanted to go there
Solidarity	Utterances that confirm or recognize shared or common experiences or feelings	S1: I was born here, but my mom is from El Salvador S2: Me too, I mean my mom is from another country
	Recognizing shared experiences and shared identities (e.g., as children of immigrants, members of same graduating class, shared affinity with academic or favorite pastimes)	S3: That class is so hard S4: Yeah I know I'm with you on that
	Affirming peers' perceptions of their experiences	S5: When I came to [high school], I was the little… I was the lost puppy…I was like… S6: You were like me. S5: I didn't talk to anybody S6: same
	Acknowledging common struggles as language learners who make mistakes	S5: When I came here, I didn't know English… my English was so bad S6: Your English is better than my Spanish, I make more mistakes than you
	Seeking to "even out" differences together	S7: Wow, you're older than me. ((laughter)) S8: yes, for 3 months I guess. ((laughter)) S7: That's not fair((laughter)) S8: ((laughter)) But you're taller. S7: Yeah, I had a growth spurt. S8: That's good.((laughter)) S7: Yeah((laughter))

Code	Definition	Examples of episodes
Support	Showing encouragement or positive feedback	S1: Good try! S2: Thanks for your help
	Recognition of linguistic or academic expertise	S1: You can do it, yeah you can do it. S2: I cannot do it in Spanish. S3: Yes, you can do it
	Encouragement for partner to continue speaking	S4: I want you to ask me in Spanish. I want to hear you.
	Allowing partners to continue or have a turn speaking	S5: *Yo viajo…viajo*, right? *viajo?* S6: *Viajé… viajaste? Viajé* S5: Yeah, I went to France … *Yo via…*
	Helping a peer finish his/her sentence by offering word choices, repairing syntax or recasting	*jaste*, er, yeah right?
Impatience, lack of support, ridicule	Not allowing partner to talk	S1: *Qué más?* S2: What?
	Making fun of partner speaking L2	S1: What else? S2: Don't go Spanish on me.
	Expressing a lack of awareness of partner's contribution	S1: I'm asking a question. S3: She just said, "*Qué más?*"((laughter))
	Disrespecting peer's linguistic resources	S4: '*Como es [high school name]?*' S5: '*[high school name] es muy divertido y tenemos…* S4: ((laughter making fun of S5's prounciation)) S5: Stop making fun of me((laughter)) S6: Stop…no, don't S5: Oh my goodness.

* *Note.* S1 = student 1, S2 = student 2 in a dyad. Double space indicates a new episode between other students.

Findings

Findings revealed how adolescent peers of complementary language backgrounds mediated their interactions, using social tools, or relationship-building discourse. Students' interactions provided many opportunities to engage in language exchange by asking questions about language, generating and appropriating new vocabulary, evaluating word choice and using cross-linguistic comparisons for meta-linguistic analysis. However, the opportunity for students to get to know each other as social individuals was often more important than the task at hand. We found great variability in terms of frequency of LREs and willingness to elaborate language across student pairs depending on their degree of social cohesiveness, which developed through their discourse. In our coding of transcripts, we found a positive relationship between the frequency of social discourse moves and the frequency of LREs. Students were more likely to participate in LREs if they also participated in social discourse moves.

Figure 1 is based on our dataset of 33 transcriptions across 12 sessions, and each data point in the plot represents a transcription of one pair's interaction. For clarity of this quantitative analysis, we collapsed all of the discourse moves coded as *social inquiry*, *solidarity*, and *support* into one category. Across the 33 transcripts analyzed, we coded 539 LREs, 185 episodes of *social inquiry*, 93 episodes of *solidarity* and 440 episodes of *support* (or a total of 718 social discourse moves). As Figure 1 shows, the interactions with more social discourse moves also included more LREs (R squared value of 0.321 indicates a positive relationship). Additionally, we identified 39 episodes of "impatience/lack of support/ridicule". In transcripts with several instances of ridicule moves (more than 10), we found the number of LREs was also significantly lower (less than 5).

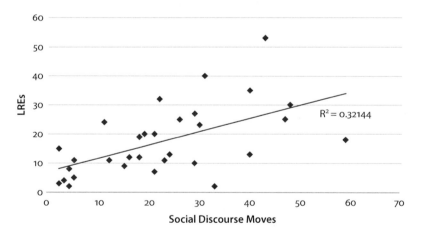

Figure 1. LRE and social discourse co-occurrence in transcribed interactions

Looking at the coding patterns across our event maps, we found LREs were interwoven with discursive moves of *social inquiry, solidarity* and *support*. We found students' *social inquiries* were a way to open conversation and consequently ask questions about language. As students used their L2 to find out more information about their partners, they often paused to ask a question about language form or lexical appropriateness. Since the learning activities invited the students to reflect on common experiences at school (e.g., "What do you remember about your first day or first weeks at school?"), this precipitated further *social inquiry* initiated by the students and was consequently followed by additional discursive moves of *support* and *solidarity*. In most cases LREs were followed by discursive moves of *support*. Discursive moves of *support* were common among the students as a way to encourage participation and use of the target language. These instances of *support* opened the floor for more LREs since students were encouraged to seek further help from students who were recognized as experts to continue with the activity in the L2. Across the transcriptions, we found discursive moves of *solidarity* were connected to common affiliations or loyalties. The students also used discursive moves of *solidarity* and *support* to strengthen social networks or invite peers to be part of the school community. We argue that these social discourse moves created a more collaborative environment (Naughton 2006) or collaborative mindset (Sato & Ballinger 2012), which has been shown to facilitate more effective peer feedback.

For this chapter, we selected excerpts from transcripts that illustrate how students use *social inquiry, solidarity*, and *support* in their discourse and how this is connected with opportunities to engage in languaging, or thinking about language together. The excerpts below came from two different sessions and are representative of the kinds of interactions we observed throughout the sessions.

Social inquiry builds solidarity and affords opportunities to understand how to use the target language

Excerpts 1, 2, and 3 below are from a session (recorded on 02/25/2011) in which students were given a "think/write, pair, share" activity guided by the following discussion question: "What do new students (coming from middle school or arriving from other countries) need to know about [Southwoods] High School?" Students responded to discussion questions first in writing (in their target language) and then they shared their responses orally with partners and asked each other for help improving their writing in the target language.

In this recorded interaction, three girls were working together: (1) Natalí, a bilingual expert; (2) Karen, an English expert; and (3) Cecilia, a Spanish expert. Natalí used mostly Portuguese at home, but claimed to be English dominant since she had emigrated from Brazil five years prior and was no longer designated to receive ESOL services. Natalí drew upon her literacy and communication skills in Portuguese to learn Spanish in class, and she reported using Spanish fluently (relying upon Portuguese cognates) with her Spanish-dominant/bilingual friends. Karen, U.S. born and English dominant, had completed Spanish level 2. Cecilia had emigrated from Mexico three years ago and was enrolled in ESOL level 3. Although all three students had different learning needs, their interaction afforded opportunities to simultaneously learn and use their target languages.

At the beginning of this session, the girls wrote their answers and began to read their writing out loud to themselves. Before they started with the questions in the assignment, Natalí began by using *social inquiry* when she asked Cecilia about her arrival to the U.S. Natalí followed her question by briefly sharing her own immigration story, which created *solidarity* among the girls from the beginning of their conversation[6]. This *social inquiry* afforded opportunities for languaging when Cecilia asked for clarification about Natalí's use of the verb "*venir*" and reformulated this verb in her response (e.g., "Natalí: –*Cuando venistes[sic] a los Estados Unidos?* [When did you come to the U.S.?], Cecilia: –*Cuando vine?* [When did I come?]"). Throughout this interaction, we observed multiple opportunities for noticing language and offering feedback, and we observed that these opportunities were interwoven with relationship-building.

Excerpt 1. *"OK, let's talk"* (from Transcript 02/25/11)

Time on audio	Transcript line	Original utterance	English gloss (as needed)
04:30	33	Natalí: Ok, we got to talk	
	34	Karen: Ok, let's talk	
	35	Natalí: just have a conversation in Spanish	
	36	Natalí: *Te gustas* [sic] *Southwoods?*	*Do you like Southwoods?*
	37	Cecilia: *Sí*	*Yes*
	38	Natalí: *Que ano* [sic] *estas aquí....* ((Cecilia looks confused because does not pronounce ñ)) *um.... que clase eres?* Like what grade are you? How do you say that in Spanish?	*What year [sic] are you here...* *um... what class are you?*
05:00	39	Cecilia: *En qué grado estás?*	*What grade are you?*
	40	Natalí: *En qué grado?* ok	*What grade?*
	41	Cecilia: *once*	*eleven*
	42	Natalí: *once?*	*eleven?*
	43	Cecilia: *Sí y tú?*	*yes, and you?*
	44	Natalí: You're in the same grade as her ((pointing to Karen))	
	45	Cecilia: *En qué grado estas?* ((looking at Karen))	*What grade are you?*
	46	Natalí: *Once*	*eleven*
	47	Karen: *once*	*eleven*
	48	Natalí: *yo soy* [sic] *doce*	*I'm [sic] twelve*
	49	Cecilia: *Doce?*	*twelve?*
	50	Natalí: *Si. Ultimo año. Yay!*	*Yes. Last year. Yay!*
	51	Cecilia: Which grade are you in?	

---

6. This occurred 3 minutes into the transcription, but was not included in the excerpts here due to space limitations.

At the beginning of Excerpt 1, Natalí expressed her desire to "just have a conversation in Spanish" (line 33–35), signaling her interest in practicing Spanish while getting to know each other. Natalí used her target language (Spanish) to initiate *social inquiry* to find out her partners' grade level and to determine their shared experiences. Her questions about social identity opened space for questions about language – as her question about grade level flowed into "how do you say that in Spanish?" This opened up a new opportunity for Natalí and Karen to hear Cecilia model Spanish syntax and offer new lexicon during the conversation. Although Natalí made errors (using *soy* instead of *estoy*), Cecilia followed up with clarification questions in her target language (English), which also afforded Natalí another opportunity to re-use the word *año* that she had mispronounced earlier.

Excerpt 2. *"Whoo progress!"* (from Transcript 02/25/11)

Time on audio	Transcript line	Original utterance	English gloss (as needed)
07:00	70	Cecilia: *no tengas miedo de ser tu mismo* (Reading what Karen has written on paper, "don't be afraid to be yourself")	*don't be afraid of being yourself*
	71	Karen: Hmm?	
	72	Natali: *No tengas::*	*don't be (or don't have)*
07:30	73	Cecilia: *::No tengas*	*don't be*
	74	Natalí: *medo* ((with Portuguese pronunciation))	*afraid (fear)*
	75	Karen: um, what?	
	76	Natalí: *medo*	*afraid*
	77	Cecilia: *mie̱do*	*afraid*
	78	Natalí: Oh yeah *miedo*, *medo* is in Portuguese, *medo*	*afraid, afraid is in Portuguese, afraid*
	79	Karen, Cecilia, Natalí: ((laughter))	
	80	Cecilia: *Miedo de ser*	*afraid of being*
	81	Karen: mmhmm?	
	82	Cecilia: *De ser… tu mismo*	*of being … yourself*
	83	Karen: hmm?	
	84	Cecilia: *Tu, t-u*, yeah	*your, y-o-u-r*
	85	Natalí: *mismo*	*self*
	86	Cecilia: *mismo*	*self*
	87	Natalí: whoo ((exhale)) progress! ((smiling & celebrating Karen's complete written sentence in Spanish))	
08:00	88	Karen: I know, right?((laughter))	

Discursive support creates safe space to ask questions and take risks using language

In Excerpt 2, Natalí and Cecilia built off of each other's utterances as they helped Karen to co-construct her writing in Spanish. Karen had the following phrase written on her paper in English, "Don't be afraid to be yourself." Cecilia offered her a quick translation (line 70), which Karen did not understand. Recognizing her confusion, Natalí acted as a mediator and scaffolded Cecilia's translation by breaking it down into smaller phrases thereby making it more comprehensible. Even as Natalí was teaching Karen, Cecilia was teaching Natalí when she corrected her use of *medo* vs. *miedo* [to be afraid]. As a multilingual, Natalí used multiple languages as tools for analysis (English was used to express her metalinguistic awareness of the differences between Spanish and Portuguese). Cecilia and Natalí echoed each other's utterances as they co-constructed the sentence. The students showed metalinguistic and metacognitive awareness with a discursive move of *support*. For example, line 87–88 shows that Natalí celebrated her peer's "progress" and recognized the hard work they all went through together to accomplish the writing of this sentence in Spanish.

Excerpt 3. *"It's really hard to learn another language"* (from Transcript 02/25/11)

Time on audio	Transcript line	Original utterance	English gloss (as needed)
	119	Cecilia: Do you understand songs in Spanish?	
	120	Natalí: I understand more than I speak. *Yo compriendo [sic] me*, how do you say I… more? ((laughter))	*I understand mo(re)*
	121	Cecilia: ((laughter))*Entiendo más de lo que hablo*	*I understand more than what I speak.*
12:00	122	Natalí: *Yo hablo Portugués…Yo hablo portugués, español, inglés y francés*	*I speak Portuguese… I speak Portuguese, Spanish, English, and French*
	123	Cecilia: You speak French, really? I'm learning French	
	124	Natalí: French is easy. I speak Portuguese, so it's easy	
	125	Cecilia: cause you speak Portuguese, so it's easy French for you, "*pero*" not for me… Portuguese is your first language right?	*"but"*
	126	Natalí: mmhmm, English second, Spanish third, French fourth	

Time on audio	Transcript line	Original utterance	English gloss (as needed)
12:30	127	Karen: For me? English first, Spanish second((laughter))	
	128	Natalí: That's the bad thing about speaking English. That's the bad thing about English. It's really hard to learn another language after.	
	129	Karen: But then you learn another language, say you speak another language then every other language is easier xxx…	
	130	Natalí: But English is really hard.	
13:00	131	Natalí: I think it's because like the way we speak, like our, Spanish or Portuguese we don't xx…	
	132	Cecilia: How about schedules ((referring back to assignment))	
	133	Natalí: I think they would know schedule, I would think ((referring to the word, "schedule"))	
	134	Cecilia: I didn't, I don't know the word in Spanish((laughter))	
	135	Mr. Laurent: *Hor…*	*Sche(dule)…*
	136	Cecilia: *Horarios*, oh yeah((laughter))	*Schedules*
	137	Natalí: I think they would know schedule at least. That's like one word I knew when I got here. That was my first word, was you know 'schedule'? Yeah, here's the schedule, 500 classes,	
	138	Karen: My first word was xx [inaudible] in Spanish	
	139	Cecilia: My first word in English was xxxx [inaudible]	

In Excerpt 3, Cecilia initiated another discursive move of *social inquiry* when she asked Natalí if she understood songs in Spanish. Natalí responded first in English then took a risk by responding in her target language, Spanish, which allowed her to recognize her own language gap and to ask another language related question. Cecilia offered a fluent Spanish model and also used her target language, English, when using another discursive move of *social inquiry* to ask about which languages her partners speak (lines 119–127).

As they realized they both shared the common experience of being multilingual language users (Martin-Beltrán 2013), they used translanguaging practices

(Canagarajah 2011; García 2009), shuttling back and forth fluidly between Spanish and English even within one speech turn. As the students considered the meaning of "schedule", they drew upon both languages and realized that this was a tricky concept in either language because of the situated meaning of this word specific to a school context. They also showed evidence of languaging (Swain 2006) as they externalized their thinking about their language use and the learning of languages and generated *solidarity* as they shared their "first words" in a second language (lines 137–139). Finally, the students finished their activity with a discussion in which they shared their different language expertise and discussed how difficult learning a language can be, expressing *support* for Cecilia, who was still learning English. This discursive negotiation of *support* and *solidarity* opened a safe space for interactions with peers and new possibilities to engage in metalinguistic conversations.

Discursive support leads to solidarity and further questions about language

Excerpts 4 and 5 below come from a different session (recorded 03/08/2011), in which students were asked to do a "think/write, pair, share" activity responding to the following question, "What do you remember about your first day or first weeks at [Southwoods]?" After the students wrote responses on their own paper individually, the students were supposed to ask their partners this question in their target language. Mary, an English expert, was U.S. born and English dominant and was studying Spanish (level 3 of 5) when she joined the LA program. Patricia, a Spanish expert, had emigrated from El Salvador four months prior and was enrolled in ESOL (level 2 of 5). These girls were highly engaged in their conversations as they had fun engaging in social inquiry.

Excerpt 4. *"You did a good try"* (from Transcript 03/08/11)

Time on audio	Transcript line	Original utterance	English gloss (as needed)
01:00	3	Patricia: I want you to ask me in Spanish. I want to hear you.	
	4	Mary: Ok((laughter)) Ok, um, alright. *Qué es lo que visite [sic] o oiste?*	*What did you see [sic] or hear?*
	5	Patricia: *Um, vi a varia, varias jóvenes, asi que al principio me daba miedo porque son gigantes, asi. Y pensé, que no sé…. no estaban buenos…((laughter))*	*I saw several young people, so at the beginning I was scared because they are giants, so. And I thought that I don't know… they weren't good.*

Time on audio	Transcript line	Original utterance	English gloss (as needed)
	6	Mary: ((laughter))ok, so you said… what again?	
	7	Patricia: *Vi a varios jóvenes* and *maestros.*	*I saw many young people and teachers.*
	8	Mary: *Jóvenes?*	*young people?*
	9	Patricia: Yeah, it means young people.	
	10	Mary: There's a lot of young people here?	
	11	Patricia: yeah	
	12	Mary: Okay.	
01:43	13	Mary: How do you say noticed?	
	14	Patricia: mmm, I don't know…	
	15	Mary: ((laughter))	
	16	Patricia: I don't know, the xxx?	
02:00	17	Patricia: How did you feel?	
	18	Mary: um…I was happy.	
02:30	19	Mary: um… *Cómo te sentiste?*	*How did you feel?*
	20	Patricia: *Al principio, sentí un poco incómoda pero ya después me acostumbré*	*At the beginning I felt a little uncomfortable but later I got used*
	21	Mary: Ok, your turn.	
	22	Patricia: With whom did you speak?	
	23	Mary: Like with whom? My friend?	
	24	Patricia: yeah	
	25	Mary: Ok, yeah, my friends I guess.	
03:00	26	Mary: *Con quién hablaste?*	*Who did you talk to?*
	27	Patricia: Um, *primero con el* "counselor." *No sé como se dice en español, consejera?* I guess.	
	28	Mary: Uh yeah, I think so.	
	29	Patricia: *Primero con el consejera y después con unas niñas y entonces hicieron mis amigas .*	*First with the counselor and later with some girls and then they became my friends.*
	30	Mary: I don't know how to spell counselor((laughter))…counsa…	
	31	Patricia: *Jera*	*(coun) selor*
03:30	32	Mary: *Jera?*	*(coun) selor?*
	33	Patricia: *jera… "jota"*	*(coun) selor… jay ((letter used in the Spanish word))*
	34	Mary: How do you write it? [Patricia writes it out on Mary's paper] Oh.	

(continued)

Excerpt 4. (*continued*)

Time on audio	Transcript line	Original utterance	English gloss (as needed)
	35	Patricia: You did a good try.	
	36	Mary: I was a failure, horrible.	
	37	Mary: So, um, what grade are you in? Like grade… are you a senior?	
04:00	38	Patricia: I'm…9th?	
	39	Mary: How old are you?	
	40	Patricia: 14	
	41	Mary: Same((laughter)) same age, yeah.	
	42	Patricia: Are you in 9th too?	
	43	Mary: yeah	
	44	Patricia: oh	
	45	Patricia: What class do you have after this?	
	46	Mary: I have um…geometry after, math. It's horrible. ((laughter))	
	47	Patricia: ((laughter)) Yeah ((laughter)) Where are you from?	
04:30	48	Mary: My mom, she's from West Africa and my dad is from Illinois. Where are you from?	
	49	Patricia: I'm from El Salvador.	
	50	Mary: Oh, okay, I always wanted to go there.	
	51	Patricia: Really?	
	52	Mary: Yeah, yeah like my friends would bring me things like from El Salvador and it was really cool.	

After reading the discussion prompt, Patricia responded in her target language, and encouraged Mary to produce her target language. She used a discursive move of *support* when she offered her partner a turn and said, "I want you to ask me in Spanish. I want to hear you". When Mary asked the question in Spanish, Patricia showed she understood Mary's attempt to use Spanish by responding in fluent Spanish. In this interaction, she introduced new vocabulary (*jóvenes*) and modeled usage of the imperfect and preterit tenses (which had caused confusion in an earlier session). They co-constructed their answers as Mary asked for clarification and rephrased Patricia's comment in English to check for understanding (line 10). Throughout the interactions, the students playfully took turns talking, which was signaled by discourse moves of *support* such as "OK your turn!" offering each other space to practice the target language.

In line 27, Patricia also demonstrated *solidarity* with Mary when she admitted her own uncertainty about how to translate the English word "counselor", which they both used in this context. When Patricia explained that she did not know the word for "counselor" in her expert language, she called attention to language and this opened space for Mary to also use a similar phrase "*no sé cómo se dice*" [I don't know how to say it] later in their interaction. Although Mary had not used the word "*consejera*" before this interaction, she agreed with Patricia's translation, which she understood from the context. Patricia's translanguaging practices offered a language bridge (using both languages "counselor" and "*consejera*" in context) and the insertion of an English word acted as an anchor to allow Mary to understand the longer phrase in Spanish.

In line 30, as Mary was recording Patricia's response, she recognized that she did not know how to spell this new word offered by her partner. Mary used English at first (avoiding Spanish) and then tried to say it in Spanish (laughing and hedging). Patricia helped Mary to pronounce the word and to recognize the form of the word by writing it on the paper as a mediational tool. In line 35, Patricia uses *support* or reassurance to Mary when she said "you did a good try," but Mary humbly admitted her struggles with the language. The girls established solidarity by admitting their own flaws and by referring to common struggles and challenges in high school. For example, later in their interaction, Mary mentioned her horrible experience in math, and both girls complained about teachers until finally Patricia declared, "I'm with you on that," followed by shared laughter. Not only did these discursive moves lighten the tone of their interaction, but they also created a context of trust in which further LREs and collaboration could occur. In fact, in the interaction following this excerpt, we found the students engaged in ten more LREs.

In line 37, Mary engaged in *social inquiry* and positioned her partner as an "upperclassman" when she asked if Patricia was a senior (considered a high compliment among adolescents). Mary laughed when she found out that they were both the same age and in the same grade. Patricia asked where Mary was from, and instead of simply stating that she was born in the United States, Mary shared her family's immigration heritage to show her *solidarity* with Patricia, who had recently immigrated to the United States. When Patricia shared that she was from El Salvador, Mary commented that she always wanted to go there. Mary used a discursive move of *support* when she showed appreciation for Patricia's home country and affinity with Patricia when she explained that she had friends who also had Salvadoran connections by adding "it was really cool."

Excerpt 5. *"Do you want to talk in Spanish?"* (from Transcript 03/08/11)

Time on audio	Transcript line	Original utterance	English gloss (as needed)
	104	Patricia: So do you want to talk in Spanish?	
	105	Mary: uh, I will do my best ((laughter)).	
	106	Patricia: Ok, um.. *Tu has ido de viaje a otro pais?*	*You have traveled to another country?*
	107	Mary: *Si, yo viajo…viajo, "right"? viajo?*	*Yes, I travel, travel, right?, travel?*
	108	Patricia: *Viajé… viajaste? Viajé*	*traveled (1st person) … traveled? (2nd person) traveled (1st person)*
	109	Mary: yeah… um, let's see, France.	
09:30	110	Patricia: *amigos?*	*friends?*
	111	Mary: Hmm	
	112	Patricia: What did you say?	
	113	Mary: Oh France, France.	
	114	Patricia: To visit France?	
	115	Mary: Yeah, I went to France … *Yo via… jaste, er,* yeah right?	*I tra…veled (using 3rd person verbal form)*
	116	Patricia: *Tu… Yo viajé.*	*You … I traveled*
	117	Mary: *Yo viajé a Senegal,* "which is in um Africa". *Yo viajé …* let's see Spain "y" I don't remember, Canada, I think.	*I traveled to Senegal … … I traveled …*
	118	Patricia: Where?	
	119	Mary: Canada…and you… *"y tu"?*	*… and you?*
	120	Patricia: *Yo, solo un pais que esta cerca de ahí que se llama Guatemala* and *aca, los Estados Unidos,* that's it.	*Me, only to a country that is close there, which is called Guatemala and here, the United States*
10:00	121	Mary: That's it. Well you've been to Guatemala…is it nice there? I've never been to any South American countries before.	

While they used predominately English for much of their *social inquiry* discourse earlier in the session, Patricia tried to shift the language use when she offered discursive *support* to her partner as she encouraged Mary to speak Spanish (line 104). Creating this supportive context allowed space for Mary to ask additional questions about language (e.g., in line 107 when she asked for feedback and clarification of verb form *"viajo"* [to travel]). Patricia offered the past tense form in first person and second person (line 108). Mary tried to appropriate the form offered by Patricia when she used the second person form (see line 115), but Patricia redirected Mary by offering the first person form as a model (line 120, "*yo viajé*").

Throughout the rest of their interaction, they engaged in several LREs including negotiation about verb tense and lexicon, which offered additional opportunities to produce synonyms and to discuss subtle differences in word choice. Although much of this conversation could be considered "off-task" because they were not following the assignment, this was an authentic opportunity for communication in each of their target languages. They shared their loyalties for World Cup soccer teams, and asked each other about traveling with family. They seemed to have fun finding out each other's birthday, they laughed about each other's siblings, and even joked about who was taller and older. These moves back and forth could be understood as the opposite of one-up-manship, as one girl complimented her partner, her partner came back with a different compliment (i.e., even though one is older, the other is taller). They played with status and power to keep each other on equal terms in this relationship.

Finally, at the end of the session, both girls shared laughs and said, "It was nice to meet you." This simple social greeting acknowledged that this interaction was more than a task but an authentic social interaction and opportunity to make a new friend in high school. We argue that these opportunities to build relationships with students of different ethno-linguistic backgrounds opened up new possibilities to use and learn target languages together.

We found that this dialogue was full of linguistic and social affordances for both students as they asked questions of each other in terms of language and social life. We observed Patricia encouraging Mary to use Spanish and Patricia presenting many language learning affordances for Mary in terms of introducing and using new vocabulary and syntax. The interaction also afforded Patricia many opportunities to use her target language, English, and they both drew upon bilingual language resources and translanguaging practices to engage in questions about language.

In their interviews, students explained how the LA program provided unique opportunities to interact with and begin meaningful relationships with students from ethnolinguistic backgrounds. In their evaluation of the program, 90% of the students responded that they had "made a new friend" and they explained that their favorite part of the program was talking with "friends of my age" in Spanish and English. This corroborated our findings from our discourse analysis of the transcripts, which showed how adolescents foregrounded interpersonal and relationship-building purposes for communication.

Conclusions

Our study sheds light on the kinds of social discourse adolescent peers use in their interactions, which has been neglected in previous research. Our findings show that as the students used social discourse to build relationships with their interlocutors, they were more likely to engage in languaging (Swain 2006; Swain & Deters 2007). Initiating questions about language or correcting a peers' language could be perceived as risky, yet greater instances of languaging (operationalized as LREs) occurred when students used discursive moves of *social inquiry, solidarity* and *support*.

As students admitted their own mistakes and shared struggles while negotiating for *solidarity*, we found that they opened space for others to participate in mutual learning opportunities, thereby allowing each other to grow while they were in their ZPD (Martin-Beltrán 2014; Donato 2004; Foster & Ohta 2005; Kowal & Swain 1997; Ohta 2000). Our study contributes to sociocultural research by examining how relationship-building discourse serves as a mediational tool that affords language knowledge co-construction (Swain, Brooks, & Tocalli-Beller 2002). Our study contributes to peer interaction research by attending to relationship-building (or *comity*) in relation to languaging.

Our study reveals how students discursively construct *comity* (Aston 1993) through discursive moves of *social inquiry, support* and *solidarity*; and furthermore, how constructing *comity* affords opportunities for language learning in interactions among linguistically diverse adolescent peers. Aston (1993) argued that negotiation for solidarity and support will fail if experiences and affective ties are not shared. Our study contributes to this theory by shedding light on how interlocutors can discover shared experiences and establish affective ties. We offer the term *social inquiry* to expand this understanding and shed light on when and for what purposes adolescent peers use social discourse in their interactions. We recognize the limitations of this study in terms of understanding learning and recognize that future research is needed to examine *comity* in peer interaction in relation to language learning outcomes.

Pedagogical implications

Prior research has confirmed the positive relationship between peer interaction and language learning, and often assumed that simply placing students in pairs will create a context for feedback, comprehensible input and opportunities to produce language. Because a person's willingness to use language and ask questions is dependent on social context and social relationships, we argue that students need to know more about their interlocutors to understand the variety of language to speak and the kind of feedback they can offer.

We argue that students' social discourse moves created a more collaborative environment (Naughton 2006) or collaborative mindset (Sato & Ballinger 2012), which has been shown to facilitate more effective peer feedback. If educators acknowledge the importance of interpersonal relationships in classrooms, they can strengthen the foundations of language learning. The study has implications for teachers in other contexts (both dual language and traditional second language classrooms) to become aware of the ways peers can build *comity* during their interactions. Using social discourse in interactions may create a more fertile context for language use and risk taking, especially among adolescent language learners (for whom socialization is often a priority). Teachers should create opportunities for students to engage in authentic *social inquiry* both before and during peer interactions to encourage students to use the target language and to question language form and function. Teachers can use discussion prompts that elicit sharing of personal experiences among peers as they collaborate. For example, in our study we found that discussion activities that invited the students to reflect on shared experiences at school precipitated further social inquiry and additional discursive moves of *solidarity* and *support*. For beginning students, it may be helpful to provide sentence frames or phrases that are examples of social discourse (such as those in Table 1).

Previous research has shown that students benefit from systematic and strategic preparation prior to participation in peer interaction activities, such as instructing students to give corrective feedback (Gielen, Peeters, Dochy, Onghena, & Struyven 2010; Sato & Lyster 2012) and introducing interaction strategies (Ballinger 2013; Naughton 2006; Sato & Ballinger 2012). Our findings also recommend incorporating modeling of social discourse into this preparation. Teachers can model social discourse moves by role playing to offer examples of discursive moves of *support, solidary, social inquiry* and contrasting cases.

By modeling negotiation for *solidarity* and *support* in teacher-student discourse, teachers may encourage this discourse in peer interaction and thereby afford further opportunities for language learning. It is important to recognize all learners have room to grow (see Martin-Beltran 2013), and all need to *use* language to learn and to interact with others. In many classrooms, teachers often focus on the transaction of information or goal-oriented speech to accomplish a task or to give peer corrective feedback. Focusing on "right" answers or task completion in interactions glosses over the fact that much of our every day speech is about building interpersonal relationships or *comity* (Aston 1993). To ignore this function of language in second language learning contexts is to ignore one of the fundamental purposes for human communication. If these relationships are foundational, neglecting the development of these relationships may constrain opportunities for learning in interaction. Therefore, if educators are to support youth learning language in their formative years, we need to offer spaces to develop and recognize the benefits of social discourse rather than dismiss such behavior as "off-task." Teachers must consider ways to harness social discourse to connect with and expand opportunities for language learning among peers.

Acknowledgements

This research was funded through the National Academy of Education and Spencer Foundation Postdoctoral Fellowship. Thank you to Eliza Hughes and Alexandra Ralph for outstanding research assistance. We are indebted to the students and teachers at "Southwoods" who brought life to the Language Ambassadors.

References

Atkinson, D. (2010). Extended, embodied cognition and second language acquisition. *Applied Linguistics*, 31(5), 599–622. doi:10.1093/applin/amq009

Aston, G. (1993). Notes on the interlanguage of comity. In G. Kasper & S. Blum-Kulka (Eds.), *Interlanguage pragmatics* (pp. 224–250). Oxford: Oxford University Press.

Aston, G. (1998). Introduction. In G. Aston (Ed.), *Negotiating service* (pp. 1–23). Bologna: Editrice CLUEB.

Ballinger, S. (2013). Towards a cross-linguistic pedagogy: Biliteracy and reciprocal learning strategies in French immersion. *Journal of Immersion and Content-Based Language Education*, 1(1), 131–148. doi:10.1075/jicb.1.1.06bal

Ballinger, S., & Lyster, R. (2011). Student and teacher language use in a two-way Spanish/English immersion school. *Language Teaching Research*, 15, 289–306.

Block, D. (2003). *The social turn in second language acquisition*. Edinburgh: Edinburgh University Press.

Breen, M. P. (2001). Overt participation and covert acquisition in the language classroom. In M. P. Breen (Ed.), *Learner contributions to language learning: New directions in research* (pp. 112–140). Harlow, UK: Longman Pearson Education.

Canagarajah, S. (2011). Codemeshing in academic writing: Identifying teachable strategies of translanguaging. *Modern Language Journal*, 95, 401–417. doi:10.1111/j.1540-4781.2011.01207.x

Castanheira, M. L., Crawford, T., Dixon, C. N., & Green, J. L. (2001). Interactional ethnography: An approach to studying the social construction of literate practices. *Linguistics and Education*, 11(4), 353–400. doi:10.1016/S0898-5898(00)00032-2

Castanheira, M. L., Green, J., Dixon, C., & Yeagerb, B. (2007). (Re) Formulating identities in the face of fluid modernity: An interactional ethnographic approach. *International Journal of Educational Research*, 46(3), 172–189. doi:10.1016/j.ijer.2007.09.005

Cole, M. (1996). *Cultural psychology: A once and future discipline*. Cambridge, MA: Harvard University Press.

Corsaro, W. A. (1981). Entering the child's world: Research strategies for field entry and data collection in a preschool setting. *Ethnography and language in educational settings*, 117–146.

Dalton-Puffer, C. (2005). Negotiating interpersonal meanings in naturalistic classroom discourse: Directives in content-and-language-integrated classrooms. *Journal of Pragmatics*, 37(8), 1275–1293. doi:10.1016/j.pragma.2004.12.002

Donato, R. (2004). Aspects of collaboration in pedagogical discourse. *Annual Review of Applied Linguistics*, 24, 284–302. doi:10.1017/S026719050400011X

Engeström, Y. (1987). *Learning by expanding. An activity-theoretical approach to developmental research*. Helsinki: Orienta-Konsultit Oy.

Firth, A., & Wagner, J. (2007). Second/foreign language learning as a social accomplishment: Elaborations on a reconceptualized SLA. *The Modern Language Journal*, 91(s1), 800–819. doi:10.1111/j.1540-4781.2007.00670.x

Foster, P., & Ohta, A. S. (2005). Negotiation for meaning and peer assistance in second language classrooms. *Applied Linguistics*, 26(3), 402–430. doi:10.1093/applin/ami014

García, O. (2009). *Bilingual education in the 21st century: A global perspective*. Malden, MA: Wiley-Blackwell.

García Mayo, M. P. (2005). Interactional strategies for interlanguage communication: Do they provide evidence for attention to form? In A. Housen & M. Pierrard (Eds.), *Investigations in instructed second language acquisition* (pp. 383–405). Berlin: Mouton de Gruyter. doi:10.1515/9783110197372.3.383

Gass, W. H. (1985). *Habitations of the word: Essays*. New York, NY: Simon and Schuster.

Gass, S. M., & Selinker, L. (2008). *Second language acquisition: An introductory course* (3rd ed.). New York, NY: Routledge.

Gielen, S., Peeters, E., Dochy, F., Onghena, P., & Struyven, K. (2010). Improving the effectiveness of peer feedback for learning. *Learning and Instruction*, 20(4), 304–315. doi:10.1016/j.learninstruc.2009.08.007

Goffman, E. (1971). *Relations in public: Microstudies of the Public Order*. New York, NY: Basic Books.

Gutiérrez, K. (2008). Developing a sociocritical literacy in the third space. *Reading Research Quarterly*, 43(2), 148–164. doi:10.1598/RRQ.43.2.3

Gumperz, J. J. (Ed.). (1982a). *Language and social identity* (Vol. 2). Cambridge University Press.

Gumperz, J. J. (1982b). *Discourse strategies* (Vol. 1). Cambridge University Press. doi:10.1017/CBO9780511611834

Cook-Gumperz, J. (Ed.). (1986). *The social construction of literacy* (Vol. 3). Cambridge University Press.

Gumperz, J. J. (1992). Contextualization and understanding. In A. Duranti & C. Goodwin (Eds.), *Rethinking context: Language as an interactive phenomenon* (pp. 229–252). Cambridge: Cambridge University Press.

Hatch, E. (1992). *Discourse and language education*. Cambridge: Cambridge University Press.

Ivanič, R. (1994). I is for interpersonal: Discoursal construction of writer identities and the teaching of writing. *Linguistics and Education*, 6(1), 3–15. doi:10.1016/0898-5898(94)90018-3

Kirkland, D. E. (2009). Standpoints: Researching and teaching English in the digital dimension. *Research in the Teaching of English*, 44(1), 8–22.

Kowal, M., & Swain, M. (1997). From semantic to syntactic processing: How can we promote it in the immersion classroom? In R. Johnson & M. Swain (Eds.), *Immersion Education: International Perspectives* (pp. 284–309). New York, NY: Cambridge University Press. doi:10.1017/CBO9781139524667.022

Lantolf, J. (2000). *Sociocultural theory and second language learning*. Oxford: Oxford University Press.

Leech, G. N. (1983). *Principles of pragmatics*. London: Longman.

Llinares, A., & Pastrana, A. (2013). CLIL students' communicative functions across activities and educational levels. *Journal of Pragmatics*, 59(A), 81–92. doi:10.1016/j.pragma.2013.05.011

Long, M. H. (1996). The role of the linguistic environment in second language acquisition. In W. Titchie & T. K. Bhatia (Eds.), *Handbook of language acquisition: Vol. 2. Second language acquisition* (pp. 413–468). San Diego, CA: Academic Press.

Long, M., & Porter, P. (1985). Group work, interlanguage talk, and second language acquisition. *TESOL Quarterly*, 19, 207–228. doi:10.2307/3586827

Mackey, A. (2007). *Conversational interaction in second language acquisition: A collection of empirical studies*. Oxford: Oxford University Press.

Mackey, A. (2012). *Input, interaction and corrective feedback in L2 classrooms*. Oxford: Oxford University Press.

Mackey, A., Gass, S. M., & McDonough, K. (2000). How do learners perceive interactional feedback? *Studies in Second Language Acquisition*, 22, 471–497. doi:10.1017/S0272263100004022

Mackey, A., & Goo, J. (2007). Interaction research: A meta-analysis and research synthesis. In A. Mackey (Ed.), *Conversational interaction in second language acquisition: A collection of empirical studies* (pp. 407–452). Oxford: Oxford University Press.

Martin-Beltrán, M. (2010). Positioning proficiency: How students and teachers (de)construct language proficiency at school. *Linguistics and Education*. 21(4), 257–281. doi:10.1016/j.linged.2010.09.002

Martin-Beltrán, M. (2013). I don't feel as embarrassed because we're all learning: Discursive positioning among adolescents becoming multilingual. *International Journal of Educational Research*, 62, 152–161 doi:10.1016/j.ijer.2013.08.005

Martin-Beltrán, M. (2014). "What do you want to say?" How adolescents use translanguaging to expand learning opportunities. *International Multilingual Research Journal*, 8(3), 208–230. doi:10.1080/19313152.2014.914372

Moje, E. B., Ciechanowski, K. M., Kramer, K., Ellis, L., Carrillo, R., & Collazo, T. (2004). Working toward third space in content area literacy: An examination of everyday funds of knowledge and Discourse. *Reading Research Quarterly*, 39, 38–70. doi:10.1598/RRQ.39.1.4

Moll, L. (2010). Mobilizing culture, language, and educational practices: Fulfilling the promises of Mendez and Brown. *Educational Researcher*, 39(6), 451–460. doi:10.3102/0013189X10380654

Naughton, D. (2006). Cooperative strategy training and oral interaction: Enhancing small group communication in the language classroom. *The Modern Language Journal*, 90(2), 169–184. doi:10.1111/j.1540-4781.2006.00391.x

Ohta, A. S. (2000). Re-thinking interaction in SLA: Developmentally appropriate assistance in the zone of proximal development and the acquisition of L2 grammar. In J. P. Lantolf (Ed.), *Sociocultural theory and second language learning* (pp. 51–78). Oxford: Oxford University Press.

Pica, T. (1994). Research on negotiation: What does it reveal about second-language learning conditions, processes, and outcomes? *Language Learning*, 44(3), 493–527. doi:10.1111/j.1467-1770.1994.tb01115.x

Philp, J., Walter, S., & Basturkmen, H. (2010). Peer interaction in the foreign language classroom: What factors foster a focus on form? *Language Awareness*, 19(4), 261–279. doi:10.1080/09658416.2010.516831

Rouhshad, A & Storch, N. (2016). A focus on mode: Patterns of interaction in face-to face and computer-mediated contexts. In M. Sato & S. Ballinger (Eds.), *Peer interaction and second language learning: Pedagogical potential and research agenda* (pp. 267–289). Amsterdam: John Benjamins.

Rogoff, B. (1990). *Apprenticeship in thinking: Cognitive development in social context.* Oxford: Oxford University Press.

Sato, M. (2013). Beliefs about peer interaction and peer corrective feedback: Efficacy of classroom intervention. *The Modern Language Journal*, 97(3), 611–633.
    doi:10.1111/j.1540-4781.2013.12035.x

Sato, M., & Ballinger, S. (2012). Raising language awareness in peer interaction: A cross-context, cross-methodology examination. *Language Awareness*, 21(1–2), 157–179.
    doi:10.1080/09658416.2011.639884

Sato, M., & Ballinger, S. (2016). Understanding peer interaction: Research synthesis and directions. In M. Sato & S. Ballinger (Eds.), *Peer interaction and second language learning: Pedagogical potential and research agenda* (pp. 1–30). Amsterdam: John Benjamins.

Sato, M., & Lyster, R. (2012). Peer interaction and corrective feedback for accuracy and fluency development. *Studies in Second Language Acquisition*, 34(4), 591–626.
    doi:10.1017/S0272263112000356

Spradley, J. P. (1980). *Participant observation.* New York, NY: Holt, Rinehart and Winston.

Storch, N. (2002a). Patterns of interaction in ESL pair work. *Language Learning*, 52(1), 119–158.
    doi:10.1111/1467-9922.00179

Storch, N. (2002b). Relationships formed in dyadic interaction and opportunity for learning. *International Journal of Educational Research*, 37(3-4), 305–322.
    doi:10.1016/S0883-0355(03)00007-7

Storch, N. (2008). Metatalk in a pair work activity: Level of engagement and implications for language development. *Language Awareness*, 17, 95–114. doi:10.2167/la431.0

Swain, M. (1985). Communicative competence: some roles of comprehensible input and comprehensible output in its development. In S. Gass & C. Madden (Eds.), *Input in second language acquisition* (pp. 235–253). Rowley, MA: Newbury House.

Swain, M. (2006). Languaging, agency and collaboration in advanced second language learning. In H. Byrnes (Ed.), *Advanced language learning: The contribution of Halliday and Vygotsky* (pp. 95–108). London: Continuum.

Swain, M., Brooks, L., & Tocalli-Beller, A. (2002). Peer-peer dialogue as a means of second language learning. *Annual Review of Applied Linguistics*, 22, 171–185.
    doi:10.1017/S0267190502000090

Swain, M., & Deters, P. (2007). "New" mainstream SLA theory: Expanded and enriched. *Modern Language Journal*, 91(4), 820–836. doi:10.1111/j.1540-4781.2007.00671.x

Swain, M., & Lapkin, S. (1998). Interaction and second language learning: Two adolescent French immersion students working together. *The Modern Language Journal*, 82(3), 320–37.
    doi:10.1111/j.1540-4781.1998.tb01209.x

Swain, M., & Lapkin, S. (2002). Talking it through: Two French immersion learners' response to reformulation. *International Journal of Educational Research*, 37(3–4), 285–304.
    doi:10.1016/S0883-0355(03)00006-5

Swain, M., & Lapkin, S. (2013). A Vygotskian sociocultural perspective on immersion education: The L1/L2 debate. *Journal of Immersion and Content-Based Language Education*, 1(1), 101–129. doi:10.1075/jicb.1.1.05swa

Titscher, S., Wodak, R., Meyer, M., & Vetter, E. (2000). *Methods of text and discourse analysis*. London: Sage

van Lier, L. (1998). The relationship between consciousness, interaction, and language learning. *Language Awareness, 7*, 128–145. doi:10.1080/09658419808667105

van Lier, L. (2000). From input to affordance: Social-interactive learning from an ecological perspective. In J. Lantolf (Ed.), *Sociocultural theory and second language learning* (pp. 245–259). Oxford: Oxford University Press.

Wertsch, J. V. (1985). *Vygotsky and the Social Formation of Mind*. Cambridge, MA: Harvard University Press.

Vygotsky, L. (1978). *Mind in society*. Cambridge, MA: Harvard University Press.

Appendix

Transcription conventions

Bold text	Focus vocabulary word
?	rising intonation at end of sentence
!	increased volume and tone of excitement
.	falling intonation
,	continuing intonation
-	abrupt cut off
::	double column indicated overlapping speech
<u>Underline</u>	stress given to this word or phrase
…	micro-pause less than 1 second
(1 sec)	pause, silence indicated by number of seconds
(())	comments about gesture, facial expression, eye gaze, body, posture
italics	utterance in Spanish and translation of utterance originally in Spanish in separate column
[*brackets*]	translation of utterance in Spanish in transcripts where English gloss column in not included
"quotations"	indicate student reading directly from the book
xxx	unintelligible/ inaudible approximately one syllable per x

CHAPTER 13

Peer interaction while learning to read in a new language

Martha Bigelow and Kendall King
University of Minnesota

This chapter examines second language (L2) peer oral language interaction between two learners engaged in a partner reading activity. The data come from an English language arts class for newcomers in an all-immigrant high school in the U.S. Students arrive in this beginner-level, English language arts class with widely disparate experiences with formal schooling and print literacy, as well as with different first languages and oral English language skills. The year-long class focuses on developmental English language and literacy skills, and the students and teacher absorb and accommodate newcomer students each month. The data presented in this chapter highlight the peer work between two asymmetrically-paired, female adolescent students: an Amharic newcomer with prior schooling in Ethiopia and beginning-level oral English skills, and a Somali speaker with stronger English language skills but very low print literacy and no formal schooling before arriving to the U.S. Through an analysis of their interactions in one paired reading session, we describe how these two students use their language and literacy skills to complete a reading task and in doing so, we consider the complexities of how asymmetrically paired students engage in everyday classroom tasks and the learning opportunities therein.

Introduction and literature review

Peer interaction is widely believed to be beneficial for second language (L2) learners. Research on peer interaction indicates that it has the potential to provide students with opportunities to negotiate understandings of meaning and form (Philp, Walter, & Basturkmen 2010); to notice aspects of the new language (e.g., lexical, syntactic, phonological, pragmatic) (Izumi 2002; Izumi & Bigelow 2000; Izumi, Bigelow, Fujiwara, & Fearnow 1999; Philp 2003); and to engage in the many processes and facilitative benefits that linguistic production offers L2 learners (Ballinger 2013; de Bot 1996; Iwashita 1999; Shehadeh 2001, 2003; Sato & Ballinger 2012; Swain 1985, 1993, 1995; Swain 2000). Furthermore, a great deal

DOI 10.1075/lllt.45.14big
© 2016 John Benjamins Publishing Company

of research has explored interaction with respect to the influence of interlocutors' roles, relationships, and proficiency levels (Plough & Gass 1993; Storch 2002; Sato & Viveros 2016; Tedick & Young 2016) and task features (Revesz 2009; Robinson, Ting, & Urwin 1995; Swain & Lapkin 2001) on interactions and L2 learning opportunities. Overall, the linguistic and interpersonal demands of tasks have been well documented in the research literature and are recognized as having great potential for promoting peer interaction and language learning (Gass & Mackey 2007). However, as argued below, the way that materials are used by learners while engaging in tasks (Guerrettaz & Johnston 2013) remains less explored and learners' interactions while using these materials in everyday classroom settings have been less frequently analyzed. Also unexplored is how learners' very low levels of print literacy and formal schooling influence peer interaction.

Learners who are new to print literacy are also new to the many strategies for comprehending text. They are still developing the ability to attend to the sounds of language as distinct from meaning. They are also in the process of building their knowledge about functions, structures, print conventions, and knowledge of how different texts work. Emergent readers are still learning onset-rime blending, individual sound blending, and blending and segmenting of compound words (see Vinogradov 2008 for a description of older emergent readers). These skills need to be taught, which means that they must be integrated into basic literacy instruction, often in classes with mixed literacy levels. Therefore, it is inevitable that, even with the most carefully differentiated lesson plan, students will be asked to work together across dramatically mismatched literacy levels, with texts that are either too difficult or too easy for them. In addition to literacy level, there are multiple considerations and complications to any classroom task. For instance, peer interactions and task work often take place in a context in which partners' skills and identities are assumed, negotiated, or resisted (Pavlenko & Blackledge 2004). Learners have agency as they (dis)engage in classroom language learning, which might maximize or minimize the intended benefits of the task. For example, students often use preferred strategies to complete a task (e.g., ask the teacher), (re)define roles assigned by the teacher (e.g., read silently rather than aloud or vice versa), and even change the task as it unfolds (Cohen 2006; Ehrman & Oxford 2011).

While there are many pedagogical suggestions about designing second language tasks designed to maximize learning, there are relatively few descriptive studies of naturally occurring peer interaction in classrooms (Philp, Walter, & Basturkmen 2010). Although there are notable exceptions (e.g., Foster & Ohta 2005; Sato & Lyster 2012; Storch & Aldosari 2013), overall, most peer-interaction studies rely on researcher-created, not teacher-created, tasks and/or are implemented in laboratory-like settings or at best, in a way that simulates a classroom.

Thus, data collection often occurs outside of regular class time, and participants are typically adult volunteers, who are more likely to carefully attend to instructions and to comply with the parameters of the study. Equally important, most of the current findings on peer interaction are derived from studies using participants who (a) have high levels of formal schooling and high levels of print literacy in their home languages (e.g., Donato 1994); (b) are engaged primarily in second (or third) language learning, not language *and* initial literacy learning (e.g., Storch 2002); (c) are asked to complete narrowly designed tasks (e.g., 'spot the difference' tasks), as opposed to longer, broader, more complex tasks that are common to everyday classrooms such as reading a story and answering questions (e.g., Philp 2003); and (d) are roughly equally matched in terms of language and literacy skills (e.g., see Oliver 2000 for an excellent comparison of adults and children). Without including more diverse learners in the enterprise of understanding peer interaction, the question of transferability or generalizability of the findings to date remains, at best, unanswered, and at worst, highly problematic. This study aims to bring the issue of limited formal schooling and low print literacy into peer interaction research.

In this chapter, we analyze two students' interaction while carrying out a partner reading activity. This sort of interaction differs markedly from traditional oral tasks such as picture drawing or opinion-exchange. Most crucially, the text the participants read together exerts a powerful mediating force in the interaction because of joint attention on the printed word. Within a Vygotskian analytical framework, learning cannot be understood without reference to the context within which it occurs. Many researchers have used Vygotskian theories to understand peer interaction (e.g., Forman & Cazden 1985; Tudge 1990; Zhu & Mitchell 2012) because it provides tools to focus on multiple layers of an event – the interpersonal, the interactional, the intertextual, and the intercultural. Sociocultural theory, particularly Vygotsky's concepts of mediation and the zone of proximal development (ZPD), have been widely used and adapted to explore L2 learning in many settings and with learners of all ages (Cazden 1994; de Guerrero 1994; Guerrero & Villamil 1994; de Guerrero & Villamil 2000; Kowal & Swain 1994; McCafferty 1994; Washburn 1994). While Vygotsky used the ZPD as a tool for understanding the mental age levels of a child in order to predict their educative potential, much like IQ testing, present-day researchers have adopted this construct to help examine how learners' potentially support and scaffold each other, and negotiate the task at hand.

In the partner reading task we analyze here, the book shapes their interaction and the potential learning that the task has to offer. However, we know of no research that explores second language peer interaction in which lack of print literacy was recognized or problematized with respect to task design or dyadic pairing of adolescent or adult language learners. Furthermore, it is often assumed that student pairs of different skills levels have the potential to turn a peer interaction experience into a mutually beneficial learning opportunity for both. For instance, in L2 classrooms, placing students in groups with mixed levels of proficiency in the target language has long been recommended as a means to promote meaningful interaction and learning (e.g., Echevarria, Vogt, & Short 2014). However, more recent research has called mixed grouping into question, at least for some types of learners (Young & Tedick 2016).

The tendency to exclude certain learner populations and to rarely use routine classroom contexts and everyday tasks such as that described here is highly problematic for a field such as SLA, which strives toward universal generalizations about the nature of language learning (Bigelow & Tarone 2004, 2012; Pettitt & Tarone 2015). This is particularly salient in light of the substantial evidence that L2 learners without alphabetic print literacy skills tend to process oral language differently than those with print literacy, and further, to use different strengths and strategies (Tarone, Bigelow, & Hansen 2009) than those with print literacy. This work suggests important differences in cognitive processing for literate and non-literate L2 learners. Meanwhile, other research points to learners' differences in terms of their understanding of the relevance of decontextualized activities so common in Western schooling traditions, their interpretations of abstraction (e.g., mapping a story onto a plot diagram), and more broadly, of their culture-specific ways of viewing and being in the world (Bigelow & King 2014; Watson 2010).

This chapter begins to address some of these gaps by closely examining peer interaction between two immigrant adolescent female students, one of whom has very low print literacy and little prior schooling. Despite the long-standing (UNESCO 1951), collective academic and policy recognition that learning to read in a L2 is more challenging than learning to read in one's mother tongue, students with little or no home language literacy are commonly placed in L2 classrooms around the world (King & Benson 2008). For adolescent and adult learners, the process of learning to decode and encode alphabetic script is particularly difficult as the slow, laborious process of doing so often does not result in a recognizable word or meaningful sentence. Furthermore, developing the fluency needed to comprehend text can be particularly challenging (August & Shanahan 2006). Students without print literacy are typically integrated into beginning-level language classes, which often include literate students. Therefore, teachers are left attempting to design instruction to meet the developing literacy and language needs of all their students. This study attempts to shed light on how two beginners with very different backgrounds negotiate a partner reading activity, and potentially support each other in both L2 and literacy learning.

In light of this research and the gaps we have identified, this chapter addresses three questions for two learners with varied first and second language literacy skills: (1) How do the two participants with vastly different literacy levels engage with the task and support each other's engagement towards task completion? (2) What varied roles and participation structures are created as the two participants work on the task? and (3) How do the participants' respective literacy, linguistic, academic, and social strengths and challenges shape how this peer interaction unfolds and the learning opportunities therein?

Methodology

In this study, we explored how the learners participated in a partner reading task. The task, described in detail below, was designed by the teacher to encourage students to co-read a short book and to engage in open-ended comprehension discussions.

Methodological framework

We examined the data in a way that would account for the three aspects central to task completion: (a) the book, (b) the students' physical interactions with the book using their hands and "a driver" (a piece of paper to keep the reader on the correct line of text), and (c) their verbal utterances. We qualitatively analyzed how the task evolved from beginning to end. For instance, we coded the transcript in terms of how the students worked with each other – who helped who, how and when. In other words, who supplied a word, who asked for a word, and how comprehension was co-constructed. This analysis thus drew upon both cognitive and sociocultural research paradigms to understand how learners with divergent levels of formal schooling, literacy, and L2 skills support each other toward task-completion. The analysis was cognitive because we documented and described how the participants decode and comprehend the text. This mixed approach draws from the cognitive foundations of learning to read which dominate reading research (e.g., Kamil, Pearson, Moje, & Afflerbach 2011) with a long tradition of research on reading strategies and reading comprehension. In addition, we drew upon sociocultural traditions as we analyzed how the participants engage in the reading task, and with each other. In addition, this analysis was based on the assumption that reading occurs in a social context, past and present, and often involves interactions with the text and other people (e.g., Bloome & Egan-Robertson 1993; Wood, Bruner & Ross 1976).

Research context

The data for this study were collected in an urban, all-immigrant high school we call Franken International. Franken is located in a mid-size U.S. city with substantial Somali and Latino populations. The vast majority of students at Franken International are English learners who arrived in the U.S. as adolescents or young adults. Their ages span from 14 to 21 years, with 21 being the age at which students are no longer eligible for services in K-12 settings in the state. Many Franken International students are experiencing formal schooling for the first time. During the 2010–2011 academic year, when the study took place, there were ten full-time teaching staff working with about 150 students, 90% of whom were eligible for free or reduced price lunch. The tone of the school was close-knit, friendly and upbeat. Students and staff routinely greet and banter with each other; students are supportive and, for instance, quick to help new arrivals 'learn the ropes'.

We focused our data collection in two beginning-level ESL classes. The teacher, who is certified in K-12 ESL and reading, generously welcomed us into her class and allowed us to approach her students as potential participants. She has a high level of intercultural competence, based on our many observations of how she interacted with students of different backgrounds. She welcomed students' languages into the instructional space and was respectful of students. Both class periods were focused on developmental literacy skills (including vocabulary, grammar, and phonics), and the most recent arrivals to Franken International were assigned to this class. New arrivals often joined the class each week and it was common for students to leave Franken for many reasons (e.g., to transfer to another school, leave the country, leave school to work). Despite students' beginning-level English proficiency, the teacher regularly tried to include higher order and often very abstract language arts skills such as plot analysis, as well as materials she thought would be culturally familiar (e.g., the folktale genre).

Participants: Ayan and Aisha

Ayan was 15 at the time of the study and in her second year in this introductory English class. Franken International was her first formal schooling experience. Ayan was outgoing and talkative (in Somali) and was often redirected back to her work by the adults in the room. She did her classwork intensely, with a lot of obvious effort. Ayan caught our attention immediately as she frequently solicited support from us, the teacher, and fellow students. We also noticed that students rarely turned to her for help, and she was never, in our time there, asked to help a more recently arrived student. She had acquired many emergent-reader skills and concepts such as understanding that text flows from left to right, that letters transform into sounds which blend together to form words, and that text carries meaning. While she still struggled with English literacy skills, she had mastered many aspects of 'doing school' (Roy & Roxas 2011; Bigelow & King 2014) and she often seemed more concerned with the performance of good student behavior (e.g., following instructions, listening) or figuring out ways to complete a task (e.g., borrowing a student's worksheet to copy), and she seemed less interested in comprehending the task content. We noticed that her English writing skills and productive oral skills were among the weakest in the class, and she frequently received support from the Educational Assistant. Ayan also attended an additional, smaller literacy class later in the day to help her develop basic literacy skills. While Ayan was a proficient speaker of Somali, we had no evidence that she could read or write in Somali. We administered a Somali literacy test with her and she was unable to complete any part of the assessment including writing her name, age, or address. The assessment was conducted in the school library with Somali peers nearby, who tried to help her get started on this test. Even with assistance, she did not produce any written Somali. She was also reluctant to do any part of the written English literacy test. She did the English reading activities very slowly, with much sub-vocalization and little confidence. At the close of the study (and end of the academic year), students were asked to write in response to three prompts ('*In some ways, this year was hard / fun / surprising. For example: I….*'). Ayan's only responses were "I don't math because it is dificalt for me. I don't socialstudies beause it is hard. I don't know English. I don't know science."

The other member of the dyad, Aisha, arrived one month before this interaction was recorded. While there were other Ethiopian students in the class, she was the only Amharic speaker. She spoke in a quiet voice but smiled often and seemed comfortable in the class. She was 19 years old at the time and reported that she had started school when she was eight years old and had not missed any formal schooling. She had not yet graduated from high school in Ethiopia, which is why she enrolled at Franken. When we assessed her literacy in Amharic, she demonstrated fluent and confident home language reading and writing skills. She clearly had mastered the basic literacy skills that our assessment was designed to measure. She was also comfortable with the routines of schooling – doing worksheets, following instruction, and conforming to general classroom learning expectations. She reported that her school in Ethiopia was similar to Franken in many ways and that she had studied English before she came to the United States.

Data collection and task description

While the project yielded many hours of field notes, videos, and documents, this chapter presents analysis of one 34 minute audio-video recording of peer inter-action during a particular partner reading activity between two students: Ayan and Aisha. This video-recording of these two particular students was conducted during routine work on a regular classroom task designed by the teacher. The researcher was holding the camera while providing support during the reading task. The video was shot close up, largely focusing on the participants' hands as they helped each other to complete the task. About two-thirds of the way into the task, an Educational Assistant also came over to check the students' progress and comprehension, thus also shaping how the task was engaged in and completed.

During this partner reading, the class of approximately 20 students were paired in dyads according to the classroom seating arrangement. The teacher did not re-arrange students, but asked those who normally sat with each other to do the activity together. Ayan and Aisha, like the other dyads in the class, were given one book to share. The story was a folktale called *Anansi and the Pot of Beans* (Norfolk & Norfolk 2006). The teacher instructed pairs to read each page in the following way: one student was to move a "driver" (piece of construction paper the length of the page) down each line of text as the other student read. The expecta-tion was that they would switch roles, including switching who held the driver, and re-read the same page. Before moving to the next page, they were asked to dis-cuss the question, "What happened?", presumably to aid comprehension, prompt oral interaction, and encourage the development of comprehension strategies. Students had done this same task before with other books and the teacher mod-eled it again before the task started, presumably for newcomers. Upon completing the book reading, students were asked to answer three comprehension questions on a worksheet.

Anansi and the Pot of Beans is based on an African folktale about a trickster spi-der who cannot resist his grandmother's beans. The story is classified as appropriate for pre-K to third grade reading and interest levels (Guided reading level: K; Lexile Measure: 540L). The class had discussed other folktales previously and most were becoming familiar with concepts such as plot, setting, characters, and moral of the story. In the days following the interaction presented here, the class continued to work on plot structure by creating a diagram showing rising action, climax and reso-lution of the story. These activities were part of a multiple-month unit on folktales, a focus that was intended to link in culturally compatible ways with students' experi-ences with similar genres in the oral modes. A choice such as this has the potential to link home and school settings, and thus potentially contributes to a curriculum that is culturally responsive (Gay 2000; Ladson-Billings 1995; Moje & Hinchman 2004).

Data analysis

In contrast to many other studies of peer interaction and task-based language learning in which learners tend to engage in narrowly defined tasks that target specific language skills such as metalinguistic knowledge (Gutierrez 2008), pragmatics, intercultural learning (East 2012), or grammatical features (Shintani 2012), the present task analysis focuses on the routine classroom literacy activity of reading a book aloud together. We chose to focus on this type of reading task as it was a common learning activity, both in this site (Bigelow & King 2014) and elsewhere (Bigelow 2010). We chose this particular piece of data because our goal was to understand how two students, who had varied levels of literacy as well as differences in their first and second language skills, support each other while managing and completing a task such as this.

The analysis of the transcribed video-recording focuses on Ayan and Aisha's interaction with each other and with the text (Erickson 1992). We examined how they negotiated their roles in the task and how they stayed engaged throughout the task. We also sought to analyze how the students' academic or personal strengths, dynamics, or challenges seemed to shape the interaction. Of particular interest were the ways in which their varied language and literacy skills might impact engagement with the task. To this end, we viewed the transcript and video with an eye to the different sorts of interactions between the girls, and quantified word suppliances, as detailed below. The close-up video allowed us to track how the oral interactions corresponded with the physical pages and text of the *Anansi* book (Garcez 1997). The transcripts analyzed below include the researcher (Bigelow) and the Educational Assistant (Jane), as well as the two students. Our analysis focused not only on the language used between and among the girls and the adults, and between the girls and the text, but it also incorporated aspects of their body language and physical control of the task. We examined where participants' hands were on the page as well as other behaviors such as tracking the text with their fingers, tapping the page, and using the piece of paper to further mediate the progression of the task.

Two constructs emerged as important analytically: participant structures and suppliances. Participant structures have been defined as the respective roles and patterns of engagement of individuals in an activity (Cazden 1986; Erickson 1982; Philips 1972). In the present case, as evident below, participant structures were determined by how the students' reading aloud was organized across the task (e.g., one girl as reader and one as 'audience'). We segmented and analyzed the transcript to correspond to each page of the book as well as by the distinct participation structure that qualitatively emerged through the analysis of turns.

Suppliances, in turn, refer to the solicited or unsolicited provision of the next word(s) on the printed text to the reader. (These are sometimes referred to in elementary education circles as 'tolds'.) Suppliances potentially function in multiple ways, for instance, as a means to facilitate and demonstrate shared attention on the printed text or as a means to minimize learner frustration and accelerate reading rate. For learners such as Ayan, who are still developing the ability to decode in a language they are not proficient in, suppliances might also potentially support comprehension by providing oral access to an unfamiliar word, and thus might speed up the rate of reading aloud. Suppliances likely do less to help her to develop and practice use of meaning, syntax and visual cues and strategies (Schwartz 1997). The general advice to parents[1] and teachers is that novice readers benefit from 'sounding it out' (e.g., supplying the word thus has the potential to minimize self-confidence and undermine independent reading skills) (Taylor, Hanson, Justice-Swanson, & Watts 1997; Ehri 2005). In our analysis, we coded for instances when the reader received a word from someone (suppliances); when the learner was prompted to attend; when there were explicit requests for assistance; and when there was manipulation of the materials (e.g., turning pages, pointing to text, moving the driver).

Findings

In analyzing how the participants engaged with the text and each other, we found that in working on the assigned task of reading the 32-page folktale, these two asymmetrically paired students engaged in four different participation structures, each of which unfolded spontaneously. Below we describe in broad terms how Aisha and Ayan constructed these different participation structures, and collaboratively moved across them as they work, with great effort, towards task completion.

Participation structure 1 (*story pages 1–6*)

Initially, and for the first six pages of the text, both students read each page in turn, that is, first Aisha read the page, then Ayan read the same page aloud (as indicated by grey shading for both students in Table 1). Yet for all six pages the asymmetry in reading fluency was stark with Aisha reading quickly, fluently, and with generally

---

1.   See this website for an example of advice often given to parents about best practices in early literacy support: http://www.momadvice.com/post/helping_your_child_read.

appropriately pacing intonation (e.g., pausing between clauses, rising intonation with questions). Ayan, in contrast, was more hesitant, and less fluent in her oral production. Ayan's pauses elicit multiple, frequent word suppliances (i.e., the provision of the next word(s) on the printed text) by Aisha and by the researcher, Bigelow, as quantified in Table 1.

Table 1. Overview of participation structure 1

Page of book	1	2	3	4	5	6	totals
Aisha outloud reading and suppliances received			1				2
Ayan outloud reading and suppliances received	9	6	8	4	5	1	33

As evident in Excerpt 1 below, Ayan's oral reading of the text was highly supported and scaffolded, while also frequently interrupted as she was rarely given time needed to attempt to sound out a word. Here, Aisha quickly reads page 2 of text; the students then quickly switched roles.

Excerpt 1 (see Appendix 1 for transcription conventions)

Time	Turn	Participant	
2:08	1	Aisha	[using finger to follow words above driver, which is moved and held by Ayan] grandma spider said anansi. do you have any work for me today. Sure, said grandma spider. I want you to plant some beans in the my garden.
2.22	2	Ayan	grandma spider said anansi do you have…. (2 sec)
2.38	3	Martha (author)	any.
2.40	4	Ayan	any work xxx [unintelligible]
2.49	5	Aisha	today
2.50	6	Ayan	today xxx [unintelligible]
2.55	7	Martha	sure,
2.56	8	Ayan	sure said grandma spider. i want you to
3.08	9	Martha & Aisha	plant.
3.09	10	Ayan	Plant
3.13	11	Martha	some.
3.16	12	Ayan	some …(8 sec)
3.26	13	Martha	beans.
3.27	14	Ayan	[taps finger on word] beans in my garden [following with finger]

Of the 26 words on this page, Ayan received suppliances for 6 of them, that is in turns 3 5, 7, 9, 11, and 13. As detailed above, suppliances refer to the provision of the next word(s) on the printed text, and as such, potentially function in multiple ways, for instance, to promote comprehension, accelerate reading rate, minimize frustration, or undermine confidence and the development of independent reading skills. In addition, it is clear that Ayan's accuracy in decoding the text was quite low; she received suppliances for 26% of the words on this page but seems to recognize few. The Individual Reading Inventory (Betts 1946) estimates that readers reach the frustration level when they know 90% or fewer words they are reading. Ayan had clearly reached this level based on her rate of reading, pauses and lack of appropriate spacing or intonation, yet she persisted through the task.

Across this first participation structure, this pattern remained constant with Ayan receiving suppliances for roughly a quarter of all words. Over these first five pages of text (121 words total), Ayan receives 33 word suppliances (a rate of 27%). Eleven were supplied by Bigelow, and 22 by Aisha. In contrast, when Aisha read these same 121 words, she received only two suppliances, one from Bigelow and one from Ayan ('ground'). These suppliances can be interpreted as the result of Ayan's slow reading rate and/or possibly, to Aisha's desire to move the task along or lack of patience. Furthermore, Ayan and Aisha were not reading strategically. For instance, neither was initiating self-repair or coaching the other in decoding strategies. And no prompts supported readers' monitoring (e.g., *does that make sense?*) or searching (e.g., *what can you try?*) strategies (Schwartz 2005).

The asymmetry between the students was most evident in this structure in terms of reading fluency, but it was also apparent with respect to who is managing the task. Contrary to what might be expected, Ayan, the weaker reader, exerted greater control and management of the task. For instance, Ayan managed the task physically: turning the pages of the book and transferring the 'driver' back and forth between the students. She also occasionally prompted Aisha for a reading cue, e.g., tapping her finger on the word. Finally, although not evident in the transcript here, we found that in this first participation structure, Ayan was a far more active participant in the summary/comprehension discussions prompted by Bigelow, with Ayan participating in three out of four of these, and Aisha only once. Across the task, these summaries mostly took the form of very brief reports (e.g., after the first two pages, Bigelow asks, "Ok, what happened?" Ayan responds, "The first Anansi grandma home." Bigelow expanded, "mhm he went to his grandma's house." Ayan says 'yes', and they return to the reading task).

Participation structure 2 (*story pages 7–11*)

While the first participation structure allowed the students to progress in the task, it was also quite slow; the students worked for more than ten minutes to read just five of the 32 pages of the book, and had a total allotted time of just thirty minutes for the task. This is perhaps why, after page six, they moved into the second and more expedient participation structure, where each girl read two pages in turn (see Table 2 where shading again indicates who read each page).

Table 2. Overview of participation structure 2

Page of book	7	8	9	10	11	totals
Aisha outloud reading and suppliances received	1					1
Ayan outloud reading and suppliances received			1	23		24

Here Aisha still provided extensive word suppliances, and to a much greater extent, supported Aisha's decoding through shadow-reading, or at times simultaneous, voice-over reading. Bigelow, in turn, provideed no word suppliances here. As evident in Excerpt 2, the students moved into this new structure with no discussion or meta-commentary about the task.

Excerpt 2

Time	Turn	Participant	
10:09	1	Aisha	grandma spider come to the porch with a large pitcher of fresh lemonade. and called to him. anansi, here is a cool drink for you.
10:30	2	Aisha & Ayan	grandma. spider. came. to:: the porch. with. a large pitcher of fresh lemonade and called to:: him. anansi, here is a cool. drink. for. you. [words read one by one then they move to next page]
11:06	3	Aisha	thank you grandma. as he drank the cold, sweet
11:17	4	Martha	lemonade.
11:19	5	Aisha	lemonade. I'm making. your favorite meal said grandma. I am cooking spicy beans. they'll be ready soon for our lunch
11:38	6	Martha	what happened ayan? [Ayan pounds desk lightly with her fist.]
11:42	7	Ayan	[unintelligible, pointing at the pictures] anansi
11:50	8	Aisha	[unintelligible] drink
11:56	9	Martha	good.
11:59	10	Ayan	thank you. [laughing] [Ayan misses her turn to read and the students turn the page]
12:11	11	Aisha	I love your spicy beans. said anansi he finished his lemonade and went back to his work. grandma spider returned to the kitchen.
12:31	12	Ayan	[she's moving the driver herself and following along with her finger at the same time] grandma. spider. looked. for her bean spices, but the tins were empty. she called anansi I need spices. I must … (2 sec.) go to the mar…(2 sec.)
13:17	13	Aisha	market.

Aisha read page five, and then Ayan, rather than read page five, immediately moved to page six, a change in the established protocol. Aisha received support in a different way here as well. Rather than being supplied words one by one, Aisha read in tandem with Ayan, with Aisha's voice predominant. They continued this pattern of taking turns reading until the end of page seven (line 5), when Bigelow prompted them for a comprehension discussion (line 6). Here, Ayan lightly pounded her fist, perhaps realizing the established pattern has been violated, or perhaps, as suggested by her laughter and 'thank you' (line 10), that she had found a way to get through reading more quickly and minimize the amount of aloud reading she would need to do.

The students continued this back and forth reading pattern for 5 pages. Notable here was that they moved into reading two pages each prior to switching reader roles. They took turns seamlessly with few prompts and apparent joint control, albeit with little evidence of enjoyment or interest. Although not evident in the transcript here, we found that they both participated more evenly in the comprehension discussions although they were rather brief and basic, revealing little comprehension of the print or the pictures.

Participation structure 3 (*story pages 12–16*)

At page 12 and continuing through page 16 of the text, the students initiated a new participation structure, wherein Ayan read outloud, with help from Aisha and from the roaming Educational Assistant, Jane (Table 3).

Table 3. Overview of participation structure 3

Page of book	12	13	14	15	16	Totals
Aisha outloud reading and suppliances received						0
Ayan outloud reading and suppliances received			2	4	5	11

Here Ayan took over oral reading, and in contrast to previous structures, managed the driver independently. She had full physical possession of the book, and driver, and was pointing with her fingers as she moved through the text. The dynamic here switched, in part because Jane (who previously had been moving around the room helping other groups), came over and stood near the girls' desks. At the same time, Aisha began to look at the accompanying worksheet for this task and attended less to Ayan's outloud reading. While the students had been moving towards more extended, uninterrupted reading of larger segments of text, Jane disrupted this pattern by inserting comprehension checks or pronunciation recasts (see Excerpt 3).

Excerpt 3

Time	Turn	Participant	
19:22	1	Ayan	anansi bl...(1 sec.)
19:23	2	Aisha	Blew
19:24	3	Jane	blew [pointing to the word]
19:26	4	Ayan	blew on the hot beans and tasted them. ahhhhhh he slur,
19:50	5	Jane	slu::rped, like ahhhhh, slu::rped.
19:57	6	Ayan	he. spooned and blew. slurp..slurp...he spooned
20:09	7	Aisha	spooned.
20:10	8	Ayan	spooned and blew and slurped up
20:16	9	Aisha	spoonfuls.
20:17	10	Ayan	spoonfuls of the beans
20:24	11	Martha	what happened?
20:29	12	Ayan	[pointing to the pictures] happened eat. anansi. up the beans. that's it.
20:34	13	Jane	what's he doing here what action is that? [pointing to the picture]
20:39	14	Ayan	the beans. slurp the beans. slurp the beans.
20:44	15	Jane	taste is t-t-t-t
20:45	16	Jane	what's this? [EA makes sound of blowing]
20:48	17	Ayan	hot.
20:49	18	Jane	blowing?
20:50	19	Ayan	blow
20:51	20	Jane	blew. good.
20:53	21	Ayan	[Ayan turns the page]

Here Ayan is working her way through page 15. Aisha provided three individual word suppliances here: 'blew' (turn 2), 'spooned' (turn 7), 'spoonfuls' (turn 9). In contrast to other participation structures, Jane also supplied words (e.g., 'slurped' turn 5, and 'blowing', turn 18). Jane inserted herself more fully into the interaction in a few different ways: she pointed to the pictures; she also acted out and tried to clarify a potentially confusing word 'slurped' (turn 5); and lastly, she attempted to check or deepen vocabulary comprehension by quizzing for meaning (e.g., "What's this?", blowing air and asking students to name the action) (turn 16) and then evaluating their answer ('good', turn 20). This initiation-response-evaluation sequence temporarily diverted the girls' attention away from the reading task. Notable in this participation structure were the same pattern of Ayan controlling the task and using the resources at hand (Aisha, Jane, the driver, her fingers, etc.) to continue towards task completion.

Participation structure 4 (*story pages 17–32*)

A fourth and final structure was established at page 17 of the text, when Ayan and Aisha began, and then completed the book, with parallel independent reading. Here (see Table 4), word suppliance was reduced further for Ayan, as the pressure to complete the task increased and the students began to co-read.

Table 4. Overview of participation structure 4

Page of book	17–34	23	24	25–30	31	32	totals
Aisha outloud reading and suppliances received							0
Ayan outloud reading and suppliances received			2		1		3

Here we see how Aisha and Ayan used their respective strengths, namely Ayan's task management skills, and Aisha's oral reading fluency, to complete the book reading. As evident in Excerpt 4 below, Ayan, while not the dominant reader, pushed to complete the reading.

Excerpt 4

Time	Turn	Participant	
21:51	1	Ayan & Aisha	[reading with Aisha] Anansi, took off his hat and filled with steaming beans
22:16	2	Aisha & Ayan	as he put the lid back on the beans he. heard. shouts. from the
22:35	3	Ayan	hey! why looking at this one?
22:37	4	Aisha	[laughs]
22:39	5	Ayan & Aisha	… the garden. hey hey hey hey get out of grandma spider's garden
22:52	6	Ayan & Aisha	anansi saw a flock of birds eating the beans he had just planted. some of the neighbors were, waving, and yelling. the scared birds flew through the open kitchen window. the neighbors ran to the porch and pounded on the door. get out of grandma's kitchen you nasty birds! anansi, let us in to help you [slow decoding word by word]
23:50	7	Ayan	to help you [Ayan turns over the driver to Aisha]
23:56	8	Aisha	[clearly and fluently] anansi didn't know what to do. he had to hide the beans. anansi let us in the neighbors yelled. the birds screeched and flapped and anansi looked around quickly. anansi did the only thing he could think to do. he pulled the hat full of hot beans on his head and opened the door. [Ayan taps on the page]
24:35	9	Martha	she wants you to go fast. [laughter]

Time	Turn	Participant	
24:39	10	Aisha	the neighbors come in yelling and sc…(1 sec)
24:48	12	Martha	screaming
24:52	13	Aisha	screaming and chasing out the flapping birds
24:56	14	Martha	flapping birds
			[Ayan is turning pages, using the driver, and pointing to the words for Aisha to read. Ayan is subvocalizaing]
24:58	15	Aisha	flapping birds.

Ayan and Aisha engaged here, and for the remainder of the book, in mainly independent but parallel, overlapping reading. Aisha was the more audible (louder and clearer) reader but both students engaged with the text. What was very salient here were the ways that Ayan pushed Aisha to read aloud and to continue to focus. For instance, at turn 3, she said to Aisha, whose attention had shifted to the worksheet, "hey why you looking at this one?" in an attempt to redirect Aisha's attention to the book, and to continue to receive support. Ayan's question here was notable in a few ways. First, for its pragmatic complexity and indirect politeness strategies: while this was stated as a question, it was really a direct request for Aisha to move back to the reading task. It was also notable as the first explicit comment about task management, and one of the few authentic, spoken interpersonal exchanges between them (aside from Ayan's 'thank you' to Aisha [turn 10, Excerpt 2 above]). This comment reflects Ayan's stronger English language oral speaking skills and her reliance on Aisha to decode, but also likely her more extensive experience with U.S. school tasks such as this.

Aisha and Ayan continued to read in tandem, with Ayan 'driving' via the colored paper, following the words together and with overlapping, but generally synchronized voices, until turn 7, when Ayan turned the driver over to Aisha. This seemed to serve as a cue for Aisha to read more audibly and independently. Her pace quickened but Ayan also continueed to read and follow along, moving her lips as she decodes, subvocalizing. At page 22, Ayan taped the page, prompting Aisha to increase her pace, a message confirmed by Bigelow (turn 9). Ayan took control again of the driver and managed the task more directly by turning the page, moving the driver, and pointing to words for Aisha to read, as Ayan followed along subvocalizing. They continued in this manner until the close of the text.

Summary of findings

Overall, our analysis demonstrates the ways that these two asymmetrically paired students engaged in four different participation structures, each of which unfolded spontaneously. Aisha and Ayan constructed these different participation structures collaboratively as they worked towards task completion. We found that Ayan and Aisha brought complementary skills to the reading task, which were in part due to their different prior experiences with schooling and print literacy, but also no doubt related to their more recent experiences in U.S. schools as well as their individual personalities. Ayan used her tenacity to 'do school,' and to make use of the resources (including people) around her, to successfully complete the task. Aisha heavily supported Ayan's reading through word suppliances and voice over, a function of her stronger print literacy skills, while Ayan supported Aisha's engagement through joint attention and leading of summary discussions, a likely function of her greater experience in U.S. classrooms and English language conversation skills. As we suggest below, it is likely that the task design, and the commitment the girls had to each other, the teacher, and the endeavor of being students at this school influenced the participants' willingness to engage in the activity (Turner 1995).

Discussion

This chapter has examined how learners with varied first and second language literacy skills engage with each other and the task in light of their varied backgrounds, task constraints, and asymmetrical pairing. We discuss each in turn below and focus on the learning opportunities therein.

It is crucial to consider is the impact of the book on the activity and the potential learning opportunities it provided. The book was a powerful, even overwhelming, mediating factor in the type of peer interaction that occurred. As the interaction was tightly focused on decoding the written text, there was little negotiation for meaning. This decoding and reading aloud produced word suppliances when the reader paused or prompted. This limited focus on meaning or negotiation might be due to the participants' desire to push toward task completion without the need for confirming or checking comprehension. Or, if there was comprehension of the text, the participants possibly assumed they shared the same interpretation of the text and did not necessarily need to clarify or negotiate the meaning of the text. The reading comprehension checks by Bigelow (e.g. *What happened?*) also offered few opportunities for this dyad to negotiate meaning. The fact that there was so little meaningful interaction suggests that this task, at least as performed here, was not particularly facilitative of second language learning (Gass & Mackey 2007). However, while not promoting meaningful interaction or negotiation of meaning, it is possible that the task served as mechanism to review a text already read, to practice a procedure for learning to read (partner reading), or to practice decoding.

Furthermore, in terms of developing literacy skills, we maintain that Ayan and Aisha's participation in the task was likely of little benefit to either. If the students had read this book independently, they each would have likely spent very little time with the text – for Aisha, because it was too easy and for Ayan, because it was too hard. For both girls, albeit for different reasons, the *Anansi* text was a suboptimal choice for fostering meaning-making literacy skills. The classroom setting of this task might have leveraged the participants' desire to participate in literacy activities, and the commitment they seem to have to each other to complete assigned tasks, and potentially to further develop their literacy skills. Nevertheless, neither girl was equipped to optimally support the development of reading skills in the ways that an experienced teacher might; this includes providing support for meaning making, print decoding, and prompting learners to monitor comprehension (Schwartz 2005). Indeed, successful completion of the task required very little meaning making or real learning; Ayan and Aisha were busy, 'on-task', and compliant with teacher directions here (Berliner 1990), but this work was unlikely to promote their English reading skills.

Within a sociocultural or Vygotskian framework (e.g., Lantolf & Thorne 2006), human action is directed or mediated by motives, and arises out of need, all within intersections of social relationships and cultural phenomena. If we conclude that the partner reading activity did little to help Ayan and Aisha learn to read in English, then we need to explore other motives or needs that the task fulfilled which propelled them towards task completion. For instance, perhaps they needed to act like readers and be part of a classroom of students who were learning English and learning to read. Such an interpretation is supported by Ayan's redirection comment to Aisha ("hey! why looking at this one?"). Or perhaps they felt obligated to each other or to the researcher with the camera. Perhaps the feeling of participating (mostly) as requested by the teacher reveals Ayan and Aisha's trust in the teacher and their belief that by following the teacher's instructions, they will become better readers, learn English, be successful in the class, and presumably in school. The task, after all, is rather long and dull, yet the girls stick with it. While all – or some varied combination of these motives – were likely in play, this analysis highlights the hard work that many language learners do, often without clear motives or well defined learning objectives. Furthermore, with respect to second language learning from a sociocultural perspective, these data provide a clear example of how learners can productively work together (with a variety of good intentions and motivations), yet the nature of the task and skill asymmetries result in few opportunities for second language learning.

Also important here are the insights provided by this data on the impact of asymmetrical pairing on interactional patterns and their potential impact on learning. We found that while there was little negotiation for meaning as defined in the L2 literature, there was a great deal of collaboration in setting up roles, participation structures, and work towards task completion. Ayan and Aisha constructed four different participation structures across this task. These participation structures allowed for different interactional moves and roles, in response to task and material constraints as well as their own skills and strengths.

Across the four structures Aisha took on the role of 'expert decoder' by reading fluently, supplying words for Ayan, and voicing decodes more audibly during parallel reading. Ayan took the role of 'expert task manager'. She prompted Aisha to stay focused; issued indirect requests for suppliance of words she needed; offered meta-comments about the task; maintained physical control of task resources (e.g., turning pages, pointing to words, managing the driver), and participated in comprehension discussions (although often minimally). As suggested here, and documented elsewhere (see Bigelow & King 2014), Ayan's strengths were in 'doing school', that is, in figuring out how to complete requirements which might, or might not, involve learning but always involve some sort of busy work (e.g., copying, doing a worksheet). Ayan was clearly the weaker reader but had a more dominant personality during the interaction. While we saw on multiple occasions that she struggled to stay on track in class, this task seemed to help her stay focused due to the use of the driver, as a tool, and the close involvement of a more proficient peer. Although Aisha has stronger oral reading skills, and much more extensive previous experiences with literacy, her way of interacting with Ayan was more accommodating and even passive at times. As Storch and Aldosari (2013) have suggested, it may be that the dyadic pairing (e.g., collaborative, dominant/passive, expert/novice) is as important, if not more important than the proficiency level of learners in determining task engagement.

This detailed analysis of two students doing a single reading task adds an additional dimension to existing literature on dyadic task completion. As noted above, much of the existing literature is based on studies that include only learners who have high levels of formal schooling and high levels of print literacy in their home languages; are engaged primarily in second (or third) language learning, not learning language *and* initial literacy simultaneously; are roughly equally matched in terms of language and literacy skills; and are asked to complete narrowly designed tasks (e.g., 'spot the difference' tasks). The everyday example analyzed here, in turn, examines a longer, broader, more complex task that is common to everyday classrooms. Here we see how students engage with a task fully, to their best ability and successfully (in terms of completion), yet their opportunities for second language learning, and for negotiation for meaning, are constrained by their differential skill sets and personalities as well as by the nature of the task.

The findings from this analysis thus complicate the notions of 'expert' and 'novice' and the potentially complementary strengths of learners. For instance, in these data, we saw how the more 'novice' reader (Ayan) managed the task, while the 'expert' reader accommodated to a particular reading style. These findings also highlight learners' own agency in figuring out how to complete a task in a way that worked for them (in light of time limitations and their own needs and skills as L2 readers). These data also provide an example of the fluidity of interactional structures within one clearly defined task, and serves as a reminder of the creativity of students in determining how to complete a given task and the wide variation in how this might be accomplished. Finally, as suggested above, despite being a requirement of the task, there was very little comprehension discussion, a fact which calls into question how meaningful that part of the task was, and pushes us to consider other ways in which this might have been structured. The learners, as inexperienced readers, might not have invested in the comprehension portion of the task, but rather in the goal of completing the task, given the absence of any other purpose set out for them to read this story.

Conclusion and pedagogical implications

Peer interaction and task-based language learning have been important constructs within the field of language teaching and learning because of their potential to maximize classroom language learning by engaging learners in language use, problem solving, and potentially higher order thinking. For these reasons, language teachers often strive to increase the amount of learner interaction in their classroom. This can be accomplished with supportive or scaffolded teaching practices, such as breaking tasks into phases with pre-teaching key lexical or syntactic structures, offering models of outcomes, task repetition, and offering learners clear instructions for how to work together, as well as an authentic purpose for the task (see McCormick Calkins 2000, for an example of a research-based book with generally accepted strategies for teaching reading).

We maintain that it is possible for there to be learning benefits for both members of an asymmetrically paired dyad with dramatically different language proficiency and literacy levels. Yet, as we reflect on the literacy development opportunities of the task, our analysis suggests that this particular partner-reading task may not have facilitated literacy acquisition or second language development for either student, as implemented. There are glimmers of amusement in the transcript, as might be expected with a comical folktale, but for the most part, the participants completed the task by largely going through the motions of the task without visibly making much meaning from the text. How could it have been different? Ayan would benefit from texts that would allow her to recognize a much higher percentage of words and to engage common emergent reading strategies such as combining beginning sounds with picture clues and context clues, both of which have the potential to help her become a fluent reader. Aisha would have benefitted from a different, more advanced-level text, and the opportunity to read silently with a clear academic or aesthetic purpose.

The partner reading task did, however, serve other purposes besides practicing English reading. There were opportunities for both Ayan and Aisha to help assist each other in 'doing school'. They enacted multiple roles and identities throughout the task and with a great deal of effort they were able to have the satisfaction of completing the task, even if this was mainly symbolic and not maximally beneficial to either of them. Perhaps this outcome was possible because Ayan and Aisha agreed to work collaboratively, more or less according to the task instructions, and this could contribute in some way to self-efficacy as students, if not as readers. It is our hope that the participants have further opportunities to read level-appropriate texts across many genres and those that are of high interest to them. To maximally engage and motivate learners, the purpose of the reading activity could be more authentic. For instance, orally recounting a folktale for entertainment or reading a store's website for hours of operation are examples of reading for authentic, or real, out-of-school purposes. Perhaps reading in school could include not only age and developmentally appropriate texts, but also motivating purposes to read. Many and varied reading opportunities that are collaborative, multilingual, and individual would likely offer Ayan and Aisha the avenues toward being able to comprehend high school content. It is possible for these type of literacy activities to occur in a classroom setting while simultaneously supporting Ayan and Aisha's developing identities as good readers, students and valuable and contributing members of the learning community.

Acknowledgement

We are grateful to Kate Stemper and Melissa Engman for helping us think through ways sociocultural theory applies to reading instruction in this task; to Annie Delbridge and Kristi Bergeson for insights into Ayan and Aisha's reading proficiency and learning needs, from a literacy standpoint; and to Jenna Cushing-Leubner, Mary Lynn Montgomery, Stephanie Owen-Lyons, Yi-Ju Lai, Margaret Martin, and Jen Vanek for their insightful critiques and comments. Thanks to the volume editors, anonymous reviewers, and to Catherine Lilly for helpful suggestions.

References

August, D., & Shanahan, T. (Eds.). (2006). *Developing literacy in second-language learners: Report of the National Literacy Panel on Language-Minority Children and Youth*. Mahwah, NJ: Lawrence Erlbaum Associates.

Ballinger, S. (2013). Towards a cross-linguistic pedagogy: Biliteracy and reciprocal learning strategies in French immersion. *Journal of Immersion and Content-Based Language Education*, 1(1), 131–148. doi:10.1075/jicb.1.1.06bal

Berliner, D. (1990). What's all the fuss about instructional time? In M. Ben-Peretz & R. Bromme (Eds.), *The nature of time in schools: Theoretical concepts, practitioner perceptions* (pp. 3–35). New York, NY: Teachers College Press.

Betts, E. A. (1946). *Foundations of reading instruction, with emphasis on differentiated guidance*. New York, NY: American Book Company.

Bigelow, M. (2010). *Mogadishu on the Mississippi: Language, racialized identity, and education in a new land*. New York, NY: Wiley-Blackwell.

Bigelow, M., & King, K. (2014). Somali immigratn youths and the power of print literacy. *Writing Systems Research*, 6(2), 1–16.

Bigelow, M., & Tarone, E. (2004). The role of literacy level in SLA: Doesn't who we study determine what we know? *TESOL Quarterly*, 39(1), 689–700.

Bigelow, M., & Tarone, E. (2012). A research agenda for second language acquisition of pre-literate and low-literate adult and adolescent learners. In P. Vinogradov & M. Bigelow (Eds.), *Low educated second language and literacy acquisition, 7th symposium* (pp. 157–181). Minneapolis, MN: University of Minnesota Printing Services.

Bloome, D., & Egan-Robertson, A. (1993). The social construction of intertextuality in classroom reading and writing lessons. *Reading Research Quarterly*, 28(4), 304–333. doi:10.2307/747928

Cazden, C. B. (1994). Language, cognition, and ESL literacy: Vygotsky and ESL literacy teaching. *TESOL Quarterly*, 28(1), 172–176. doi:10.2307/3587207

Cazden, C. G. (1986). Classroom discourse. In M. C. Wittrock (Ed.), *Handbook of research on teaching* (3rd ed., pp. 432–463). New York, NY: MacMillan.

Cohen, A. D. (2006). The learner's side of foreign language learning: Where do styles, strategies, and tasks meet? *International Review of Applied Linguistics in Language Teaching*, 41(4), 279–291.

de Bot, K. (1996). The psycholinguistics of the output hypothesis. *Language Learning*, 46, 529–555. doi:10.1111/j.1467-1770.1996.tb01246.x

de Guerrero, M. C. M. (1994). Form and functions of inner speech in adult second language learning. In J. P. Lantolf & G. Appel (Eds.), *Vygotskian approaches to second language research* (pp. 83–116). Norwood, NJ: Ablex.

de Guerrero, M. C. M., & Villamil, O. S. (1994). Social-cognitive dimensions of interaction in L2 peer revision. *The Modern Language Journal*, 78(4), 484–496. doi:10.1111/j.1540-4781.1994.tb02065.x

de Guerrero, M. C. M., & Villamil, O. S. (2000). Activating the ZPD: Mutual scaffolding in L2 peer revision. *The Modern Language Journal*, 84(1), 51–68. doi:10.1111/0026-7902.00052

Donato, R. (1994). Collective scaffolding in second language learning. In J. P. Lantolf & G. Appel (Eds.), *Vygotskian approaches to second language research* (pp. 33–56). Norwood, NJ: Ablex.

Echevarria, J., Vogt, M., & Short, D. (2014). *Making content comprehensible for elementary English learners.* Boston, MA: Pearson.

East, M. (2012). Addressing the intercultural via task-based language teaching: Possibility or problem? *Language and Intercultural Communication* 12(1), 56–73. doi:10.1080/14708477.2011.626861

Ehri, L.C. (2005). Learning to read words: Theory, findings, and issues. *Scientific Studies of Reading*, 9(2), 167–188. doi:10.1207/s1532799xssr0902_4

Ehrman, M., & Oxford, R. (2011). Adult language learning styles and strategies in an intensive training setting. *The Modern Language Journal*, 74(3), 311–327. doi:10.1111/j.1540-4781.1990.tb01069.x

Erickson, F. (1982). Classroom discourse as improvisation: Relationships between academic task structure and social participation structure in lessons. In L.C. Wilkinson (Ed.), *Communicating in the classroom* (pp. 153–181). New York, NY: Academic Press.

Erickson, F. (1992). Ethnographic microanalysis of interaction. In M.D. LeCompte, W.L. Millroy, & J. Preissle (Eds.), *The handbook of qualitative research in education* (pp. 201–225). San Diego, CA: Academic Press.

Foster, P., & Ohta, A. (2005). Negotiation for meaning and peer assistance in second language classrooms. *Applied Linguistics*, 26(3), 402–430. doi:10.1093/applin/ami014

Forman, E.A., & Cazden, C.B. (1985). Exploring Vygotskian perspectives in education: The cognitive value in peer interaction. In J.V. Wertsch (Ed.), *Culture, communication, and cognition: Vygotskian perspectives* (pp. 323–347). Cambridge: Cambridge University Press.

Garcez, P.M. (1997). Microethnography. In N. Hornberger & D. Corson (Eds.) *Encyclopedia of language and education* (pp. 187–196). Dordrecht: Springer. doi:10.1007/978-94-011-4535-0_18

Guerrettaz, A.M., & Johnston, B. (2013). Materials in the classroom ecology. *The Modern Language Journal*, 97(3), 779–796. doi:10.1111/j.1540-4781.2013.12027.x

Gutierrez, X. (2008). What does metalinguistic activity in learners' interaction during a collaborative L2 writing task look like? *The Modern Language Journal*, 92(4), 519–537. doi:10.1111/j.1540-4781.2008.00785.x

Gass, S., & Mackey, A. (2007). Input, interaction and output in second language acquisition. In B. VanPatten & J. Williams (Eds.), *Theories in second language acquisition: An introduction* (pp. 175–200). Mahwah, NJ: Lawrence Erlbaum Associates.

Gay, G. (2000). *Culturally responsive teaching: Theory, research, and practice.* New York, NY: Teachers College Press.

Iwashita, N. (1999). Tasks and learners' output in nonnative-nonnative interaction. In K. Kanno (Ed.), *The acquisition of Japanese as a second language* (pp. 31–52). Amsterdam: John Benjamins. doi:10.1075/lald.20.06iwa

Izumi, S. (2002). Output, input enhancement, and The Noticing Hypothesis: An experimental study on ESL relativization. *Studies in Second Language Acquisition*, 24, 541–577. doi:10.1017/S0272263102004023

Izumi, S., & Bigelow, M. (2000). Does output promote noticing and second language acquisition? *TESOL Quarterly*, 34(2), 239–278. doi:10.2307/3587952

Izumi, S., Bigelow, M., Fujiwara, M., & Fearnow, S. (1999). Testing the output hypothesis: Effects of output on noticing and second language acquisition. *Studies in Second Language Acquisition*, 21(3), 421–452. doi:10.1017/S0272263199003034

Kamil, M.L., Pearson, P.D., Moje, E.B., & Afflerbach, P. (Eds.). (2011). *Handbook of reading research*, vol. IV. New York, NY: Routledge.

King, K. A., & Benson, C. (2008). Vernacular and Indigenous literacies. In B. Spolsky & F. M. Hult (Eds.), *Blackwell handbook of educational linguistics* (pp. 341–354). Malden, MA: Blackwell. doi:10.1002/9780470694138.ch24

Kowal, M., & Swain, M. (1994). Using collaborative language production tasks to promote students' language awareness. *Language Awareness*, 3(2), 73–93. doi:10.1080/09658416.1994.9959845

Ladson-Billings, G. (1995). Toward a theory of culturally relevant pedagogy. *American Educational Research Journal*, 32(3), 465–491. doi:10.3102/00028312032003465

Lantolf, J., & Thorne, S. (2006). *Sociocultural theory and the genesis of second language development*. Oxford: Oxford University Press.

McCafferty, S. G. (1994). The use of private speech by adult ESL learners at different levels of proficiency. In J. P. Lantolf & G. Appel (Eds.), *Vygotskian approaches to second language research* (pp. 117–134). Norwood, NJ: Ablex.

McCormick Calkins, L. (2000). *The art of teaching reading*. Upper Saddle River, NJ: Pearson.

Moje, E. B., & Hinchman, K. (2004). Culturally responsive practices for youth literacy learning. In T. L. Jetton & J. A. Dole (Eds.), *Adolescent literacy research and practice* (pp. 320–350). New York, NY: The Guilford Press.

Norfolk, B., & Norfolk, S. (2006). *Anansi and the pot of beans*. Atlanta, GA: August House.

Oliver, R. (2000). Age differences in negotiation and feedback in classroom and pairwork. *Language Learning*, 50(1), 119–151. doi:10.1111/0023-8333.00113

Pavlenko, A., & Blackledge, A. (Eds.). (2004). *Negotiation of identities in multilingual contexts*. Clevedon, UK: Multilingual Matters.

Pettitt, N., & Tarone, E. (2015). Following Roba: What happens when a low-education mutilingual learns to read. *Writing Systems Research*, 7 (1), 20–38.

Philips, S. (1972). Participation structure and communicative competence: Warm Springs children in community and classroom. In C. Cazden, V. John, & D. Hymes (Eds.), *Functions of language in the classroom* (pp. 329–342). New York, NY: Teachers College Press.

Philp, J. (2003). Constraints on "noticing the gap" nonnative speakers' noticing of recasts in NS-NNS interaction. *Studies in Second Language Acquisition*, 25(1), 99–126. doi:10.1017/S0272263103000044

Philp, J., Walter, S., & Basturkmen, H. (2010). Peer interaction in the foreign language classroom: What factors foster a focus on form? *Language Awareness*, 19(4), 261–279. doi:10.1080/09658416.2010.516831

Plough, I., & Gass, S. (1993). Interlocutor and task familiarity. In G. Crookes & S. Gass (Eds.), *Tasks and language learning: Integrating theory and practice* (pp. 35–56). Clevedon, UK: Multilingual Matters.

Revesz, A. (2009). Task complexity, focus on form, and second language development. *Studies in Second Language Acquisition*, 31(2), 437–470. doi:10.1017/S0272263109090366

Robinson, P., Ting, S., & Urwin, J. (1995). Investigating second language task complexity. *RELC Journal*, 25, 62–79. doi:10.1177/003368829502600204

Roy, L. A., & Roxas, K. C. (2011). Whose deficit is this anyhow? Exploring counter-stories of Somali Bantu refugees' experiences in "doing school". *Harvard Educational Review*, 81(3), 521–541. doi:10.17763/haer.81.3.w441553876k24413

Sato, M., & Ballinger, S. (2012). Raising language awareness in peer interaction: A cross-context, cross-method examination. *Language Awareness*, 21(1-2), 157–179. doi:10.1080/09658416.2011.639884

Sato, M., & Lyster, R. (2012). Peer interaction and corrective feedback for accuracy and fluency development: Monitoring, practice, and proceduralization. *Studies in Second Language Acquisition*, 34(4), 591–262. doi:10.1017/S0272263112000356

Sato, M. & Viveros, P. (2016). Interaction or collaboration? The proficiency effect on group work in the foreign language classroom. In M. Sato & S. Ballinger (Eds.), *Peer interaction and second language learning: Pedagogical potential and research agenda* (pp. 91–112). Amsterdam: John Benjamins.

Schwartz, R.M. (1997). Self-monitoring in beginning reading. *The Reading Teacher*, 51(1), 40–48.

Schwartz, R.M. (2005). Decisions, decisions: Responding to primary students during guided reading. *The Reading Teacher*, 58(5), 436–443. doi:10.1598/RT.58.5.3

Shehadeh, A. (2001). Self- and other-initiated modified output during task-based interaction. *TESOL Quarterly*, 35(3), 433–457. doi:10.2307/3588030

Shehadeh, A. (2003). Learner output, hypothesis testing and internalizing linguistic knowledge. *System*, 31(2), 155–171. doi:10.1016/S0346-251X(03)00018-6

Shintani, N. (2012). Input-based tasks and the acquisition of vocabulary and grammar: A process-product study. *Language Teaching Research* 16 (2), 253–279.

Storch, N., & Aldosari, A. (2013). Pairing learners in pair work activity. *Language Teaching Research*, 17(1), 31–48. doi:10.1177/1362168812457530

Storch, N. (2002). Patterns of Interaction in ESL Pair Work. *Language Learning*, 52(1), 119–158. doi:10.1111/1467-9922.00179

Swain, M. (1985). Communicative competence: Some roles of comprehensible input and comprehensible output in its development. In S. Gass & C. Madden (Eds.), *Input in second language acquisition* (pp. 235–253). Rowley, MA: Newbury House.

Swain, M. (1993). The output hypothesis: Just speaking and writing aren't enough. *The Canadian Modern Language Review*, 50(1), 158–164.

Swain, M. (1995). Three functions of output in second language learning. In G. Cook & B. Seidlhofer (Eds.), *Principle and practice in applied linguistics: Studies in honour of H.G. Widdowson* (pp. 125–144). Oxford: Oxford University Press.

Swain, M. (2000). The output hypothesis and beyond: Mediating acquisition through collaborative dialogue. In J. Lantolf (Ed.), *Sociocultural theory and second language learning* (pp. 97–114). Oxford: Oxford University Press.

Swain, M., & Lapkin, S. (2001). Focus on form through collaborative dialogue: Exploring tasks effects. In M. Bygate, P. Skehan & M. Swain (Eds.), *Researching pedagogic tasks* (pp. 99–118). New York, NY: Longman.

Tarone, E., Bigelow, M., & Hansen, K. (2009). *Literacy and second language oracy*. Oxford: Oxford University Press.

Taylor, B.M., Hanson, B., Justice-Swanson, K.J., & Watts, S. (1997). Helping struggling readers: Linking small group intervention with cross-age tutoring. *The Reading Teacher*, 51, 196–209. doi:10.1598/RT.51.3.4

Tudge, J. (1990). Vygotsky, the zone of proximal development, and peer collaboration: Implications for classroom practice. In L.C. Moll (Ed.), *Vygotsky and education: instructional implications and applications of sociohistorical psychology*. (pp. 155–174). Cambridge: Cambridge University Press. doi:10.1017/CBO9781139173674.008

Turner, J. (1995). The influence of classroom contexts on young children's motivation for literacy. *Reading Research Quarterly*, 30(3), 410–441. doi:10.2307/747624

Vinogradov, P. (2008). "Maestra! The letters speak." Adult ESL students learning to read for the first time. *Minne/WITESOL*, 25. Retrieved from: http://minnetesoljournal.org/wp-content/uploads/2015/11/TESOL-2008.pdf

Washburn, G. N. (1994). Working in the ZPD: Fossilized and nonfossilized nonnative speakers. In J. P. Lantolf & G. Appel (Eds.), *Vygotskian approaches to second language research* (pp. 69–82). Norwood, NJ: Ablex.

Watson, J. (2010). Interpreting across the abyss: A hermeneutic study of initial literacy development by high school English language learners with limited formal schooling. (Unpublished doctoral dissertation), University of Minnesota, Minneapolis, MN.

Wood, D., Bruner, J. S., & Ross, G. (1976). The role of tutoring in problem solving. *Journal of Child Psychology and Psychiatry*, 17(2), 89–100. doi:10.1111/j.1469-7610.1976.tb00381.x

Young, A. & Tedick, D. J. (2016). Collaborative dialogue in a two-way Spanish/English immersion classroom: Does heterogeneous grouping promote peer linguistic scaffolding? In M. Sato & S. Ballinger (Eds.), *Peer interaction and second language learning: Pedagogical potential and research agenda* (pp. 135–160). Amsterdam: John Benjamins.

Zhu, W., & Mitchell, D. A. (2012). Participation in peer response as activity: An examination of peer response stances from an activity theory perspective. *TESOL Quarterly*, 46(2), 362–386. doi:10.1002/tesq.22

Appendix 1

Transcription conventions

CAPS	spoken with emphasis (minimum unit is morpheme)
.	falling intonation at the end of words
,	rising intonation at the end of words
?	rising intonation in clause
->	continuing or flat intonation (as in lists)
!	animated tone, not necessarily an exclamation
::	elongated sound
[]	transcriber's comment
… (.x)	pause and estimate of length

EPILOGUE

New pathways in researching interaction

Jenefer Philp
Lancaster University

Introduction

What is exciting about this edited collection on peer interaction is the range of research presented here: it reflects a burgeoning interest in an area little considered even 15 years ago. In this final chapter, I highlight some of the ways in which the research on peer interaction takes us along new paths in exploring instructed language learning, and enlarges our view of learning opportunities in the classroom. These include, as Sato and Ballinger set out in their introductory chapter, insights into: interactional patterns and learner characteristics; tasks and interactional modalities; and learning settings.

This volume shifts our focus from teacher-fronted interaction to peer interaction, and draws us to consider quite a different side of instructed language learning. Speaking about the classroom in general, Breen (1985), foregrounds social relationships between peers as being at the heart of learner behaviour and outcomes. He reminds us that "(h)ow and why learners do what they do will be strongly influenced by their situation, who they are with, and by their perceptions of both" (138). Breen's reminder is evident in much of the research documented in the current volume. This research involves a range of age groups, from younger learners to adolescents to adults, and represents a variety of instructional settings, including two way immersion (e.g., Young & Tedick); foreign language (e.g., Sato & Viveros); L1 primary school classes (e.g., Bigelow & King); and CMC (e.g., McDonough, Crawford, & Vleeschauwer). The studies vary too in task type, task complexity and modality, training, proficiency, and language focus. Nevertheless, we find that in the majority of studies, relations between peers stand out as a recurring focus, and we are left with a strong suspicion that peer relations might, for all our research in other directions, be a critical feature that mediates the relative effectiveness of peer interaction for learning. Although they are often elusive in experimental studies, the social goals and relations between peers seem all too obvious in descriptive classroom-based studies.

DOI 10.1075/lllt.45.15phi

This collection highlights the distinctive possibilities that peer interaction offers to learning. These possibilities include a potential for greater autonomy and heightened involvement in the learning process, where learners must rely on their collective resources, rather than on the teacher. This body of research may also lead us to consider how peer interaction contrasts with and complements teacher-fronted or teacher-learner interaction (Batstone & Philp 2013; Philp, Adams, & Iwashita 2014), an area for future research. I will begin by thinking about the character of learning (Sfard 1998), specific to language learning, and methods for investigating learning within the context of peer interaction. I then focus on two themes that emerge across studies in this research: the social nature of peer interaction and engagement in peer interaction. I finish with a brief discussion of the role of the teacher for peer interaction.

Describing and exploring learning in the context of peer interaction

Batstone and Philp (2013) note the multi-participant nature of classroom inter-action, and the variability in who is involved in interaction at different times, whether in teacher-led whole class interaction, pair and group work or private conversations between peers, or teacher and student(s). These differing kinds of talk contribute to each learner's experience as a whole; with "layers of related inter-actions working in parallel, (…) each play a part in the kind of affordances pro-vided" (121). These learning affordances can be complimentary: One interaction may spark enquiry or lead to noticing a problem or a gap to be resolved, that is, it provides the catalyst for potential change (Schmidt 2001); Another interaction may actually provide the solution or a part-solution to a difficulty engendered in a past encounter; Yet other interactions may allow learners the chance to re-engage with a semi-familiar form (Nation 2007; Schmitt 2008), and further proceduralize the development of their receptive or productive skills (DeKeyser 2007).

In any class, teacher-led and peer-directed interactions have distinctive char-acteristics. In contrast to the asymmetric nature of the teacher-learner relationship, peer interaction is typically more symmetric in terms of participant contributions because of the relative equality between learners in terms of their age, authority and proficiency. This is particularly so for children (Laursen & Hartup 2002), but less the case in adult learning settings where learners and teacher may share a similar age and maturity level. This equality allows for the possibility of exploring and experimenting, for trial and error, because the other participants may know no better. They may be able to help but, crucially it is because their contribution remains refutable, malleable, open for co-construction that it is most useful: con-flict in understanding provides a catalyst for change (De Lisi & Golbeck 1999; see also Philp et al. 2014; Sato & Ballinger 2016, for a review of differences between teacher-student and student-student interactions). What this suggests is that these distinctive relationships mean teacher-learner and peer interaction likely contribute to the learning process in complementary ways (see Gibbons 2003; Mercer 2008, for two very worthwhile discussions of teaching-and-learning in the classroom). For example, teacher-student interaction provides a context in which students can receive dependable feedback on their L2 use, reliable models to draw on, and expert scaffolding where help is needed. Peer interaction, where supportive and collaborative in mindset (Ballinger 2013), provides a context for experimenting, for "playing" with language, for articulating initial ideas and hypotheses: peers provide the place to try things out, and for time on task to practice undaunted.

Sfard (1998) characterises two views of learning in terms of "participation" and "acquisition", and cautions against limiting our view of learning to just one or the other. In SLA research, we are starting to see a greater tolerance for inclusion of both views (Hulstijn et al. 2014), and this is reflected in this volume, with both perspectives represented in the research: we see learning measured and described for different purposes.

Sociocultural approaches

Many chapters describe learning from a sociocultural perspective, largely because at its Vygotskian core is the inherently social nature of language and learning as well as the interdependence of the social and the cognitive (Hogan & Tudge 1999; Lantolf 2000). This is evident in the use of the "zone of proximal development" (ZPD) as a dynamic measure of learning – the notion that learning is not best measured by a single individual effort, but is captured too by what can be accomplished with a co-participant. It highlights the enabling of progress to higher levels of thinking, problem solution and language use, through the social support of co-construction. Through help that is within the range the learner is approaching but as yet unable to attain, we see what that learner will ultimately be able to do unassisted (Daniels 2011; Vygotsky 1978).

The metaphor of the scaffold (Wood, Bruner & Ross 1976) is appropriate for language learning: the learner, whether child or adult, is enabled through the particular help of a co-participant to create the meaning they wish to express, or complete the task required. This help is contingent on the needs of the learner – almost like filling in additional stepping stones to bridge links that are too far apart – each stone chosen to fit the need. However, a potential problem is the overuse of the term "scaffolding". Where the term scaffolding is used generically for any kind of assistance, such as providing peer correction, spelling a word, looking up a word in the dictionary, we lose the explanatory power of this term. The value of "scaffolding" is that it allows us to see the dialogic nature of a particular type of interaction, in which the more expert interlocutor provides guidance that is cali-brated to the specific needs of the learner engaging with a specific task.

While there are many ways scaffolding is understood and operationalised in the literature, I highlight three prominent models here, used in educational psy-chology and/or applied linguistics. First, Wood, Bruner, and Ross (1976) in their original use of the term scaffolding, identify six functions of scaffolding, which are based on parental assistance of pre-school children's problem solving of a wooden puzzle, and which may be enacted through non-verbal means (see Gibbons 2003 for an application in a primary school class). In another model, Aljaafreh and Lantolf's (1994) operationalisation of scaffolding is more clearly language-related and tailored to the purpose of providing assistance by an expert tutor to an adult language learner. In their model, scaffolding involves graduated help that is con-tingent on the needs of the learner and transpires through dialogic interaction. These first two conditions are shared by a third conceptual model of scaffolding; that of van de Pol, Volman, and Beishhuizen (2010), who describe scaffolding in L1 school settings. They identify three key characteristics of scaffolding. The first is fading, in which the teacher increasingly reduces degree of support (similar to Aljaafreh and Lantolf's graduated help). The second involves contingency, that is, the degree of support provided depends upon what arises: it is particular to the needs of the individual at particular points in time during the task or activity. The third involves transfer of responsibility. This last characteristic emphasizes the end goal of ZPD: ultimately the student demonstrates the ability to take responsibil-ity for her own learning. Each of these three models, consistent with Vygotsky's original conception of ZPD, entail dialogic assistance between expert and novice – teacher/tutor/ adult and student/child – not between peers. However, they pro-vide a useful starting point for considering the incidence of scaffolding between peers (as opposed to other types of peer assistance). In this collection, scaffolding among peers is predominantly identified through analysis of language related epi-sodes (LREs) (Swain & Lapkin 1998) to describe the co-construction of language and mediation of successful task completion. If scaffolding can occur between learners, as suggested by Donato's (1994) research on "collective scaffolding" (see also Storch 2001, 2002, 2009) as well as by many of the studies in this volume (e.g., Baralt, Gurzynski-Weiss, & Kim, Chapter 8; Bigelow & King, Chapter 13; Martin-Beltrán, Chen, Guzman, & Merrills, Chapter 12; Rouhshad & Storch, Chapter 10; Sato & Viveros, Chapter 3; Young & Tedick, Chapter 5), how is it best operationalised? Should it be distinguished from other kinds of peer assistance? Further research to develop the theoretical construct and operationalisation of scaffolding in peer interaction would be particularly fruitful in building more of an understanding of the nature of scaffolding for language learning, and, specifically for language learning during peer interaction.

Vygotsky's work provides us with insights into the potential of dialogic interaction during asymmetric relationships, including heterogeneous peers working together. A Piagetian perspective is useful for considering interaction between child and adolescent homogenous peers because of the emphasis placed on the balance of existing and new knowledge, where challenges to existing knowledge act as a catalyst to development. Duchesne, McMaugh, Bochner, and Krause (2013) explain that peer interaction provides an ideal context for peers to "expand their ideas, overcome conflicts (disequilibrium) and to achieve shared solutions (equilibrium) that are more mature than individual efforts" (78) (see also, Brown, Metz, & Campione 1996). Thus, both conflict and cooperation are important for conceptual learning to occur from peer interaction (De Lisi & Golbeck 1999). For this reason, Philp and Duchesne (in press) suggest, "It is the way in which peers interact around agreement or disagreement that is central to the effectiveness of the interaction for learning". As many of the studies in this volume conclude of the patterns of interaction between peers, a high degree of mutuality is most effective for learning. This could be attributed to the benefits of symmetric interaction noted above (see Baralt et al.; Choi & Iwashita; Martin-Beltran et al.; Moranski & Toth; Rouhshad & Storch; Sato & Viveros; Young & Tedick this volume).

Cognitive approaches

While sociocultural approaches and the use of qualitative analyses help us to see the dynamic aspect to learning within interactional spaces, the important work of more cognitivist experimental studies help us to predict likely outcomes of different task conditions and modalities, with obvious applications both for theory and pedagogy. For example, García Mayo and Azkarai (Chapter 9) used quantitative methods to investigate how task modality (written vs. oral) might impact use and outcomes of LREs, as well as degree of engagement among 44 adult EFL learners. This allowed them to differentiate between effects of modality and task for incidence and resolution of LREs, and level of engagement. They found significant differences on LREs with respect to modality, and on depth of engagement with respect to task.

Loewen (2005) usefully used teacher-student form-focused episodes where students received incidental focus on problems in their output, to identify deficiencies in L2 knowledge. Based on these episodes, he created tailor-made post-tests. However, as the content of these episodes arising from classroom conversation was unpredictable, pre-testing was not possible. Such individualized testing can be optimal for identifying benefits of interaction, yet weakened without the use of pre-tests to gauge learners' baseline knowledge. Swain (2001) used LREs during dyadic tasks (dictogloss and jigsaw task) to create post-tests, and developed pre-test data based on a pilot of the two tasks used to gauge learners' former knowledge. Fernández Dobao (Chapter 1) resolves the problem by predicting probable areas of difficulty with particular lexical items, based on task content, and presumably the same could be attempted with particular grammatical forms. Interestingly, these pre-tests enabled Fernández Dobao to differentiate between new knowledge and consolidation of knowledge of lexical items. This kind of testing of baseline knowledge could be further developed through reference to theoretical work – for example, vocabulary knowledge, both receptive and productive (e.g., Nation 2013), or explicit versus implicit knowledge of grammatical forms (Ellis, Loewen, Elder, Erlam, Philp, & Reinders 2009). Such research provides the balance to more qualitative work that, through detailed description and analysis, captures the messy complexity of peer interaction, learning, and individual variability. This balance is reflected in mixed methods research, as described below.

Mixed methods approaches

What the learner can achieve through collaboration with others is the kind of learning characterized by Sfard's (1998) "participation metaphor." That is, learning through participation. In this collection, learning as participation is often explored through LREs (Swain & Lapkin 1998). This is quite different to the construct of learning described by an "acquisition metaphor", as something individually possessed, and often tested through unassisted performance, for example in a pre and post-test. While these metaphors of learning are associated with different theoretical paradigms, they can reflect different aspects of learning, and different stages in the learning continuum (as Fernández Dobao suggests in Chapter 1). In this way we may identify change over time both through gain scores on tests, as well as through progression in the amount and kind of assistance needed for particular accomplishments. Finding ways to capture these different aspects of the learning process requires innovative techniques and receptivity to the possibilities afforded by different theoretical paradigms (see Hulstijn et al. 2014 for discussion). Some of these innovations are described in Sato and Ballinger's introduction, while others are discussed in this chapter as they relate to the themes of learning, social relations, and engagement.

In contrast to earlier research on peer interaction, and consistent with a change of focus in the field of SLA to learners' involvement in processes of learning, we find in this collection fewer experimental studies, and more classroom-based non-interventionist research. Future research could make more use of mixed methods, using both qualitative and quantitative approaches in the same study, or in a sequence of related studies. Gass and Mackey (2015) suggest "a major advantage of mixed methods research is to gain a richer and more fulsome picture of the phenomenon under investigation" (288). Baralt et al.'s study (Chapter 8) provides a taste of the possibilities afforded by mixed methods research, particularly when the research draws on theory-driven models to operationalise key constructs. In this case, the researchers build on experimental work on effects of task complexity (Baralt 2013, 2014; Robinson & Gilabert 2007) to then qualitatively explore task outcomes, modality, and engagement, the latter construct based on Svalberg's (2012) model. Their findings highlight social relations between learners as an oft hidden variable in task outcomes. Having reflected on ways of looking at learning, using the metaphors of participation and acquisition, the next section of this chapter focuses on two themes that emerge from the research in the 15 studies presented here: social relations and engagement.

Social relations and learning through peer interaction

Consistent with current trends in research on interaction and L2 learning (Mackey, Abbuhl, & Gass 2012), we see an increased use of more introspective tools in current research. These allow for the possibility of qualitatively exploring inter-relationships between learners, as well as individual learner variables such as motivation, anxiety, attitudes and beliefs specific to a particular class or experience. Breen (1985) reminds us that behaviour needs to be explored in tandem with perceptions. It is not enough to describe what learners do in order to understand how they learn, because their own perception of the situation, attitudes and beliefs all impact on their experience. In recognising the large part played by the participants themselves – as social people who know one another to varying degrees, who work well together (or not), who share a history in some part – it becomes more apparent that classroom-based research preserves existing relationships between participants of a class, and in this regard provides a different picture from laboratory studies that must rely on random volunteers brought together for a short and well controlled study. However, the social aspect to peer interaction is as yet a largely unexplored area in research specific to instructed language learning (for exceptions, see work among child peers in L1 settings, e.g. Philp & Duchesne 2008; Toohey 2000).

A number of the studies in this collection focus on social relations, and draw from a range of models and constructs, including social interdependence theory

(Roseth, Johnson, & Johnson 2008; see Sato & Viveros Chapter 3); positioning theory (Davies & Harré 1990; see Young & Tedick Chapter 5); and Aston's (1993) concepts of comity, solidarity, and support (see Martin-Beltrán et al. Chapter 12). Young and Tedick's (Chapter 5) study with 10–11 year old students, examines collaborative dialogue through the qualitative analysis of LREs, using recursive coding to identify how learners position themselves and others as they enact novice and expert roles during group work. The use of focal students allowed for the comparison of patterns of interaction across groups, contrasting how the same students behaved amongst different peers, and contrasting groups of similar and differing proficiency level (see also Choi & Iwashita Chapter 4). Young and Tedick highlight one of the potential difficulties in heterogeneous groups (O'Donnell 2006); peer interaction can inhibit learning, and be a negative experience for the participants. In their study, the contributions of a less proficient learner were devalued by his peers, and he was belittled throughout. Among homogenous groups more positive group dynamics appeared; learners worked collaboratively, reflecting even participation and a shared focus.

Other researchers in this volume explore social relations through descriptions of how students work with one another on tasks, and centre on patterns of interaction (Storch 2002), mostly focusing on mutuality and equality (Moranski & Toth, Chapter 11; Rouhshad & Storch, Chapter 10). Rouhshad and Storch's innovative study reminds us that social relations are one mediating factor among others in effective peer interaction. In their study, they did not explore relationships between learners (but see Baralt et al. Chapter 8). However, by tracking patterns of interaction between dyads across modalities (FTF and SCMC), they found greater collaborative patterns among F2F pairs than SCMC pairs, and greater resolution of LREs. Here, modality and patterns of interaction appear to intersect: physically working together appears to foster more focus on language form, and a greater commitment to resolving difficulties that arise.

Taken together, these studies point to social relations as one factor we cannot afford to ignore, either as researchers or teachers, when considering the effectiveness of peer interaction, its strengths and potential limitations. This volume suggests many promising directions for further research on peer social relations and L2 learning across different age groups (younger learners, adolescents and adults). The use of theoretical models from other disciplines, and the adoption of focal participants in the design as a means of tracking across partners and task conditions has been particularly fruitful. This research would be likely enhanced by cross-disciplinary research, involving expertise from related fields such as social sciences, psychology and education.

Engagement in peer interaction

Perhaps partly due to these shifts in focus and understanding, it is only in the past decade that we have come to see explorations of learner engagement in studies of instructed language learning, and it is well represented in this collection. Intuitively, most classroom teachers and researchers would assert the importance of engagement for learning, and research bears this out, with robust links found between engagement and learning (e.g. Furlong & Christenson 2008; Gettinger & Ball 2007; Christenson, Reschley, & Wylie 2012). However, often, the word engagement tends to be used ubiquitously in a generic sense and is not theorised or operationalised specifically for language learning. Exceptions include Storch (2008), Dörnyei & Kormos (2004), Svalberg (2012), and Baralt et al. (Chapter 8). Learner engagement is certainly an area requiring greater "conceptual and operational clarity" (Martin 2012: 303). It is useful to turn to the field of educational psychology for a greater wealth of research on engagement, as reflected by a recent handbook on the topic (Christenson et al. 2012). There it is described as a multidimensional construct (Fredricks, Blumenfeld, & Paris 2004), although scholars from different theoretical perspectives and instructional contexts differ as to description of the number and nature of these dimensions. In this volume, we have seen a range of factors that mediate learning between peers. Understanding engagement as multidimensional allows us to bring together attention to form with the affective, psychological and social dimensions that support effective learning.

For the most part, SLA research to date primarily concerns learners' *cognitive* engagement with language (see Svalberg 2012 for an exception). This relates to the noticing, use and discussion of language form during pair and group work, predominantly using collaborative writing tasks such as dictogloss. As we see in this volume, with the focus on language learning and peer interaction, engagement is not only cognitive, but also behavioural, social and emotional. This is consistent with current descriptions of the construct of engagement within the field of education (for review, see Philp & Duchesne, in press). Many of the indicators of engagement in the educational psychology literature overlap with ways in which applied linguistics have described a focus on language among learners in peer interaction. In the following, I draw links between the research carried out in the fields of education and applied linguistics and suggest ways in which education-based research using the construct of engagement can inform research in the field of applied linguistics.

Cognitive engagement relates to the processing of information and conceptual ideas. It involves metacognitive strategies such as planning, monitoring, and evaluating. Storch (2008) identifies two levels of engagement in metalanguage use in a pair writing task. Elaborate engagement is described as intense discussion of

language forms, whereas limited engagement involves simply repeating, acknowl-
edging or ignoring a peer's suggestion (see Rouhshad & Storch, Chapter 10). This
is consistent with constructs of cognitive engagement, and involves many of the
indicators seen in Helme and Clarke's (2001) study of engagement in a mathematics class. Like Storch, and García Mayo and Akarai (Chapter 9), they also made a
distinction in level of engagement according to relative depth of processing. The
researchers operationalised cognitive engagement through behavioural indicators,
such as verbalizing thinking and self-monitoring (versus superficial approaches
such as copying or repeating information, and avoiding effort). In group settings,
these indicators include questioning, completing peer utterances, exchanging
ideas, explaining or providing information, justifying an argument, and using
gestures that reflect cognition (see Churchill, Okada, Nishino, & Atkinson 2010).
Some of these indicators are also evident in Moranski and Toth's (Chapter 11)
analysis of learners' depth of processing during group work to derive rules relating
to the use of the Spanish reflexive pronoun *se*. Their analysis, based on Craik and
Lockhart's model (1972) in effect, describes cognitive engagement.

In a study of motivational factors affecting task performance, Dörnyei and
Kormos (2000) describe learner engagement by quantity (*number of words* and
turns). Essentially this measures the behavioural dimension of engagement.
However, measures of behavioural engagement can also go beyond quantity of on-
task and off-task behaviour. Other studies include conduct, persistence and effort
(Reschly & Christenson 2012), that is, quality as well as quantity of time spent on
task. Sato and Viveros' (Chapter 3), measure of "task-related collaboration (TRC)"
reflects behavioural engagement. Learners demonstrated engagement with the
task by deliberating over what was required, and by negotiating and assigning roles
and responsibilities. As Sato and Viveros note, these TRCs also reflected relational
patterns between students as a context in which participants might assert dominance, choose to opt out, or work collaboratively. Potentially then, TRCs may also
provide a window onto social engagement.

Cognitive and behavioural engagement are the dimensions that tend to be
explored in applied linguistics research. However they do not capture the affective
and/or social aspects to interaction among peers that are vital to engagement, all
the more so, I would argue, for younger and adolescent learners for whom peers
matter so much (Dunn 1999; Hartup 1989, 2011).

When we consider how important relations between learners appear to be
for effective interaction, whether among children, adolescents or adults (Philp &
Duchesne 2008; Philp & Mackey 2010; Rouhshad & Storch, Chapter 10; Sato &
Viveros Chapter 3), it is perhaps not surprising that, in the context of academic
settings, Pekrun and Linnenbrink-Garcia's (2012) model of engagement includes
a social-behavioural dimension. They suggest positive indicators such as actively

supporting peers' engagement, respecting others, and working cohesively and negative indicators such as social loafing, or reducing effort by having others do the work, discouraging participation, disrespecting peers and showing low group cohesion.

In this collection, two studies of heterogeneous groupings in two-way immersion classes provide examples of the social dimension of engagement/disengagement, although they are not identified as such. Martin-Beltrán, Chen, Guzman, and Merrills (Chapter 12) provide ample evidence of social engagement among young adolescent learners during tasks, as participants negotiate identity and social relationships within the peer group. They note that "the opportunity for students to get to know each other as social individuals was often more important than the task at hand" (329). Their coding of social discourse moves (social inquiry, solidarity and support) provides a useful starting point for operationalising aspects of social engagement in this context. Complimenting this is the research by Young and Tedick described above, among younger learners. They found reciprocity and cohesive interaction among homogeneous groups, yet low group cohesion, and disrespect for lower proficiency members in other groups.

In the context of academic settings, Pekrun and Linnenbrink-Garcia (2012) see emotional engagement as vital, working through both a positive/negative dimension (e.g., enjoyment vs boredom) and an activating / deactivating dimension. In this way, students' positive and negative emotions (e.g. feeling relaxed or frustrated) can either activate or deactivate engagement depending on the specific emotion.

While there is little consideration of social and emotional dimensions of engagement in research on instructed language learning (see Svalberg 2009, 2012 for an exception), the contribution of these dimensions to engagement is very apparent in a number of studies here. Baralt, Gurzynski-Weiss, and Kim's (Chapter 8) innovative study comparing engagement (Svalberg 2009) of foreign language learners in SCMC and F2F settings reflects this. As discussed earlier, they found that modality makes a difference to how learners work together. Their study also suggests that peer relations during the interaction are paramount to adult learners: there were clear differences in affective state and patterns of interaction between the SCMC groups, who were unused to working together, and the F2F group, who were familiar with one another. By considering affective and social engagement alongside learners' focus on language (cognitive engagement) during task interaction, they were able to go beyond a surface comparison of task performance (difference in modality outcomes) to a recognition of the complex affective and social factors also at work.

How students interact with one another will influence their language learning through the extent and quality of the reflection, practice and feedback this interaction offers. In turn, their interaction and learning experiences are affected through the relationships they develop with one another, and their patterns of relating to one another. In a study of peer learning in a maths class, Hogan and Tudge (1999) conclude, "The greater the extent to which partners are involved in the task *(behavioural engagement)*, treat it as a joint endeavour *(social engagement)*, and come to a shared understanding *(cognitive engagement)*, the more likely it seems to be that children will learn" (61: annotations added in italics).

Engagement with language is clearly a rich area for future research on classroom interaction, important both for SLA theory and pedagogy. As Janosz (2012) argues, it is vital to define engagement specific to the particular context of learning – in our case, to language learning. For example, Storch (2008) distinguishes between elaborate and limited levels of engagement, identified in LREs. García Mayo and Azkarai (Chapter 9) provide a more elaborated coding system, distinguishing between "ignored" and "addressed" to indicate that learners did pay attention to the problem although it was not resolved.

Fernández Dobao's (Chapter 1) identification of the role taken by each participant within an LRE is highly productive in describing participation, differentiating the roles of trigger, observer, contributor and solver. Comparison of participation roles with test scores (vocabulary targeted by LREs) demonstrated comparable gains for the silent learners, suggesting "they were actively engaged with the vocabulary being discussed" (388). This study highlights the need for triangulating the data on engagement. Adopting a multidimensional model of engagement for interaction research will require a range of measures in addition to the analysis of LREs. Visual cues such as eye gaze, facial expression, body language and gesture, as well as pitch of voice and energy levels can be indicative of engagement. In addition, the use of introspective measures such as stimulated recall (Gass & Mackey 2000; Philp & Mackey 2010) or post-task questionnaires and interviews (Baralt et al. Chapter 8; Sato 2013) provides triangulation.

The role of the teacher in peer interaction

The role of teachers in peer interaction is not a focus in the research presented here, yet it is vital to effective peer learning (O'Donnell 2006; Mercer 1996). This is an obvious area for future research. What is the part played by the teacher? The answer is a complex one, differing widely according to learners' age, social context, task, and learning goals. As O'Donnell (2006) cautions "[d]ifferent choices in peer learning activities require teachers to take different stances with respect to the students, tasks and outcomes" (796). These roles range from pedagogic roles such as drawing learners' attention to language forms and main ideas, modelling language use, resolving linguistic issues and providing advice or feedback to class-room management issues. Two key teacher roles are evident in this volume: foster-ing a positive classroom climate and selecting and structuring activities in ways that scaffold successful collaborative task completion.

Effective peer interaction necessitates a positive classroom environment (e.g., Mercer 1996; O'Donnell 2006; Dörnyei & Maldarez 1997; Salmon 2000). Based on research among adolescent learners in [L1] school settings, Shim, Kiefer, and Wang (2013) suggest that a positive "classroom peer climate", where learners share positive perceptions of reliance on others for support and feel safe to voice their efforts or needs, is vital to fostering help-seeking among peers (290). Shim et al., referring to social interdependence theory (Roseth, Johnson, & Johnson 2008), emphasize the role of the teacher in creating tasks with cooperative goal structures (rather than competitive or individual goal structures) for this age group. This is consistent with the findings of some of the studies in this volume that suggest mutuality and a "collaborative mindset" (Ballinger 2013) are most likely to foster the kind of peer interaction most productive for language learning (see also Sato & Ballinger 2012). Like Ballinger (2013), the studies of Dobao (Chapter 1), Sato and Viveros (Chapter 3), Young and Tedick (Chapter 5) also highlight the role of the teacher in fostering this attitude of respect and support between peers. This provides an interesting contrast to Fujii, Mackey, and Ziegler's study in which adult learners are given explicit training on how to be more effective interlocutors in terms of negotiating communication difficulties, and providing feedback to one another. The two roles are coupled in a study by Dawes (2004) in which L1 learners in primary science classes were trained to use exploratory talk (Mercer 1996) in pair and group work with peers. This training emphasised group over individual achievement, and the need for collaboration. Students were explicitly taught the skills and the language to ask questions, elicit elaborative responses and defend their own ideas, as well as to value the contribution of all group members. Younger learners benefited from the modelling of questions and reasoning, ("What do you think? Why?"), learning to be accountable for ideas ("because…"), using active listening ("Say that again?"); valuing others' ideas ("We need your opinion"); and engaging in joint decision making, ("Do we all agree?") (Dawes 2004: 686).

Based on the studies here, we argue that coaching learners in how to be effective collaborators and interactors is important for adult, adolescents and young learners alike, in face-to-face and online environments (see Sato & Lyster 2012). The find-ings of the two studies that compare F2F and CMC settings (Baralt et al., Chapter 8; Rouhshad & Storch, Chapter 10), imply a need for considerable groundwork in online classes to foster group identity, and to place value in working together and providing support for one another (see De Smet, Van Keer & Valcke 2008; Salmon 2000 for discussion of the role of the teacher/moderator in this process).

Finally, to make the most of the complementarity of peer interaction and other teacher-led talk in the classroom, the teacher's role is vital: in setting up the task, in providing sufficient and appropriate support beforehand, and during peer interaction, as well as following up peer talk by foregrounding successes and addressing difficulties. Bigelow and King's (Chapter 13) study of two heterogeneous adolescent learners reading together underlines the need for teachers to monitor mismatched pair work and to address difficulties that are beyond the scope of the learners' competencies (whether linguistic, cognitive or social). Similarly, Young and Tedick (Chapter 5) highlight the danger of leaving heterogeneous groups simply to their own devices, assuming peer scaffolding will transpire. Like Sato and Viveros (Chapter 3), their study suggests an active role for the teacher, including the need for careful preparation in training students, in selection and structuring of the activities, and in subtle monitoring of peer work.

In this final chapter, I have chosen to discuss two of the themes running through the 15 studies in this volume: social relations; and learner engagement in peer interaction. It is clear that we should not neglect the relationships between learners, neither as teachers nor as researchers (Storch & Aldosari 2013). I've also suggested that we can pay more attention to commonly used terms, such as "scaffolding" and "engagement" in order to be more precise in the focus of our research, and clearer in our constructs. There are certainly many more insights to be gleaned, for example, regarding corrective feedback, the effects of task variables such as modality, and learner variables such as proficiency and age. This valuable collection of research not only helps to clarify but also to extend our understanding of the potential of peer interaction. It serves to point us along new paths for researching interaction, in terms of focus, theory and research methods specific to peer interaction in different settings, for differing purposes and among different age groups.

References

Aljaafreh, A., & Lantolf, J. (1994). Negative feedback as regulation and second language learning in the zone of proximal development. *The Modern Language Journal*, 78(4), 465–483. doi:10.1111/j.1540-4781.1994.tb02064.x

Aston, G. (1993). Notes on the interlanguage of comity. In G. Kasper & S. Blum-Kulka (Eds.), *Interlanguage pragmatics* (pp. 224–250). Oxford: Oxford University Press.

Ballinger, S. (2013). Towards a cross-linguistic pedagogy: Biliteracy and reciprocal learning strategies in French immersion. *Journal of Immersion and Content-Based Language Education*, 1(1), 131–148. doi:10.1075/jicb.1.1.06bal

Baralt, M. (2013). The impact of cognitive complexity on feedback efficacy during online versus face-to-face interactive tasks. *Studies in Second Language Acquisition*, 35, 689–725. doi:10.1017/S0272263113000429

Baralt, M. (2014). Task sequencing and task complexity in traditional versus online classes. In M. Baralt, R. Gilabert, & P. Robinson (Eds.), *Task sequencing and instructed second language learning* (pp. 95–122). London: Bloomsbury.

Baralt, M., Gurzynski-Weiss, L., & Kim, Y. (2016). The effects of task complexity and classroom environment on learners' engagement with the language. In M. Sato & S. Ballinger (Eds.), *Peer interaction and second language learning. Pedagogical potential and research agenda.* Amsterdam: John Benjamins.

Batstone, R., & Philp, J. (2013). Classroom interaction and learning across time and space. In K. McDonough & A. Mackey (Eds.), *Second language interaction in diverse educational contexts* (pp. 109–128). Amsterdam: John Benjamins. doi:10.1075/lllt.34.09ch6

Bigelow, M., & King, K. (2016). Peer interaction while learning to read in a new language. In M. Sato & S. Ballinger (Eds.), *Peer interaction and second language learning. Pedagogical potential and research agenda.* Amsterdam: John Benjamins.

Breen, M. (1985). The social context for language learning—a neglected situation? *Studies in Second Language Acquisition*, 7, 135–158. doi:10.1017/S0272263100005337

Brown, A., Metz, K. E., & Campione, J. C. (1996). Social interaction and individual understanding in a community of learners: The influence of Piaget and Vygotsky. In A. Tryphon & J. Voneche (Eds.), *Piaget-Vygotsky: The social genesis of thought* (pp. 145–170). London: Psychology Press.

Choi, H., & Iwashita, N. (2016). Interactional behaviours of low-proficiency learners in small group work. In M. Sato & S. Ballinger (Eds.), *Peer interaction and second language learning. Pedagogical potential and research agenda.* Amsterdam: John Benjamins.

Christenson, S. L., Reschly, A. L., & Wylie, C. (2012). *Handbook of research on student engagement.* New York, NY: Springer. doi:10.1007/978-1-4614-2018-7

Churchill, E., Okada, H., Nishino, T., & Atkinson, D. (2010). Symbiotic gestures and the Socio-cognitive Visibility of Grammar in Second Language Acquisition. *The Modern Language Journal*, 94(2), 234–253. doi:10.1111/j.1540-4781.2010.01019.x

Damon, W., & Phelps, E. (1989a). Critical distinctions among three approaches to peer education. *International Journal of Educational Research*, 58, 9–19. doi:10.1016/0883-0355(89)90013-X

Daniels, H. (2011). Vygotsky and psychology. In Goswami, U. (Ed.), *The Wiley-Blackwell handbook of childhood cognitive development* (2nd ed.). Malden, MA: Wiley-Blackwell.

Davies, B., & Harré, R. (1990). Positioning: The discursive production of selves. *Journal for the Theory of Social Behaviour*, 20(1), 43–63. doi:10.1111/j.1468-5914.1990.tb00174.x

Dawes, L. (2004). Talking and learning in classroom science. *International Journal of Science Education*, 26(6), 677–695. doi:10.1080/0950069032000097424

DeKeyser, R. (2007). Conclusion: The future of practice. In R. DeKeyser (Ed.), *Practice in a second language* (pp. 287–304). Cambridge: Cambridge University Press.

De Lisi, R., & Golbeck, S. L. (1999). Implication of Piaget's theory for peer-learning. In A. M. O'Donnell & A. King (Eds.), *Cognitive perspectives on peer-learning* (pp. 3–38). Mahwah, NJ: Lawrence Erlbaum Associates.

De Smet, M., Van Keer, H., & Valcke, M. (2008). Blending asynchronous discussion groups and peer tutoring in higher education: An exploratory study of online peer tutoring behaviour. *Computers and Education* 50(1), 207–223. doi:10.1016/j.compedu.2006.05.001

Donato, R. (1994). Collective scaffolding in second language learning. In J. P. Lantolf & G. Appel (Eds.), *Vygotskian approaches to second language research* (pp. 33–56). Norwood, NJ: Ablex.

Dörnyei, Z. & Kormos, J. (2000). The role of individual and social variable in oral task performance. *Language Teaching Research* 4(3), 275–300. doi:10.1177/136216880000400305

Dörnyei, Z., & Malderez, A. (1997). Group dynamics and foreign language learning. *System*, 25(1), 65–81. doi:10.1016/S0346-251X(96)00061-9

Dunn, J. (1999). Siblings, friends, and the development of social understanding. In W. A. Collins & B. Laursen (Eds), *Relationships as social contexts* (pp. 263–279). Mahwah, NJ: Lawrence Erlbaum Associates.

Duchesne, S., McMaugh, A., Bochner, S., & Krause, K. (2013). *Educational psychology for learning and teaching*. Melbourne: Cengage Learning Australia.

Ellis, R., Loewen, S., Elder, C., Erlam, R., Philp, J., & Reinders, H. (2009). *Implicit and explicit knowledge in second language learning, testing and teaching*. Clevedon, UK: Multilingual Matters.

Fernández Dobao, A. (2016). Peer interaction and learning: A focus on the silent learner. In M. Sato & S. Ballinger (Eds.), *Peer interaction and second language learning: Pedagogical potential and research agenda*. Amsterdam: John Benjamins.

Fredericks, J., Blumenfeld, P., & Paris, A. (2004). School engagement: Potential of the concept, state of evidence. *Review of Educational Research*, 74(1), 59–105. doi:10.3102/00346543074001059

Fujii, A., Ziegler, N., & Mackey, A. (2016). Peer interaction and metacognitive instruction in the EFL classroom. In M. Sato & S. Ballinger (Eds.), *Peer interaction and second language learning: Pedagogical potential and research agenda*. Amsterdam: John Benjamins.

Furlong, M., & Christenson, S. (2008). Engaging students at school and with learning: A relevant construct for all students. *Psychology in the Schools*, 45, 365–368. doi:10.1002/pits.20302

García Mayo, M. P., & Azkarai, A. (2016). EFL task-based interaction: Does task modality impact on language-related episodes? In M. Sato & S. Ballinger (Eds.), *Peer interaction and second language learning: Pedagogical potential and research agenda*. Amsterdam: John Benjamins.

Gass, S. M., & Mackey, A. (2000). *Stimulated recall methodology in second language research*. Mahwah, NJ: Lawrence Erlbaum Association.

Gettinger, M., & Ball, C. (2007). Best practices in increasing academic engaged time. In A. Thomas & J. Grimes (Eds.), *Best practices in school psychology V* (pp. 1043–1075). Bethesda, MD: National Association of School Psychologists.

Gibbons, P. (2003). Mediating language learning: Teacher interactions with ESL students in content-based classroom. *TESOL Quarterly*, 37(2), 247–273. doi:10.2307/3588504

Hartup, W. W. (1989). Social relationships and their developmental significance. *American Psychologist* 44, 120–126. doi:10.1037/0003-066X.44.2.120

Hartup, W. W. (2011). Critical issues and theoretical viewpoints. In K. H. Rubin, W. M. Bukowski, & B. Laursen (Eds.), *Handbook of peer Interactions, relationships and groups* (pp. 3–19). London: The Guildford Press.

Helme, S., & Clarke, D. (2001). Identifying cognitive engagement in the mathematics classroom. *Mathematics Education Research Journal*. 13(2), 133–153. doi:10.1007/BF03217103

Hellermann, J. (2008). *Social actions for classroom language learning*. Clevedon, UK: Multilingual Matters.

Hogan, D., & Tudge, J. (1999). Implications of Vygotsky's theory for peer learning. In S. O'Donnell & A. King (Eds.), *Cognitive perspectives on peer learning* (pp. 39–66). Mahwah, NJ: Lawrence Erlbaum Associates.

Hulstijn, J., Young, R., Ortega, L., Bigelow, M., DeKeyser, R., Ellis, N., Talmy, S. (2014). Bridging the gap: Cognitive and social approaches to research in second language learning and teaching. *Studies in Second Language Acquisition*, 36, 1–61. doi:10.1017/S0272263114000035

Janosz, M. (2012). Part IV commentary: Outcomes of engagement and engagement as an outcome: Some consensus, divergences, and unanswered questions. In S. L. Christenson, A. L. Reschly & C. Wylie (Eds.), *Handbook of research on student engagement* (pp. 695–703). New York, NY: Springer. doi:10.1007/978-1-4614-2018-7_33

Kormos, J. & Dörnyei, Z. (2004). The interaction of linguistic and motivational variables in second language task performance. *Zeitschrift für Interkulturellen Fremdsprachenunterricht* [Online], 9(2). Retrieved from: http://zif.spz.tu-darmstadt.de/jg-09-2/beitrag/kormos2.htm

Lantolf, J. (2000). *Sociocultural theory and second language learning.* Oxford: Oxford University Press.

Laursen, B., & Hartup, W. (2002). The origins of reciprocity and social exchange in friendships. In B. Laursen & W. Graziano (Eds.), *Social exchange in development* (pp. 27–40). San Francisco, CA: Jossey-Bass.

Loewen, S. (2005). Incidental focus on form and second language learning. *Studies in Second Language Acquisition* 27(3), 361–386. doi:10.1017/S0272263105050163

Loewen, S., & Wolff, D. (2016). Peer interaction in F2F and CMC contexts. In M. Sato & S. Ballinger (Eds.), *Peer interaction and second language learning. Pedagogical potential and research agenda.* Amsterdam: John Benjamins.

Mackey, A., & Gass, S. M. (2015). *Second Language Research* (2nd ed.), Mahwah, NJ: Lawrence Erlbaum Associates.

Mackey, A., Abbuhl, R., & Gass, S. (2012). Interactionist approach. In S. Gass & A. Mackey (Eds.), *The Routledge handbook of second language acquisition* (pp. 7–23). New York, NY: Routledge.

Martin, J. (2012). Part II Commentary: Motivation and engagement: Conceptual, operational, and empirical clarity. In S. L. Christenson, A. L. Reschly, & C. Wylie (Eds.). *Handbook of research on student engagement* (pp. 303–311). New York, NY: Springer. doi:10.1007/978-1-4614-2018-7_14

Martin-Beltrán, M., Chen, P. J., Guzman, N., & Merrills, K. (2016). How adolescents use social discourse to open space for language learning during peer interactions. In M. Sato & S. Ballinger (Eds.), *Peer interaction and second language learning. Pedagogical potential and research agenda.* Amsterdam: John Benjamins.

McDonough, K., Crawford, B., & De Vleeschauwer, J. (2016). Thai EFL learners' interaction during collaborative writing tasks and its relationship to text quality. In M. Sato & S. Ballinger (Eds.), *Peer interaction and second language learning. Pedagogical potential and research agenda.* Amsterdam: John Benjamins.

Mercer, N. (2008). The seeds of time: Why classroom dialogue needs a temporal analysis. *Journal of the Learning Sciences,* 17(1), 33–59. doi:10.1080/10508400701793182

Mercer, N. (1996). The quality of talk in children's collaborative activity in the classroom. *Learning and Instruction,* 6(4), 359–377. doi:10.1016/S0959-4752(96)00021-7

Moranski, K., & Toth, P. (2016). Small-group meta-analytic talk and Spanish L2 development. In M. Sato & S. Ballinger (Eds.), *Peer interaction and second language learning. Pedagogical potential and research agenda.* Amsterdam: John Benjamins.

Nation, P. (2013). *Learning vocabulary in another language.* Cambridge: Cambridge University Press.

Nation, P. (2007). The four strands. *Innovation in Language Learning and Teaching,* 1(1), 2–13. doi:10.2167/illt039.0

O'Donnell, A. M. (2006). The role of peers and group learning. In P. Alexander & P. Winne (Eds.), *Handbook of educational psychology* (pp. 781–802). Mahwah, NJ: Lawrence Erlbaum Associates.

Pekrun, R., & Linnenbrink-Garcia, L. (2012). Academic emotions and student engagement. In S. L. Christenson, A. L. Reschly & C. Wylie (Eds.), *Handbook of research on student engagement* (pp. 259–282). New York, NY: Springer. doi:10.1007/978-1-4614-2018-7_12

Philp, J., Adams, R., & Iwashita, N. (2014). *Peer Interaction and second language learning*. New York, NY: Taylor & Francis.

Philp, J., & Duchesne, S. (2008). When the gate opens: The interaction between social and linguistic goals in child second language development. In J. Philp, R. Oliver, & A. Mackey (Eds.), *Second language acquisition and the younger learner. Child's play?* (pp. 83–103). Amsterdam: John Benjamins. doi:10.1075/lllt.23.07phi

Philp, J., & Duchesne, S. (in press). Exploring engagement in tasks in the language classroom. *Annual Review of Applied Linguistics*, 36.

Philp, J., & Mackey, A. (2010). Interaction research: What can socially informed approaches offer to cognitivists (and vice versa)? In R. Batstone (Ed.), *Sociocognitive perspectives on language use and language learning* (pp. 210–228). Oxford: Oxford University Press.

Reschly, A. L., & Christenson, S. L. (2012). Jingle, jangle and conceptual haziness: Evolution and future directions of the engagement construct. In S. L. Christenson, A. L. Reschly, & C. Wylie (Eds.). *Handbook of research on student engagement* (pp. 1–19). New York, NY: Springer. doi:10.1007/978-1-4614-2018-7

Robinson, P., & Gilabert, R. (2007). Task complexity, the Cognition Hypothesis and second language learning and performance *International Review of Applied Linguistics*, 45, 161–176.

Roseth, C. J., Johnson, D. W., & Johnson, R. T. (2008). Promoting early adolescents' achievement and peer relationships: The effects of cooperative, competitive, and individualistic goal structures. *Psychological Bulletin*, 134, 223–246. doi:10.1037/0033-2909.134.2.223

Rouhshad, A., & Storch, N. (2016). A focus on mode: Patterns of interaction in face-to-face and computer-mediated contexts. In M. Sato & S. Ballinger (Eds.), *Peer interaction and second language learning. Pedagogical potential and research agenda*. Amsterdam: John Benjamins.

Salmon, G. (2000). *E-moderating: The key to teaching and learning online*. London: Kogan Page.

Sato, M. (2013). Beliefs about peer interaction and peer corrective feedback: Efficacy of classroom intervention. *The Modern Language Journal*, 97(3), 611–633. doi:10.1111/j.1540-4781.2013.12035.x

Sato, M., & Ballinger, S. (2012). Raising language awareness in peer interaction: A cross-context, cross-method examination. *Language Awareness*, 21(1-2), 157–179. doi:10.1080/09658416.2011.639884

Sato, M., & Ballinger, S. (2016). Understanding peer interaction: Research synthesis and directions. In M. Sato & S. Ballinger (Eds.), *Peer interaction and second language learning: Pedagogical potential and research agenda*. Amsterdam: John Benjamins.

Sato, M., & Lyster, R. (2012). Peer interaction and corrective feedback for accuracy and fluency development: Monitoring, practice, and proceduralization. *Studies in Second Language Acquisition* 34(4), 591–626. doi:10.1017/S0272263112000356

Sato, M., & Viveros, P. (2016). Interaction or collaboration? The proficiency effect on group work in the foreign language classroom. In M. Sato & S. Ballinger (Eds.), *Peer interaction and second language learning: Pedagogical potential and research agenda*. Amsterdam: John Benjamins.

Schmidt, R. (2001). Attention. In P. Robinson (Ed.), *Cognition and second language instruction* (pp. 3–32). Cambridge: Cambridge University Press. doi:10.1017/CBO9781139524780.003

Schmitt, N. (2008). Review article: Instructed second language vocabulary learning. *Language Teaching Research*, 12, 329. doi:10.1177/1362168808089921

Sfard, A. (1998). On two metaphors for learning and the dangers of choosing just one. *Educational Researchers*, 27, 4–13. doi:10.3102/0013189X027002004

Shim, S. S., Kiefer, S. M., & Wang, C. (2013). Help seeking among peers: The role of goal structure and peer climate. *The Journal of Educational Research*, 106(4), 290–300. doi:10.1080/00220671.2012.692733

Storch, N. (2001). How collaborative is pair work? ESL tertiary students composing in pairs. *Language Teaching Research*, 5, 29–53. doi:10.1177/1362 6880100500103

Storch, N. (2002). Patterns of interaction in ESL pair work. *Language Learning*, 52, 119–158. doi:10.1111/1467-9922.00179

Storch, N. (2008). Metatalk in a pair work activity: Level of engagement and implications for language development. *Language Awareness*, 17, 95–114. doi:10.2167/la431.0

Storch, N. (2009). *The nature of pair interaction. Learners' interaction in an ESL class: its nature and impact on grammatical development.* Saarbrücken, Germany: VDM Verlag.

Storch, N., & Aldosari, A. (2013). Pairing learners in pair work activity. *Language Teaching Research*, 17(1), 31–48. doi:10.1177/1362168812457530

Svalberg, A. (2009). Engagement with language: Developing a construct. *Language Awareness*, 18(3-4), 242–258. doi:10.1080/09658410903197264

Svalberg, A. (2012). Thinking allowed: Language awareness in language learning and teaching: A research agenda. *Language Teaching*, 45(3), 376–388. doi:10.1017/S0261444812000079

Swain, M. (2001). Examining dialogue: Another approach to content specification and to validating inferences drawn from test scores. *Language Testing*, 18(3), 275–302.

Swain, M., & Lapkin, S. (1998). Interaction and second language learning: Two adolescent French immersion students working together. *The Modern Language Journal*, 82(3), 320–337. doi:10.1111/j.1540-4781.1998.tb01209.x

Toohey, K. 2000. *Learning English at School.* Clevedon, UK: Multilingual Matters.

Van de Pol, J., Volman, M., & Beishuizen, J. (2010). Scaffolding in teacher-student interaction: A decade of research. *Educational Psychological Review*, 22, 271–296. doi:10.1007/S10648-010-9127-6

Vygotsky, L. (1978). *Mind in society: The development of higher psychological processes.* Ed. and trans. M. Cole, V. John-Steiner, S. Scribner, & E. Souberman. Cambridge, MA: Harvard University Press.

Wood, D., Bruner, J., & Ross, G. (1976). The role of tutoring in problem solving. *Journal of Psychology and Psychiatry*, 17, 89–100. doi:10.1111/j.1469-7610.1976.tb00381.x

Young, A., & Tedick, D. (2016). Collaborative dialogue in a two-way Spanish/English immersion classroom: Does heterogeneous grouping promote peer linguistic scaffolding? In M. Sato & S. Ballinger (Eds.), *Peer interaction and second language learning. Pedagogical potential and research agenda.* Amsterdam: John Benjamins.

Index